HOW TO COOK MEAT

OTHER BOOKS BY CHRIS SCHLESINGER
AND JOHN WILLOUGHBY

The Thrill of the Grill
  Techniques, Recipes, and Down-Home Barbecue

Salsas, Sambals, Chutneys & Chowchows
  Intensely Flavored "Little Dishes" from Around the World

Big Flavors of the Hot Sun
  Hot Recipes and Cool Tips from the Spice Zone

Lettuce in Your Kitchen
  Where Salad Gets a Whole New Spin and Dressings Do Double Duty

License to Grill
  Achieve Greatness at the Grill with 200 Sizzling Recipes

How *to* Cook Meat

CHRIS SCHLESINGER *and*
JOHN WILLOUGHBY

WW **William Morrow**
An Imprint of HarperCollins*Publishers*

HarperCollins books may be purchased for educational, business, or sales promotional use. For information please write: Special Markets Department, HarperCollins Publishers Inc., 10 East 53rd Street, New York, NY 10022.

FIRST EDITION

Original food photographs copyright © 2000 by Beatriz Da Costa

Book design by Richard Oriolo

Illustrations by Jennifer Harper
additional illustrations by Alexis Seabrook

Printed on acid-free paper

Library of Congress Cataloging-in-Publication Data

Schlesinger, Chris.
    How to cook meat / Chris Schlesinger and John Willoughby—
1st ed.
        p.   cm.
Includes index.
ISBN 0-688-16199-5
1. Cookery (Meat)   I. Willoughby, John.   II. Title.

TX749 S263 2000
641.6'6—dc21

00–062482

00 01 02 03 04   P I D   10 9 8 7 6 5 4 3 2 1

To Roscoe, Jake, and Sherman,
true connoisseurs of finely prepared meat

CONTENTS

ACKNOWLEDGMENTS

As usual, there are more people who helped make this book than we can possibly thank, but we want to single out a few.

From Chris
Thanks to the staff at my restaurants for taking up the slack so I had the time to do this book. At the East Coast Grill, I'd particularly like to thank Maureen Rubino, my general manager; her assistant, Erin; Owen Tilly, the chef; as well as Eric, Seth, Elmer, Amilcar, and all the rest of the staff. At the Back Eddy, my thanks to general manager Sal Liotta and chef Aaron DeRego along with Nigel, Brian, and the rest of the gang. I'd also like to thank Jimmy Burke and Bob Kinkead, my pals, mentors, and colleagues through the years, for all the teaching, eating, drinking, and laughing. And finally thanks to my coauthor, Doc, for his ability, agility, and intestinal fortitude and for tolerating a sometimes petulant, sometimes confused, and always lazy partner. As usual, a pleasure and an honor.

From John (Doc)
Thanks to all of my colleagues at *Cook's Illustrated* magazine, and in particular Chris Kimball, Jack, Kay, Adam, Barbara, Amy, Dawn, Julia, India, Bridget, and Henrietta for their support and tolerance. Thanks to Mark Bittman for his ever-present comradeship and inspiration. And, of course, thanks to my coauthor, Chris, for his alacrity, perspicacity, all-around ebullience, and ability to put up with my irksome habits and occasionally alarmist nature. The pleasure and honor, truly, are mine.

From both of us
Our thanks to Nancy Kohl and Kirsten Mikalson, without whom this book would not exist—their hard work, diligence, and ability to tolerate ever-changing surface conditions

on the road to completion were essential and guarantee them a bright future in this business; to Kay Rentschler, not only for her indispensable help in the conceptual formulation of this book but also for her expertise in the flavors of the Austro-Hungarian Empire; to our indefatigable agent Doe Coover, an evergreen source of inspiration and encouragement; to her colleague Frances, for always taking our calls cheerfully no matter how grumpy we might be; to Doug Bellow, Dana Van Gorder, Carl Taplin, Tom Huth, and in particular Michael Otten for testing and retesting our recipes in their home kitchens.

At HarperCollins, thank to our original editor, Justin Schwartz, for helping translate our eager enthusiasm into what we hope is a useful book; to the ultimate closer, Harriet Bell, for her drive and vision; to Adrian Zackheim for his support and his inspirational display of two-fisted eating at the East Coast Grill last February; to Leah Carlson-Stanisic for making a complicated concept into a clear and readable design; and to Judith Sutton for coralling our errors.

Thanks also to John Dewar, the world's finest butcher, for his patient guidance at our early morning sessions; to Paul Derber, supplier of high-quality meats, for his lucid explanations; to Dr. Terry Dockerty and the National Cattlemen's Beef Association for generously allowing us to use their expert photographs of various cuts of beef, pork, lamb, and veal; to the National Livestock and Meat Board for putting out clear, concise, and helpful guides that are worth their weight in gold to anyone who wants to know even more about meat; and to Dave Griffin of Texas A&M University for organizing and presenting the highly informative Beef 101 course.

Finally, thanks to our extended family—Rick, Susan, Tommy, Lizzie, Steve, and Chris's wife, Marcy, for their unwavering love and friendship.

HOW TO COOK MEAT

All THE MEAT THAT'S FIT *to* EAT

Let's face it, meat tastes great. From steaks to chops, ribs to roasts, it has a direct, hits-you-where-you-live appeal that cannot be denied.

So it's no surprise that when we think of our favorite food experiences, meat usually played the major role. Eating that first super-flavorful fat-edged prime rib as a young boy was a culinary rite of passage. Then there was the first spit-roasted whole pig, the crackling-crisp skin contrasting beautifully with the rich, buttery, smoky tendrils of the inner meat. A roast leg of lamb, slathered with a paste of garlic, rosemary, and lemon juice, was the clearest memory of a childhood trip to Greece. And how many times have we celebrated a gorgeous summer day with a cold beer and a perfectly grilled double-thick T-bone steak, rich and juicy inside and charred just right on the outside?

Obviously, we love meat. And with this book, we want to share that love with you, to give you an even deeper appreciation of the flavor that you already savor—because red meat is a bedrock part of our culinary heritage, a taste that is right down in our genes.

But we're not blind to all the nutritional information that is going around today concerning red meat. We agree that the typical American diet probably includes too much of it. In fact, that's how this book got started in the first place. We were concerned about our own meat consumption and decided to try to make the meat we ate really count. This had the ironic effect of raising our appreciation and our dedication to proper preparation of meat. Once we gave up the lousy ham sandwiches and the fast-food burgers, we found ourselves becoming more enamored of not only roasts and steaks, but also some of the overlooked and less popular cuts. Pretty soon cuts like short ribs, veal breast, and fresh ham began to gain ground as new favorites.

When we started exploring meat in this way, it led us to both rediscovering some old classics and appreciating the way meat is used in other cultures, where the roasts and steaks of European-derived cuisines are almost unknown. This opened up a whole new world to us, and we want to share that world with you. We want to share the classic cuts, we want to share the international favorites, and we want to share the overlooked cuts, the unpolished gems of the meat world.

At the same time, we want to teach you how to cook every cut exactly right. Because if you're going to eat less meat, then it's even more important that you derive maximum enjoyment from every experience.

There's actually a lot to be said for red meat in a nutritional context too. It remains the single most nutrient-dense, efficient food delivery system available to human beings. It contains all the essential amino acids (those are the ones that our bodies need but cannot synthesize from other foods) and, more important, it contains each in exactly the proportion that our bodies require it. Red meat is also an unrivaled source of iron and crucial trace elements such as zinc and copper, along with vitamins B_6 and B_{12}. As for saturated fat, many cuts are leaner these days, and even within current nutritional guidelines you can eat ten ounces of lean red meat every day and not exceed the recommended fat intake.

Meat is also a core part of the human experience, intricately intertwined with our history as a species. Hunter-gatherers weren't hunting for vegetables, after all, and the need to band together to hunt for meat was the primary motivation for the early social bonds that eventually created civilization. Anthropologists vary in their estimation as to whether the eating of meat represents humans' desire to show their power over animals or to identify with them, but they all agree that it has a deep-seated relevance to our understanding of our place in the natural world.

As Americans, we are particularly meat-oriented, because our country has perhaps the most consummate carnivore history of all. Native Americans had always hunted and eaten meat, and European settlers took to the practice with a passion. In their native countries meat had for the most part been a privilege of wealth. But in this new land, game was astonishingly plentiful, and with the vast amount of land available, the new Americans began raising both cattle and hogs in large quantities. Europeans who visited colonial America consistently marveled at the amount of meat consumed by the average citizen. Like rice in much of Asia, meat became the center of our national dinner plate.

The odd thing, though, is that despite its prominent place in our national diet, many of us don't know all that much about meat anymore.

During the culinary revolution that has swept the United States over the past couple of decades, the greatest attention has been paid to products once less commonplace in the American kitchen. Greens, grains, and vegetables of all kinds have rightfully been praised, explained, and brought to a well-deserved place of greater significance on our plates. But that led to a certain amount of indifference about some aspects of meat cookery. We know about steaks and chops, and we have some idea about roasts, but braises and stews and many lesser-known cuts have fallen into disrepute or neglect.

As a result, most Americans tend to go to the grocery store and pick out the same cuts of meat they always have, then take them home and cook them the same way their parents did. This is a shame, both because meat has changed in character and because folks are losing out on a whole world of excellent culinary opportunities. It is our fond hope that this book will help remedy that.

To that end, part of what we want to do with this book is to help expand your meat horizons. Steaks are wonderful, but we want to enjoy rich, flavorful stews simmering on the stove as well as juicy roasts coming out of the oven, hearty braised meat dishes and smoky grilled chops with spicy salsas. We want to eliminate the false notion that there is a hierarchy of meats. Stew meat is not worse than tenderloin, it's just different. If you cook it right, it can become a dish that is every bit as enticing and satisfying in its own way as a succulent filet mignon. Remember that a hierarchy of price does not really reflect a hierarchy of value; it's all a matter of knowing which cut should be matched with which cooking method.

When you start looking at meat this way you not only end up with some outstanding food, you get some side benefits along the way as well. The less highly regarded cuts of meat tend to be less expensive, for one thing. For another, they allow you to feel virtuous, because you are being a responsible consumer by using all the resources the animal has to offer, rather than just a select few. Besides all that, these cuts are fun to cook. For a better idea of what we're talking about here, check out our Top 5 Favorite Cuts in the recipe chapter for each meat. There are some super-expensive cuts in those lists, for sure, but you'll also find some of these unpolished gems. We're big fans of pork butts, for example, we love shoulder lamb chops, and we're excited about beef skirt steaks. These types of overlooked cuts are, we believe, one of the real strengths of this book.

The bottom line is that this book is a celebration of meat. We want to help you get the most out of it and enjoy every aspect of it, from buying it to cooking it to eating it. We want to be sure that every time you bring a meat dish to the table, it more than satisfies your memories and your expectations.

What better place to start than at the meat counter?

MEET MEAT

There is a lot of good meat out there, and there are a lot of neat, fun, and tasty ways to cook it. So, walking up to the meat counter should be an occasion for excitement. But even for an experienced cook, it can often be a prelude to bewilderment instead.

And why not? At any given time, there are about a hundred and fifty separate cuts of red meat on display in the meat section of an average large supermarket. Not only that, but the same cut may have a different name depending on the state, the city, or even the particular shop where you're buying it. Some differences are geographic. Until recently, for instance, butchers in Kansas City called the boneless top loin steak a Texas strip, while those in Texas (and much of the rest of the country) referred to it as a New York strip, and in New York, they called it a Kansas City strip. Other cuts of meat, like Boston butt and picnic shoulder, derive their names from butchering practices of the distant past. There are also plenty of local names that were coined simply because they're more enticing than the more "clinical" names. In much of the South, for instance, the beef chuck neck pot roast is known as a bell roast because it comes from the part of the neck where the cow's bell used to hang. All in all, meat industry experts estimate that there are over a thousand different names used for the three hundred or so standard cuts of red meat in this country.

So, the real question is, how do we make sense of all this?

Well, clearly there's no way you can learn every local name for every cut of red meat. And since language tends to evolve, it's very likely that people are going to keep on making up new names for cuts of meat as the years go by. We've tried to make the whole situation as clear as possible by giving you lists of all the names these cuts are presently known by, plus pictures of all of them as they look in the market. But it's also very helpful to learn a few basic characteristics of the various parts of the animals. That way you can make good use of the standard labels applied to packaged cuts of meat in almost every market in this country—and you will also know which cooking method works with which cut.

THE BIG PICTURE

Here's the story, generally speaking.

When an animal is butchered, it is first separated into a number of large sections called the "primal cuts." These are then broken down into smaller sections known as "subprimals," and the subprimals in turn are divided into retail cuts—steaks, chops, roasts, and all the rest.

But of course you won't see these primal cuts in the supermarket. Instead, you'll see all those individual retail cuts into which the primals are ultimately separated—the roasts, steaks, brisket, and so on.

So how do you put these two together? Well, we're going to try to make it easy for you, because it actually can be pretty complicated. I (Chris) remember being in culinary school trying to figure out where all the dozens of different cuts of beef came from on the cow and becoming increasingly confused, along with most of my classmates. To make it clearer, our instructor followed a pedagogical plan that is used in cooking schools all over the country—he tried to relate the parts of the cow to parts of the human body. As gross as it may seem, it was pretty effective. I told the instructor that he should get a raincoat and paint it with a diagram showing which part of his body translated to which part of the cow, then put it on whenever we started talking about beef cuts.

Even today, though, after all the years I've spent cutting up and cooking beef, I can still get confused about what cut comes from which part of the steer. In an effort to simplify this, to make it less abstruse, less obtuse, and generally easier to remember, we recommend you divide each animal into four basic parts and then give each of them a descriptive name. So, for example, we like to divide the steer into the chuck, which we call the Tough But Flavorful section; the rib, or Big Money Section; the loin, which we dub the Steak Section; and the round, known to us as the Roast Section.

Of course, this is an oversimplification with plenty of exceptions and qualifications, but that's how we think of the animal, and it's actually pretty helpful in keeping things straight. Why bother, you ask? Well, because many of the flavor and texture characteristics of a particular cut of meat are determined by the primal cut it comes from. The less exercise a particular part of an animal gets, the more tender the cuts from that part of the animal are going to be. For all four-legged animals, the back, which includes the rib and loin sections, does the least work in moving the animal around and so is the most tender. The most tender part of the animal overall is the section just to the front of the loin, known as the rib section, which produces the prime rib roast. The loin yields those incredibly tender steaks—the porterhouse, the T-bone, the filet mignon, the New York strip. Next on the descending tenderness scale comes the sirloin, which is the part between the loin and the rump. Cuts from the leg and hip (the round) are made up of larger muscles with little fat and a good amount of connective tissue, so they are not all that tender while cuts from the shoulder and neck of the animal are, for the most part, tougher yet. Meat that comes from the foreshank, breast, and side is usually the gnarliest of all.

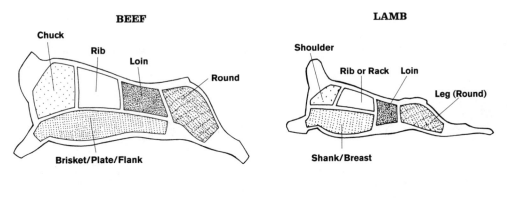

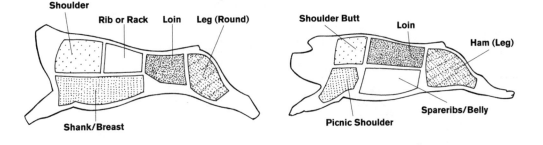

Now for the cooking methods. Tender cuts are best cooked with dry-heat methods like grilling, sautéing, roasting, and broiling, while tougher cuts do best with moist-heat methods like braising and stewing.

Put these two dynamics together and it means that, in general, cuts from the loin and rib are usually grilled, sautéed, roasted, or broiled; cuts from the leg are often roasted and sometimes braised or stewed; cuts from the shoulder are often braised or stewed and sometimes roasted; and cuts from the foreshank, breast, and side are most often braised or stewed.

Of course, within these general parameters there are many levels of complication. We delve into those in the section of each recipe labeled "The Cut." But in general, these guidelines hold pretty firm.

BEEF Short Loin Steaks and Roasts

Porterhouse Steak

T-Bone Steak

Tenderloin Steak
(Filet Mignon)

Top Loin Steak
(Boneless)

LAMB Loin Chops and Roasts

Loin Chop   Double Loin Chop

VEAL Loin Chops and Roasts

Loin Chop   Kidney Chop

PORK Loin Chops and Roasts

Tenderloin, Whole

Top Loin Chop
(Boneless)

Butterfly Chop

Loin Chop

In trying to explain all of this, we've found it helpful to compare cuts taken from the same sections of different animals. So let's look at a cut taken from the loin section, also known as the short loin. Let's take the beef porterhouse steak as our point of comparison. From the other three animals, the equivalent cut would be the veal, lamb, or pork loin chop. All four cuts are very tender, all four have portions of two separate muscles separated by a bone, and all four are best cooked with direct dry-heat methods such as grilling or broiling.

It gets more complicated than this for other sections of the animals, but the point is the same: If you understand the way the cut from one animal works, you basically understand them all.

Once you have this down, you can learn a lot from the labels on packages of meat in the supermarket. A few years ago in an attempt to cut down on the confusion about which cut is what, the National Livestock and Meat Board came out with label standards that are increasingly used around the country. In large type—usually at the bottom of the label, below the weight, price per pound, total price, and sell-by date—you will find the type of meat (e.g., pork), the primal cut from which the particular cut came (e.g., loin), and the name of the particular cut (e.g., tenderloin roast). So, in the case of this example, you know that this comes from a part of the animal that is very tender—and therefore should be cooked using a dry-heat method like grilling or roasting.

The dynamic of matching meat to method is so crucial to cooking meat right that we have organized this whole book around it. For each of the four types of meat, the recipes are divided by the size and texture of the cuts. The categories include "Large Tender" cuts such as loin and rib roasts; "Large Tough" cuts such as shoulder roasts and brisket; "Small Tender" cuts such as chops and steaks; and "Small Tough" cuts, which for the most part refer to stew meat, usually taken from the shoulder or leg. (The organ meats such as liver or sweetbreads, also known as offal, have their own separate category.) Most of the cuts of meat within each category are cooked with the same cooking method.

NEGLECTED GEMS

But as with any set of rules, this one has exceptions. Here you will find many of the neglected and underused cuts, the undiscovered gems of meat cookery that bring surprising rewards to the intrepid cook who seeks them out.

To show you what we mean, let's take a look at another section of all four animals, the upper section of the shoulder. Despite the fact that most cuts from the shoulder are relatively tough and need long, slow cooking, there are a couple of cuts here that are actually excellent for grilling. They are the beef, veal, and pork blade steaks and the lamb blade chop. They all come from the top of the shoulder near the neck, and they all have the same deep, rich flavor as other cuts from this part of the animal, but they are also tender enough to go on the grill. Since not many people know about them, they are also very inexpensive. These blade cuts are particular favorites of Chris's because they are the continuation of the rib, the most expensive section of each animal. Now, the muscles from the rib area don't stop just because they move into the shoulder; they merely begin to change somewhat in character. So the first couple of blade lamb chops next to the rib, for instance, are actually very similar to your high-priced rib lamb chops, with a little more chew but a lot smaller price tag.

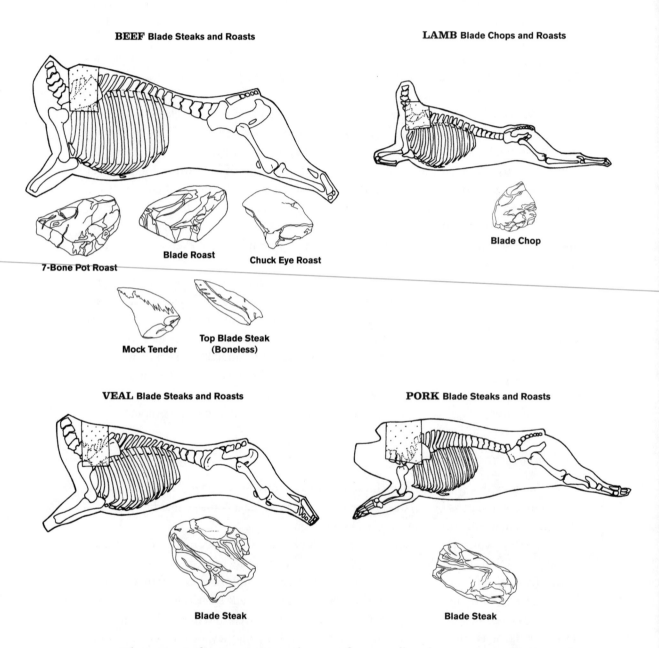

BEEF Blade Steaks and Roasts

LAMB Blade Chops and Roasts

7-Bone Pot Roast

Blade Roast

Chuck Eye Roast

Blade Chop

Mock Tender

Top Blade Steak
(Boneless)

VEAL Blade Steaks and Roasts

PORK Blade Steaks and Roasts

Blade Steak

Blade Steak

These types of cuts are among the most fun as well as the most rewarding to cook, and as we go through each animal, we'll point them out to you. Put them together with the more well known popular cuts, and you're going to have a meat repertoire that will keep you going for a long time.

MAKING A CHOICE

Let's say you know that you're going to be grilling, which calls for a small tender cut of meat, and you want to buy a really good chop or steak to throw on the fire. How do you go about picking one?

There are several factors that go into making this choice. You may want to consider the grade of the meat, you definitely need to check out its physical appearance, you might want to consider "brand," and you should decide whether you will look for it in a supermarket or at a butcher shop.

GRADES OF MEAT

The grading of meat is a concept that most people have heard about but are a bit fuzzy on. The confusion comes, it seems to us, from a popular but mistaken notion that the grade of meat has something to do with whether or not it is safe to eat. It doesn't.

Meat is subjected to far more regulation and official evaluation than any other food in this country. It is a very safe product. (If you want to know about a dangerously unregulated industry, let's talk seafood.) Since 1906, it has been mandatory that all meat be inspected by the United States Department of Agriculture (USDA) at the packing plant to be sure that it is produced under sanitary conditions and is not spoiled or contaminated. But that doesn't have anything to do with grading. All meat, whatever the grade, should be equally safe for consumption.

Grading is a voluntary program. If the producer wants to pay the USDA, a grader will come to the plant and grade the meat. The reason the producer might do this is because grade is an attempt to communicate to consumers the likely palatability of a particular piece of meat—its tenderness, juiciness, and flavor.

Meat grades are based on age (younger meat is more tender and therefore considered better) and the degree of intramuscular fat, or marbling (meat with more marbling is juicier and more flavorful and therefore considered better). There are eight possible grades for beef, running from "Prime" at the top to "Canner" at the bottom. Veal and lamb have fewer grades and pork has a different system altogether.

But grading is actually much less important to your daily meat buying than you might think. Only the top three grades—Prime, Choice, and Select—appear at meat counters or in butcher shops. The others are just not high enough quality for consumers to buy.

And practically speaking, the grade of the meat is only an issue for most of us consumers when it comes to beef. Veal, lamb, and pork all come from animals that are considerably younger when slaughtered, which means that their meat is naturally more tender and intramuscular fat is not so relevant a consideration. You may occasionally see these meats with grades indicated in the market, but that is more the exception than the rule. So, for more on grading, refer to page 41 in our Beef chapter.

PHYSICAL APPEARANCE

More important than grading when choosing an individual piece of meat are muscle color, texture, fat color, and amount of fat, all of which differ somewhat from animal to animal. Pointers and tips about these qualities and exactly what to look for in each type of meat and in each particular cut are included in the individual chapter introductions as well as in the section labeled "The Cut" that accompanies each recipe.

BRANDING

Sometimes you will come across what is known as "branded" meat. As with grading, this is a factor that most often applies to beef. The brand in question can either be that of a specific producer or of a specific breed, such as Angus or Hereford in cattle. We believe that branding will probably become more common for all types of red meat in the coming years. The only way to find out whether a meat bearing the brand name of a specific producer is consistently of higher quality than unbranded meat is to try the meat for yourself. The same is true of breed branding, although that does seem a more reliable guide, at least when it comes to beef.

Before too long, we may well be seeing another more sophisticated type of branding. The technology is at hand that will allow breeders to do an analysis of the genetic makeup of a piece of meat and to accurately predict the tenderness as well as the flavor qualities of meat that comes from animals with that same genetic makeup. All meat from those animals can then be given a branded identity with a virtual money-back guarantee of the quality of the meat. We're not sure how we feel about applying all this high technology to what should basically be a primal eating experience, but keep your eye out for it in any case.

SUPERMARKET OR BUTCHER?

A more practical question is whether you should shop for meat at a butcher or at a supermarket. The choice really depends on several factors, including what particular cut of meat you're looking for and how much you want to pay. Butcher shops tend to be a bit more expensive, but they're also going to have the obscure cuts, and they will be happy to give you really thick versions of even the more commonly available selections. Besides that, the guy behind the counter is going to be very knowledgeable and therefore helpful if you're a bit unsure of what you're looking for.

On the other hand, not everyone has a butcher store conveniently close to them, and there are many cuts of meat that you can easily get in perfectly good quality at the supermarket.

We've tried to help you with this choice throughout the book by pointing out those cuts of meat that you are likely to find only in the butcher shop, so you will be aware of this in advance and won't be disappointed at the supermarket. But we also encourage you to venture out there and figure out for yourself when to use each meat-buying option. In our experience this is a good thing, not only because supermarket butchers and specialty butchers serve different purposes but because butchers are generally pretty funny guys, and if you go in and talk to them you'll often find the experience amusing as well as educational.

To illustrate, let us tell you how we buy meat.

I (Chris) generally buy my meat from John Dewar, a fantastic custom butcher who services many of the finest hotels and restaurants in Boston, including the East Coast Grill, but also has a retail business. So when I want a piece of meat, I'll call up John and order a 2-pound T-bone or a crown roast or a giant loin-end standing rib for Christmas dinner or a steamship round of veal to impress my new in-laws. I know I'll always get top quality and exactly what I want, because John delivers the very best. In your town you probably have an upscale butcher something like this, the guy you can call on the phone who will go out of his way to help you find what you want.

On the other hand, I (Doc) count on John for special occasions, but for the most part I get my meat from Larry, the butcher at the supermarket a few blocks from my house. Our relationship has definitely changed over the past couple of years. The first time I walked in and asked for a skirt steak, for example, he looked me straight in the eye and said, "Buddy, I've been working here for three years and I've never even *seen* a skirt steak."

Now, there were many possible replies to that, but none of them was going to get me the steak I wanted. So I thought about it for a minute, then asked what he had in the case that was really great. He grudgingly allowed as how they happened to have some fresh leg of lamb from Vermont that for some reason no one was buying. I figured I could shift gears and test a few lamb recipes, so I asked him if he could take one of the legs, cut about four thick steaks from the center, a couple of chops from the sirloin end, and the rest into cubes for shish kebab. He cocked his head, gave me a kind of quizzical look, and then said, "Yeah, sure, that's no problem."

At that moment, I think his idea of me changed from pain in the butt to someone who might be interesting to work with, and I knew I was going to get some good lamb for dinner. I've gone back there consistently over the past couple of years, and now when I walk up to the counter—after Larry makes some crack about being fresh out of lamb's brains—we settle down to see what he can get me that will work for the dish I have in mind. I never did get any skirt steak from Larry, but he did once put aside some fresh ham hocks that came in because he figured I'd probably find it interesting to cook with them. He was right.

So our advice is to make the most of the supermarket meat counter. Challenge the guy behind the counter and see if he will rise to the occasion. Ask him specifically for what you want and see what happens. Some butchers may look at you as if you were crazy, but others will be the happiest supermarket butchers in the world because they get to cut something special for someone who will actually appreciate it, rather than putting the same old stuff into the same old plastic wrappers.

Go ahead and ask for the two-inch-thick pork chop. Find out if, when you come in next week, the butcher could have a five-pound boneless rib roast or a giant T-bone steak for two, ready for you. You've got nothing to lose by asking, and there's a fair chance that you could end up with the equivalent of a butcher shop right in your own supermarket.

A LITTLE SCIENCE: GETTING THE BEST
FLAVOR FROM TODAY'S MEAT

Wherever you get your meat, it is going to be considerably different from the meat our grandparents cooked. This is good in some ways and bad in others, but in any case, it has definite implications not only for the particular cut of meat you buy, but also for how you cook it.

Over the past several decades, meat producers have responded to consumer health concerns by modifying breeding and feeding programs in order to produce leaner animals. The results of these efforts have been the most dramatic in pork, in which the fat content of some cuts (mostly from the loin) has been reduced by almost 60 percent in the past quarter century. But today's beef and lamb are also leaner. (Veal has always been relatively lean for red meat.)

This is definitely a positive development in terms of healthfulness. But in terms of sheer sensual enjoyment, it has been a mixed blessing, largely because of the various roles that fat plays in meat.

There are two basic types of fat in meat: intermuscular fat, which is found between and around the muscles, and intramuscular fat, which is within the muscles themselves. Intermuscular fat can usually be trimmed off if you wish, with little effect. But intramuscular fat, also known as marbling, plays several important roles in our enjoyment of meat.

First, when the meat is cooked, the intramuscular fat melts and slips in between the muscle fibers, lubricating them and making them tender. Second, this fat stimulates our salivary glands as we eat, which makes the meat seem juicy as we chew it. Finally, and probably most important, intramuscular fat carries flavor. Meat scientists even theorize that it is the fat that most distinguishes the flavor of one type of red meat from another.

In other words, the less intramuscular fat in a given piece of meat, the less flavorful, tender, and juicy it will be. This is why in days past, when having too much fat in the diet was not considered a problem, cooks engaged in a practice called barding, in which they actually inserted long thin strips of pork fat into lean cuts of meat to improve its gustatory qualities.

All of this does not mean that today's meat is flavorless or boring. But it does mean that the leaner cuts of meat—which also come from more tender parts of the animal, the loin and rib areas—tend to have less robust flavor and somewhat less satisfying "mouth feel" than they did in the past.

On the whole, this seems to be a reasonable trade-off for the health benefits, particularly since there are several ways to address this somewhat lower "flavor quotient" in today's meat. To begin with, it's probably best not to cook lean cuts as long as our grandmothers may have. Without fat to lubricate it, the meat dries out faster and also loses some of its flavor. In the recipes in this book, we have adjusted the cooking times accordingly.

Another way to address the issues raised by lower-fat meat is to look for other qualities that make meat flavorful. Here are three good options.

THE FLAVOR/TENDERNESS NEXUS

Americans in general tend to equate tenderness with quality in meat, but that is not the whole story. Don't get us wrong—we appreciate a super-tender beef tenderloin or lamb loin chop as much as the next person. But we would also like to encourage you to look at meat from the standpoint of valuing the whole animal. If you do so, you'll find that most cuts have some excellent qualities you can appreciate.

In fact, we have found that there is a pretty strong inverse relationship between flavor and tenderness. In other words, the tougher the cut of meat, the more likely it is to have deep, rich flavor. There is a reason, for instance, that osso buco, made from the tough shank, is among the very most popular veal dishes. And, in our experience, you'll never get more satisfying beef flavor than from tough cuts like short ribs or oxtail.

This flavor/tenderness trade-off is familiar to chefs and food scientists alike, but the reason behind it remains somewhat mysterious. In his seminal book *On Food and Cooking,* for example, Harold McGee observes that exercise, which toughens the muscles of animals, also contributes to their flavor. He ascribes this phenomenon to some combination of the nature of tissue cells and the concentration of fat, but he also admits to being somewhat mystified.

Taking advantage of this flavor dynamic usually requires long, slow cooking with moist heat to make the meat more tender. Sometimes, as with the lamb shoulder chops we mentioned earlier, it also means accepting a bit of chewiness. That is a different quality from stringiness or toughness, and it is one we actually enjoy in many cuts of meat.

Some people recommend marinating tougher cuts as a means of making them more tender, but we don't agree. In our experience, marinating only makes the surface of meat mushy and does little to tenderize the interior. We occasionally marinate for flavor, but don't expect it to tenderize.

BETTER ON THE BONE

Another flavor-enhancer is to cook meat on the bone. Apart from the pure primal satisfaction of the bone-in approach, we believe it actually makes the meat taste a little better.

We spent a fair amount of time trying to figure out just why this might be, but without much luck. We asked dozens of scientists, butchers, and just plain old meat eaters about this. Almost to a person, they agreed with our assessment of this issue, but they had little in the way of scientific explanation.

Culinary experts and laboratory scientists at the National Cattleman's Beef Association suggested that it might have to do with the marrow in bones. Marrow has highly concentrated flavor, and they theorized that some of the marrow might seep from the bones into the surrounding meat during cooking, intensifying its taste. This makes sense to us, but when we tried this theory out on some of our butcher friends, they pointed out that even thinner nonmarrow bones, such as those in a rib or a porterhouse steak, sweeten the flavor of meat.

Professor William Mikel of the University of Kentucky thought perhaps it might have to do with differing rates of heat transfer around the bone. In other words, since bone does not heat up as quickly as the meat itself, it may provide the juices with a place to concentrate during the most intense heat of cooking. This squares with our own personal theory, which is that since the bone is surrounded with more capillaries than other parts of the meat, you end up with more juices, and therefore more flavor, in the meat nearest the bone.

Whatever the scientific explanation, it is far less important than the simple pleasure of eating meat on the bone. Try it and we bet you'll agree.

BROWN IS GOOD

There is one final flavor booster that is perhaps the most important of all. Whether you are eating meat bone-in or boneless, whether you choose tough cuts or tender ones, it is crucial to give the meat a good sear at the beginning of cooking.

Despite what you may have heard, searing does not seal moisture inside the meat. What searing does do, though, is create an intense layer of deep flavor on the outside of meat, which in turn adds an unbelievable amount of flavor to the whole dish.

This is one of the secrets of people who cook for a living. Hanging out with professional cooks, two things you notice is that every time they approach a stove they're not only going to make a huge mess (which they generally clean up, to be fair) but if there is meat involved in the meal, at some point you're going to have to open the kitchen windows and turn off the smoke alarms. Unfortunately, we have found that many home cooks tend to shy away from browning meat really well, either from fear of overcooking the outside of the meat or from a dislike for the spattering that sometimes accompanies high-heat searing. Get over it. You really need to sear meat (except veal) until it has a good dark brown coat on all sides.

The reason for this has to do with the ways that sugars and proteins act when they are heated together. The name for this phenomenon is the "Maillard reaction," after the French doctor who first analyzed it back in 1912. Busily investigating amino acids, Maillard stumbled across the fact that when carbohydrates and proteins are heated together, sugars (from the carbohydrate) and amino acids (from the proteins) combine to form new but unstable chemical structures. As the heat continues to be applied, these compounds in turn break down, producing literally hundreds of new by-products, each of which has a distinctive taste and aroma. As a result, food subjected to this process gains a whole new layer of rich, deep, complex flavors.

So start to think of a well-seared, slightly crusty, brown exterior as a forecast of deep flavor rather than a reproach for overcooking. To aid in browning, always dry the meat well before you sear it. To cut down on spattering, use a pot with sides at least five inches high when browning meat for stews and braises; when using a sauté pan, you can always try using one of those mesh spatter shields. And if you become faint of heart, just repeat to yourself the flavor mantra, "Brown is good, brown is good." You're going to have much better meat dishes if you do.

WHEN IS IT DONE?

Knowing when something is done to your liking is perhaps the single most important aspect of being a good cook. Like every other food that is subjected to heat, meat will be underdone, underdone, underdone, done, then overdone. In other words, the window of perfect doneness is a small one, and you need to learn how to jump right through it when it opens.

The way to do this varies depending on the cut of meat you're cooking. For roasts, you need a thermometer; for braises, a fork is still the most reliable tool; for smaller pieces of meat, we favor the classic "nick, peek, and cheat" method. The details of each of these methods are explained in the individual sections in "Methods of Meat Cookery," below.

We realize, too, that the point at which something is "done" is not the same for all of us. We believe that you should eat meat the way you like it, not the way you're told to like it. If you want your meat well-done, by all means cook it that way. After all, you're the one who paid for it.

On the other hand, this is our book, so the recipe instructions are generally given for cooking meat the way we like it. We prefer beef rare to medium-rare, but on the rare side; veal medium-rare to medium, but on the medium side; pork medium; and lamb medium-rare. So that's what you'll find in our recipes. But we also give guidelines for those of you who want to cook any of those meats more or less.

It's also true that one person's rare may be another's medium-rare. The table below shows what we mean when we use these terms. The temperatures are the temperatures at which the meat should be removed from the heat; the temperature will rise 5 to 7 degrees as the meat rests—an important reason why you should be sure to give the meat a rest before eating it.

	TEMPERATURE WHEN REMOVED FROM HEAT SOURCE	FINAL APPEARANCE
Rare	120°F	Raw center
Medium-Rare	126°F	Red center, slightly warm
Medium	134°F	Pink center
Medium-Well	150°F	Hint of pink in center
Well-Done	160°F	Cooked throughout; no pink in center

PUTTING THE FIRE TO IT: METHODS OF MEAT COOKERY

Determining when meat is done is the end of the cooking process. Selecting the right method for the particular cut of meat is the beginning. In between is another critical part—applying the principles of the particular cooking method correctly.

The sections below explain the hows and whys of each of these techniques. Most of the principles are at least as old as Escoffier, but we've tried to highlight what we have learned over the past couple of years about just how to apply each method to the cooking of meat. We've included a little science when we thought it would make the reasons behind the procedures clearer. In many ways, this is the heart of the book. Read it, and you'll be a great meat cook in no time.

ROASTING

To us, there's nothing more mouthwatering than a big, juicy, perfectly seared roast emerging from the oven. From medieval times, when a "joint" was the center of every banquet worth attending, right on down to the Sunday dinners and holiday feasts of our youth, roasts have always had a special standing as not only luxurious and celebratory, but completely delicious. Not to mention that they often produce some very high-quality leftovers.

Another reason for the enduring popularity of roasts is that they are very simple: Just put that meat in the oven and go about your other business as it cooks.

Despite this simplicity, though, the ability to roast well has long been considered a crucial test of a cook's skill. Brillat-Savarin, the famous and very influential nineteenth-century French gourmand, even went so far as to say that roasting was an innate skill that determined whether you would be a good cook or not; if you were unlucky enough not to be born a roaster, there was no way you could be taught. Even though at that time "roasting" meant turning meat on a spit over an open fire, we still think that Brillat-Savarin was off-base. Instead, we go along with that other celebrated Frenchman of the nineteenth century, Auguste Escoffier, the chef who basically codified Western culinary techniques. "One may become a good roaster," he said, "with application, observation, care, and a little aptitude."

Actually, we don't even think you need much aptitude if you just pay some attention to what you're doing.

The first step is picking the right cut of meat, which is very simple. As a dry-heat cooking method, roasting is suitable only for relatively tender cuts. Because it is a rather slow cooking process, it is also best for large cuts of meat, those that take a while to cook all the way through.

With the meat chosen, you are ready to roast. Our approach, which we think will give you excellent results, may be a little different from the style that you're used to. It may seem a bit mysterious. But it is actually quite simple. The three key points are: Sear the meat at a high oven temperature, finish roasting at a low to moderate temperature, and estimate the cooking time not by weight, but by mass.

Let's take the last point first. One culinary myth that has resulted in many an unsatisfactory meal is the idea that you should cook a roast for "X" minutes per pound. Please forget that. It just doesn't make sense. What matters in determining roasting time is not so much the weight of the roast, but its size and shape. This is particularly true of roasts from the loin and the rib, which tend to be oblong in shape. For roasts from the round and chuck, which are usually rolled and tied, there is a closer (although far from exact) correlation between weight and cooking time.

Here's an example. Say you have one tenderloin that is six inches long and about two inches in diameter, and another that is a foot long and also about two inches in diameter. The second one weighs about twice as much as the first, but do you really think it will take twice as long to cook? No way. It will actually take almost exactly the same amount of time, because it is about the same thickness. If, on the other hand, you took two tenderloins, stacked them on top of each other, and tied them together, it would indeed take about twice as long to roast as a single tenderloin, because the combined pieces of meat would be twice as thick. It is the mass and shape, not the weight, that is the best indicator of cooking time.

So from now on when you look at a roast in the market, don't think of it as so many pounds; instead, think of how it relates in size and shape to a familiar object like a milk carton. That will be a much better rough guide to how long it will take to cook. Of course, its exact cooking time will vary depending on the degree of doneness you are looking for, but this will provide you with a general idea. More importantly, it will start you thinking about mass rather than weight when cooking roasts. So here are approximate cooking times, geared toward having the meat medium-rare, for roasts that look like they are about the size of these containers, assuming that you use our approach of searing hard and then cooking low:

CONTAINER SIZE	APPROXIMATE COOKING TIME
1 quart	30 to 40 minutes
½ gallon	45 minutes to 1 hour
Gallon jug	2 to 2½ hours

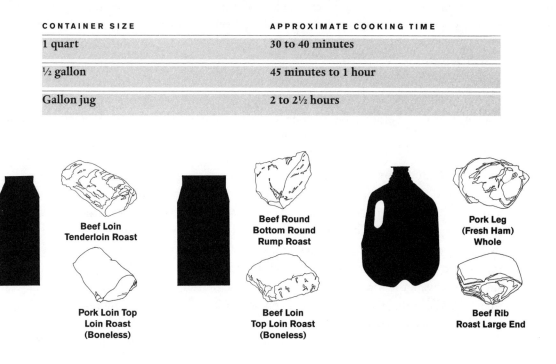

Beef Loin
Tenderloin Roast

Pork Loin Top
Loin Roast
(Boneless)

Beef Round
Bottom Round
Rump Roast

Beef Loin
Top Loin Roast
(Boneless)

Pork Leg
(Fresh Ham)
Whole

Beef Rib
Roast Large End

As for the high-then-low oven temperature, we use this approach for two reasons: It's simple and it works really well. An initial high heat searing is essential to a good roast. Some people like to sear their roasts on top of the stove, but we think that cooks are more likely to sear long enough to get a nice dark crust if they can simply put the meat in the oven and let it brown.

But if you then continue to roast a large piece of meat at a high oven temperature, it will tend to lose too much fat and moisture and get dry. Roasting at a low to moderate oven temperature, about 300°F, keeps the meat tender and juicy. This is particularly important for larger roasts.

Another important step in roasting actually comes after the meat is out of the oven: Let it rest for a while before you carve and serve it. This may go against your feeling that food should be served hot right out of the oven, but here patience is definitely a virtue. Good cooks have long known that allowing cooked meat to rest is important, but in recent years, food scientists like our friend Harold McGee have provided scientific backup for the firsthand observations of experienced cooks. Here's the low-down.

As the proteins in meat heat up during cooking, they coagulate, which basically means that they uncoil and bond with each other. As this happens, the proteins squeeze out some of the liquid that was held in their coiled structures and in the spaces between the individual molecules. The external heat from the cooking source then drives the freed liquid toward the center of the meat. (It is this process that allows professional cooks to judge the degree of doneness of a piece of meat just by pressing on it with a finger; the more the proteins have coagulated, the firmer and, therefore, the more done the meat is.) But this coagulation process is at least partially reversible. As the meat rests and cools somewhat after coming out of the oven, the ability of the protein molecules to hold moisture increases, and some of the liquid is redistributed and reabsorbed by those molecules. As a result, less juice will run out when you cut the roast. This, in turn, makes for juicier and more tender meat on the plate.

So be patient and let that roast have a rest. You will often need the time anyway, to make a simple sauce from the pan drippings. And on those occasions when everything else is actually ready for dinner, use the time to have another beverage of your choice with your guests.

Roasting Techniques

The essential first step in roasting meat is to preheat the oven to a high temperature (we like 500°F). While the oven is preheating, you can pat the roast dry and season it generously with salt and pepper. Now put it in the hot oven and sear it really well. Browning a roast in the oven generally takes about 20 minutes, but, as always, you should use visual clues rather than set times to determine when the cooking task has been accomplished. In this case, the clue is simple: You want the roast to be dark brown on the outside. If you look in the oven after 10 minutes and find that the roast is getting too brown, turn the temperature down a bit; if you check the roast after 20 minutes and it is not dark enough, keep on searing until it is.

Once the meat is well browned, turn the oven down to 300°F. At this point, add any vegetables that you want to roast alongside the meat but that you did not want to subject to the initial high heat. Then just let that meat cook.

About 15 minutes before you think the roast will actually be done, start checking its state of doneness with a meat thermometer. This is the best way to figure out if your roast is done, and it's important to do it right and get an accurate reading. To make sure you're at dead center of the roast, poke the thermometer all the way through to the other side, then draw it back to the midpoint. Wait for 5 seconds (count it out), and you should get an accurate read. When cooking bone-in roasts, be sure you're not touching the bone, which would give you a screwy reading.

When the roast is done to your liking—and that's easy to know: 120°F is rare, 126°F is medium-rare, 134°F is medium, and 160°F is well-done—take it out of the oven, cover it loosely with foil to keep it warm, and let it rest for 10 to 20 minutes.

When you take the roast out of the pan, you'll usually see some very dark brown bits stuck to the bottom of the pan. Because of the browning reactions that have taken place during the initial searing and long roasting, these bits are very flavorful. Often, though not always, you will want to take advantage of that. To do so, simply spoon off the fat from the pan, put the pan on the stove over medium-high heat, add some flavorful liquid like stock or wine, and bring the liquid to a simmer, scraping the bottom of the pan to incorporate the browned bits. Many classical recipes call for thickening the liquid with flour or butter at this point, but we usually prefer to just let it simmer until the liquid is reduced and the flavor is concentrated—then, skim off the film, strain out the solids, and you've got your jus.

You're done. Slice the meat into thick slices if it's a very tender cut such as prime rib or tenderloin, thinner slices for tougher roasts such as chuck roast. Now pour some of the jus (if you've made it) over it, and serve it up with the rest of the jus on the side. That's real eating.

BRAISING

Although braising may sound foreign to some of you, it really isn't. What we're talking about here is a lot of variations on the theme of pot roast: Basically, braising is cooking food in a relatively small amount of liquid in a closed container over a relatively long period of time. Like barbecuing, braising is a "slow and low" method.

Next to grilling, braising may be our favorite cooking method for meat. This is because the primary goal of braising meat is to transform tough into tender, a process that creates a very tasty meal indeed.

The cuts of meat most suitable for braising come from the parts of the animal's body—primarily the shoulder and parts of the leg—used in moving around. This means they contain a lot of the connective tissue called collagen. To make such cuts tender, it is necessary to melt the collagen, transforming it into gelatin. Braising is particularly effective at doing this because the meat cooks at a relatively low temperature for a long time. If the meat were cooked at a higher temperature, the collagen would be steamed away; if it were cooked for a shorter period of time, the collagen would not melt.

Meats for braising also need to have a relatively high proportion of intramuscular fat. This is important, because the fat keeps the meat moist during the long, slow cooking process.

When braising, there are really only three fundamental rules to follow, all related to the fact that braising is a variant of boiling.

First, because boiling water never gets above 212°F degrees and browning does not begin to take place below 325°F degrees, braising food will not brown it. Therefore, it is very important that you start out by putting a good strong sear on whatever you are going to braise. This creates a concentrated layer of flavor that will later be diffused throughout the broth, flavoring the entire dish. Similarly, be sure to dissolve the brown bits that are left on the bottom of the pan after searing, again because their intense flavors will permeate the broth during the long cooking.

Second, since water stays at the same temperature as long as it continues to boil, no talent or effort is required on the part of the cook to keep food that is being braised at a constant, even temperature for a long period of time with no threat that the exterior will burn. This is fortunate, because the single most important aspect of braising is to cook the food long enough to reach tenderness, a point that is appraised not by internal temperature but by texture.

Finally, snugness is important in two ways when braising. The meat should fit snugly into the pan, so that a small amount of liquid will come about halfway up the sides of the meat, and the lid should fit snugly on the pan so the upper part of the meat is cooking in steam.

Like stews, braises are even better if made a day ahead of time. This has two advantages. First, since braising is a long, slow process, it's hard to have braised dishes on weeknights—unless you cook them one night and eat them the next. Second, most cuts of meat that are suitable for braising contain quite a lot of fat. If you refrigerate the dish overnight, you can then simply remove the layer of fat that will form on top of the liquid and discard it before reheating the dish.

Braising Techniques

First you want to dry the meat well, season it well, and—using a pot that will hold the meat snugly—brown it very well. For the large pieces of meat that are typical of braises, we find that searing takes about 15 minutes, which is probably longer than you might think. But don't hesitate—it will be worth it. When the meat is nicely browned, take it out of the pot.

Next, you want to brown any aromatic vegetables (onions, garlic, carrots, celery, etc.) that you are using. To do this, you'll typically need only a couple of tablespoons of fat in the pot. So if the meat you have just browned was fatty, you'll need to pour out some of the excess fat; if, on the other hand, the meat was lean, you may need to add a bit of oil to the pot. Then go ahead and brown the vegetables.

At this point, you will probably notice a bunch of browned bits stuck to the bottom of the pot. In French cooking, this stuff is called *fond,* and it is definitely not something you want to clean out of the pot. It is intensely flavorful due to the browning reactions that have taken place during searing. What you want to do is loosen and dissolve those brown bits in liquid so their flavor will be diffused throughout the dish as it cooks. This is called "deglazing." So you add the liquid to the pot and, as you heat it to a simmer, use a wooden spoon to scrape up all those browned bits.

Now you're ready to return the meat to the pot, along with any other vegetables you want to add. Just nestle the meat right in there, then check to see that it is covered about halfway by the liquid. If the amount of liquid called for in the recipe is too much or too little, make the adjustment by using less or more. After all, few pieces of meat are exactly the same size, so the amount of liquid we call for is only an approximation.

When the liquid has come back to a simmer, skim any film off the surface, cover the pot, and put it in a 300°F oven. You could cook the meat on top of the stove, but we prefer using the oven because it provides a more even heat that surrounds the pot, rather than coming only from the bottom.

Now you're basically done. Just let the meat cook and, about 15 minutes before the point at which we suggest it may be done, start checking it. The best way to determine doneness with braised meat is to stick a large fork straight down into the meat and try to lift it out of the pan. If you can't do so because the meat won't hold the fork, then it has reached the state our grandmothers called "fork-tender," and it's ready to eat. Remember, you are cooking past the point of doneness to the point of tenderness.

When the meat is done, you'll also want to check the braising liquid. Often it will have all the flavor you want, and you'll be ready to serve the dish. Sometimes, though, you may feel that it should have a more intense flavor. No problem. Simply take the meat out of the pot, set it on a platter, and cover it loosely with foil. Now put the cooking pot on the stove over medium-high heat, bring the braising liquid to a boil, and reduce it until it is flavorful enough for your taste. Either way, you will want to do a final seasoning of the braising liquid with salt and pepper.

Now, carve the meat into thick slices, pour the braising liquid into a big gravy boat, and you're ready to eat some incredibly flavorful, really tender meat.

GRILLING, SAUTÉING, AND BROILING

It will come as no surprise to any of you who have read our other books that grilling is our absolute favorite cooking method. There's nothing like the thrill of cooking over live fire, and nothing like the taste of food that is cooked this way. A juicy, perfectly seared piece of fire-cooked meat coming off the grill is about as close to culinary perfection as we can imagine.

We're not going to go into a lot of detail about grilling here, because there simply isn't room to deal with all the many manifestations of this most exciting of cooking methods. (If you're interested, you might want to check out our previous book *License to Grill*.) But we are going to give what we consider to be the most helpful general guidelines, which apply not only to grilling but also to sautéing and broiling.

We're combining these three cooking methods here because the principles of all three are the same. They are all dry-heat cooking techniques in which meat (in this case) is cooked quickly over direct, intense heat. This means that they are all best suited to cooking relatively small, very tender cuts of meat: small because the high heat would cause a large piece of meat to burn on the outside well before it was cooked on the inside, tender because the quickness of the process does not allow time for any connective tissues to break down during cooking.

Whichever of these high-heat cooking methods you use, it is usually best to buy thick. That way, you can sear the meat nicely on the outside without overcooking it on the inside. You'll notice that we almost always call for steaks, chops, and other tender cuts of meat that are at least 1½ inches thick and sometimes as much as 2 inches or even more. We understand that there are variations in the thicknesses of these cuts and that you may not be able to find, for example, a 2-inch-thick porterhouse steak. We are giving you the ideal. But if you can't find it, just buy the thickest you can get a hold of and adjust the cooking time accordingly.

Since searing is the essence of all three cooking methods, the first step for all of these techniques is to make sure the heat is high before you start cooking the meat.

For grilling, that means building a fire about half an hour before you start cooking so the flames can die down and the coals can become covered with gray ash. At that point, you need to check the temperature of the fire to be sure it is just right; most meats should start out over a hot fire, but some need medium-high. We also recommend that you usually build a two-level fire, with one side of the grill hot and the other side cooler. That way, if the meat starts to burn on the outside before it is cooked through, you can move it to the cooler side.

For sautéing, be sure that you use only a little bit of oil, really just enough to film the surface of the pan—you want the meat to sear, not fry. Heat the oil over medium-high heat until it is very hot, almost smoking, before you add the meat.

For broiling, be sure that you preheat the broiler before you start cooking.

Another key to these cooking methods is to flip the meat only once while it is cooking. If you keep flipping it back and forth, not only do you interfere with the proper formation of the sear, you also disrupt the process of driving the juices to the center of the meat. Don't think, either, that you have to cook meat for an equal amount of time on both sides. You can cook it for 70 percent of the time on one side and 30 percent on the other side and it will come out just fine. The point at which you should flip is not necessarily the midpoint of the cooking process, but the point at which the first side achieves the sear you want it to have.

As with other cooking methods, a primary aspect of perfect grilling, sautéing, and broiling is knowing when the meat is done to your liking. Some people recommend using a thermometer to check doneness for meats cooked with these methods, but we prefer more direct methods.

One option is the "hand method," which many professional chefs use. This means that you poke the meat and compare it to the feeling of various parts of your hand: You start with rare, which feels like the connective tissue between the ball of your thumb and the knuckle of your index finger, and progress to very well done, which feels like the base of the ball of your thumb. It's fun to use this method, and we recommend you poke meat when you're cooking it so that you begin to learn about this method from personal experience. But it's very hard to do when you're cooking just one dish. It makes much more sense for professionals, who can compare dozens or even hundreds of similar cuts of meat in a single evening.

Let us explain by example. When I (Chris) was working at the Diplomat Hotel in Florida in 1976, on one Saturday night in February, I was assigned the "steak station." That evening I cooked nothing but sirloins, and I sent out 373 steaks, not one of which was returned for being incorrectly done. This feat is still legend in southern Florida and, although I was only a twenty-two-year-old culinary student at the time, it remains one of my personal career highlights. On the other hand, I'm not allowed to cook steaks at my sister's house, because I always overcook them. So as you can see, it's easy to use the hand method when you're cooking one steak after another after another, but when you're cooking only one or two you tend to misjudge.

So we recommend that you learn the touch method as you go along, but for everyday use, we suggest what we call the "nick, peek, and cheat" method. As the name implies, you simply pick up one of whatever you are cooking, nick it slightly with a knife so you can look inside, and check its state of doneness. That's all there is to it. No guesswork, no intricate techniques. It couldn't get much easier—or more accurate.

Despite that, though, many home cooks shy away from this method. One reason is that somehow the idea has taken hold that it is not good to handle food while it is being cooked. Not true. Check out any professional cook, and you will notice that he or she is constantly touching what they are cooking. Another reason people avoid the "peek and cheat" method is the myth that cutting into a piece of food lets all the juices run out. Again, not true. Some juices do escape, but it's not like putting a hole in a balloon; the very small amount of juice you may lose pales in comparison to the prospect of serving raw or burned food.

With the tender cuts of meat that are cooked with any of these three methods, doneness is a matter of taste, with opinions running the gamut from dead raw to gray throughout. This makes it easy: Simply look inside to see if the meat is done to your liking. Remember, though, that the meat will continue to cook a bit after it is removed from the heat, a phenomenon known as "carryover cooking." So, if you want your meat medium-rare, for example, remove it when it still looks rare.

Grilling/Sautéing/Broiling Techniques

Begin by making sure that your fire is hot, the oil in your sauté pan is almost smoking, or your broiler is fully preheated.

While the heat source is heating up, dry the meat well and season it generously with salt and pepper. Then place it on the grill, add it to the pan, or put it in the broiler, making sure in all cases that you do not crowd the pieces of meat. If you do, the meat will not sear well.

When the meat is well seared on the first side (however long that may take), turn it to cook the other side. Don't keep flipping it back and forth.

If at some point you decide that the meat is cooking so fast that it will burn on the outside before cooking through, move it to the cool side of the grill, turn down the heat under the sauté pan, or turn the broiler to low if you have that option. When grilling, though, resist the temptation to use the cover when cooking small cuts of meat. Since they are only on the grill a short time, they will pick up an unpleasant flavor from the inside of the cover. If you feel you need to cover the meat so it cooks through more thoroughly, use a metal pie plate or disposable aluminum pan.

That's about all there is to it—another reason we are so fond of grilling and its cousin cooking methods. As with all other cooking methods, check for doneness early and often, using the "nick, peek, and cheat" method. When the meat is done one level less than you want it to be when you eat it, remove it from the heat and let it rest for 5 minutes. Then serve it and eat it. It doesn't get much better than that.

STEWING

Nothing is quite so homey and comforting as a meat stew. Precisely because the cooking method is so imprecise—you put some pieces of meat and a bunch of other ingredients in a pot, cover them with liquid, and cook until they're done—stews have a reassuring aura of hearty, down-home simplicity. Since the flavor of the meat permeates the entire dish as it slowly simmers, stews also have a long and honorable history of making a little bit of meat go a long way.

The principles of stewing are very much like those of braising: The long, slow moist-heat cooking transforms much of the connective tissue in tough pieces of meat into gelatin, making the meat far more tender. The primary difference between the two cooking methods is that stewing uses smaller pieces of meat and a larger amount of liquid, enough to completely cover the meat and other ingredients. In other words, if braising is wading, then stewing is swimming.

When it comes to choosing meat for stews, you usually have two options. You can either buy prepackaged "stew meat" or buy a larger piece of meat and cube it yourself. The obvious advantage of the first option is convenience, and we are certainly in favor of that. But there is also a definite advantage to cutting up the meat yourself.

Certain cuts of meat, mostly from the shoulder, and from the leg in some animals, are ideal for stewing. They have plenty of connective tissue to provide flavor, along with enough fat to keep the meat moist during the long, slow cooking. Chances are that when you buy prepackaged meat some of it comes from these cuts, but, since most prepackaged stew meat consists of trimmings left over from any relatively gnarly cut after the butcher has fashioned the larger cuts from it, you will probably be getting a mixture of bits from several parts of the animal. So to be sure that you are getting the best meat for stews, buy that larger piece and cut it up yourself. This also allows you to cut it into relatively large cubes, which gives the meat a more significant presence in the stew. To us, that makes for a more satisfying eating experience.

Stewing Techniques

As with all other methods of cooking meat, stewing starts out with drying the meat, then seasoning it liberally and browning it well. Drying is particularly important here. Moisture on the surface of meat would cause the hot oil to splatter, and when using small pieces of meat, there is more opportunity for the oil to splatter up between them rather than just around the edges as with a larger piece.

It is also important that you do not crowd the meat in the pot when browning. If you do, the meat will not get hot enough and it will begin to exude too much liquid to brown well. So be sure that the cubes of meat do not touch each other, even if this means that you need to brown the meat in batches rather than all at once.

You also want to check to be sure the oil is hot enough before you begin browning the stew meat. To do this, put a single piece of meat in the pot when you think the oil is hot enough. If it does not sizzle the moment it hits the pot take it out and wait for the oil to heat up more. On the other hand, if it spits, sputters, and smokes, the oil is too hot; remove the pot from the heat and let it cool slightly.

After browning the meat, you'll want to adjust the amount of fat in the pot, then brown the aromatic vegetables and deglaze the pot, just as you do when braising. Then put the meat back into the pot and add enough liquid to just cover all the ingredients. If the amount of liquid specified in the recipe is not enough, simply add more of the appropriate stock, wine or beer, or water.

After skimming any film off the top of the liquid, reduce the heat to low and simmer slowly until the meat is done. As with other cooking methods, the times that we give in the recipes are only approximations, and the only way to be sure when any particular stew is done to your liking is to check early and often. With stews, the method of doing this is supremely straightforward: Take out a piece of meat and taste it. It should be tender rather than chewy.

When the meat is done, the stew is almost ready. Because we like the dynamic of adding something fresh and bright to long-cooked stews, we often toss in a bit of citrus juice or fresh herbs or something of that nature right at the end. After that, it's just a matter of adjusting the seasoning with salt and pepper, skimming any film from the surface, and serving it up.

Thick or thin, many stews are excellent served just as is. But some are even better when served over a starch such as rice or with potatoes. We'll give you advice in this department in each stew recipe, but feel free to improvise as you please. After all, it's your stew.

TOP 5 TIPS FOR COOKING MEAT

We've given you a lot of information in the preceding pages, and we hope that it has been useful. But for ourselves, we find it also helps to have the most important basics in condensed form. So here are our fundamental, highly important tips for cooking meat. If you follow them, you are going to end up with some pretty fine meat on your plate.

1. *Use the right method for the right meat.*

We've said it before and now we'll say it again: It is crucial that you match the method to the meat: cook tender cuts with dry heat, tougher cuts with moist heat.

2. *Use plenty of kosher salt and freshly cracked black pepper.*

When we say "sprinkle generously," we mean it. Nothing brings out meat's rich flavors like salt, and as for fresh pepper, we think it is one of the few ingredients for which there is no substitute. It is a whole different animal from preground, and well worth the small amount of extra effort.

3. *Sear the meat longer than you think you should.*

Look for a dark brown sear on the outside of the meat, not just a light golden hue. And for best results, always dry the meat well before searing it.

4. *Check for doneness early and often.*

There are plenty of variables in cooking, from the particular piece of meat you buy to the pot you use to the stove you cook on. That means that the times given in recipes are only guidelines. Start checking for doneness well before the recommended cooking time is up, and check frequently after that.

5. *Get to know your butcher.*

Since buying good-quality meat is the first step to a good meal, this may be the most important tip of all. As with fishmongers or farmers or cheese sellers, having a personal relationship with a butcher is an invaluable help.

COOK'S NOTES

START WITH SALT

Forget about that old rule that you don't salt meat just prior to cooking because it draws out moisture. The small amount of fluid drawn to the surface by salt is more than compensated for by the fact that the salt has a chance to interact with the meat and amplify its flavors. Because the moisture drawn to the surface contains proteins, early salting also intensifies the browning process. We prefer kosher salt for a number of reasons, primarily because it seems to have a deeper flavor than regular salt and its large crystals make it easier to judge just how much salt you're adding when you use your fingers—which is the best and most fun way to do it. (By the way, when making any of our recipes that call for a set amount of salt, as opposed to "to taste," be aware that regular table salt has about twice as much salt per volume as kosher salt.)

AGING, NO

Aged meat is not the same as old meat. Aging is a process by which meat (almost always beef) is allowed to sit over a number of days exposed to the air in conditions of carefully controlled temperature, humidity, and air circulation. As moisture evaporates and certain enzymes go to work on the meat's protein, the meat becomes more tender and gains a deeper, more concentrated flavor.

It is theoretically possible to age meat at home in your refrigerator, but it's not such a great idea. Too many things can go wrong along the way, and you are likely to end up with meat that is spoiled rather than properly aged. In our opinion, the eating of aged beef is an experience best reserved for restaurant dining. Since this is a book about home cooking, that's really all we have to say about it.

FREEZING, YES

Freezing meat, on the other hand, is a fine idea for the home cook. Meat freezes well—some types better than others—and doing so lets you take advantage of good prices when you see them. It also lets you hang on to meat that you buy and then can't use as quickly as you thought you would. Of course, no meat that has been frozen and then thawed will ever be exactly the same quality as the fresh version, but if you take a few precautions along the way, it can be pretty close.

The two key points here are to take the meat from fresh to frozen as quickly as possible and to keep air from getting to the meat while it is in the freezer. To accomplish the first goal, set your freezer on the lowest (coldest) setting. While the optimal temperature for freezing meat is 0°F, many home freezers operate closer to 10° to 15°F; the lower you can set yours, the better. For the second goal, wrap the meat in a double layer of either freezer paper or plastic wrap, not aluminum foil, which tends to become brittle and crack when frozen. Try to wrap the meat as tightly as you can, so that as little air remains inside the package as possible. It's also a good idea to get some freezer tape if you're going to be freezing a lot of meat. Unlike regular tape, it will stay on the package even at freezing temperatures, and it is specially made for writing on, so you can label and date the packages.

Even if you don't buy special freezer tape, do label and date packages of meat before you put them into the freezer. A label is important because it keeps you from being faced with a mystery package when your memory fails you a few weeks or months later. A date is important because oxidation and dehydration of meat continue very slowly even at freezing temperatures, so you don't want to leave the meat in the freezer forever. The optimal approach is to use meat within a month or two of the time you put it in the freezer, simply because you are not going to be able to wrap it tightly enough to get all of the air out. It's acceptable, though, to keep pork frozen for up to 6 months, veal and lamb for 9 months, and beef up to a year.

To thaw meat, take it out of the freezer, put it on a plate, and let it thaw overnight in the refrigerator. Thawing it at room temperature is too inviting to bacteria, and thawing in the microwave gives you mushy meat. Many books advise that twenty-four hours is sufficient to thaw meat, but we have found that this is true only of smaller cuts; roasts may take considerably longer. Since there is nothing more annoying than going to prepare the roast and finding it still frozen at the center, we recommend giving large roasts a couple of days to thaw.

Doneness

You'll notice that in the case of tender cuts of meat such as roasts, steaks, and chops, we don't follow the USDA guidelines in terms of how long the meat should be cooked. There is a simple reason for this: In our opinion, the guidelines instruct you to cook meat until it is overdone. Follow them, and the meat will be dry and relatively flavorless. There is no good restaurant in the country that follows the USDA guidelines, and neither do we.

The exception to this rule is ground meat. With larger cuts, there is no way for airborne bacteria or germs to get inside the meat. Any that are on the outer surface will be killed by the high heat of searing, and much lower cooking temperatures are high enough to kill the food-borne pathogens that might be inside the meat. With ground meat, on the other hand, every bit of the meat has been exposed to possible contamination by airborne pathogens. That means you really do have to be concerned about cooking the meat well enough to kill all those nasty bugs.

STORAGE

You want to watch out for keeping meat, either fresh or cooked, in the refrigerator for too long. All fresh meat should be wrapped quite tightly before being refrigerated, but different meats keep for different lengths of time. As a rule of thumb, veal should only be kept refrigerated for a day or two, while pork can be kept there for 2 to 3 days, and beef and lamb can go for 3 to 4 days. For the most part, organ meats, which are quite perishable, should be refrigerated for only a day or so. After that, it's cook it or freeze it.

Once cooked, meat will last for 4 or 5 days in the refrigerator if well covered.

PORTION SIZE

Our recipes call for traditional portions of meat, but you can easily adjust this to suit your own diet. We may say, for example, that a 3-pound pork loin roast serves 4 to 6; but if you are eating less meat these days, you can serve it to 8 or even 10 guests. If you want a pork roast but you're not having that many people over for dinner, don't worry—we provide ideas for using the leftovers too.

THE TOOLS YOU NEED

You don't need many tools to cook meat, and you probably already have most or all of them. So, assuming that you already have the standard big items (a stove, a grill) and small items (wooden spoons, a ladle, sharp knives), here are the other tools and pans you should have on hand to make the recipes in this book.

TONGS: The single most used tools in both of our kitchens are our long-handled, spring-loaded tongs. They are ideal for flipping small items in the sauté pan, moving things around on the grill, plucking cubes of meat out of stews to test their doneness, and even for turning small roasts. We recommend that you have several pairs on hand.

MEAT THERMOMETER: When you're dealing with a large roast there is no good way to accurately judge its state of doneness except with a meat thermometer. This is one place where it is worth spending some money and getting a good one. We generally prefer the dial thermometers to the digital instant-read variety because, in our experience, they tend to be longer-lasting and more reliable. Admittedly they may not be as easy to read with absolute precision, but then a difference of half a degree in meat temperature is not a big deal anyway.

That said, there is one style of digital-style thermometer that you might want to check out if you cook a lot of roasts. Usually referred to as a "thermometer/timer," it consists of a thermometer/timer unit that is connected to a probe by a long wire. To use it, you push the probe into the roast, put the roast in the oven, and set the thermometer/timer unit, which sits on the counter, to the internal temperature you want the roast to cook to. When the roast reaches that temperature, the timer buzzes. The down side of this is that, since you are not opening the oven door to check the temperature, you do not see the meat at all, which can be a slight problem because there are factors other than temperature (e.g., color) that you might want to assess. On the other hand, it is definitely convenient.

ROASTING PANS: It's a good idea to have a couple of roasting pans, one large and one medium-sized. You will need the larger one for things like leg of lamb, but if you put a smaller roast into a pan that is way too big for it, the juices will probably burn in the large empty areas around the meat. Get roasting pans that are heavy enough so they can be used on top of the stove as well as in the oven. That way you can make the jus right in the roasting pan rather than a saucepan, which increases your dishwashing tasks.

ROASTING RACK: If you put a roast on a rack rather than just on the bottom of the pan, it cooks a lot more evenly, because the hot air can circulate all around it. Also, it won't burn on the bottom. It's best to get a sturdy rack.

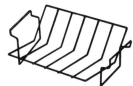

DUTCH OVEN OR OTHER HEAVY-BOTTOMED POT: A Dutch oven is nothing but a wide deep pot with a lid and handles. The important part of this pot—what makes it different, for example, from a stockpot—is that it always has a heavy bottom. That means you can use it to brown meat on the stove over high heat, then add liquid and braise or stew the meat along with other ingredients. Since browning the meat well is crucial to the flavor of stews and braises, a pot of this type is pretty close to essential.

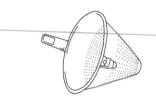

SAUTÉ PANS: You will need a large sauté pan, and you should probably have a small one too. Be sure that they are ovenproof so that you can brown meat on the stove and then put it in the oven in the same pan. Again, this will cut down on the amount of dishwashing you have to do—and that's about the only part of cooking that is no fun. We particularly like those big black cast-iron sauté pans and skillets. They're heavy, but they conduct heat remarkably efficiently and evenly and they are indestructible.

STOCKPOT: You'll need a stockpot if you're going to make your own stock, and it is also useful for blanching vegetables.

HEAVY-DUTY FORK: This can be either one of those giant two-pronged forks that come with a knife as a carving set or just a large serving fork. The purpose of it is to test the doneness of braised meats: if the meat falls off the fork, it's done.

CHINA CAP: Not essential but nice to have around, this is a large conical fine-mesh metal strainer that is very handy for straining braising liquids.

The *The* STOCK EXCHANGE: REAL KITCHEN *Solutions*

When French cuisine came to America, there was a lot of talk about fine homemade stocks being the indispensable basis for great food. This certainly makes sense in the context of French cooking, because that cuisine revolves around the "mother sauce" system, and a mother sauce not only requires a stock, it depends upon it for its depth of flavor. As a result, cooking instructors in this country constantly hammered on the importance of real homemade stock.

There's no doubt that this is an important concept. But it is also a little Franco-centric. After all, there are many fine cuisines in which stock is far from central. Besides, in today's world, the practicalities involved in making a stock are difficult for most people. If we were to insist that our dishes only be made with homemade stock, a lot of these excellent dishes would simply not get cooked. So we're taking a different position on the stock question. We acknowledge its importance as a base for braises, stews, and soups, but we're looking at it more from the point of view that it is important to use *some* flavorful liquid as this base. Now, there are many different ways to get a flavorful liquid into the pot, and we like to think that our dishes can be very successful whether you make your own stock in the classic tradition, use souped-up canned chicken broth, or even just go with plain old canned broth "as is." And in most cases, you will be braising or stewing in the liquid anyway, so the cooking process itself will add plenty of flavor to it.

Our advice, then, is this: If you have a roast chicken, throw the carcass in the freezer; then you can always use it later to make a stock. In fact, get in the habit of doing the same thing any time you have leftover bones from meat, or chicken wing tips, or even just the odd piece of meat. Even if you don't feel up to going the whole nine yards, you can adopt our favorite approach: Take some canned chicken stock and enrich it with the standard aromatic vegetables (carrots, celery, onion) plus any piece of meat or bones that you have left over or have frozen from previous cooking sessions.

But the decision is really up to you. Listed in descending order of flavor intensity, here are your stock options. If you don't have time or inclination to make the best, just substitute one farther down the line.

STOCK OPTIONS

THE REAL DEAL: This is the classic approach, which will yield an intensely flavorful liquid. Basically, you toss meaty bones and vegetables together in a roasting pan and roast them in a hot oven until they caramelize and turn a dark, nutty brown. You then dump the roasted mixture into a stockpot, add water, and simmer for a few hours. Strain out the solids, and you end up with a golden-brown stock that's practically rich enough to call a soup. If you cook it long enough, the bones will give up enough gelatin so that the stock gels completely when it's chilled. This is the good stuff. We encourage you to make it whenever you have bones on hand, or time to spare, then freeze it in relatively small, airtight containers. It will keep for 2 to 3 months.

SUPER-CHARGED CANNED BROTH: If you just don't have the time or inclination to make your own stock, the next-best option is to doctor up some canned chicken broth. Toss your meat and vegetable scraps—bones from a roast, the ends of an onion, celery tops, parsley stems, whatever you come up with as you prep the rest of your recipe ingredients—into a medium saucepan with a bit of oil and brown them over medium heat for 8 to 10 minutes. Then pour in your favorite low-salt canned broth, add a bay leaf and some peppercorns, and simmer over low heat on a back burner as long as possible, until you need it for the recipe. Strain out the solids, and it's ready to use. It won't have the great color or richness of stock made with roasted bones, but the flavor will be deeper and more complex than broth straight from the can.

NO-STOCK STOCK: Even if you don't have canned stock, you can still make the most out of those meat and vegetable trimmings. Follow the same procedure as in Super-Charged Canned Broth above, but substitute wine, beer, or even water for the canned broth.

CANNED CHICKEN BROTH: Use it straight from the can . . . it's better than plain water. It is also more flavorful than canned beef broth, and much easier to get your hands on than lamb or veal stock. We advise you to use a low-salt version, since you may be reducing it quite a bit, a process that causes full-salt versions to end up being way too salty.

OTHER LIQUIDS: Sometimes stock is not required to make a flavorful liquid for a stew or braise. Wine, beer, and fruit juices all add a lot of flavor to the pot. Our favorite is beer, since it has a particular affinity for meat and adds real body to the liquid as well. Beer is particularly handy in those situations when you have used some stock but don't have any more, and the dish needs more liquid. Don't fuss, just toss in a beer.

WATER: No explanation needed. It's got no flavor, it's got no body, but making a stew or braise with water is better than not making it at all.

The Real Deal Recipe

4 pounds meaty raw beef, pork, lamb, or veal bones, depending on the type of stock you are making (or chicken backs, necks, and giblets)

2 tablespoons olive oil (optional)

1 large onion, unpeeled, quartered

2 stalks celery, roughly chopped

2 medium carrots, roughly chopped

2 tablespoons tomato paste

$\frac{1}{2}$ cup dry white wine (or substitute dry red wine, beer, or water)

10 black peppercorns

1 bay leaf

4 sprigs fresh thyme (or $\frac{1}{2}$ teaspoon dried thyme)

10 sprigs fresh parsley

Kosher salt and freshly cracked black pepper to taste

2 cloves garlic, unpeeled (optional)

3 to 4 quarts cold water

1. Preheat the oven to 500°F. Place a large roasting pan in the oven to preheat.

2. Rinse the bones and dry them well. Add the oil to the pan if you are using it, then add the bones, vegetables, and tomato paste. Roast until the bones and vegetables are well browned and caramelized, 20 to 30 minutes.

3. Transfer the contents of the roasting pan to an 8-quart stockpot and place the roasting pan on the stove. Add the wine to the roasting pan and bring to a simmer over medium-high heat, stirring to dissolve the brown crusty stuff in the bottom of the pan. Add to the stockpot, along with the remaining seasonings.

4. Add enough cold water to cover the ingredients by a few inches, partially cover the pot, and bring to a simmer. Simmer beef stock for about 6 hours, chicken, lamb, pork, or veal stock for about 4 hours, skimming any scum that rises to the surface and adding hot water if the liquid evaporates below the surface of the ingredients. Do not allow the stock to boil.

5. When the vegetables and bones have given up all the flavor they can, remove the pot from the heat. Place a colander over another large pot or saucepan and pour the stock into it. Lift out the colander and discard the solids. Strain the stock again, through a fine-meshed sieve this time, to remove any remaining solids. Taste and correct the seasoning, then chill. When the stock is cold, remove the layer of fat that will have formed on the surface.

BEEF: AMERICA'S MEAT

No doubt about it, Americans love beef. **For reasons of geography, history, and cultural identity, beef has become the emblematic food of** our country. For reasons of personal background, we're hooked on it too.

Being raised in Iowa, I (Doc) grew up to the sound of T-bone steaks sizzling and spitting in the broiler. Those fat steaks, cut from local steers and stored in our family spot at the meat locker downtown just off Main Street, were the default meal, the one my parents made when they wanted something really good but didn't want to put a lot of work into it. Stately rib roasts were the culinary centerpiece of choice for non-holiday celebrations, and pot roasts in various guises were the gold standard for warming winter meals. We even had barbecued beef ribs, though it required a drive to Lincoln, a town of about four hundred people located some ten miles from our house, where we could sample Carl's locally famous version.

And anybody who knows me (Chris) very well at all knows that if I am allowed to select the restaurant where we go to dinner, I will almost always be choosing a place where I can get a shrimp cocktail, a baked potato, a green salad, and a big, juicy steak. That's the food of my tribe (the WASP). Roast beef on Sunday with my grandparents, steak on the weekends with my family, hamburgers for lunch almost every day—that's my culinary heritage.

When I think of beef, I think of all the steaks, from sirloin to Delmonico to strip to skirt, and even the grilled round steak that sustained me for a period in my youth. I think of braised brisket, juicy roast rump, and tender braised short ribs. I remember the steamship rounds I carved as a buffet worker in Miami Beach, the hundreds of sirloin steaks I cooked at a dinner theater where I once worked, the fifteen prime ribs I would roast every night at the resort hotels. If you ask me, to be a professional cook in America is to work with a lot of beef, and to live in America is to eat a lot of beef.

Now, we don't mean to give the impression that only Americans are fond of beef. No less an authority than Carême, the great nineteenth-century French chef, declared beef "the soul of cooking," and it's an important part of the daily culinary repertoire in countries from Vietnam to Argentina. But when you're cooking beef in America, you've definitely got the home court advantage.

The standard explanation for the popularity of beef among Americans is that the first colonists, being from England, had an unusual fondness for it, which they passed on to their descendants. There is some truth to that, but not much; in fact, the English of that day liked mutton as much as beef. The real source of our national obsession with beef lies much farther west, in Mexico and present-day Texas.

When Spanish missionaries fanned out from Mexico through the southwestern United States, they brought cattle with them. As they later retreated from these missions, they left the cows behind. By the early eighteenth century, there were large herds of wild cattle roaming through the region. Known as Texas longhorns, they had developed, over many generations of long-range foraging in scrubland, an ability that would prove pivotal to the future of America: They could walk all day through all kinds of weather without tiring.

The ranchers who corralled and redomesticated these animals decided to put the walking prowess of their new breed to good use. They resolved to walk them all the way from their grazing lands in Texas to the ready markets to the north. Thus began the amazing American phenomenon that is the source of much of our national mythology, the "cattle drive."

By any measure, these drives were monumental endeavors. Starting from the enormous ranches in Texas, a handful of cowboys would drive huge herds of up to twenty-five hundred cattle as far as fifteen hundred miles, a journey that could take two, three, or even four months. Although the life of the cowboys was actually rather squalid, dirty, and unpleasant, these ornery cusses seized the imagination of a country still trying to define its destiny. Their feats became legendary and, for better or worse, the ideals of independence, rugged individualism, and can-do optimism that are at the heart of America's self-image were largely formed in and around the cattle drive. Along the way, beef became forever entwined with our sense of national identity.

The next stage was considerably less romantic. Seeing an opportunity for profit, wealthy entrepreneurs from Europe and the East bought up huge tracts of land in the West and Midwest and set about creating an industry out of a legend. Before long, a new form of restaurant, the steak house, became all the rage from New York to San Francisco. America had begun its love affair with beef. Today, it is our country's most popular meat by a wide margin.

Like pork, though, today's beef is considerably different from the beef that our ancestors ate.

In the 1960s, nutritionists and others began to raise health concerns about the amount of saturated fat in the American diet, particularly from beef. The resulting demand for healthier beef caused producers to embark on an intensive program designed to come up with a less fat-laden product.

Their efforts have worked remarkably well. Through crossbreeding, modifications in feeding programs, and more extensive trimming of external fat prior to sale, producers have reduced the fat in today's beef by 27 percent compared to twenty years ago. Of course, this makes for a somewhat less flavorful and less tender product. The beef industry has tried to address the tenderness issue by bringing cattle to slaughter earlier. To deal with the somewhat lower flavor quotient, we recommend the tactics described earlier in the book: Use some of the tougher but more flavorful cuts, cook bone-in cuts, and sear hard at the beginning of cooking.

Rich, juicy, eminently adaptable, and possessed of a unique, deep flavor, beef is the taste of home to many Americans. Fortunately, there are plenty of ways to enjoy it. The huge variety of choices and the high quality that is routinely available make beef a very good place to start experimenting with all kinds of cuts.

ABOUT CUTS OF BEEF

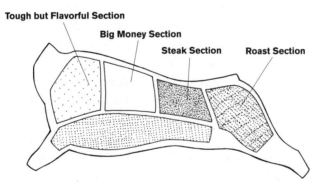

Because a steer is so much larger than a lamb or a pig, its muscles are separated into many more individual cuts. That translates into a whole lot of options at the meat counter; you could cook beef every night of the week for months without repeating yourself. It also translates into a confusing situation. So, let's start by sorting out the parts of the steer and what well-known cuts come from each one.

The steer is divided into four main parts: the chuck, which is the shoulder and arm from the neck back through the first five ribs; the rib, which includes the rib cage from the sixth through the twelfth ribs; the loin, which is the center and rear section of the back; and the round, which is the butt and leg. When a steer is butchered, it is cut lengthwise in half, creating two sides of beef. Each of these is then cut into the four cuts we just described, making a total of eight per steer. These are the primal cuts.

In line with our "keep it simple" approach to understanding parts of meat animals, we recommend you think of the four major sections of the steer like this: the chuck, which happens to be the primal that we champion, is the Tough But Flavorful Section; the rib is the Big Money Section; the loin is the Steak Section; and the round is the Roast Section.

The chuck, which is the equivalent of your neck, upper arms, and shoulders, is a tough part of the steer, riddled with connective tissue developed by the exercise involved in moving the animal around. This part of the beast is a primary source of ground beef as well as stew meat. It is also the source of relatively large cuts, such as 7-bone blade roast and chuck shoulder roast, that are perfect for braised dishes like pot roast. The brisket, which is at the bottom of the chuck, is also a great piece of meat for braising. Going against type, there are also a couple of relatively tender large cuts in the chuck, including the chuck eye roast and the chuck top blade steak.

Next comes the rib, which is the equivalent of your rib cage. This area is far more tender than the chuck, in fact the most tender part of the whole animal. It includes the very pricey standing rib roast, a.k.a. prime rib, which is why we call this the Big Money Section. If you cut the standing rib roast into steaks, you get Delmonico, or rib-eye, steaks, which are among our favorites. The tough but meaty ends of the ribs become short ribs. (You can also get short ribs from the chuck, but don't worry about that at this point.)

The loin, which corresponds to your lower back, is also very tender. The three primary sections of the loin are the top loin muscle, the tenderloin muscle, and the sirloin, which corresponds to the hip. Here is where you get all the steaks you know best, from filet mignon to porterhouse to T-bone and all the variations on sirloin steak.

Finally comes the round, which is the equivalent of your butt and leg. This is the one primal cut that is sometimes used as a retail cut—if you have ever been at a buffet where a guy in a funny little white hat was carving up what looked like a giant leg, you have actually seen a round. But, like the other primals, the round is usually carved up into smaller sections. Most of them are suitable for roasting, including the eye round roast, rump roast, and top round roast. You also see a steak come out of here for summer grilling, along with some stew meat and some braising cuts from the bottom round. This is also another major source for ground beef.

By this point, you should have a general idea of how the cow is divided up. So let's look in a little more detail at the cuts in terms of how they are best cooked, which is the way you'll actually deal with them in your kitchen.

When it comes to roasts, you have to start with the Monarch of Roast Beef, the standing rib roast. As you now know, this majestic cut comes from the rib section of the cow. With its wonderfully rich, beefy flavor, it is a bedrock American favorite, fit for any celebratory occasion. Roasts taken from the short loin area, including the Châteaubriand, the full tenderloin, and the top loin roast, are also right up there in terms of both tenderness and flavor. For a slightly less exalted but still excellent roast, try the tender rump roast, the surprising chuck eye roast, and the classic eye of round, ideally suited for roast beef sandwiches.

For braising and stewing, the chuck is the section to turn to time after time. From chuck arm roasts to beef shoulder pot roast to the full and half brisket, cuts from this part of the beast have a tremendous amount of full, deep flavor. They are excellent choices for long, slow moist cooking, an approach that turns them from tough and gnarly to tender and succulent. Short ribs, which can come from several different parts of the steer, have all of these same flavor virtues plus a bone, which is always an added advantage. Cuts from the bottom round, such as the bottom round steak, are also good braising material, although a little chewier than those from the chuck.

In the same way, just about any cut from the chuck, when cut into cubes, makes wonderfully flavorful stew meat. If for some reason you can't locate a decent cut of chuck, top and bottom round also work well in stews.

When you're talking about grilling, sautéing, or broiling beef, you're talking about steaks. Of course the best known of these come from the Steak Section, the loin, and in particular from the short loin, which is the portion of the loin nearer the front of the steer. When the extremely tender tenderloin muscle from this area is cut into steaks, it becomes filet mignon. The top loin muscle, when cut into steaks, is the ever-popular New York strip, which also goes by many other names. The legendary porterhouse and T-bone steaks are cut vertically from the top to the bottom of the short loin, so they include portions of both the top loin and the tenderloin muscle. From the sirloin, the rear section of the loin, come the best-value steaks in terms of price, sometimes a little chewy but with really good flavor. Sirloin steaks come in many varieties. If cut in the traditional way, they are named for the portion of the bone they contain. If cut in the modern boneless fashion, they are named for the particular muscle that they come from, primarily top sirloin and bottom sirloin. Steaks from other sections of the cow include the very flavorful Delmonico from the rib area, the surprisingly tender chuck top blade steak, and the top round steak, the only cut from the round that achieves the tenderness quotient needed for high-heat cooking.

There are also several steaks that do not fit the traditional image because they are relatively long, flat pieces of meat. These steaks—the flank, the skirt, and the hanger steak—all run more or less horizontally along the sides of the steer. All three have recently gone from neglected to very popular. We are big fans of the skirt steak and the flank steak, both of which have tremendous flavor and enough fat to make them juicy. The hanger steak, on the other hand, goes in our category of world's most overrated steaks, along with the newly popular tri-tip.

Before we leave the tender cuts of beef, we want to say a word or two about doneness and thickness.

When we cook tender cuts of beef, the roasts and the steaks, we like them rare to medium-rare, but on the rare side. Because this is our book, the recipes are geared to that state of doneness. But just because that's our preference doesn't mean you have to go along with it. Each recipe also gives instructions for cooking the meat longer, so go ahead and cook it to whatever degree of doneness you fancy. Just remember that as the meat sits after it comes out of the oven or off the fire, it is going to move up about one degree of doneness. So if you want your steak medium, remove it from the heat when it's medium-rare.

Speaking of steaks, you will notice that we usually specify very thick ones in our recipes. That's because with a nice thick piece of meat you can get a good strong sear on the exterior without overcooking the interior. We encourage you to seek out a butcher who will cut steaks thick for you. But if that doesn't work out, you can go with a thinner version and just shorten the cooking time. In that case, though, be particularly sure you check for doneness early and often so you don't take your meat past the point you want it to be.

The one cut of beef we do cook more thoroughly is ground beef. This can come from virtually any part of the steer, but most often it is from the round or the chuck. Again, the best quality in terms of flavor and meat/fat ratio comes from the chuck. We like to combine this super-popular meat with spicy flavors.

Finally, there are the so-called variety cuts of beef. Although not for everybody, they are actually quite delicious when you give them a chance. From tripe to beef heart to tongue to the meltingly tender, supremely indulgent marrow from the shin bone, every one of them is well worth exploring. Not to be forgotten is the oxtail, actually the tail of the steer, which has powerful beef flavor and is becoming increasingly popular as more cooks realize its taste potential.

The basic message here is that if you like meat, there is some cut of beef out there that is going to be calling your name every time you stroll up to the meat counter or walk in the door of the butcher shop. The only thing you have to do is pick it out.

OUR TOP 5 FAVORITE CUTS OF BEEF

1. **3-pound porterhouse steak**

2. **Rump roast**

3. **Delmonico steak**

4. **Brisket**

5. **Skirt steak**

BUYING BEEF

The large selection of beef cuts is a great resource for the cook but, as we said above, it can also create a lot of confusion. Since there are so many distinct ways to separate the many muscles that make up a steer, butchers in different locations have developed quite different approaches. Beef is not butchered the same way in Italy and France as it is in this country, for example, and yet another method is used in South America.

There's no need to go that far afield to find variations, though. Butchers on the East Coast tend to cut beef somewhat differently from those in the West. That means, for instance, that the tri-tip roast is commonplace in San Francisco supermarkets but rarely seen in markets in Boston. Butchering techniques also change over time. The sirloin, which a few years ago was routinely cut into bone-in steaks, is now most often made into boneless cuts with very different names. (See page 100 for more details.)

What this all means is that, particularly when it comes to beef, it pays to get to know your butcher. If you don't have a butcher shop handy, this is the time to strike up a relationship with the guy behind the meat counter in the supermarket. Challenge him to help you out, and the chances are good that he will respond with enthusiasm. The ability of supermarket butchers to supply exactly the cut of beef you want is limited by the fact that much of their meat comes from the supplier prebutchered and wrapped in Cryovac, but a little effort will get you more than you might suppose.

In addition to locating the particular cut that you want, there are a number of factors to consider in selecting the individual piece of meat. Let's start with the USDA grade, because beef is the one meat where this is actually a relevant factor for the consumer. As we mentioned earlier, the USDA grade is an indication not of the safety of the meat, but of its palatability—in other words, how much you will like it when you bite into it. The assumption is that beef that is younger and that has more intramuscular fat (marbling) will be more tender, juicy, and flavorful and therefore more appealing.

Grading is voluntary and the producer has to pay the USDA to do it. But since there is such a wide variety of tenderness and quality in beef, it is worth it for the producers more often than not. Beef can receive one of eight grades, but only the top three—Prime, Choice, and Select—are of high enough quality to be sold in supermarkets and butcher shops, so those are the only ones you need to consider.

In point of fact, you can pretty much forget about Prime beef for home cooking. You will rarely find it even at high-end butcher shops. Only about 2 percent of all beef receives that rating, and most of it is sold to upscale restaurants and steak houses here and in Japan.

But that still leaves you with a very good option. USDA Choice beef remains the standard of excellence in most of the world, and 45 percent of meat that is actually graded receives the Choice designation. Our advice (which you should feel free to ignore, of course) is to seek out Choice beef when you can find it. It is particularly important when buying tender cuts of meat such as a big, thick porterhouse steak or a standing rib roast, where the degree of marbling will really make a very noticeable difference. When it comes to the tougher cuts of beef, on the other hand, Select is quite suitable.

But that's not quite the whole story, as I (Doc) found when I took a "Beef 101" course sponsored by Texas A & M University. Along with the other students, I got to evaluate a steer on the hoof, assign it a USDA grade after it was slaughtered, and finally cut it into primal cuts, a process that professionals refer to as "fabrication."

In the process of doing all this, I discovered something about quality grades that makes common sense, but that I had not thought about before: There is almost as much leeway within the grade as between grades. Professionals talk not just about "Choice" beef, but about "High Choice," "Choice," and "Low Choice." In the supermarket or butcher shop, though, those gradations are lost, and all you get is the designation of "Choice." This means that it makes sense to look carefully at individual pieces of meat even if they are graded the same. For the same money, you may be able to pick out a porterhouse that has a moderate amount of marbling, versus one that has only a small amount. The difference in tenderness and juiciness will be substantial. So when buying steaks, in particular, look for a good amount of white fat distributed evenly inside the muscle in small flecks and streaks. This is the ideal of marbling.

But what about beef that is not marked with any grade in the market? Well, much of it is what people in the business call "No Roll." What this means is that the beef in question was not high enough quality to receive a grade of either Prime or Choice, which are the two grades that command a premium price. Therefore, the packer told the USDA inspector not to bother rolling his official grading stamp down the carcass. The No Roll beef sold in markets in this country is almost uniformly Select.

Another option when buying beef is to choose a so-called branded meat. Like grading, branding is much more prevalent with beef than with other meats. The brand can refer to a specific producer, such as Nieman Ranch, or a specific breed, such as Angus or Hereford. Only by tasting the meat in question can you decide whether it is worth buying a particular brand. In our opinion, breed branding is a somewhat more reliable guide, since several cattle experts told us that the #1 predictor of high-quality, well-marbled beef is the breed of the steer from which the meat comes. We recommend you try any specific branded breeds you see in the market, then decide for yourself what you think.

There are also some general guidelines when buying beef, regardless of grade or brand. Always look for meat that is a rich cherry or slightly brownish red in color, with a relatively thin layer of external fat that is white rather than brownish or darkened. The surface of the beef should look moist but not wet or sticky, and if you are buying prewrapped beef, beware of those with a lot of liquid in the container, which generally means the meat has been frozen and then thawed. Above all, beef should smell fresh, with no sour or stale odors.

Beef stores better than other red meats. It will keep in the refrigerator, tightly wrapped, for three to four days, and can be frozen, again tightly wrapped (see page 27) for up to a year. Because it does slowly lose moisture in the freezer, though, it's best to use it after a month or two.

As we hope we've shown, there are many good reasons why beef is America's favorite red meat. So drop that old notion of the hierarchy of values, and you'll find yourself ending up with an awful lot of great meals. You may only have beef once or twice a week, but if you pay a little attention to how you buy and cook it, you're definitely going to enjoy it every time.

RECIPES FOR
LARGE TENDER CUTS OF BEEF

Grill-Roasted Rib Roast (Prime Rib) with Potato-Garlic Hobo Pack, Sour Cream, and Bacon Bits

Boneless Rib Roast "Prime Rib–Style" au Jus with Yorkshire Pudding

Cumin-Crusted Roasted Châteaubriand with Wild Mushrooms and Madeira

Sage-Rubbed Roasted Loin of Beef with Shallot-Bourbon Sauce

Grill-Roasted Whole Loin of Beef with Yellow Tomato–Ginger Jam

Garlic-Studded Roasted Eye of Round with Sweet Potatoes and South American Parsley-Caper Sauce

Latin-Flavored Roasted Chuck Eye Roast with Lime-Chipotle Marmalade and Fried Plantains

Rump Roast on a Bed of Red Onions, Leeks, and New Potatoes

10 STEPS TO GREAT ROASTED BEEF

1. Preheat the oven.

2. Dry the meat.

3. Season the meat well.

4. Put the roast on a rack in a roasting pan, set on the middle shelf of the preheated oven, and sear it.

5. Turn down the oven temperature.

6. Add the vegetables, if any.

7. Check for doneness early and often.

8. Transfer the meat to a platter, cover loosely with foil, and allow to rest for 10 to 20 minutes, depending on size.

9. Pour off the excess fat from the pan, add stock, deglaze, and simmer to reduce the liquid.

10. Carve and serve, passing the jus separately.

Grill-Roasted Rib Roast (Prime Rib) with Potato-Garlic Hobo Pack, Sour Cream, and Bacon Bits

SERVES 6 TO 8

This is the Big Daddy of roast beef, the most expensive and the most well marbled cut of them all. When cooked over live fire so that it picks up a nice smoky flavor, it is about as fine an eating experience as a carnivore can imagine. We call here for a bone-in roast, which is better suited to the rigors of grill-roasting than the boneless version, and accompany it with a hobo pack that's an updated version of the classic roast beef accompaniment, baked potatoes with sour cream and bacon.

As always when grill-roasting, be sure that no part of the meat is directly over the coals. It's also a good idea to put the thicker side of the roast toward the fire for three quarters of the cooking time, then turn it around.

If you have butcher's twine, tie the roast at both ends, simply making loops of twine parallel to the bone. This helps ensure that the outer flap of meat doesn't pull away from the rib-eye muscle during cooking. It's mostly a matter of appearance, so it's not crucial, but it does give you a better-looking roast in the end.

If you don't want to mess with a charcoal fire, you can do both the rib roast and the hobo pack in the oven at a straight 400°F, increasing the cooking times by about 10 percent. Or (a better choice), you can grill-roast the beef but serve it with a straight-up baked potato.

One 4-rib rib roast, about 6 to 8 pounds
6 tablespoons kosher salt
6 tablespoons freshly cracked black pepper

FOR THE HOBO PACK
6 large baking potatoes, washed and quartered lengthwise
16 garlic cloves, peeled
1/4 cup roughly chopped fresh sage
1/3 cup olive oil
Kosher salt and freshly cracked black pepper to taste

FOR THE GARNISH

1 cup sour cream

½ cup minced fresh chives

8 slices bacon, cooked until crisp and crumbled

1. Light a fire on one side of a large kettle grill, using about enough charcoal to fill a large shoe box.

2. Dry the roast with paper towels, then rub it all over with the salt and pepper, pressing gently to be sure that it adheres. When the fire has died down and the coals are covered with white ash, place the roast bone side down on the side of the grill away from the coals, being very careful that none of the meat is directly over the coals. Put the lid on the grill and open the vents about one quarter of the way. Cook, adding a handful of fresh charcoal about every 30 minutes, until the roast is done the way you like it, about 1 hour and 40 minutes to 2 hours for rare. To check for doneness, insert a meat thermometer into the dead center of the roast and let it sit for 5 seconds, then read the temperature: 120°F is rare, 126°F is medium-rare, 134°F is medium, 150°F is medium-well, and 160°F is well-done; we like to pull it at 122°F. When the roast is done to your liking, remove it from the grill, cover it loosely with foil, and allow it to rest for 20 minutes or so before carving.

3. While the roast is cooking, make the hobo packs: Tear off eight sheets of heavy-duty foil, each about 2 feet long, and stack them one on top of the other. Arrange half the potatoes, garlic, and sage in the center of the top sheet, drizzle with half of the olive oil, and season with salt and pepper. Fold up the top four sheets of foil around the vegetables one after the other, turning the package one quarter turn after each one and making sure that each sheet is well sealed around the vegetables. Repeat this process with the remaining potatoes, garlic, and sage.

4. Place the hobo packs in the coals around the periphery of the fire, where the heat is less intense. Pile the coals up around the packs and cook until the potatoes are tender, about 40 minutes.

5. Remove the hobo packs from the coals, unwrap the packages, and garnish the potatoes with the sour cream, chives, and bacon.

6. Slicing between the ribs, cut the beef into big thick slices. Serve accompanied by the potatoes.

COOK ONCE, EAT TWICE

Leftover prime rib makes the best cold roast beef sandwich in the entire world. Or you can do as Chris's grandmother did— cut up the leftover beef and toss it with lettuce and a vinaigrette for an excellent lunch salad. If you're a fan of bones, try leaving a bit of extra beef on the ribs and roasting them in a 350°F oven for about 20 minutes, then gnawing off the meat. Now, there's a real treat.

This is the justly famed "prime rib," the same cut that is used for the Grill-Roasted Rib Roast (page 44), but with the bones removed. Since "prime" really refers to the USDA grade, we just call it a rib roast.

As with the Grill-Roasted Rib Roast, there is really no substitute for this magnificent cut of meat.

Boneless Rib Roast "Prime Rib–Style" au Jus with Yorkshire Pudding

SERVES 8 TO 12

This is the prime rib out of central casting, the King of Roast Beef. Here we use the boneless version, which is easier for inside cooking, and roast it on a bed of vegetables so that it creates a lot of flavorful pan drippings to make a delicious *jus,* the French term for the natural juices that come out of a piece of meat as it cooks. We like to leave the jus nice and light in texture, just reduced slightly rather than thickened with flour and butter.

We accompany the beef here with the traditional British Yorkshire pudding, which is not a pudding at all, but sort of a cross between a soufflé and a popover. To give the Yorkshire pudding a nice, puffy consistency as well as a richer flavor, we heat up some of the fat from the beef in a muffin tin, then pour the pudding batter on top of the hot fat and return it to the oven. Just be careful not to spill the fat when you are moving the muffin tin around.

If you're looking for a shortcut here, you can skip the Yorkshire pudding and just serve the beef by itself, or accompany it with corn muffins or store-bought dinner rolls.

One 8-pound boneless rib roast
1/2 cup kosher salt
1/2 cup freshly cracked black pepper
2 medium onions, peeled and thickly sliced
2 large carrots, peeled and diced large
3 stalks celery, diced large
2 plum tomatoes, cored and diced large
10 garlic cloves, peeled

FOR THE YORKSHIRE PUDDING
4 large eggs
1 1/2 cups milk
1 1/2 cups all-purpose flour
3/4 teaspoon kosher salt, or to taste

FOR THE SAUCE
1/2 cup dry red wine
3 cups beef stock (or see Stock Options, page 32)
Kosher salt and freshly cracked black pepper to taste

1. Preheat the oven to 400°F.

2. Dry the meat with paper towels, then rub it all over with the salt and pepper, pressing gently to be sure they adhere. Place the meat on a sturdy rack in a medium roasting pan and arrange the onions, carrots, celery, tomatoes, and garlic around it. Place in the oven and cook until well browned, about 20 minutes. Reduce the oven temperature to 300°F, stir the vegetables around, and roast until the meat is done the way you like it. Start checking for doneness after 1 hour, but with a roast of this size it may take about an hour and 20 minutes for rare. To check for doneness, insert a meat thermometer into the dead center of the roast and let it sit for 5 seconds, then read the temperature: 120°F is rare, 126°F is medium-rare, 134°F is medium, 150°F is medium-well, and 160°F is well-done; we like to pull it at 122°F.

3. Meanwhile, make the Yorkshire pudding batter: In a medium bowl, beat the eggs until foamy. Add the milk and whisk to combine. Add the flour and salt and stir just to combine. Cover and refrigerate.

4. When the roast is done, remove it from the pan, cover it loosely with foil, and set it aside to rest for 20 minutes or so. Raise the oven temperature to 450°F.

5. Skim the fat off the juices in the roasting pan and reserve; set the pan of drippings aside. Pour about ¼ cup of the skimmed fat into a 12-cup muffin tin, dividing it evenly among the cups. Put the muffin tin into the oven for 3 to 5 minutes to get the fat hot, then pour the cold batter into the cups on top of the fat—watch out for spattering—filling each cup about three quarters full. Put the muffin tin back into the oven and bake for 15 minutes. Reduce the oven temperature to 350°F and bake for about 15 minutes more, until the puddings are puffy and dark golden brown.

6. While the puddings are baking, place the roasting pan, with the drippings, over high heat. Add the wine and bring to a simmer, stirring to dissolve the brown crusty stuff in the bottom of the pan. Add the beef stock, bring back to a simmer, and reduce by about one third, 10 to 15 minutes. Season the sauce with salt and pepper and strain it into a gravy boat; discard the vegetables.

7. Carve the beef into slices about 1 inch thick and serve with the Yorkshire pudding to soak up the jus.

THE CUT

To get a Châteaubriand, you cut off the head of the tenderloin, then cut off some slices for filet mignon, then cut out a section that you roast and call Châteaubriand. The tenderloin is the least-used muscle in the cow, so it is extremely tender. Like the prime rib, this is a very deluxe, very expensive cut of beef, which makes it worthwhile to go to your butcher rather than trying to find it in the supermarket.

OTHER NAMES

Filet mignon roast, full tenderloin roast.

OTHER CUTS YOU CAN USE

You won't be substituting anything for this. Often imitated but never duplicated, the beef tenderloin has no substitutes.

Cumin-Crusted Roasted Châteaubriand with Wild Mushrooms and Madeira

SERVES 4

If the prime rib is the King of Roast Beef, then the Châteaubriand, which is the French name for a roast cut from the center of the tenderloin of beef, is the Prince. Maybe even the Heir Apparent. This is incredibly tender and has a very delicate beef flavor, so we just roast it with some vegetables, then serve it with a rich sauce of mushrooms and Madeira. To give it a touch of the exotic, though, we added a simple coriander rub for the exterior of the beef.

One 2½-pound center-cut beef tenderloin roast

¼ cup kosher salt

¼ cup freshly cracked black pepper

¼ cup cracked coriander seeds

1 onion, peeled and diced small

1 carrot, peeled and diced small

1 stalk celery, diced small

1½ pounds wild mushrooms of your choice (porcini, portobellos, chanterelles, morels, shiitakes, etc.), stems removed and reserved, thinly sliced

1 plum tomato, cored and diced small

3 tablespoons olive oil

FOR THE SAUCE

2 cups beef stock (or see Stock Options, page 32)

2 tablespoons unsalted butter

1 small red onion, peeled and diced small

⅓ cup Madeira wine

Kosher salt and freshly cracked black pepper to taste

1. Preheat the oven to 500°F.

2. Dry the meat with paper towels, then rub it all over with the salt, pepper, and coriander, pressing gently to be sure they adhere. Place the roast on a sturdy rack in a medium roasting pan. Scatter the onion, carrot, celery, mushroom stems, and tomato around the meat and drizzle the olive oil over the vegetables. Place in the oven and roast until the meat is well browned, about 20 minutes. Reduce the oven temperature to 300°F, stir the vegetables around, and roast until the meat is done to your liking,

15 to 25 minutes more for rare. To check for doneness, insert a meat thermometer into the dead center of the roast and let it sit for 5 seconds, then read the temperature: 120°F is rare, 126°F is medium-rare, 134°F is medium, 150°F is medium-well, and 160°F is well-done; we like to pull it at 122°F. When the meat is done to your liking, remove it from the pan, cover it loosely with foil, and allow it to rest for 10 to 20 minutes while you prepare the sauce.

3. Place the roasting pan with the vegetables in it on the stove over medium-high heat. Add the beef stock and bring to a boil, then reduce the heat to medium and simmer for 15 minutes, stirring to dissolve the brown crusty stuff in the bottom of the pan. Strain and reserve the stock; discard the vegetables.

4. In a large sauté pan, melt the butter over medium heat. Add the red onion and cook, stirring occasionally, until translucent, 7 to 9 minutes. Add the mushrooms and cook, stirring occasionally, until they are cooked but not mushy, 5 to 7 minutes more. Add the Madeira and simmer until slightly reduced, 3 to 5 minutes. Add the reserved stock and simmer for 3 minutes more. Season with salt and pepper.

5. Slice the beef into slices about 1 inch thick and serve with the sauce.

COOK ONCE, EAT TWICE

This beef is so tender you can cut it with a fork. If you cooked your Châteaubriand rare, you can take advantage of its texture by slicing any leftovers very thin and serving them carpaccio-style, sprinkled with salt and pepper, drizzled with really good olive oil, and dotted with grated Parmesan cheese and/or capers. Oh, yeah.

OTHER NAMES

Beef top loin roast.

OTHER CUTS YOU CAN USE

You can substitute a rib roast (prime rib) or basically any tender boneless beef roast such as the tenderloin, bottom sirloin, or even the chuck eye roast.

BUTCHERSPEAK

With this cut, you probably want to ask the butcher for a rib end rather than a loin end, which we prefer because it is slightly more tender. Also, ask him to leave a good $1/4$ inch of fat on the roast. You might also see a whole strip loin in the supermarket, which you can use in this recipe if you're cooking for a larger group.

Sage-Rubbed Roasted Loin of Beef with Shallot-Bourbon Sauce

SERVES 6

A beef loin is such a magnificent piece of meat that it is usually cut up into steaks, but here we use it as a deluxe roast. Before roasting, the meat is rubbed with a little sage and garlic to give it a nice crust. It is served with a newly classic American pan sauce that I (Chris) learned from my friend and mentor Bob Kinkead, now chef/owner of Kinkead's in Washington, D.C. Be careful when you put the bourbon back on the stove when making the sauce, because you will get a flare-up of flames. But don't worry, this is just the alcohol burning off, and it will die down quickly.

$1/2$ cup kosher salt

$1/2$ cup freshly cracked black pepper

$1/2$ cup chopped fresh sage

$1/4$ cup chopped garlic

One 4- to 5-pound boneless top loin roast

2 medium onions, peeled and thickly sliced

2 medium carrots, peeled and diced large

3 stalks celery, diced large

2 plum tomatoes, cored and diced large

3 tablespoons olive oil

FOR THE SAUCE

3 cups beef stock (or see Stock Options, page 32)

2 tablespoons unsalted butter, plus (optional) 2 tablespoons, cut into 2 chunks

$1/3$ cup minced shallots

1 cup bourbon

$1/3$ cup roughly chopped fresh parsley

Kosher salt and freshly cracked black pepper to taste

1. Preheat the oven to 500°F.

2. In a small bowl, combine the salt, pepper, sage, and garlic and mix well. Dry the meat with paper towels, then rub it all over with this mixture, pressing gently to be sure it adheres. Place the roast on a sturdy rack in a medium roasting pan. Rub the onions, carrots, celery, and tomatoes with the olive oil, then scatter them around the meat. Place in the oven and roast until the meat is well browned, about 20 minutes. Reduce the oven temperature to 300°F, stir the vegetables around, and continue to roast until the meat is done to your liking, about 30 to 40 more minutes for rare. To check for doneness, insert a meat thermometer into the dead center of the roast and let it sit for 5 seconds, then read the temperature: 120°F is rare, 126°F is medium-rare, 134°F is medium, 150°F is medium-well, and 160°F is well-done; we like to pull it at 122°F. When the roast is done, remove it from the pan, cover it loosely with foil, and allow it to rest for 20 minutes or so while you prepare the sauce.

3. Pour off and discard the fat from the roasting pan, leaving the vegetables as well as the brown stuff stuck to the bottom of the pan. Place the roasting pan on the stove over medium-high heat, add the beef stock, and bring to a simmer. Continue to simmer, stirring to dissolve the brown crusty stuff in the bottom of the pan, until reduced by about half, 10 to 15 minutes. Strain and reserve the stock, discarding the vegetables.

4. In a large sauté pan, melt the 2 tablespoons butter over medium heat. Add the shallots and cook, stirring occasionally, until translucent, 7 to 9 minutes. Take the pan completely away from the stove (unless you want singed eyebrows) and add the bourbon. Return the pan to the heat and simmer for 3 to 5 minutes. Add the reserved stock and simmer until reduced by half, about 7 minutes more. Remove from the heat and add the remaining 2 tablespoons butter bit by bit if desired, stirring until it melts completely. Stir in the parsley and season with salt and pepper.

5. Cut the roast into slices about ½ inch thick and serve, passing the sauce on the side.

COOK ONCE, EAT TWICE

Leftovers from this roast can be used in the same way as those from the prime rib (page 46) or Châteaubriand (page 48). Or you can just slice the meat and serve it cold with some grainy mustard, a loaf of good bread, and some salad, and you've got yourself a very classy lunch.

See Sage-Rubbed Roasted Loin of Beef (page 000) for a description of this cut and how to buy it. In many larger supermarkets, this cut will be set out all Cryovacked and ready to go. A raw pound will end up yielding about 12 ounces of cooked meat, so if you've got heavy meat eaters, you should figure a full pound of uncooked meat per person.

OTHER CUTS YOU CAN USE

You can substitute any tender beef roast in this recipe, adjusting the cooking time according to the size, of course.

Grill-Roasted Whole Loin of Beef with Yellow Tomato–Ginger Jam

SERVES 10 TO 15

When I'm feeding a large group, I (Chris) like to serve a roast rather than individual steaks, because that way you can focus all of your cooking attention on a single piece of meat. And this is just the roast to make. It's a very impressive outdoor roast and a sure way to win friends and influence people. The spice mix, which is a variation on the classic Southern barbecue spice rub, has some nice sweetness along with its spiciness, and it forms a fantastic crust on the outside of the meat as it cooks. To complement the roast's rich, deep, smoky flavor, we serve a kind of sweet-and-sour tomato jam alongside it.

You are grill-roasting here, so when you put the meat on the grill, be sure that none of it is directly over the fire. If it is, the fat and juices dripping into the fire will create smoke with an unpleasant flavor (as opposed to the delicious smoke flavor that comes from the coals themselves). For even cooking, it's also a good idea to switch the roast around, end to end, once about halfway or so through the cooking process.

You can serve this roast without the jam, but the two are so great together that it makes more sense to make the jam ahead if you think you will be pressed for time. It will keep, covered and refrigerated, for 4 to 5 days. The jam is also excellent with any other beef dish, so if you make a double batch, you are likely to use it up with no problem.

Try serving this with baked beans and coleslaw for a down-home, country-style meal that will knock their socks off.

FOR THE JAM

¼ cup olive oil

1 large red onion, peeled and thinly sliced

2 tablespoons minced garlic

3 tablespoons minced fresh ginger

½ cup dark raisins

5 medium yellow tomatoes, cored and diced large (or substitute red tomatoes or 2 pints yellow cherry tomatoes, quartered)

1 cup white vinegar

½ cup orange juice

⅓ cup lightly packed brown sugar

2 tablespoons ground coriander

¼ cup fresh lime juice (about 2 limes)

Kosher salt and freshly cracked black pepper to taste

¾ cup kosher salt

¾ cup freshly cracked black pepper

½ cup paprika

¼ cup ground cumin

¼ cup ground coriander

¼ cup sugar

One 12-pound whole beef loin, fat trimmed to ½ inch

COOK ONCE, EAT TWICE

You can slice any leftover portion of this roast very thin and serve it up as a kind of super-classy barbe-cue sandwich on white bread with coleslaw and a little hot sauce.

1. Make the jam: In a large a sauté pan, heat the oil over medium-high heat until hot but not smoking. Add the onion and cook, stirring frequently, until golden brown, 11 to 13 minutes. Add the garlic, ginger, and raisins and continue cooking for 1 minute. Add the tomatoes, vinegar, orange juice, brown sugar, and coriander and simmer, stirring occasionally, until the mixture has a jamlike consistency, about 30 minutes. Remove from the heat, add the lime juice, season with salt and pepper, and set aside. (You can store the jam in the refrigerator, covered, for up to 5 days.)

2. In a small bowl, combine the salt, pepper, paprika, cumin, coriander, and sugar. Dry the meat with the paper towels, then rub it all over with this mixture, pressing gently to be sure it adheres.

3. Light a fire in a large kettle grill, with the coals well over to one side of the grill, using about enough coals to fill a shoe box.

4. When the fire has died down and the coals are covered with white ash, place the roast on the side of the grill away from the coals, being careful that none of the meat is directly over the coals. Put the lid on the grill, opening the vents about one quarter of the way. Cook, adding a handful of fresh charcoal about every 30 minutes, until the meat is done to your liking, about 50 to 70 minutes for medium-rare. To check for doneness, insert a meat thermometer into the dead center of the roast and let it sit for 5 seconds, then read the temperature: 120°F is rare, 126°F is medium-rare, 134°F is medium, 150°F is medium-well, and 160°F is well-done; we like to pull it at 122°F. When the roast is done, take it off the grill, cover it loosely with foil, and allow it to rest for 20 minutes or so before carving.

5. Cut the beef into slices about ¼ to ½ inch thick and serve with the tomato-ginger jam.

The eye round, which comes from the hip of the cow, is a bit chewy. Since it has very little intramuscular fat, it also has less beefy flavor than other cuts. However, it is an inexpensive way to get a roast beef and it is nice sliced very thin and used, like "deli" roast beef, for sandwiches. Since it has so little fat, it is best not to cook it past rare or medium-rare. One of the great advantages of this roast is that you can get it anywhere; it would not be all that surprising to see it show up at a convenience store.

OTHER NAMES

Round eye pot roast.

OTHER CUTS YOU CAN USE

You can substitute any beef roast here with excellent results. We particularly like the roasts in the sirloin area, such as the bottom round rump roast and the top round roast in this recipe.

Garlic-Studded Roast Eye of Round with Sweet Potatoes and South American Parsley-Caper Sauce

SERVES 6 TO 8

Our friend Bill Cramp does not cook a lot, but one thing he is an expert on is roast beef sandwiches, his absolute favorite food. At least twice a month, Cramp will cook an eye round roast and put it in the refrigerator so he can make sandwiches whenever he likes. Over many years of this habit, Cramp has developed the theory, which we share, that the cooking time for roasts depends not on weight, but on shape. Eye round roasts are always roughly the shape of a smallish football, so no matter how many pounds a particular roast may weigh, Mr. Cramp, who likes his meat very rare, always cooks it for exactly one hour.

You can follow Mr. Cramp's style if you like, or you can use a meat thermometer and make sure the roast is done to your liking before taking it out of the oven. We can only say that the reason we use this cut as a dry-cooked roast, while other cooks might find it too tough, is because on those frequent occasions when Mr. Cramp brings a cold eye round roast to our poker nights, it is exceedingly popular and disappears like magic.

Here we pair this relatively inexpensive roast with a flavorful parsley-caper sauce that is a favorite in Argentina and Uruguay, both countries where beef is king. It is super-delicious on any kind of beef, and it's also great drizzled over these roast sweet potatoes.

One 5-pound beef eye of round

10 garlic cloves, peeled and halved lengthwise

¼ cup kosher salt, plus more to taste

¼ cup freshly cracked black pepper, plus more to taste

¼ cup ground cumin

4 large sweet potatoes, peeled and halved lengthwise

3 tablespoons vegetable oil

Kosher salt and freshly cracked black pepper to taste

FOR THE SAUCE

½ cup roughly chopped fresh parsley

1 tablespoon minced garlic

¼ cup capers, rinsed and drained

⅓ cup extra virgin olive oil

¼ cup red wine vinegar

Kosher salt and freshly cracked black pepper to taste

1. Preheat the oven to 500°F.

2. Dry the meat with paper towels. With a paring knife, make 20 small slits in the surface of the roast, and push a piece of garlic into each one. Rub the roast all over with the salt, pepper, and cumin, pressing gently to be sure they adhere. Place the roast on a sturdy rack in a medium roasting pan and place in the oven.

3. Once the roast goes in the oven, rub the sweet potatoes with the vegetable oil and sprinkle them generously with salt and pepper. After 10 minutes, open the oven, place the sweet potatoes around the roast, and cook for 10 minutes longer.

4. Reduce the oven temperature to 300°F and continue roasting until the meat is done to your liking, about 50 minutes total cooking time for rare. To check for doneness, insert a meat thermometer into the dead center of the roast and let it sit for 5 seconds, then read the temperature: 120°F is rare, 126°F is medium-rare, 134°F is medium, 150°F is medium-well, and 160°F is well-done; we like to pull it at 122°F. When the meat is done to your liking, remove it from the oven, cover it loosely with foil, and let it rest for 20 minutes or so while you make the parsley sauce.

5. In a small bowl, combine the parsley, garlic, capers, olive oil, and red wine vinegar, mix well, and season with salt and pepper.

6. To serve, slice the meat very thin against the grain. Drizzle the meat and sweet potatoes with parsley sauce, and pass the remaining sauce on the side.

COOK ONCE, EAT TWICE

This cut of beef was born to be roasted on the weekend, put in the refrigerator, and used for roast beef sandwiches morning, noon, or midnight. Or try it as a substitute meat in a Head Cheese Reuben (page 158).

THE CUT

This is basically a boneless rib roast cut from the center (the "eye") of the first five ribs. It comes from the chuck, or forequarter, of the cow. This is an area where the muscles work pretty hard to move the cow around, so chuck has a whole lot of flavor but is not always real tender. Because of this, many cooks would not choose to use a section of the chuck as a roast. But this particular cut makes a great roast, and in fact it may well be the very best value in the cow—it is both very flavorful and quite tender.

OTHER NAMES

Inside chuck roll, boneless chuck roll, boneless chuck fillet.

OTHER CUTS YOU CAN USE

You can substitute any beef roast here.

BUTCHERSPEAK

If you go to a butcher shop and ask for this cut, you will definitely be impressing the butcher, because he'll know that you are in search of one of the great underappreciated cuts of meat.

Latin-Flavored Roasted Beef Chuck Eye Roast with Lime-Chipotle Marmalade and Fried Plantains

SERVES 6

We like to think of this dish as a "bargain roast in designer clothes." It has a wonderful combination of flavors from Latin America. If you can get hold of whole cumin and coriander seeds, by all means use them, and crack the coriander seeds yourself—they really contribute a wonderful aroma and flavor to the dish. To crack coriander seeds—or any other spice seeds, for that matter—you can either use a pepper mill set on the very coarsest setting, or you can put the seeds on a cutting board and roll back and forth over them with the edge of a small sauté pan or frying pan.

As for the chipotles, we are going to admit here, for the first time in public, that canned chipotles in adobo sauce are our absolute favorite chiles. They have a deep, penetrating smoky heat that makes just about any dish taste better. And while the fried plantains may seem a bit difficult, after you've made them once, you will want to be making them all the time. They are really pretty easy, and not only do they taste great, but smashing them lets you work out some of the stress of daily life.

If you don't have time to make the marmalade, you could substitute a quick fresh preparation like Tomato-Cucumber Relish (page 275) or your favorite fresh salsa.

FOR THE MARMALADE

4 plum tomatoes, cored, peeled, and diced large

2 small limes, halved lengthwise and very thinly sliced

1¼ cups sugar

1 tablespoon minced canned chipotles in adobo

1 tablespoon adobo sauce from the chipotles

2 tablespoons fresh lime juice (about 1 lime)

Kosher salt to taste

¼ cup paprika

½ cup cumin seeds, toasted in a dry skillet over medium heat, shaken frequently, until fragrant, 3 to 5 minutes

⅓ cup cracked coriander seeds

¼ cup kosher salt

¼ cup freshly cracked black pepper

One 3½- to 4-pound beef chuck eye roast

FOR THE PLANTAINS

2 cups vegetable oil

2 green plantains, peeled and cut into 2-inch rounds

Kosher salt and freshly cracked black pepper to taste

1. Make the marmalade: In a medium saucepan, combine the tomatoes, sliced limes, and sugar. Cook slowly over low heat, stirring occasionally, for about 3 hours, until thick, glossy, and pretty much the consistency of jam.

2. Add the chipotles, adobo sauce, lime juice, and salt and mix well to combine. Set aside to cool to room temperature. (You can store the marmalade in the refrigerator, covered, for up to 2 weeks.)

3. Preheat the oven to 500°F.

4. In a small bowl, combine the paprika, cumin seeds, coriander seeds, salt, and pepper and mix well. Dry the meat with paper towels, then rub it all over with this mixture, pressing gently to be sure it adheres. Place the roast on a sturdy rack in a medium roasting pan and roast until the meat is well browned, about 20 minutes. Reduce the oven temperature to 300°F and continue roasting until the meat is done to your liking, about 30 minutes more for rare. To check for doneness, insert a meat thermometer into the dead center of the roast and let it sit for 5 seconds, then read the temperature: 120°F is rare, 126°F is medium-rare, 134°F is medium, 150°F is medium-well, and 160°F is well-done; we like to pull it at 122°F. When the roast is done to your liking, remove it from the oven, cover it loosely with foil, and let it rest for about 20 minutes while you prepare the plantains.

5. In a small saucepan, heat the oil until very hot but not smoking. Drop the plantain rounds into the oil 4 or 5 at a time and cook until well browned, 2 to 3 minutes. Remove them from the oil and drain on paper towels or a brown paper bag. Then place each fried round on a work surface and, using a heavy object such as a small cutting board or sauté pan, apply steady pressure to mash it as flat as a pancake. Put the mashed plantain sections back into the hot oil, 2 or 3 at a time, and cook for 2 minutes or so, until the entire surface is golden brown. Remove, drain on paper towels or a brown paper bag, and season liberally with salt and pepper.

6. Thinly slice the meat (about ¼ inch thick) against the grain and serve with the fried plantains and marmalade.

The name says it all here—this cut comes from the rump of the cow. To our taste buds, this is the most flavorful as well as the most tender cut from the round, which is the hind-quarters of the beast from the ankle to the rump. You can find this cut relatively easily in a supermarket.

OTHER CUTS YOU CAN USE

You can substitute any of the beef round roasts, such as the beef round tip roast or the beef round bottom roast, as well as boneless chuck eye roast.

Rump Roast on a Bed of Red Onions, Leeks, and New Potatoes

SERVES 6

The first time we made this straightforward dish, there were six of us eating dinner together, and every one of us made the same comment: "Now, *this* is what roast beef should taste like." That doesn't necessarily mean that this is the absolute "best" roast beef (whatever that might be), but it does mean that this is the texture and flavor our taste memories call up when we imagine a beef roast. We're willing to bet that they will match yours too. The vegetables in this dish are also outstanding, because as the roast cooks, its juices seep out and are absorbed by the vegetables around it. When you want a classic roast beef, this is it.

Serve this with a big green salad and a side of Hoppin' John (page 421).

One 4- to 5-pound beef rump roast, well trimmed

2 tablespoons kosher salt, plus more to taste

2 tablespoons freshly cracked black pepper, plus more to taste

2 medium red onions, peeled and thinly sliced

5 leeks (white part only), cleaned well and cut into very thin strips

¼ cup minced garlic

4 plum tomatoes, cored and diced medium

12 red new potatoes (about the size of golf balls), halved

¼ cup olive oil

⅓ cup roughly chopped fresh herbs: any one or a combination of parsley, basil, oregano, and/or sage

¼ cup fresh lemon juice (about 1 lemon)

1. Preheat the oven to 500°F.

2. Dry the meat with paper towels, then rub it all over with the salt and pepper, pressing gently so they adhere. Place it on a sturdy rack in a medium roasting pan and roast until it is well browned, about 20 minutes.

3. Meanwhile, in a large bowl, toss the onions, leeks, garlic, tomatoes, and potatoes with the olive oil and salt and pepper to taste. When the roast reaches the 20-minute mark, reduce the oven temperature to 300°F, arrange the vegetables in the roasting pan around the meat, and continue roasting until the meat is done to your liking, 40 to 50 minutes longer for rare. To check for doneness, insert a meat thermometer into the dead center of the roast and let it sit for 5 seconds, then read the temperature: 120°F is rare, 126°F is medium-rare, 134°F is medium, 150°F is medium-well, and 160°F is well-done; we like to pull it at 122°F. When the roast is done to your liking, remove it from the oven, cover it loosely with foil, and let it rest for 20 minutes or so.

4. While the roast is resting, toss the vegetables with the herbs and lemon juice and correct the seasoning if needed.

5. Thinly slice the roast against the grain. Place a portion of the vegetable mixture on each plate, fan the meat slices out over it, and serve.

COOK ONCE, EAT TWICE

If you happen to have fewer people come to dinner than you expected, so that you have not only meat but some of the vegetables left over, you can cut everything into rough cubes, toss it all in a hot sauté pan with a couple of minced chile peppers, and have yourself a really fine hash. Like the other beef roasts, this also makes wonderful sandwiches the next day.

RECIPES FOR
LARGE TOUGH CUTS OF BEEF

10 STEPS TO GREAT BRAISED BEEF

1. Dry the meat.

2. Season the meat well.

3. Sear the meat hard.

4. Transfer the meat to a platter, adjust the amount of fat in the pot, and sauté the aromatics and vegetables.

5. Deglaze the pot with some of the liquid.

6. Return the meat to the pot along with enough liquid to cover it about halfway.

7. Bring to a simmer, skim off the film, cover the pot, and place in a 300°F oven.

8. Check for doneness early and often: Look for "fork-tender."

9. Skim the fat and any film from the liquid and, if you want, remove the meat and reduce the liquid; season to taste.

10. Carve the meat and serve with the braising liquid on the side.

Old-fashioned Braised Beef with Herbed Potato Dumplings and Horseradish Sauce

SERVES 6

This is a pretty classic approach to a large, relatively tough but flavorful cut of beef. We like to use a cut from the chuck because it has plenty of good flavor, and the long, slow cooking makes it tender. It also has enough fat to keep it from drying out.

The braising liquid here is very flavorful, and it's great to have some nice spongy dumplings to really soak up that tasty liquid. The dumplings will turn out best if you cook the potatoes ahead and refrigerate them overnight.

¼ cup vegetable oil, or more if needed

One 3½- to 4-pound boneless beef shoulder roast

Kosher salt and freshly cracked black pepper to taste

2 medium onions, peeled and diced large

2 carrots, peeled and diced large

4 stalks celery, diced large

4 allspice berries

2 bay leaves

Stems from 1 bunch parsley

Big pinch of black peppercorns

About 5 cups beef stock (or see Stock Options, page 32)

FOR THE SAUCE

½ cup sour cream

3 tablespoons prepared horseradish

¼ cup roughly chopped fresh dill

¼ cup fresh lemon juice (about 1 lemon)

Kosher salt and freshly cracked black pepper to taste

FOR THE DUMPLINGS

2 to 3 large eggs

2 pounds baking potatoes, cooked in their jackets in salted water until tender, drained, and refrigerated overnight

2 to 2½ cups all-purpose flour

1 tablespoon kosher salt

2 teaspoons freshly grated nutmeg

3 to 4 fresh chives, finely chopped

2 tablespoons finely chopped fresh parsley

THE CUT

We are calling for a boneless beef shoulder here. There are several cuts that come from the shoulder and work really well in this application; our favorites are the arm pot roast and the shoulder pot roast. This is definitely a supermarket cut.

OTHER NAMES

For arm pot roast, chuck arm roast; for shoulder pot roast, honey cut cross-rib roast, shoulder roast, English roast.

OTHER CUTS YOU CAN USE

You can use pretty much any boneless cut from the shoulder or neck of the cow here, particularly those with "pot roast" in their name. These include the neck pot roast, 7-bone pot roast, under blade pot roast, cross-rib pot roast, and top blade pot roast.

1. Preheat the oven to 300°F.

2. In a 5-inch-deep Dutch oven or other large ovenproof pot with a lid, heat the oil over medium-high heat until very hot but not smoking. Dry the meat with paper towels, sprinkle it generously with salt and pepper, place it in the Dutch oven, and brown well, 5 to 8 minutes per side. When it is nicely browned, transfer the meat to a platter.

3. Pour off the fat or add oil to the pot as needed so you have a total of about 2 tablespoons in the pot. Add the onions, carrots, and celery and cook, stirring occasionally, until the onions are lightly browned, 11 to 13 minutes.

4. Return the beef to the pot and add the allspice, bay leaves, parsley stems, and peppercorns. Add enough stock to come halfway up the sides of the meat (about 4 cups). Bring to a simmer, scraping any browned bits off the bottom of the pan. Skim any scum off the surface, then cover, place in the oven, and cook until the meat is very tender, 2 to 2½ hours. Begin checking for doneness after 2 hours. To check for doneness, plunge a fork straight down into the meat and try to pull the fork out. If the fork slides out easily, the meat is done; if the meat hangs on to the fork, give it more time.

5. While the meat is braising, make the sauce and dumplings. For the sauce, combine all the ingredients in a medium bowl and mix well. Cover and refrigerate until serving time.

6. For the dumplings, crack 2 eggs into a large bowl and beat them lightly with a fork. Peel the potatoes and press them through a potato ricer (or finely grate them by hand) into the bowl with the eggs. Add 2 cups of the flour and the salt, nutmeg, chives, and parsley. Work the ingredients together to form a firm dough, adding another egg, lightly beaten, if the dough is too dry.

7. Before forming the dumplings, give the dough a "test run": Bring a small pot of water to the boil. With wet hands, form a 2-inch round dumpling and drop it into the boiling water. If the dumpling falls apart, work a bit more flour into the dough; if not, form about 15 more 2-inch dumplings. Place the formed dumplings on a baking sheet, cover, and set aside until the meat is done.

8. When the meat is done, remove it from the pot, cover it loosely with foil, and set it aside. Skim the fat from the braising liquid and strain the liquid into a large saucepan. Add the remaining 1 cup stock to the braising liquid and bring to a boil over high heat. Add 2 tablespoons salt and drop in the dumplings one at a time. Reduce the heat to a simmer and let the dumplings poach gently until they float to the surface, about 12 to 15 minutes. As they are done, remove them from the pot with a slotted spoon.

9. Slice the meat into ½-inch-thick slices and arrange on individual plates. Top each serving with 2 piping-hot dumplings and a spoonful of the chilled horseradish sauce and serve at once, passing the braising liquid separately.

Cuban-Style Braised Beef Blade Steak with Olives, Raisins, and Fried Sweet Potatoes

SERVES 4

When we think of braises, we tend to think of European-style dishes, but this one has a definite Cuban beat. With the raisins and olives and the beefy chuck meat, it has a great combination of sweet and earthy flavors, and the fried sweet potatoes round it all out. We would serve this with a simple salad of arugula, tomatoes, and blue cheese.

2 tablespoons olive oil

One 2½- to 3-pound bone-in beef blade steak (or other bone-in chuck steak), 2 to 3 inches thick

2 tablespoons cumin seeds (or 1 tablespoon ground cumin)

2 tablespoons kosher salt

2 tablespoons freshly cracked black pepper

2 cups dry red wine

1 cup tomato juice

½ cup roughly chopped pitted green olives (with or without pimientos)

⅓ cup dark raisins

FOR THE SWEET POTATOES

2 large sweet potatoes

¼ cup vegetable oil

Kosher salt and freshly cracked black pepper

1. Preheat the oven to 300°F.

2. In a 5-inch-deep Dutch oven or other large ovenproof pot with a lid, heat the oil over medium-high heat until very hot but not smoking. Dry the meat with paper towels and rub it all over with the cumin, salt,

THE CUT

The bone-in beef blade steak, as its name implies, comes from the blade portion of the chuck. The chuck is basically the neck, shoulder, and arm of the animal. It is ideally suited to braising, because it has plenty of good beef flavor and the long, slow cooking makes it tender. The blade steak comes from the portion of the chuck nearest to the rib section, which means it is a little bit more tender than other chuck cuts. This cut (or one of the substitutes discussed below) should be readily available at any supermarket.

OTHER NAMES

Chuck steak (or roast) 1st cut.

OTHER CUTS YOU CAN USE

Other options from the blade section of the chuck include the top blade steak, also known as the 7-bone steak, and the under blade steak, also called the California steak. Any other bone-in steak from the chuck will also work well here. You can also use any bone-in chuck roast, as long it is thin enough.

and pepper. Place it in the Dutch oven and brown well on both sides, 8 to 10 minutes per side.

3. Meanwhile, combine the red wine and tomato juice. When the meat is browned, add enough of this liquid to the Dutch oven to come halfway up the sides of the meat. (If you have some of the mixture left over, reserve it to add later; if there is not enough, just add water.) Add the olives and raisins and bring to a simmer, scraping any browned bits from the bottom of the pan. Skim any scum from the top. Cover, place in the oven, and braise until the meat is very tender, 1 to 1½ hours, checking for doneness after 1 hour. To check for doneness, plunge a fork straight down into the meat and try to pull the fork out. If the fork slides out easily, the meat is done; if the meat hangs on to the fork, give it more time.

4. While the meat is cooking, place the sweet potatoes on a small baking sheet and bake until they are easily pierced with a fork but still offer some resistance, about 45 minutes. Remove the potatoes from the oven and allow them to cool. As soon as they are cool enough to handle, cut them lengthwise into quarters.

5. When the meat is done, remove it from the cooking liquid, cover it loosely with foil, and let it rest for 10 to 20 minutes.

6. Meanwhile, taste the braising liquid; if the liquid needs more fla-vor, place the pot on the stove over medium-high heat and simmer to reduce the liquid, then season to taste. For a thicker sauce, reduce it until it coats the back of a spoon.

7. While the braising liquid is reducing, heat the vegetable oil in a large sauté pan over medium-high heat until it is very hot but not smok-ing. Add the sweet potatoes and fry until they are brown and crisp, about 3 minutes. Remove to paper towels or a brown paper bag and sprinkle with salt and pepper.

8. Cut the meat into slices about 1 inch thick, arrange on plates, and moisten with the braising liquid. Serve with the sweet potatoes, passing the remaining braising liquid separately.

Old-School Yankee Pot Roast with Root Vegetables and Fresh Tomato-Fennel Relish

SERVES 6

Some meat dishes have stood the test of time for very good reasons, and this is one of them. It is definitely a case in which the blending of several ingredients creates a whole new flavor dynamic, the earthy flavors of the root vegetables mixing wonderfully with the rich, beefy flavor of a roast that starts out a bit gnarly but ends up falling-apart tender. Here we add a relish that has some sweetness and some citrus to it, both of which help give a little jolt of flavor to the roast, rich and mellow after all that time in the oven.

Serve this with garlic bread and a salad of crisp Romaine lettuce. What more do you need?

2 tablespoons olive oil

One 4-pound boneless bottom round rump roast

¼ cup kosher salt, or more to taste

¼ cup freshly cracked black pepper, or more to taste

4 cups beef stock (or see Stock Options, page 32)

¼ cup catsup

4 cups large-diced root vegetables: any one or a combination of onions, potatoes, parsnips, turnips, rutabaga, leeks, celery root, and/or acorn or other winter squash

FOR THE RELISH

1 small tomato, cored and diced small

¼ cup finely chopped fennel

¼ cup roughly chopped fresh parsley

¼ cup fresh lemon juice (about 1 lemon)

Kosher salt and freshly cracked black pepper to taste

1. Preheat the oven to 300°F.

2. In a 5-inch-deep Dutch oven or other large ovenproof pot with a lid, heat the oil over medium-high heat until very hot but not smoking. Dry the meat with paper towels and sprinkle it with the salt and pepper, pressing gently to be sure they adhere. Place the meat in the Dutch oven and brown well, 8 to 10 minutes per side.

THE CUT

The boneless rump roast, which, as its name implies, comes from the rear hip of the animal, is a little bit more expensive than cuts from the chuck, but it will give you a very flavorful pot roast. This is a cut that should be easy to find in the supermarket.

OTHER NAMES

Round tip roast, back of rump roast.

OTHER CUTS YOU CAN USE

Any of the pot roast cuts from the blade, shoulder, or arm sections of the chuck will also work just fine here. Also, see Pot Roast Options (page 68) for more possibilities.

COOK ONCE, EAT TWICE

This is a wonderful dish when reheated. Or, if you have leftover beef along with a few vegetables, use them as substitute ingredients in A Severe Tongue Hashing (page 156).

3. Meanwhile, combine the stock and catsup and mix well. Add enough of this mixture to the Dutch oven to come halfway up the sides of the meat. (If you have some of the mixture left over, reserve it to add later; if there is not enough, add some water or beer.) Bring to a simmer and skim any scum from the surface. Cover, place in the oven, and braise until the meat is very tender, 2 to 2½ hours. After 1 hour and 15 minutes, add the root vegetables to the pot; after 2 hours, begin checking the meat for doneness. To check for doneness, plunge a fork straight down into the meat and try to pull the fork out. If the fork slides out easily, the meat is done; if the meat hangs on to the fork, give it more time.

4. While the meat is cooking, make the relish: In a small bowl, combine the tomato, fennel, parsley, lemon juice, and salt and pepper. Mix well and set aside.

5. When the meat is done, remove it and the vegetables from the pot, transfer to a platter, and cover them loosely with foil. Skim the fat from the cooking liquid. Taste the liquid, and if you think it needs more flavor, place the pot on the stove over medium-high heat and simmer to reduce the liquid. For a thicker sauce, reduce it until it coats the back of a spoon. Season with salt and pepper.

6. Cut the meat into thick slices and serve with the vegetables and the braising liquid, passing the relish on the side.

Balsamic-Braised Pot Roast with Tomatoes, Lemons, Raisins, and Black Olive–Pine Nut Relish

THE CUT

See Old-fashioned Braised Beef (page 61) for details on boneless beef shoulder pot roast and how to buy it.

OTHER CUTS YOU CAN USE

A well-trimmed half brisket, a rump roast, or any of the other roasts from the blade, shoulder, or arm sections of the chuck will perform very well in this recipe. See Pot Roast Options (page 68) for more details.

SERVES 6

"Pot roast" does not always have to mean beef cooked with root vegetables. The term simply refers to a tough cut of beef that is browned, then cooked in a covered pot along with enough liquid to cover it partway. So you can add ingredients to create any flavor footprint that you want.

In this Mediterranean-style pot roast, we use several acidic ingredients that contrast with and set up the rich flavor of the long-cooked beef. Lemons, balsamic vinegar, and red wine all contribute, while sweet raisins join in on the side of the beef for a complementary flavor dynamic. To top it off, there's a fresh but earthy relish for your guests to add as they want.

To segment the lemons, peel them with a sharp knife, removing the white pith entirely. Cut between the membranes and remove each section whole, taking care to remove the seeds.

Serve this with crusty bread, Blue Cheese Mashed Potatoes (page 413), and a simple green salad.

1 cup dry red wine

¾ cup balsamic vinegar

1 tablespoon sugar

¼ cup olive oil, or more if needed

One 4- to 5-pound boneless beef shoulder pot roast

¼ cup kosher salt

¼ cup freshly cracked black pepper

2 large red onions, peeled and diced small

¼ cup minced garlic

6 plum tomatoes, cored and diced small

1 cup dark raisins

2 lemons, peeled, cut into segments, seeded (see headnote)

1 to 2 cups beef stock (or see Stock Options, page 32)

Kosher salt and freshly cracked black pepper to taste

FOR THE RELISH

1 cup roughly chopped pitted black olives

¼ cup pine nuts, toasted in a 350°F oven until lightly browned, about 10 minutes

1 cup roughly chopped fresh basil or parsley

¼ cup extra virgin olive oil

Kosher salt and freshly cracked black pepper to taste

1. Preheat the oven to 300°F.

2. In a medium bowl, combine the wine, vinegar, and sugar. Mix well to dissolve the sugar and set aside.

3. In a 5-inch-deep Dutch oven or other large ovenproof pot with a lid, heat the oil over medium-high heat until very hot but not smoking. Dry the meat with paper towels, then rub it all over with the salt and pepper, pressing gently to make sure they adhere. Place the roast in the pot and brown it well on all sides, about 10 minutes total. When the meat is browned, transfer it to a platter and set it aside.

4. Pour off the fat or add oil to the pot as needed so you have a total of about 2 tablespoons in the pot. Add the onions and cook, stirring occasionally, until translucent, 7 to 9 minutes. Add the garlic and cook, stirring, for 1 minute more.

COOK ONCE, EAT TWICE
If you have very juicy tomatoes, there will be quite a lot of braising liquid with this dish, so there may be some left over when the roast has all been eaten. Freeze it, then thaw it when you want some incredibly flavorful gravy to put over potatoes but don't want to do any work.

5. Return the meat to the pot and add the tomatoes, raisins, lemons, and wine-vinegar mixture. Add enough stock so that the liquid comes about one quarter of the way up the sides of the meat (the tomatoes will quickly give off more liquid). Bring to a simmer, scraping any browned bits from the bottom of the pot. Skim any scum off the surface. Cover, place in the oven, and cook until the meat is tender, 2 to 2½ hours. Begin checking for doneness after 2 hours. To check for doneness, plunge a fork straight down into the meat and try to pull the fork out. If the fork slides out easily, the meat is done; if the meat hangs on to the fork, give it more time.

6. While the meat is cooking, make the relish: In a medium bowl, combine the olives, pine nuts, basil, olive oil, and salt and pepper and mix well.

7. When the meat is done, remove it from the pot, cover it loosely with foil, and set aside. Skim the fat from the braising liquid and taste the liquid. If it needs more flavor, place the pot on the stove over medium-high heat and simmer to reduce the liquid. For a thicker sauce, reduce it until it coats the back of a spoon. Season to taste with salt and pepper.

8. Cut the pot roast against the grain into thick slices, spoon some of the sauce over the top, and pass the remaining sauce and the relish separately for guests to sprinkle over the beef.

POT ROAST OPTIONS

When it comes to beef pot roast, there are many cuts that will do the trick. Among the best are the cuts from the chuck (the shoulder of the cow). One excellent option is the blade roast (also sometimes known as the top blade chuck roast or the 7-blade pot roast, so called because the blade bone somewhat resembles the number 7), which is among the most tender and flavorful of all chuck pot roast cuts. Another good choice is the boneless chuck shoulder roast, which is a relatively tender and very flavorful cut taken from the back of the cow's foreleg.

But basically any cut from the chuck will make a good pot roast, so the best idea is probably to simply pick the one that is the size you are looking for. Some of the more common names used for chuck roast cuts are: arm pot roast or boneless arm shoulder roast, chuck eye or chuck eye roll, flatiron roast, cross-rib roast or shoulder clod, or just plain boneless chuck roast.

Brisket is also an excellent choice for pot roast—since it has more fat than the other pot roast cuts, it can be cooked longer without overcooking.

Another very good pot roast option is the rump roast, which comes from the round (the rear hip and leg of the cow). Other than this particular cut, though, cuts from the round tend to lack enough fat to hold up to the long, slow cooking without drying out.

Lazy Sunday Pot Roast with Caraway and Green Apples

SERVES 6

This is a recipe that I (Doc) found written in pencil on an index card tucked inside my Grandmother Schwyhart's old, worn cookbook. Like many of her best dishes, this one relies on standard components of classic German cooking put together in an interesting way. The apples are particularly nice in this dish; they puff up as they cook so they look like dumplings, and they really soak up the other flavors.

We call this "Lazy Sunday" not because Grandma Schwyhart was lazy—in her late eighties, you would still find her rising early to bake pies for "those poor shut-ins" ten years her junior—but because it takes very little effort and yields a wonderful Sunday afternoon dinner when served with Roasted Potatoes (page 414).

2 tablespoons oil, or more if needed

One 4- to 5-pound boneless cross-rib pot roast or other chuck roast

Kosher salt and freshly cracked black pepper to taste

2 medium onions, peeled, halved, and thinly sliced

½ cup cider vinegar (or substitute white vinegar)

3 bay leaves

1 tablespoon caraway seeds

¼ cup packed brown sugar

¼ cup chopped fresh marjoram (or 2 tablespoons dried marjoram)

2 to 2½ cups beef stock (or see Stock Options, page 32)

4 Granny Smith or other tart green apples, quartered, cored, and peeled

1. Preheat the oven to 300°F.

2. In a 5-inch-deep Dutch oven or other large ovenproof pot with a lid, heat the oil over medium-high heat until very hot but not smoking. Dry the meat with paper towels, sprinkle it generously with salt and pepper, place in the pot, and brown well, about 8 to 10 minutes per side. When the meat is well browned, transfer it to a platter.

3. Pour off fat or add oil to the pot as needed so you have about 2 tablespoons in the pot. Add the onions and sauté, stirring, until translucent, 7 to 9 minutes.

Boneless cross-rib pot roast comes from the arm half of the chuck. You should be able to get this cut, or some other suitable boneless chuck roast, in your supermarket.

OTHER NAMES
Boneless English roast, boneless Boston cut English roll.

OTHER CUTS YOU CAN USE
Any other boneless roast from the chuck would be delicious here. An excellent substitute, for example, is the boneless shoulder pot roast.

4. Add the vinegar and bring to a boil, scraping up any brown stuff from the bottom of the pan. Put the meat back in the pot and add the bay leaves, caraway seeds, brown sugar, marjoram, and enough stock so that the liquid comes halfway up the sides of the meat. Bring just to a simmer and skim any scum off the surface, then cover, put in the oven, and cook until the beef is fork-tender, 2½ to 3 hours. After 2 hours and 15 minutes, add the apples to the pot; after 2½ hours, remove the apples with a slotted spoon, set aside, and begin checking the meat for doneness. To check for doneness, plunge a fork straight down into the meat and try to pull the fork out. If the fork slides out easily, the meat is done; if the meat hangs on to the fork, give it more time.

5. When the meat is done, remove it from the pot, cover it loosely with foil, and let it rest for at least 10 minutes. Skim the fat from the braising liquid and taste the liquid. If it needs more flavor, place the pan on the stove over medium-high heat and simmer to reduce the liquid. For a thicker sauce, reduce it until it coats the back of a spoon. Season with salt and pepper. (You can also strain the liquid and pass it and the cooked onions separately.)

6. Cut the meat into thin slices and serve accompanied by the apples, braising liquid, and onions.

Barbecued Whole Beef Brisket with Pastrami-Style Rub and Grainy Mustard–Horseradish Sauce

SERVES 12 OR MORE

This is a classic Texas barbecue technique, but here we work a little change on it by using a spice rub more typical of pastrami, and a sauce of a style more often used with roast beef. But the brisket still has that intensely smoky flavor and the fantastic combination of a super-flavorful, crusty exterior with a moist, tender interior that defines the appeal of barbecue. Remember that you gotta have patience for this process; the longer you cook this brisket, the better it is going to be. Just make sure that you keep the fire off to one side so that the meat is never actually over the coals.

Of course, we understand there are also occasions when you don't have the time but still want the brisket, so there are some possible shortcuts. To begin with, the brine is optional here. It does give the brisket a slightly fuller flavor, but it is certainly not essential. Then, if you want to cut down your time by the fire, you can also use the Cheater's Method. To do so, get in as many hours as you can with the meat on the grill with some smoky chips, say 2 to 5 hours on the evening of the day before you want to serve the brisket. Then wrap it in foil, put it in a 200°F oven, and let it sit overnight, or up to 10 hours. That way you get some smoky flavor on the beef but don't have to spend all day tending the fire.

Serve this with fresh coleslaw, fruit salad, or a sweet potato salad.

One 8- to 10-pound beef brisket, untrimmed

FOR THE BRINE (OPTIONAL)

1 gallon water

1 cup kosher salt

¾ cup packed dark brown sugar

1 cup bourbon

¼ cup pickling spices

FOR THE RUB

½ cup kosher salt

½ cup freshly cracked white pepper (or ¼ cup ground white pepper)

1 cup freshly cracked black pepper

1 cup cracked coriander seeds (or ½ cup ground coriander)

FOR THE SAUCE

½ cup grated fresh horseradish

¼ cup white vinegar

¼ cup prepared horseradish

½ cup grainy mustard

1. Rinse the brisket under cold water and dry it with paper towels. If you are using the optional brine, combine the brine ingredients in a large bowl or pot and mix well. Place the meat in the brine and refrigerate it for 24 to 36 hours, turning occasionally. Remove the meat from the brine and pat it dry with paper towels.

2. Light a fire well over to one side of a large kettle grill, using enough charcoal to fill half a shoe box.

3. In a medium bowl, combine all the rub ingredients and mix well. Rub the brisket all over with this spice mixture, pressing gently so it adheres.

You can use a large half brisket if you adjust the other ingredients in the recipe in proportion, but that's about the only substitute here. If you do use a half, try to get the "point cut," also known as the thick cut or nose cut. It is cheaper and fattier than the "flat cut," and with this cooking method, both of those qualities are advantageous.

COOK ONCE, EAT TWICE

A sandwich made with rye bread, leftover brisket, and this mustard-horseradish sauce is about as good as it gets.

4. When the fire has died down and the coals are covered with white ash, place the meat on the side away from the coals, being careful that none of the meat is directly over the coals. Put the lid on the grill, opening the vents about one quarter of the way. Cook, adding a handful of fresh charcoal about every 30 minutes, for 8 to 16 hours, depending on how much time you want to devote to the process. (If the grill has a thermometer, keep the temperature between 180° and 220°F.) The outside of the brisket will get super-dark as it cooks, but don't worry—it's supposed to.

5. While the brisket is cooking, place the sauce ingredients in a blender and mix well. Scrape into a small bowl and set aside.

6. When the brisket is tender, remove it from the grill. To check for doneness, plunge a fork straight down into the meat and try to pull the fork out. If the fork slides out easily, the meat is done; if the meat hangs on to the fork, give it more time. Trim any excess fat off the brisket and slice it thin against the grain. Serve with the sauce on the side.

THE CUT

See Barbecued Whole Beef Brisket (page 70) for details on brisket. In this case, we suggest using the flat cut half of the brisket, rather than the point cut, since its leaner nature is a bit better for braising.

OTHER NAMES

Beef brisket first cut, beef brisket thin cut.

OTHER CUTS YOU CAN USE

A 7-bone blade chuck roast is also a good option here.

Braised Beef Brisket with Sauerkraut

SERVES 10

This is a pretty traditional German treatment for brisket, complete with onions, sauerkraut, and prunes. We add some allspice berries and cardamom to give it a slightly more dynamic flavor and use white rather than red wine to make the broth a little lighter. A half brisket will do just fine here.

This is excellent served with Parsleyed New Potatoes (page 412) and a fresh tomato and cucumber salad to contrast with the long-cooked meat.

1 small half beef brisket, about 7 pounds

Kosher salt and freshly cracked black pepper to taste

2 tablespoons vegetable oil

8 tablespoons (1 stick) unsalted butter

4 large onions, peeled and diced small

1/2 cup all-purpose flour

2 cups dry white wine

1 1/2 cups pitted prunes

4 cups sauerkraut, rinsed and drained

3 tablespoons sugar

2 small bay leaves

3 allspice berries

6 cardamom seeds, crushed

About 2 cups beef stock (or see Stock Options, page 32)

COOK ONCE, EAT TWICE
Like most braised dishes, this one reheats beautifully, but the meat also makes a great sandwich, particularly on dark bread with a little grated fresh horseradish.

1. Preheat the oven to 325°F.

2. Dry the brisket with paper towels and sprinkle generously with salt and pepper. In a 5-inch-deep Dutch oven or other large ovenproof pot with a lid, heat the oil over medium-high heat until very hot but not smoking. Add the meat and brown well on all sides, 8 to 10 minutes per side. Transfer the brisket to a plate.

3. Pour the oil out of the Dutch oven, then add the butter and melt it over medium heat. Add the onions and cook, stirring occasionally, until lightly browned, 11 to 12 minutes. Add the flour and continue to cook, stirring, for 4 minutes. Add the white wine and stir well to combine.

4. Return the meat to the pot and add the prunes, sauerkraut, sugar, spices, and enough stock so that the liquid comes about halfway up the side of the meat. Bring the liquid just to a simmer, scraping up any brown stuff from the bottom of the pan. Skim any scum from the surface. Cover the pot, place in the oven, and cook until the meat is very tender, 2 to 2½ hours. To check for doneness, plunge a fork straight down into the meat and try to pull the fork out. If the fork slides out easily, the meat is done; if the meat hangs on to the fork, give it more time. When the meat is done, remove it from the pot, cover it loosely with foil to keep it warm, and set it aside while you finish the sauce.

5. Strain the braising liquid, reserving the vegetables. Pour the strained liquid back into the Dutch oven. Skim the fat off the top and taste the liquid. If it needs more flavor, place the pot on the stove over medium-high heat and simmer to reduce the liquid. For a thicker sauce, reduce it until it coats the back of a spoon. Skim any scum off the top and season with salt and pepper, then add the vegetables.

6. Slice the brisket against the grain into thick slices. Place a few slices on each plate, ladle some sauce and vegetables over the top, and serve.

Short ribs, which are the
meaty ends of ribs, can
come from three different
places on the cow. The
ones from the chuck are
the most flavorful, and
since we actually prefer a
little more gnarl and fat in a
short rib, these are our
favorites. For those of you
who like a somewhat
leaner product, try the rib
short rib. (Short ribs from
the plate, the third option,
tend to be a bit too gnarly
even for our taste.) Of
course, none of them is
going to be really lean. But
they have a huge amount
of deep, rich, beefy flavor.

OTHER NAMES

Barbecue ribs, braising
ribs.

OTHER CUTS YOU CAN USE

Flanken-style short ribs
also work well here,
although it's more work to
get the meat off the bones.

BUTCHERSPEAK

Most supermarkets (and
many butcher shops too)
just label their short ribs as
such, with no further designation. They are most likely
to be chuck short ribs.
Those will certainly do the
job, but at a butcher shop
you can ask for short ribs
from the rib section.

Black Pepper–Crusted Wine-Braised Short Ribs with Garlic and Turnips

SERVES 4

This is a very hearty dish, with the richly flavored short ribs and all that garlic and the root vegetables. But we love turnips, onions, and garlic, particularly in the dead of winter. In fact, the flavor of the broth is so seductive that we've made this rather brothy, with more liquid than you might be used to in a dish of this type.

Short ribs come either "English-style" or "flanken-style." English are cut parallel to the rib bone and between the ribs, so they look like a rectangle of meat attached to a section of bone at the bottom. Flanken-style are cut across the rib bones, so they look kind of like a xylophone, short lengths of rib surrounded by bone. Both work equally well, but we like English-style simply because it is easier to separate the meat from the bone when you are ready to do so. They are also much easier to find at the supermarket.

When you sear this pepper-encrusted meat, it's going to create some very powerful smoke; you might want to temporarily disconnect the smoke detector, and make sure that your exhaust fan is turned to high.

Serve this with a nice hunk of warm buttered bread and Mediterranean White Bean Salad (page 424) or a side of steamed Swiss chard with a little garlic. You could also make some grits to serve under the meat and sauce.

4 to 5 pounds English-style beef short ribs, about 4 inches long

1/2 cup freshly cracked black pepper, plus more to taste

Kosher salt to taste

3 tablespoons vegetable oil

2 onions, peeled and diced small

20 cloves garlic, peeled

1 1/2 to 2 pounds turnips, peeled and diced large (you want about 3 cups)

1 tomato, cored and diced small

2 cups dry red wine

About 3 cups beef stock (or see Stock Options, page 32)

1/2 cup roughly chopped fresh parsley

1. Preheat the oven to 300°F.

2. Dry the short ribs with paper towels. Rub on all sides with the pepper and sprinkle with salt. In a 5-inch-deep Dutch oven or other large ovenproof pot with a lid, heat the oil over medium-high heat until very hot but not smoking. Add the ribs, in batches if necessary, and brown well on all sides, 10 to 15 minutes total. As the ribs are browned, transfer them to a platter.

3. Pour off all but about 2 tablespoons of the fat from the pot. Reduce the heat to medium, add the onions, and cook, stirring occasionally, until lightly browned, 11 to 13 minutes. Add the garlic and cook, stirring frequently, for 2 minutes. Add the turnips and tomato and cook, stirring, for an additional 2 minutes. Add the wine, bring to a simmer, and simmer for 10 minutes, scraping up any brown stuff from the bottom of the pan.

4. Return the ribs to the pan and add enough stock to come halfway up the sides of the ribs. Bring to a simmer and skim any scum from the top of the liquid. Cover, place in the oven, and cook until very tender, 1½ to 2 hours. To check for doneness, plunge a fork straight down into the meat and try to pull the fork out. If the fork slides out easily, the meat is done; if the meat hangs on to the fork, give it more time.

5. When the meat is done, remove the meat and turnips from the pot, cover with foil, and set aside. Skim the fat and any scum from the cooking liquid. Taste the liquid, and if it needs more flavor, place the pot on the stove over medium-high heat and simmer to reduce the liquid. Season with salt and pepper, stir in parsley, and serve the ribs and turnips hot accompanied by the sauce.

THE CUT
See Black Pepper–Crusted
Wine-Braised Short Ribs
(page 74) for more infor-
mation on short ribs and
how to choose them at
the butcher shop or supermarket.

Orange-Braised Short Ribs with Fennel Seeds and Oregano

SERVES 4

Short ribs are one of those cuts that has come into its own in American cooking over the past decade or so. These little ribs require some cooking time, and
they have quite a bit of fat in and around them, but the flavor that you get from
slow-cooking them with other intensely flavored ingredients is unbeatable.

Be sure to skim the fat from the braising liquid after cooking. Or, if you
really want to get rid of the fat, cook this dish a day ahead, cover, and refrigerate it, then remove the solidified fat from the top before you reheat it.

We like to serve these short ribs with mashed potatoes or soft polenta
so we can use the braising liquid as a super-flavorful gravy.

4 to 5 pounds English-style beef short ribs, about 4 inches long

6 tablespoon cracked fennel seeds

Kosher salt and freshly cracked black pepper to taste

3 tablespoons vegetable oil

2 medium red onions, peeled, halved, and very thinly sliced

1/4 cup minced garlic

1 to 2 teaspoons red pepper flakes, or to taste

1 cup dry red wine

1 cup orange juice

1/2 cup balsamic vinegar

1/2 cup catsup

2 tablespoons grainy mustard

1/2 cup roughly chopped fresh oregano

About 2 cups beef stock (or see Stock Options, page 32)

1. Preheat the oven to 300°F.

2. Dry the short ribs with paper towels, then rub on all sides with the
fennel seeds and salt and pepper, pressing gently so they adhere. In a 5-
inch-deep Dutch oven or other large ovenproof pot with a lid, heat the oil
over medium-high heat until hot but not smoking. Add the ribs, in batches
if necessary, and brown well, 10 to 15 minutes total; as the ribs are
browned, transfer them to a platter.

3. Pour off all but about 2 tablespoons of fat from the pot. Add the
onions and cook, stirring occasionally, until translucent, 7 to 9 minutes.
Add the garlic and red pepper flakes and cook, stirring frequently, for 2

more minutes. Add the wine, orange juice, balsamic vinegar, catsup, mustard, and mustard, and oregano and bring just to a simmer, scraping any browned bits from the bottom of the pan.

4. Add the meat along with salt and pepper to taste and enough stock to bring the liquid halfway up the sides of the ribs. Bring to a simmer and skim any scum from the top of the liquid. Cover, place in the oven, and cook until very tender, 1½ to 2 hours. To check for doneness, plunge a fork straight down into the meat and try to pull the fork out. If the fork slides out easily, the meat is done; if the meat hangs on to the fork, give it more time.

5. When the meat is done, remove it from the pot and cover it loosely with foil. Skim the fat and any scum from the cooking liquid, then taste the liquid, and if it needs more flavor, place the pot on the stove over medium-high heat and simmer to reduce the liquid. For a thicker sauce, reduce it until it coats the back of a spoon. Season to taste with salt and pepper and serve the ribs hot, accompanied by the sauce.

Puerto Rican Vinegar-Braised Flank Steak with Cabbage, Corn, and Yucca Salad

SERVES 4

If you think meat is too heavy for a hot summer day, give this recipe a try. You see this kind of dish a lot in Latin America—a relatively tough cut of beef is braised in a vinegary stock, then shredded and used as part of a flavorful dish with lots of other components. That way, you get that terrific combination of something that has been cooked for a very long time with something that has not been cooked at all. To accentuate this contrast, we use some of the braising liquid in the salad dressing.

There is a really great mix of flavors here—the richness of the beef and its syrupy, cilantro-laced sauce; the bite of lime; the earthiness of cumin; the heat of red pepper flakes; and all the fresh vegetables in the salad—not to mention the round starchiness of yucca, a bedrock Latin staple.

This is delicious with Spicy Latin Black Beans (page 423) or just a platter of chilled sliced tropical fruit and Margaritas.

THE CUT

See Fennel-Crusted Flank Steak (page 114) for details on flank steak and how to get what you want when buying it. Flank is one of those rare "both/and" cuts that can be cooked very slowly, as it is here, or very quickly, as it is in the recipe on page 114, and be delicious both ways.

OTHER CUTS YOU CAN USE

Since you want to be able to shred this meat with your fingers, the best substitute is pork butt.

FOR THE SPICE RUB

2 tablespoons minced garlic

2 tablespoons ground cumin

$1\frac{1}{2}$ tablespoons kosher salt

1 tablespoon red pepper flakes

$1\frac{1}{2}$ tablespoons freshly cracked black pepper

$1\frac{1}{2}$ tablespoons dark brown sugar

$1\frac{1}{2}$ to 2 pounds flank steak, most of the external fat removed

3 tablespoons olive oil, or more if needed

2 onions, peeled, halved, and thinly sliced

2 stalks celery, diced medium

1 carrot, peeled and diced medium

2 bay leaves

3 whole cloves

1 cup red wine vinegar

Kosher salt and freshly cracked black pepper to taste

FOR THE SALAD

1 medium yucca root (or substitute 2 medium potatoes)

3 ears corn, husked

$\frac{1}{2}$ small head white cabbage, cored and shredded

4 scallions (white and green parts), cut into thin strips

2 large red bell peppers, cored, seeded, and cut into thin strips

1 large carrot, peeled and cut into thin strips

$\frac{1}{2}$ cup extra virgin olive oil

$\frac{1}{4}$ cup fresh lime juice (about 2 limes)

Kosher salt and freshly cracked black pepper to taste

$\frac{1}{4}$ cup roughly chopped fresh cilantro (or substitute parsley)

1. Preheat the oven to 325°F.

2. In a small bowl, combine the spice rub ingredients and mix well. Dry the flank steak with paper towels, then rub it all over with this mixture, pressing to make sure it adheres.

3. In a 5-inch-deep Dutch oven or other large ovenproof pot with a lid, heat the oil over medium-high heat until very hot but not smoking. Add the flank steak and brown it well on both sides, 3 to 4 minutes per side. Transfer the steak to a platter.

4. Pour off the fat or add oil to the pot as needed so you have a total of about 2 tablespoons in the pot. Add the onions, celery, and carrot and cook, stirring occasionally, until the onions are golden brown, 11 to 13

minutes. Return the steak to the pot and add the bay leaves, cloves, vinegar, and enough water so the liquid comes about halfway up the sides of the meat. Bring to a simmer, cover, and place in the oven. Braise until the meat is tender, 1½ to 2 hours. To check for doneness, plunge a fork straight down into the meat and try to pull the fork out. If the fork slides out easily, the meat is done; if the meat hangs on to the fork, give it more time.

5. Meanwhile, at some point while the meat is braising, cook the corn and yucca: Bring a large pot of salted water to a boil over high heat. Remove the brown skin and pink underlayer of flesh from the yucca, then cut the yucca lengthwise in half and remove the fibrous center core. Cut the flesh into medium dice.

6. Add the corn to the boiling water and cook just until you can smell it, about 2 minutes. Remove from the water with tongs or a fork and rinse under cold water to stop the cooking process. Add the yucca or potatoes to the boiling water and cook until it is easily pierced with a fork but still offers some resistance, about 20 minutes. Remove, rinse under cold water, and drain. Cut the kernels from the corn. Set aside.

7. When the meat is done, remove it from the pot. Strain the cooking liquid into a saucepan, discarding the solids, and skim the fat from the surface. Reserve ½ cup of the cooking liquid for the salad dressing, and gently boil the rest over the heat until reduced to a syrupy sauce, about 10 minutes. Season with salt and pepper as needed.

8. In a large bowl, combine the corn kernels, yucca, cabbage, scallions, bell peppers, and carrot. Whisk the olive oil, lime juice, and salt and pepper into the ½ cup reserved cooking liquid. Stir in the cilantro, pour the dressing over the salad, and toss well to combine.

9. Divide the salad among individual plates. Shred the warm flank steak with your fingers and mix it with the sauce. Arrange the meat on top of the salad and serve.

COOK ONCE, EAT TWICE
Pile any leftover shredded beef onto a tortilla, top it with some of the salad, roll it up, and you've got a great lunch to eat with an ice-cold Mexican beer.

These bones may come from any of ribs 6 through 12. They have a fair amount of meat on them, but you have to do some work to get it. For us, that makes it all the more fun. You may see these bones on display in some butcher stores and supermarkets, but very often you will have to ask for them. Butchers who sell a lot of boneless rib roasts are your best bet.

Flintstones-Style BBQ Beef Ribs with Hot, Sweet, and Sour Bone Sauce

SERVES 4

This is a kind of a classic dish that I (Chris) used to eat a lot as a youngster in big steak houses. Over time, the cooks in those places would accumulate a lot of the big bones that sit under the beef rib, because they would serve the rib meat boneless. So they'd have a lot of these very flavorful bones left over, and very often they would tend to put them out in an "all you can eat" situation, because they didn't really cost the restaurant anything.

A lot of people boil these bones before they cook them, but I really like the idea of putting them in the oven and cooking them for a long time at a low temperature, since I think that gives them much better flavor.

This is not a dish for people who want tender meat; it's for those who enjoy good beef flavor and the primitive tactile experience of gnawing on bones. To me, the flavor and textural rewards are definitely worth it. It's a pretty messy situation, though, so you'll need to have a good supply of paper towels and beer on hand. In fact, it's probably best to eat this with good friends so you can get as messy as you want without worrying about it.

Watermelon and corn bread are the proper accompaniments here.

FOR THE RUB

¼ cup freshly cracked black pepper

2 tablespoons brown sugar

2 tablespoons paprika

2 tablespoons ground cumin

2 tablespoons kosher salt

5 pounds beef back ribs (about 2 racks)

FOR THE SAUCE

⅓ cup molasses

1 cup catsup

¼ cup balsamic vinegar

¼ cup fresh lime juice (about 2 limes)

½ cup orange juice

¼ cup soy sauce

2 tablespoons lightly packed brown sugar

3 tablespoons minced fresh ginger

3 tablespoons minced fresh chile peppers of your choice

¹⁄₂ cup thinly sliced scallions (white and green parts)

Kosher salt and freshly cracked black pepper to taste

1. Preheat the oven to 200°F.

2. In a small bowl, combine the rub ingredients and mix well. Rub the ribs all over with this mixture, pressing lightly to make sure it adheres, and lay them on a foil-lined baking sheet. Place in the oven and cook for 5 hours.

3. About 40 minutes before the bones are done, light a fire in your grill.

4. While the ribs are roasting, combine the sauce ingredients in a medium saucepan and simmer over low heat for 15 minutes, or until the sauce is slightly thickened. Remove it from the heat and cover to keep warm.

5. When the fire has died down and the coals are covered with white ash, cut the ribs into individual ribs and place on the grill. Grill for 5 to 7 minutes per side, or until the rub develops a crusty appearance. Brush the ribs with sauce and cook for 1 minute more, until the sauce forms a glaze. Remove the ribs from the fire and serve with the remaining sauce.

Steaks cut from the round are really too tough for grilling, broiling, panfrying, or even for roasting. They do respond well, though, to long, slow moist cooking methods such as braising. This dish makes good use of the bottom round steak, which is better for this particular application than a roast because it is not as thick. This is definitely a supermarket cut.

OTHER CUTS YOU CAN USE

You can substitute any top round steak or chuck steak here, as well as the tri-tip roast.

Sweet-and-Sour Braised Bottom Round Steak with Eggplant and Ginger

SERVES 6 TO 8

There are a lot of flavors going on in this Asian-style dish, with the rather large doses of cardamom and white pepper adding particularly exotic overtones. We think the many strong flavors all work very well together, creating a dish with plenty of layers of flavor. And then of course there is the eggplant, which kind of melts down over the long, slow cooking to create a wonderfully moist, meaty, thick sauce.

Serve this with white or brown rice and some steamed greens on the side.

One 4-pound bottom round steak, about 2 inches thick

¼ cup freshly cracked white pepper

3 tablespoons roughly ground cardamom seeds

Kosher salt to taste

3 tablespoons vegetable oil, or more if needed

2 onions, peeled and diced medium

¼ cup minced garlic

¼ cup minced fresh ginger

1 to 2 tablespoons minced fresh chile peppers of your choice

2 medium eggplants, diced medium

¼ cup tomato paste

2 cups dry white wine

About 2 cups beef stock (or see Stock Options, page 32)

6 tablespoons soy sauce

½ cup rice wine vinegar (or substitute white wine vinegar)

¼ cup packed dark brown sugar

Freshly cracked black pepper to taste

1 bunch scallions (white and green parts), very thinly sliced

¼ cup Asian sesame oil

¼ cup sesame seeds, toasted in a dry skillet over medium heat, shaken frequently, until fragrant, 3 to 5 minutes

4 dashes Tabasco

1. Preheat the oven to 300°F.

2. Dry the steak with paper towels, then rub it on all sides with the pepper, cardamom, and salt, pressing gently to be sure they adhere. In a 5-inch-deep Dutch oven or other large, ovenproof pot with a lid, heat the oil over medium-high heat until hot but not smoking. Add the steak and brown well, 10 to 12 minutes per side. Remove and set aside.

3. Pour off the fat or add oil to the pot as needed so you have a total of about 2 tablespoons in the pot. Add the onions and cook, stirring frequently, until lightly browned, 7 to 9 minutes. Add the garlic, ginger, and chiles and cook, stirring, for 2 minutes. Add the eggplant and tomato paste and cook, stirring frequently, for 4 more minutes. Add the wine, stock, soy sauce, vinegar, and brown sugar and bring just to a boil, scraping up any browned bits from the bottom of the pot.

4. Add the steak and bring just to a simmer. Skim any scum from the surface of the liquid and season to taste with salt and pepper. At this point the liquid should cover the steak about halfway; if it does not, add more stock. Cover, place in the oven, and cook until fork-tender, 1½ to 2 hours. To check for doneness, plunge a fork straight down into the meat and try to pull the fork out. If the fork slides out easily, the meat is done; if the meat hangs on to the fork, give it more time.

5. When the meat is done, transfer it to a plate, cover it loosely with foil, and let it rest for about 10 minutes. Skim the fat from the surface of the cooking liquid and season with salt and pepper, then place on the stove over high heat and reduce until slightly thickened.

6. Meanwhile, in a small bowl, combine the scallions, sesame oil, toasted sesame seeds, and Tabasco and mix well.

7. Cut the meat into thick slices and serve, topping each serving with some of the sauce and scallion mixture.

RECIPES FOR
SMALL TENDER CUTS OF BEEF

10 STEPS TO GREAT GRILLED BEEF

1. Build a two-level fire using hardwood charcoal.

2. Wait for the flames to die down and the coals to be covered with gray ash.

3. Check the temperature of the fire.

4. Dry the meat well.

5. Season the meat well.

6. Sear the meat hard over a hot fire.

7. Move the meat to the cooler part of the fire if it needs to cook more slowly (don't use the cover).

8. Flip the meat only once during cooking.

9. Check for doneness early and often (nick, peek, and cheat).

10. Remove the meat from the fire, cover with foil and allow to rest, then serve it up.

Pan-Seared Delmonico with Roasted Figs and Sherry-Parsley Sauce

Broiled Bacon-Wrapped Filet Mignon with Roasted Endive and Mushrooms and Blue Cheese Butter

Mr. Perfect Steak for Two

Black Pan-Seared Tournedos with Asparagus, Crab, and A-1 Hollandaise

White Pepper–Crusted Black-and-Blue Steak Stuffed with Spicy Sesame Spinach with Soy-Wasabi Dipping Sauce

Pan-Seared Thin Strip Loin Steak in the Style of Diane

Pepper-Crusted Grilled Strip Loin Steak with Homemade Steak Sauce and Mushroom Hobo Packs

Grilled Sirloin Steak High Plains Drifter–Style

Stir-fried Sirloin Tips with Ginger, Peanuts, and Scallions over Smoky Sesame Cabbage

Laotian-Style Aromatic Beef Salad

Grilled Polynesian-Style Tenderloin Tip Kebabs with Bacon, Pineapple, and Peppers

Herb-Crusted Grilled Top Round Steak "London Broil–Style" with Maître d'Hôtel Butter and Smoky Balsamic Onions

Seared Balsamic-Glazed Top Blade Chuck Steaks with Spinach, Lemon, and Olive Oil

Southeast Asian–Style Grilled Skirt Steak with Aromatic Greens and Ginger-Lime Dressing

Lime-Soaked, Cumin-Crusted Grilled Skirt Steak with Green Olive–Chile Relish

Sliced Grilled Skirt Steak on Greek Salad

Fennel-Crusted Flank Steak with Orange–Black Olive Relish and Spicy Mint Honey

Korean-Style Grilled Short Ribs with Ginger, Chiles, and Quick Kimchee

10 STEPS TO GREAT SAUTÉED BEEF

1. Use a big heavy sauté pan.

2. Dry the meat well.

3. Season the meat well.

4. Use only a small amount of oil.

5. Get the pan and the oil hot.

6. Don't overcrowd the meat in the pan.

7. Sear the meat hard.

8. Flip the meat only once while cooking.

9. Check for doneness early and often (nick, peek, and cheat).

10. Remove the meat from the heat, cover loosely with foil, and allow to rest, then serve.

10 STEPS TO GREAT BROILED BEEF

Check out sautéing: The steps are the same except you use a broiler pan instead of a sauté pan, preheat the broiler instead of getting the oil hot, and skip the searing step.

Delmonico is another name for a boneless rib-eye steak. Not surprisingly, this steak comes from the rib section of the cow, the same part of the beast that we know as the prime rib when it is used as a roast rather than sliced into steaks. This steak differs from steaks from the short loin (e.g., filet mignon, strip steak, porterhouse, and T-bone) because it has more streaks of fat in and around it. This gives it a truly deep, beefy flavor.

OTHER NAMES

Rib-eye steak, Spencer steak, beauty steak.

OTHER CUTS YOU CAN USE

Top loin strip steak, filet mignon, or a good sirloin steak would all work fine here. If you increase the cooking time just a bit, porterhouse and T-bone would also be great with this preparation.

Pan-Seared Delmonico with Roasted Figs and Sherry-Parsley Sauce

SERVES 4

With the rich taste of figs and the subtle tang of sherry, this dish has some classic Spanish flavors going for it. To provide a little exotica, we throw in some coriander seeds, which go very well with the figs. But center stage is ably occupied by the Delmonico, also known as the rib-eye steak. This steak not only is quite tender, but also has very rich beef flavor. It is the favorite steak of many a devoted carnivore, and in our steak pantheon it comes in second only to the T-bone and porterhouse.

As with most steaks, we like this best served with potatoes and a green salad. Outstanding choices would include Au Gratin Potatoes (page 410), Hash Browns (page 412), or plain baked potatoes and a leaf lettuce salad with a simple sherry vinaigrette.

This dish is also fantastic when grilled. Cook the steak over a hot fire for about the same amount of time as indicated here. Grill the figs around the edge of the fire, where it is cooler, until they are browned on all sides, about 3 minutes.

FOR THE FIGS

8 fresh figs, halved

1 tablespoon olive oil

Kosher salt and freshly cracked black pepper to taste

FOR THE SAUCE

1/3 cup extra virgin olive oil

1 tablespoon dry sherry

1/4 cup roughly chopped fresh parsley

1/2 small red onion, peeled and diced small

1 teaspoon minced garlic

Kosher salt and freshly cracked black pepper to taste

Four 12- to 14-ounce Delmonico steaks, 1 to 1 1/2 inches thick

Kosher salt and freshly cracked black pepper to taste

1/4 cup cracked coriander seeds (or 2 tablespoons ground coriander)

3 tablespoons olive oil

1. Preheat the oven to 400°F.

2. Rub the fig halves with the olive oil, sprinkle with salt and pepper to taste, and place cut side up on a baking sheet. Roast until they are tender but not mushy, about 20 minutes. Remove and set aside.

3. While the figs are roasting, make the sauce: In a medium bowl, whisk together all the ingredients until well combined.

4. Dry the steaks with paper towels, sprinkle them generously with salt and pepper, and rub them all over with the coriander, pressing gently to be sure it adheres. In a large sauté pan (or two sauté pans to avoid crowding), heat the olive oil over medium-high heat until very hot but not smoking. Add the steaks and cook until well seared on one side, 5 to 7 minutes. Turn and continue cooking for another 4 to 7 minutes for rare. To check for doneness, nick, peek, and cheat: Make a ¼-inch cut in the thickest part of the meat and take a peek; it should be slightly less done than you like it. When the steaks are done to your liking, remove them from the heat, cover them loosely with foil, and let them rest for 5 minutes.

5. Place a steak on each plate, along with 4 fig halves. Drizzle the steak and the figs lightly with the sauce and serve, passing the remaining sauce separately.

BUTCHERSPEAK

The Delmonico is one of those cuts that is confusing because some people also apply this name to a strip loin steak. To be sure that you get what you are looking for here, ask for a boneless rib-eye steak. That will also ensure that you get a steak that is cut from the large end of the beef rib (ribs 6 through 8) rather than the small end (ribs 9 through 12). Technically, those smaller steaks are called rib steaks rather than rib-eye steaks, and they don't have quite as deep a beefy flavor as the Delmonico.

Filet mignon is a steak cut from the center of the tenderloin. The tenderloin sits on top of the cow's back and does none of the work of moving the animal around, so it has virtually none of the connective tissues and sinews that make meat tough. It is also surrounded by fat, which contributes to its butter-soft texture. If tenderness is your Holy Grail, this is your steak.

OTHER NAMES

Tenderloin steak, filet de boeuf, tender steak, fillet steak.

OTHER CUTS YOU CAN USE

The only other cut that has the super-tender texture of the filet mignon is the tournedos, which is a steak cut from the small end of the tenderloin rather than the center, as the filet mignon is.

BUTCHERSPEAK

You can often find this cut in the supermarket, but you are probably better off going to a butcher for it. After all, this is the most expensive piece of beef you can buy, and you want to be absolutely sure to get top quality when you are laying out that kind of money. You can also try to get the butcher to give you this cut bone-in. It's a rarity, but it is a truly super cut, because the bone gives it some added flavor to go with the tenderness.

Broiled Bacon-Wrapped Filet Mignon with Roasted Endive and Mushrooms and Blue Cheese Butter

SERVES 4

Here it is, the "ne plus ultra" steak of our youth, the one that our parents ordered when they wanted to really put on the dog. The filet mignon is basically a thick piece of meat cut from the center of the absolutely most tender muscle on the cow. It is quite lean and has a very mild beef flavor. Because of this, filet mignon is often wrapped in bacon or served with a flavored butter to give it a little extra oomph in both the fat and flavor departments. Here we opt for both choices, creating an old school–type of dish like those that were the top of the line at the steak houses in our childhood.

We also roast some endive and mushrooms to go alongside the steak. The endive adds a nice edge of bitterness that contrasts nicely with the super-rich, almost unctuous quality of the bacon-wrapped, butter-topped meat.

FOR THE BUTTER

8 tablespoons (1 stick) unsalted butter, at room temperature

4 ounces blue cheese

FOR THE VEGETABLES

2 heads Belgian endive, halved

20 medium white mushrooms, stemmed

3 tablespoons olive oil

1 tablespoon minced garlic

Kosher salt and freshly cracked black pepper to taste

¼ cup roughly chopped fresh parsley or oregano

¼ cup balsamic vinegar

Four 8- to 10-ounce filet mignons, about 1½ inches thick

3 tablespoons freshly cracked black pepper

Kosher salt to taste

4 slices thick-cut bacon

1. Preheat the oven to 450°F.

2. Make the butter: In a medium bowl, combine the butter and blue cheese and mix well. Place the flavored butter on a piece of waxed paper or plastic wrap, form it into a rough cylinder, and wrap it up. Refrigerate until firm.

3. In a large bowl, toss the endive and mushrooms with the olive oil, garlic, and salt and pepper to coat thoroughly. Place the vegetables on a baking sheet and roast until the endive is slightly browned on the outside and the mushrooms look moist all the way through, about 20 to 25 minutes. When the vegetables are done, toss them in a large bowl with the herbs and balsamic vinegar. Cover with aluminum foil to keep them warm while you broil the steaks.

4. Preheat the broiler.

5. Dry the filet mignons with paper towels and sprinkle them generously with the pepper and salt. Wrap a strip of bacon around each one, securing it with a toothpick. Put them on the broiling rack, place 3 inches from the heat source, and sear well on one side, 3 to 4 minutes. Turn and continue cooking to the desired doneness, 3 to 6 minutes more for rare. To check for doneness, nick, peek, and cheat: Make a ¼-inch cut in the thickest part of the meat and take a peek; it should be slightly less done than you like it. When the steaks are done to your liking, remove them from the heat, cover loosely with foil, and let rest for 5 minutes.

6. Slice the butter into ¼-inch-thick slices. Divide the roasted vegetables among four plates, top each with a bacon-wrapped steak, and let a slice or two of the blue cheese butter melt on top.

COOK ONCE, EAT TWICE
If you have any leftovers, chop them all together for a luxurious endive-mushroom-steak hash, then top it with a bit of the blue cheese butter.

Mr. Perfect Steak for Two

SERVES 2

Meat is my (Chris's) favorite food, beef is my favorite meat, steak is my favorite beef, and T-bone or porterhouse is my favorite steak. In other words, this is the best meat in the world. In fact, I love this steak so much that when our group of friends goes on its annual pilgrimage to Costa Rica, I always take some humongous versions of these steaks along in my luggage for our first dinner on the beach.

Whichever of these two spectacular steaks you choose, it's important that it be at least 2 inches thick. That way, you can get a deep, crusty sear on the outside without overcooking the inside. To accomplish that, we use the "sear and move" technique, where we start out cooking the meat hard over a hot fire, then move it to a lower fire to finish cooking. It's crucial that you

THE CUT

This cut, which comes from the short loin section of the cow, has a large bone running down it and is actually two steaks in one. It includes a section of the ultratender tenderloin on one side of the bone and a section of the very tender top loin on the other side. And, of course, you also get the bone to chew on, which is no mean bonus.

The difference between the two bone-in steaks from this part of the cow is the size of the tenderloin portion. The porterhouse comes from the rear section of the short loin where the tenderloin muscle is thicker, so it includes a section of the tenderloin that is at least 1¼ inches across, sometimes as much as 2 inches or even more. The T-bone, cut from the center section of the loin, includes a smaller piece of tenderloin, from ½ to 1¼ inches across.

OTHER CUTS YOU CAN USE

You can substitute a boneless or bone-in rib-eye steak here.

BUTCHERSPEAK

You are probably not going to find a steak this thick in the supermarket. In fact, you may even have to call a butcher ahead of time to get it. Tell him you want a 2½-pound T-bone or porterhouse that's 2 inches thick or more, no skimping. He'll know you're a real steak fanatic.

check this cut for doneness often too, because its thickness makes it hard to judge. If you want, you could even use a meat thermometer on this one.

Since there are only four ingredients in this recipe (and since you're already going to be paying top dollar for the steak), you should use the best of each. Make sure you use coarse salt, crack the pepper just before it goes on the steak for the fullest flavor, and get some high-quality extra virgin olive oil for rubbing.

Serve this with New Potato Hobo Packs (page 442) or a baked sweet potato with maple sour cream and a nice spinach salad or some steamed spinach with garlic.

One giant 2- to 2½-inch-thick steak, either a 2½-pound T-bone or a porterhouse
¼ cup extra virgin olive oil
Kosher salt and freshly cracked black pepper to taste

1. Light a fire in your grill.

2. Pat the steak dry with paper towels, then rub it with the oil and sprinkle it generously with salt and pepper.

3. When the fire has died down and the coals are covered with white ash, check the temperature of the fire: you want a hot fire here (you can hold your hand 5 inches above the grill surface for 1 to 2 seconds). Place the steak over the hottest part of the fire and cook until well seared on one side, 6 to 8 minutes. Turn and sear the second side, again for 6 to 8 minutes. Move to a medium-hot part of the grill and cook, turning once, 10 to 15 minutes more for rare. To check for doneness, nick, peek, and cheat: Make a ¼-inch cut in the thickest part of the meat and take a peek; it should be slightly less done than you like it.

4. Remove the meat from the fire, cover it loosely with foil, and allow it to rest for 10 minutes before serving.

Black Pan-Seared Tournedos with Asparagus, Crab, and A-1 Hollandaise

SERVES 4

This is a knock-off of the famous dish called Veal Oscar, which was the toast of hotel restaurants in the early part of this century. The combination of crab and asparagus is a classic, one of those pairs of foods that somehow just seem to perfectly complement each other. They're also a nice match for the subtle, delicate flavor of the tournedos. This is an expensive dish, fun for a fancy dinner with friends, with a dash or two of A-1 sauce to cut the pretense a bit.

Speaking of which, don't be scared off by the hollandaise sauce. You know what happens if the worst disaster occurs and it breaks? Nothing. It still tastes the same, it just doesn't look as good. So, especially if you are cooking this for friends, don't give it a thought. Chances are it won't break anyway, particularly if you use a blender to make it. If you are in a hurry, though, you can make a compound butter in place of the hollandaise. Just let the butter come to room temperature, then combine it with all the hollandaise ingredients except the eggs and water and mix well.

Serve this with an arugula and blue cheese salad and crispy Roasted Potatoes (page 414) or French Fries (page 411).

FOR THE HOLLANDAISE

½ pound (2 sticks) unsalted butter

2 tablespoons warm water

3 large egg yolks

2 tablespoons fresh lime juice (about 1 lime)

3 tablespoons A-1 sauce

3 to 6 dashes Tabasco sauce

¼ cup roughly chopped fresh parsley

Kosher salt and freshly cracked black pepper to taste

¼ cup olive oil

Four 8-ounce tournedos, about 2 inches thick

Kosher salt and freshly cracked black pepper to taste

32 small stalks asparagus, trimmed, blanched in boiling water for 2 minutes, until crisp-tender, cooled in ice water, and drained

8 ounces fresh crabmeat, picked over for shells and cartilage

1 tablespoon fresh lemon juice

THE CUT

The tournedos is pretty much the same as a filet mignon. Both are cut from the tenderloin. This muscle, which runs along the top of the spine, is the least used muscle on the cow and therefore the most tender, a piece of meat so buttery that it can be cut with a fork. A tournedos is cut on the bias from the small end of the tenderloin, while a filet mignon is cut from the center of the muscle. You might find this cut in an upscale supermarket, but chances are you'll need to get it from a butcher. Since you want the meat to get nicely seared in this recipe, it is important that your tournedos actually be a full 2 inches thick.

OTHER CUTS YOU CAN USE

Filet mignon is an ideal substitute here, and you can also use boneless rib-eye steak (Delmonico) or a boneless strip loin.

1. Preheat the oven to 300°F.

2. Make the hollandaise: In a small saucepan, melt the butter over low heat.

Blender method: Place all the other ingredients in a blender, cover, and turn it on, then drizzle in the butter through the hole in the cover. The sauce will thicken. Taste and adjust the seasoning. Cover and keep in a warm place until ready to serve.

Hand method: Combine the egg yolks and water in the top of a double boiler and whisk until light and frothy. Place the top of the double boiler over barely simmering water and continue to whisk the egg mixture in a figure-eight motion until it starts to thicken, 4 to 8 minutes. When it starts to thicken, you will begin to see a figure eight on the bottom of the pan as you whisk. Remove the pan from the water and continue to whisk for about 15 seconds to prevent the eggs from getting too hot and curdling. Very gradually add the melted butter to the egg yolks, whisking constantly; if the sauce gets too thick at this point, add just a little water. When the butter is fully incorporated, whisk in the lime juice, A-1 sauce, Tabasco, parsley, and salt and pepper. Cover and keep in a warm place until ready to serve.

3. In a large cast-iron skillet or ovenproof sauté pan, heat 2 tablespoons of the olive oil over medium-high heat until very hot but not smoking. Pat the steaks dry with paper towels, sprinkle generously with salt and pepper, and add to the pan. Sear well on one side, 5 to 6 minutes, then turn and sear well on the other side, 3 to 4 minutes. Place the pan in the oven and cook for 4 to 6 minutes more for rare. To check for doneness, nick, peek, and cheat: Make a ¼-inch cut in the thickest part of the meat; it should be slightly less done than you like it. Remove the steaks from the oven, cover loosely with foil, and allow to rest for 5 minutes.

4. Meanwhile, heat a large sauté pan over medium-high heat. Add the remaining 2 tablespoons olive oil and heat until very hot but not smoking. Add the asparagus and cook, rolling it over a couple of times to cook evenly, until nicely seared, about 2 minutes. Sprinkle with salt and pepper, remove from the pan, and set aside. Add the crabmeat to the pan and sauté, stirring, until just warmed through, 30 to 45 seconds. Remove from the heat and season with the lemon juice and salt and pepper.

5. Top each tournedos with 8 asparagus spears and several tablespoons of crab, drizzle generously with the hollandaise, and serve right away.

White Pepper–Crusted Black-and-Blue Steak Stuffed with Spicy Sesame Spinach with Soy-Wasabi Dipping Sauce

SERVES 8 TO 10 AS AN APPETIZER

Here we take a double-thick boneless top loin steak, rub it with aromatic white pepper, and sear it very hard over a hot fire so that it gets a good crust on the outside but remains pretty much raw in the middle. Then we slice it paper-thin, so it is almost like seared carpaccio, if that's not a contradiction in terms. After that, we wrap it up around some spicy, sesame-flavored spinach to make a very flavorful appetizer, which we serve with a simple two-ingredient dipping sauce.

This may sound like a fair amount of work, but it's really pretty easy. Try serving this as an appetizer in front of a light fish meal.

One 2-pound boneless strip loin steak, 2½ to 3½ inches thick, fat trimmed totally

¼ cup freshly cracked white pepper

Kosher salt to taste

FOR THE SPINACH

1 pound fresh spinach, trimmed and well washed

2 tablespoons Asian sesame oil

10 dashes Tabasco sauce

1 teaspoon sugar

FOR THE DIPPING SAUCE

½ cup soy sauce

2 tablespoons wasabi powder (available in Asian markets), mixed with water to the consistency of wet sand

4 ounces pickled ginger (available in Asian markets)

1. Light a fire in your grill.

2. Pat the steak dry with paper towels, then rub it all over with the white pepper and salt. When the fire has died down and the coals are very hot, check the temperature: you are looking for a hot fire here (you can hold your hand 5 inches above the grill surface for 1 second). Place the steak on the grill and sear well on the top and bottom and two long sides,

THE CUT
This is the wildly popular top loin strip steak, cut double thick. You'll definitely have to go to a butcher to get a piece of meat this thick, but you need that thickness to get the raw-inside/seared-outside quality we're looking for. See Pepper-Crusted Grilled Strip Loin Steak (page 96) for more on this cut.

OTHER CUTS YOU CAN USE
The firm but fine-grained texture of the top loin strip is a key to this dish, so it's best to stick to that cut.

about 4 minutes on each. Remove the steak from the heat and allow to rest while you prepare the spinach.

3. Bring a large pot of salted water to a boil, and fill your sink or a large bowl with ice and water. Blanch the spinach in the boiling water for 1 minute; do not overcook, or the spinach will lose its bright color and fresh taste. Drain and immediately plunge into the ice water to stop the cooking process, then drain again and squeeze dry by the handful. (Be sure to wring the spinach dry at this point; if you leave it too moist, the final dish may have a soggy texture.)

4. In a small bowl, combine the oil, Tabasco sauce, and sugar and mix well. Add the spinach and toss, so the spinach is coated with the dressing.

5. Make the dipping sauce: Combine the soy sauce and wasabi and mix well.

6. Slice the steak very thin on the bias, against the grain. Place a piece of pickled ginger and a little bit of the spinach mixture on each slice of steak, then roll up tightly and pin together with a toothpick. Serve with the dipping sauce.

THE CUT

This is a relatively thin slab of meat cut from the top loin muscle (also known as the shell), which along with the tenderloin makes up the short loin section of the cow. Although we usually recommend that you get steaks that are at least 1½ inches thick, for this table-side prep, a thinner steak is better. And since we're using a thinner piece of steak here, you should be able to get it in your supermarket.

Pan-Seared Thin Strip Loin Steak in the Style of Diane

SERVES 4

If you're having some friends over and you want to give them a bit of a show, try this dish. It is really a trip back in time to the days of tuxedo-clad waiters who fooled around with the food at your table in order to make you feel important. But it is also a very tasty and impressive dish. Basically we're taking a boneless steak, coating it with a bit of mustard, cooking it up, and then making a quick brandy pan sauce. For all its impressive aura, it's quite easy. Just be sure that you take the pan away from the heat for 20 seconds before igniting the brandy; otherwise, you may get a big whoof of flame.

Good-quality mustard is a key to success with this dish, so don't skimp. Serve this with roast or baked potatoes and a classy green vegetable such as Roasted Asparagus (page 427) or Brussels Sprouts in Brown Butter (page 428).

Four 8-ounce strip loin steaks, about ½ to ¾ inch thick, well trimmed

Kosher salt and freshly cracked black pepper to taste

¼ cup grainy mustard

3 tablespoons olive oil, divided

FOR THE SAUCE

¼ cup finely diced shallots (or substitute red onion)

⅓ cup brandy (or dry Madeira)

½ cup beef stock (or see Stock Options, page 32)

Kosher salt and freshly cracked black pepper to taste

2 tablespoons roughly chopped fresh parsley

2 tablespoons fresh lemon juice (about ½ lemon)

OTHER NAMES

See Pepper-Crusted Grilled Strip Loin Steak (page 96).

OTHER CUTS YOU CAN USE

You can substitute any of the other very tender steaks here, such as the filet mignon or rib-eye.

1. Dry the steaks with paper towels and sprinkle generously with salt and pepper. In a shallow bowl, combine the mustard and 2 tablespoons of the oil and mix well. Add the steaks and toss them about so they get thoroughly coated.

2. In a large sauté pan, heat the remaining tablespoon of oil over medium-high heat until very hot but not quite smoking. Add the steaks (use two pans if necessary to avoid crowding) and cook until well seared on one side, 3 to 4 minutes. Turn and continue cooking for a total of 4 to 6 minutes for rare. To check for doneness, nick, peek, and cheat: Make a ¼-inch cut in the thickest part of the meat; it should be slightly less done than you like it. Remove the steaks from the pan and cover them loosely with aluminum foil to keep warm.

3. Make the sauce: Add the shallots to the pan and stir over medium-high heat for about 15 seconds. Take the pan completely away from the stove (unless you want singed eyebrows) and add the brandy. Wait for 20 seconds, then return the pan to the heat and ignite the brandy with a match, being careful that you are not leaning over the pan. When the flame dies, add the stock and bring to a simmer, scraping the bottom of the pan to dissolve the flavorful brown crusty stuff. Allow the sauce to simmer vigorously until it is reduced enough to coat the back of a spoon, about 5 to 7 minutes. Season the sauce with salt and pepper and add the parsley and lemon juice.

4. Serve the steaks with the sauce on the side.

THE CUT

This steak comes from one of the two muscles in the very tender (and pricey) short loin section of the cow. After the tenderloin is removed, the remaining short loin muscle, also known as the shell, is cut into strip steaks. They are really a great steak: tender and fine-grained, but with good flavor too.

OTHER NAMES

For boneless: ambassador steak, hotel-style steak, boneless club steak, New York strip, Texas strip, Kansas City strip; for bone-in: club steak, country club steak, shell steak, sirloin strip steak, strip steak, New York steak.

OTHER CUTS YOU CAN USE

Any tender steak would be a good substitute here, but the Delmonico (rib-eye) would be our top choice.

BUTCHERSPEAK

You can find these steaks at most supermarkets, but the key is to get a steak that is small enough to be a serving size for one but thick enough to get that great sear on the outside without overcooking on the inside. This means getting steaks from the part of the short loin closer to the rib, rather than the part closer to the sirloin. To be sure of this, you may want to go to a butcher.

Pepper-Crusted Grilled Strip Loin Steak with Homemade Steak Sauce and Mushroom Hobo Packs

SERVES 4 TO 6

The strip loin is right up there with our favorites in the steak department. I (Chris) have one about twice a week at Frank's Steak House in Cambridge, Massachusetts. I'm not alone in my enthusiasm, either; this steak is so popular that it has accumulated over a dozen vernacular names, from New York strip to country club steak to ambassador steak. Whatever you call it, it comes from the top loin muscle, so it is extremely tender and has some good, strong beefy flavor to boot.

The mushroom hobo packs that go with it are quick to put together, but they have enough earthy flavor to stand up to this awesome steak. Exotic (read expensive) mushrooms are wonderful with the steak, but button mushrooms are great cooked this way too.

It's fun to figure out how to make something that you have always bought in a bottle at the store, like catsup and mustard, so here's our homemade version of super-flavorful steak sauce to go with the excellent steak. You can keep the leftover sauce, tightly covered and refrigerated, for up to a month. Of course, if you're in a rush, you can always buy yourself a bottle of steak sauce at the market instead of making it yourself.

FOR THE SAUCE

2 tablespoons olive oil

1 medium onion, peeled and thinly sliced

1 cup shrimp shells, 1 teaspoon chopped anchovies, *or* 1 teaspoon chopped sardines (optional)

1 tablespoon minced garlic

1 tablespoon minced fresh ginger

1 tablespoon minced fresh chile peppers of your choice

1 cup white vinegar

1 cup beer of your choice

1 cup pineapple juice

½ cup molasses

3 tablespoons tomato paste

5 whole cloves

1 tablespoon ground cumin

2 tablespoons freshly cracked black pepper

1 shot bourbon (optional)

¼ cup soy sauce

1 lime, very thinly sliced

FOR THE HOBO PACKS

2 pounds mushrooms (any kind), trimmed

⅓ cup extra virgin olive oil

2 tablespoons minced garlic

¼ cup roughly chopped fresh herbs: any one or a combination of sage,
    thyme, and/or oregano

2 tablespoons dry sherry

Kosher salt and freshly cracked black pepper to taste

Four 12- to 16-ounce strip loin steaks, about 1½ inches thick

1 cup freshly cracked black pepper

Kosher salt to taste

1. Make the sauce: In a large saucepan, heat the oil over medium-high heat until hot but not smoking. Add the onion and cook, stirring occasionally, until golden brown, 11 to 13 minutes. Add the shrimp shells (or anchovies or sardines) if using them, along with the garlic, ginger, and chiles. Cook, stirring occasionally, for 2 minutes. Add the remaining sauce ingredients and bring to a boil. Reduce the heat to low and simmer gently for 2 hours, stirring every once in a while.

2. Strain the sauce, pushing on the solids with a wooden spoon to extract all the liquid. The sauce should have about the same consistency as the standard Lea & Perrins Worcestershire sauce. Set aside.

3. Light a two-level fire in your grill, putting about three quarters of the coals on one side and one quarter on the other. When the fire dies down, the coals on one side should be hot (you can hold your hand 5 inches above the grill surface for 1 to 2 seconds) and those on the other side medium-hot (you can hold your hand 5 inches above the grill surface for 3 to 4 seconds).

4. Make the hobo packs: Tear off eight sheets of heavy-duty foil, each about 2 feet long, and stack them one on top of the other. Arrange half the mushrooms in the center of the top sheet and drizzle with half of the olive oil. Sprinkle half the minced garlic, half the herbs, and half the sherry over the mushrooms and season with salt and pepper. Fold up the top four of the sheets of foil around the vegetables, one after the other, turning the package one quarter turn between each sheet and making sure that each sheet is well sealed. Repeat this process with the remaining ingredients so that you have two packs. Place the packs on the bottom of the grill off to one side, pile coals up around them, and cook for about 30 minutes, depending on the intensity of the coals.

5. Meanwhile, pat the steaks dry with paper towels and sprinkle them with the pepper and a generous amount of salt. Place them on the grill over the hot part of the fire and cook until well seared, 4 to 5 minutes per side. Move to the cooler part of the fire and continue to cook to the desired doneness, 10 to 12 minutes more cooking time for rare. To check for doneness, nick, peek, and cheat: Make a ¼-inch cut in the thickest part of the meat and take a peek; it should be slightly less done than you like it. When the meat is done to your liking, remove it from the heat, cover it loosely with foil, and let it rest for 5 minutes.

6. Unwrap the hobo packs and serve with the steaks, passing the steak sauce on the side.

Grilled Sirloin Steak High Plains Drifter–Style

SERVES 4

When we were kids, the meal that was most often held out as a treat was "a nice, thick, juicy sirloin steak." This is not surprising, since sirloin has long been the single most popular supermarket steak. But there is also something about a grilled sirloin that reminds us of the straightforward nature and robust food of the Old West—or at least the Old West that is portrayed in movies. So this is our tribute to the cowboys and their long association with beef, campfires, and forthright cooking.

Here we coat the steaks with a simple spice paste that really complements their beefy flavor. One of the main ingredients in this paste is paprika, which we think is a neglected spice. But if you want to really add some complex flavor to this dish, try to get hold of one of the artisanal dried red peppers that are beginning to appear in some markets these days. You might like the warm, earthy Aleppo pepper from Syria, the darkly sweet Urfa or berry-like Maras peppers from southern Turkey, or the intensely smoky *pimentón de la Vera* from the remote Estremadura region of Spain. Mail-order spice houses are starting to carry them, but the only place in the United States that we know of that carries all four is Formaggio Kitchen in Cambridge, Massachusetts, where our friends Valerie and Ihsan Gurdal preside over a store packed with amazing foods. (You can reach them at 888–212–3224.) On the other hand, paprika is also great.

We like to serve this with a pile of grilled red onions, a Mushroom and Kale Hobo Pack (page 443), and a platter of sliced tomatoes sprinkled with basil, salt, and pepper and drizzled with a simple vinaigrette. Now, that's a great backyard dinner.

BUTCHERSPEAK

You may well have to go to the butcher to get a sirloin steak this thick. To get the very best, ask for a bone-in round sirloin steak or a shell sirloin.

2 tablespoons minced garlic

¼ cup roughly chopped fresh oregano

2 tablespoons paprika (or dried *pimentón de la Vera*, Aleppo, Maras, or Urfa pepper if you can locate them)

2 tablespoons cumin seeds, toasted in a dry skillet over medium heat, shaken frequently, until fragrant, 3 to 5 minutes, if you want (or 1 tablespoon ground cumin)

3 tablespoons grainy mustard

¼ cup olive oil

⅓ cup red wine vinegar

One 3-pound bone-in or 2½-pound boneless sirloin steak, 1½ inches thick

Kosher salt and freshly cracked black pepper to taste

1. Light a two-level fire in your grill, putting about three quarters of the coals on one side and about one quarter on the other side.

2. In a small bowl, combine the garlic, oregano, paprika, cumin, mustard, olive oil, and vinegar and mix well. Dry the steak with paper towels, sprinkle it with salt and pepper, and then coat it generously with the spice paste.

3. When the fire dies down and the coals are hot on one side (you can hold your hand 5 inches above the grill surface for 1 to 2 seconds) and medium-hot on the other (you can hold your hand 5 inches above the grill surface for 3 to 4 seconds), place the steak on the grill directly over the hottest part of the fire and sear well on one side, 4 to 5 minutes. Turn and sear well on the second side, another 4 to 5 minutes. Move to the cool part of the fire and continue to cook until done to your liking, 10 to 12 minutes for rare. To check for doneness, nick, peek, and cheat: Make a ¼-inch cut in the thickest part of the meat and take a peek; it should be slightly less done than you like it. Remove the steak from the grill, cover it loosely with foil, and allow to rest for 5 minutes before serving.

COOK ONCE, EAT TWICE

With the flavorful spice paste on the meat, leftovers of this steak dish make a fantastic steak sandwich. All you need to add is the bread. If you have any spice paste left over, cover and refrigerate it and use it to add a ton of flavor to any type of simple grilled meat.

THE REAL DEAL ON SIRLOIN

Among all the beefsteaks, the single most popular one for home consumption is the sirloin. That makes sense, because with its price value, it is an ideal family steak. After all, if you've got a couple of bottomless-pit teenagers at the table, you're not likely to be serving up ultra pricey filet mignon (still the most popular steak in restaurants).

But sirloin can also be the most confusing steak of all. It is one of those cuts of meat that is called different names in different parts of the country, or even in the same region. As a result, buying it in the supermarket can be chancy. But here are some guidelines.

The sirloin portion of a steer falls between the luxuriously tender short loin and the rather tough rump. In other words, it is basically the hip of the animal. Because it contains the large hipbone, cutting it into retail portions can be problematic. This has led to a lot of variation, not only in individual steaks but in the whole approach to how to cut them.

In the past, butchers tended to cut the sirloin against the grain through the bone, and some old-style butchers still do so. This creates four different steaks named according to the part of the hipbone they contain. Working from front to back, they are known as pin bone, flat bone, round bone, and wedge bone sirloin steaks. Although the pin bone steak is the most tender, it also has a high proportion of bone to meat, so the best choice for a bone-in sirloin steak is the round bone. It can be quite large, running three pounds or more when cut an inch thick, and has the fewest fat seams of any bone-in sirloin steak.

Today, though, the most popular approach is to cut the sirloin with the grain, producing boneless steaks. These steaks are usually labeled according to the particular muscles from which they are cut. From the top sirloin come steaks with names like top sirloin or top butt steak, hip sirloin steak, *bifteck* sirloin steak, and center-cut sirloin steak. Although they can be a bit chewy, all of these steaks are tender enough to treat as you would steaks from the short loin: Grill or broil them and serve them up in all their juicy glory. Steaks from the bottom sirloin, usually called bottom sirloin butt or ball tip steaks, as well as steaks simply labeled "sirloin," which come from the portion of the sirloin closest to the leg, are usually a bit tougher. The best approach with these tougher steaks is to treat them like London broil: Grill them and cut them very thin against the grain.

The boneless approach to butchering the sirloin has also resulted in a very popular steak called the tri-tip. This is a small triangular muscle located at the bottom end of the bottom sirloin. In the past, when the sirloin was typically cut bone-in, this muscle was included as a small section of larger steaks. But with the boneless approach, it is cut into distinct steaks. Sometimes called culotte or triangle steaks as well as tri-tips, these steaks are particularly popular on the West Coast, where for some reason they are much more readily available than in the rest of the country. While it's not a bad steak, we think it's overrated, and wouldn't go out of our way to search for it. (If you see a tri-tip roast, though, it's worth picking up.)

But the very best "sirloin steak" of all is one that is not technically a sirloin at all. On the East Coast, butchers tend to call the ultra-tender—and pricey—top loin steak a sirloin. Another variation on this theme is the shell sirloin. These are bone-in steaks cut from the small section that connects the short loin and the sirloin, technically known as the shell loin. A shell sirloin steak will be nearly as tender as a top loin steak.

So what does all of this mean? Simply that this is one of those cases in which it pays to look carefully at the meat you are buying, since one particular steak with the name "sirloin" in its label may be very different from another.

Stir-fried Sirloin Tips with Ginger, Peanuts, and Scallions over Smoky Sesame Cabbage

---

SERVES 4

We have always been big fans of "tips," which are a staple of restaurant menus in New England. Tips are generally the pieces left over from tender cuts of beef after the butcher has sliced as many steaks as he can out of them. So it's a good way to get tender meat at a low price. Tips are also perfect for stir-fries, because you want small pieces of meat. The key here, as with any stir-fry preparation, is to use very high heat.

Serve this over white rice and you have a full meal, using the Asian approach of employing meat for flavor and texture rather than putting it at the center of the plate.

FOR THE CABBAGE

¼ cup soy sauce

¼ cup fresh lime juice (about 2 limes)

1 teaspoon red pepper flakes

½ teaspoon sugar

1 tablespoon olive oil

1 tablespoon sesame oil

2 cups very thinly sliced white cabbage

½ cup very thinly sliced red cabbage

1 small carrot, peeled and cut into matchsticks

Kosher salt and freshly cracked white pepper to taste

1 pound sirloin tips, cut into matchsticks about the size of your little finger

Kosher salt and freshly cracked white pepper to taste

1 tablespoon olive oil

2 tablespoons minced fresh ginger

1 teaspoon minced garlic

5 scallions (white and green parts), thinly sliced on the bias

⅓ cup roughly chopped peanuts, toasted in a dry skillet over medium heat, shaken frequently, until fragrant, 3 to 5 minutes

1. In a large bowl, combine the soy sauce, lime juice, red pepper flakes, and sugar. Mix well and set aside.

2. In a large sauté pan, heat the oils over high heat until very hot but not smoking. Add the white and red cabbage and carrot and cook, stirring

---

vigorously, until heated through, 2 to 3 minutes. Add to the bowl with the lime-soy dressing (set the pan aside), toss gently, and season with salt and white pepper. Set aside.

3. Dry the meat with paper towels and sprinkle it generously with salt and white pepper. Wipe out the sauté pan and return it to high heat. Add the olive oil and heat until very hot but not smoking. Add the meat and stir-fry, tossing it constantly, until it is just cooked through, about 2 to 3 minutes. Add the ginger, garlic, scallions, and peanuts, toss a couple of times to combine, and immediately remove the pan from the heat.

4. Place some of the cabbage on each plate and top with the stir-fry.

Laotian-Style Aromatic Beef Salad

SERVES 4

THE CUT
See Grilled Sirloin Steak High Plains Drifter–Style (page 98) for details on sirloin steak and how to buy it.
You can use any of the steaks cut from the sirloin for this recipe, but the best is the cut labeled simply "sirloin steak." Other good options include the shell sirloin steak and the tri-tip sirloin steak.

OTHER CUTS YOU CAN USE
Any relatively tender steak will do well here. This is also another great place to substitute the tender chuck blade steak. Tenderloin tips, sirloin tips, or even a round steak, thinly sliced, would also work fine here.

I (Doc) discovered this dish a couple of years ago on a trip to Laos with my friend Carl Taplin and Porn Chanthirath, a Laotian woman who runs the Bangkok Restaurant in Ellsworth, Maine, with her husband, Sisouk. For Porn, who was returning to her homeland for the first time after escaping in the early 1970s, this was a true emotional voyage. For Carl and me, it was a chance to see Southeast Asia at its unspoiled best. Despite the efforts of the ruling Pathet Lao party, Buddhism is still the major motivating force in this isolated, landlocked country. Perhaps as a result, the pace of life is slow, the people are incredibly gentle and friendly, and the streets of many cities are still filled with young monks in robes of various shades of orange. The food is also fantastic.

This meat salad, called *laap,* is the national dish of the country, available at every street-corner stall and open-air restaurant. It can be made with fish, pork, or water buffalo meat, for which we substitute beef. It is served—as is just about everything else in Laos—accompanied by a wicker basket of sticky rice, for which you can substitute any type of steamed white rice if you can't get sticky rice.

But sticky rice also contributes another distinctive flavor to the dish in the form of browned rice powder. To make it, you just sear sticky rice in a dry skillet, then grind it into a powder. You can make this without the browned sticky rice powder and it will still be delicious and very refreshing; it will just taste more Thai than Laotian.

¼ cup sticky rice

2 tomatoes, cored and quartered

2 cucumbers, peeled, seeded, and cut into 1-inch cubes

4 ounces green beans, blanched in boiling salted water for 3 minutes, cooled in ice water, and drained

½ cup or so fresh basil leaves

2 teaspoons vegetable oil

One 1-pound beef sirloin steak, trimmed and very thinly sliced

Kosher salt and freshly cracked black pepper to taste

1 teaspoon minced fresh red chile pepper

3 tablespoons fresh lime juice (about 2 limes)

1 tablespoon fish sauce (*nam pla*)

¼ cup minced scallions (white and green parts)

3 tablespoons roughly chopped fresh cilantro

¼ cup fresh mint leaves

Additional fresh cilantro and mint leaves for garnish (optional)

1. Make the browned rice powder: Place the sticky rice in a dry heavy sauté pan and cook over medium-high heat, stirring or shaking the pan very frequently, until the rice begins to smoke slightly and is nicely browned, 4 to 6 minutes. Remove from the heat and crush in a mortar and pestle or pulse in a spice grinder until the rice forms a coarse powder; do not grind completely fine. Set aside.

2. Arrange the tomatoes, cucumbers, green beans, and basil in separate piles on a large platter; set aside.

3. In a wok or heavy sauté pan, heat the oil over high heat until hot but not smoking. Dry the beef strips with paper towels and sprinkle them generously with salt and pepper, then add them to the pan and cook, stirring briskly, until just browned, 2 to 3 minutes. Remove from the heat, transfer to a large bowl, add the browned rice powder, and stir well to combine.

4. Add the chile peppers, lime juice, fish sauce, and scallions and stir well. Garnish with the cilantro and mint leaves, if desired, and serve, accompanied by rice and the platter of vegetables and basil so that your guests can add what they choose to the salad.

THE CUT

The thin tapered end of the tenderloin, which is the end nearest the front of the cow, is really too small and thin to cut into steaks, and it is often cut off when the whole tenderloin is sold as a roast, so the roast is of a more even thickness. So that little end is often cut into tips, which are incredibly tender. Basically what you're talking about here are filet mignon tips.

OTHER CUTS YOU CAN USE

Sirloin tips are fine, and if you can find a thick chuck top blade steak, it will also work very well here. Simply cut out the central line of gristle and cut the two halves into cubes.

BUTCHERSPEAK

A high-quality butcher is a good place to get tenderloin tips. If you don't see any in the case, you might ask him if he's planning to cut any tenderloin steaks or roasts, and, if so, if you can buy the tips.

Grilled Polynesian-Style Tenderloin Tip Kebabs with Bacon, Pineapple, and Peppers

SERVES 4

In my (Chris's) early years, one of my favorite restaurants was the Blue Hawaii in Norfolk, Virginia. It was there that I learned to love pupu platters, cheesy paper leis, tiny umbrellas in drinks, and that little blue Sterno flame on the table. This dish is a tribute to that formative restaurant.

It's important to get the thickest bacon that you can find for this kebab, then precook it a little bit so that the meat itself is cooked but the fat is still a little bit floppy. We use it in a variation of the old bacon-wrapped pineapple, but add some really tender cubes of tenderloin and a few squares of red bell pepper to transform it into a main course. The glaze we employ here is very simple to make, but it gives the kebab a ton of flavor. If the meat starts to get too dark as it cooks, it's simple enough to just move it to the edge of the fire to finish cooking. But make sure that you do get a good, solid, crusty sear on the outside, because that is what is going to give it that wonderful grilled flavor.

Try serving this with white rice or Simple Rice Pilaf (page 417) and Roasted Asparagus (page 427) drizzled with a simple vinaigrette.

4 slices thick-cut bacon or thick slices of slab bacon

FOR THE GLAZE

⅓ cup molasses

2 tablespoons fresh lime juice (about 1 lime)

3 tablespoons soy sauce

1 teaspoon red pepper flakes

2 pounds tenderloin tips, cut into 2-inch cubes

2 tablespoons sesame oil

Kosher salt and freshly cracked black pepper to taste

Sixteen 1-inch cubes fresh pineapple (about ½ pineapple)

2 red bell peppers, cored, seeded, and cut into 2-inch squares

1. Light a fire in your grill.

2. In a small sauté pan, cook the bacon over medium-high heat until it is cooked through but not crisp, about 5 minutes. Drain on paper towels or a brown paper bag, then cut into 1-inch pieces and set aside.

3. Make the glaze: In a small bowl, combine the molasses, lime juice, soy sauce, and red pepper flakes. Mix well and set aside.

4. Dry the tenderloin tips with paper towels. In a large bowl, toss the tenderloin tips with the sesame oil and salt and pepper, thoroughly coating the meat.

5. Thread the beef, bacon, pineapple, and red peppers alternately onto skewers. When the fire has died down and the coals are medium-hot (you can hold your hand 5 inches above the grill surface for 3 to 4 seconds), place the kebabs on the grill and cook, turning once, for 5 to 6 minutes per side for rare. During the last 30 seconds or so of cooking, brush the kebabs heavily with the glaze. To check for doneness, nick, peek, and cheat: Make a ¼-inch cut in the thickest part of the meat; it should be slightly less done than you like it.

6. Remove the kebabs from the grill, drizzle with the remaining glaze, and serve hot.

THE CUT
This cut comes from the round, which is the upper leg. The round has three muscles: top round, eye round, and bottom round. Only the top round is tender enough to be a worthy candidate for steak. This is definitely a supermarket cut, but if you go to a butcher (or are friendly with the supermarket butcher), you can ask for a first-cut top round steak. This is the section of the round closest to the sirloin, and it is the most tender.

OTHER NAMES

Short cut round steak, top round London broil.

OTHER CUTS YOU CAN USE

Flank steak or a true sirloin steak (see page 100 for a discussion of sirloin) would also be really good in this recipe.

Herb-Crusted Grilled Top Round Steak "London Broil–Style" with Maître d'Hôtel Butter and Smoky Balsamic Onions

SERVES 4 TO 6

Grandma Wetzler used to frequently cook top round for me (Chris) when I visited her in State College, Pennsylvania. I remember her bringing home the big hunk of meat, scoring it all over, dredging it in flour, and then frying it up in her big cast-iron frying pan. The resulting steak had a little chew to it–this is not the most tender steak in the world–but it also had a tremendous amount of flavor. Since then, I've cooked plenty of top round myself, and I've found that if you slice it very thin, it is an excellent steak. Plus, it's a great way to save some money. When I was young and on a budget, I swear I ate this steak four out of seven nights a week, and I enjoyed it every time.

If you're in a hurry, you can leave out the onions here. If you do, though, try cooking them up some other time, because they make an inspiring topping for steak of any kind.

Try this with some grilled bread, pan-roasted potatoes, and simple steamed broccoli. (The flavored butter is great on the broccoli too.)

FOR THE BUTTER

½ pound (2 sticks) unsalted butter, at room temperature

1 tablespoon minced garlic

¼ cup roughly chopped fresh parsley

2 tablespoons fresh lemon juice (about ½ lemon)

4 dashes Tabasco sauce

Kosher salt and freshly cracked black pepper to taste

3 tablespoons olive oil

2 tablespoons minced garlic

1 cup roughly chopped fresh herbs: any one or a combination of parsley, sage, rosemary, thyme, basil, and/or oregano

Kosher salt and freshly cracked black pepper to taste

One 3-pound top round steak, about 2 inches thick

FOR THE ONIONS

2 large red onions, peeled and cut into thick slices

¼ cup olive oil

Kosher salt and freshly cracked black pepper to taste

¼ cup balsamic vinegar

1 teaspoon sugar

2 tablespoons fresh lemon juice (about ½ lemon)

1. Light a two-level fire in your grill, putting about three quarters of the coals on one side and about one quarter on the other side.

2. Make the butter: In a medium bowl, combine the butter, garlic, parsley, lemon juice, Tabasco, and salt and pepper and mix well. Place the butter on a piece of waxed paper or plastic wrap, roll it into a cylinder, and refrigerate until firm.

3. In a small bowl, combine the olive oil, garlic, herbs, and salt and pepper and mix well. Dry the steak with paper towels, then rub it all over with the herb mixture, pressing gently to make sure it adheres.

4. When the fire has died down and the coals are hot on one side (you can hold your hand 5 inches above the grill surface for 1 to 2 seconds) and medium-hot on the other (you can hold your hand 5 inches above the grill surface for 3 to 4 seconds), place the steak over the hottest part of the fire and cook until well seared on both sides, 5 to 6 minutes per side. Move to the medium-hot part of the grill and cook, turning once, 4 to 6 minutes more for rare. To check for doneness, nick, peek, and cheat: Make a ¼-inch cut in the thickest part of the meat and take a peek; it should be slightly less done than you like it. When the steak is done to your liking, remove it from the grill, cover it loosely with foil, and let it rest for 5 minutes.

5. Meanwhile cook the onions: Rub the onion slices with the olive oil, sprinkle with salt and pepper, and place them on the medium-hot side of the grill. Cook until just tender and seared, 4 to 5 minutes per side. Remove from the grill and place in a large bowl. Add the balsamic vinegar, sugar, and lemon juice and toss well.

6. Unwrap the butter and cut it into ¼-inch slices. Slice the steak very thin, place it on a platter or individual plates, top with the butter slices, scatter the grilled onions over it, and serve at once.

COOK ONCE, EAT TWICE

Any leftovers can be turned into that often-denigrated but totally delicious diner classic, the Hot Roast Beef Sandwich. Just lay the beef between two slices of white bread, plop some mashed potatoes down alongside, cover them both with gravy, and have your knife and fork ready for action.

This most surprising
aspect of the top blade is
that it comes from the
chuck, or forequarter, of the
cow. Since this is the primary weight-bearing sec-
tion of the beast, cuts from
the chuck are usually very
tough, though flavorful. But
the top blade breaks this
mold. While participating in
a course at Texas A & M
University called "Beef
101," I (Doc) saw meat scientists measure beef
toughness with the help of
a highly specialized piece
of equipment. When the top
blade was put up against
all other cuts of beef, it
came in second only to the
extremely pricey tenderloin.
A blind tasting of ten cuts
of beef held at the end of
the course confirmed the
machine's evaluation: Top
blade was rated extremely
tender by all tasters. If you
can get past the line of
gristle in the center of this
cut, it is a real sleeper.

OTHER NAMES

Book steak, butler steak,
lifter steak, petite steak,
flatiron steak.

OTHER CUTS YOU CAN USE

This recipe is supremely
adaptable; any steak will
work just fine. The flank
and skirt are particularly
nice choices because they
have the same type of
deep, beefy flavor that you
get from this cut.

Seared Balsamic-Glazed Top Blade Chuck Steaks with Spinach, Lemon, and Olive Oil

SERVES 4

Like an underutilized species of fish, the underappreciated top blade chuck steak is a culinary hidden gem just waiting to be discovered. Unlike other cuts from the chuck, it is exquisitely tender; in fact, it is the second most tender piece of meat on the cow, surpassed only by the hyper-expensive tenderloin. Despite this, the top blade is only about half the price of other less tender steaks.

So, you say, there has to be a catch—and you're right. Running smack down the center of each top blade steak is a line of inedible cartilage. There are several ways to deal with this problem though. You can simply eat around the offending cartilage and leave it on your plate. Or you can do as we do in this recipe, cook the steak and then slice the cartilage out before serving. A third option is to remove this line of gristle before cooking and cut the steak into chunks for stir-fries or skewers. Any of these will give you incredibly tender beef with great flavor for relatively little money.

This is a simple preparation, but with the sweet-sour glaze and the lemon and garlic in the spinach, it has plenty of flavors going for it. We like it with French Fries (page 411).

FOR THE GLAZE

1½ cups balsamic vinegar

1 teaspoon sugar

1 tablespoon freshly cracked black pepper

Four 8-ounce top blade steaks, about 1 inch thick

Kosher salt and freshly cracked black pepper to taste

2 tablespoons olive oil

FOR THE SPINACH

2 tablespoons olive oil

1½ pounds fresh spinach, trimmed, well washed, and dried

1 tablespoon minced garlic

Kosher salt and freshly cracked black pepper to taste

2 tablespoons fresh lemon juice (about ½ lemon)

1. Make the glaze: In a small saucepan, bring the vinegar, sugar, and pepper to a boil over high heat. Reduce the heat to medium-low and simmer vigorously until the mixture is reduced by two thirds and syrupy, 30 to 40 minutes. Set aside, covered to keep warm.

2. Pat the steaks dry with paper towels, then sprinkle them generously with salt and pepper. In a large sauté pan (or two small sauté pans, to avoid crowding), heat the olive oil over medium-high heat until very hot but not smoking. Add the steaks and sear well on one side, 3 to 4 minutes. Turn and continue cooking for a total of 4 to 6 minutes for rare. To check for doneness, nick, peek, and cheat: Make a ¼-inch cut in the thickest part of the meat and take a peek; it should be slightly less done than you like it. When the steaks are done to your liking, remove them from the pan, cover loosely with foil, and set aside to rest while you prepare the spinach.

3. Wipe out the pan with paper towels and return it to medium-high heat. Add the oil to the pan. When it is hot, add the spinach and stir it like crazy until it wilts, 1 to 2 minutes. Add the garlic and cook, stirring, for another 30 seconds. Remove the pan from the heat, season with salt and pepper, and stir in the lemon juice.

4. Cut the center line of gristle out of each steak and brush each half generously with the glaze. Place a mound of spinach on each diner's plate, top with two steak halves, and serve.

Skirt steak comes from the short plate section of the cow, which is the inside of the rib on the chest. It is an odd-looking piece of meat, long and flat with a very pronounced grain. Although it can be quite tough, if you cook it quickly over high heat and then slice it very thin against the grain, you end up with tender and remarkably flavorful meat. This is the cut of meat originally used for both fajitas and Philadelphia cheese steak sandwiches, which is probably why both of those items became wildly popular.

OTHER NAMES

Fajitas meat, Philadelphia steak.

OTHER CUTS YOU CAN USE

You can use just about any steak you want in this recipe. If you want to keep it inexpensive, go with top round. Or, even better, try the super-tender but inexpensive chuck top blade steak; just be sure to remove the line of gristle running down the center.

BUTCHERSPEAK

Some butchers prefer either the inside skirt or the outside skirt. If you have a choice, go for the outside, which is a little thicker and a bit less stringy.

Southeast Asian–Style Grilled Skirt Steak with Aromatic Greens and Ginger-Lime Dressing

SERVES 4

We really love Thai-style salads in which herbs are used as greens, the dressing is highly aromatic and spicy, and the meat or fish is a building block rather than the center of the plate. Not only do they have a very vibrant flavor dynamic, but they have the added advantage of being healthful to boot. Here we use the classic Southeast Asian herb trio of mint, cilantro, and basil as greens, along with some spicy arugula. (Although you will lose some of the flavor dynamic, you can substitute the lettuce of your choice for the combination of arugula and herbs.)

For the meat, we use one of our absolute favorites, the skirt steak. To us, this is the best reasonably priced supermarket steak you can find. Because it has a higher fat content than other similar steaks, such as flank steak and hanger steak, it is more richly flavorful. When grilled and cut very thin on the bias, against the grain, it is as fine a piece of beef as you will find.

This dish is a meal in itself, with the possible addition of a bowl of brown or white rice.

¼ cup soy sauce

2 tablespoons cracked coriander seeds (or 1 tablespoon ground coriander)

2 tablespoons freshly cracked white pepper (or 1 tablespoon ground white pepper)

1½ pounds skirt steak, cut into 4 portions

FOR THE DRESSING

¼ cup olive oil

2 tablespoons sesame oil

1 teaspoon sugar

½ cup fresh lime juice (about 4 limes)

2 tablespoons minced fresh ginger

1 to 3 teaspoons finely minced fresh chile peppers of your choice

Kosher salt and freshly cracked black pepper to taste

2 bunches arugula, trimmed, washed, and dried

1 cup fresh mint leaves

1 cup fresh cilantro leaves (some stems are OK)

1 cup fresh Thai basil leaves (or substitute regular basil)

1 large carrot, peeled and cut into matchsticks

1 red bell pepper, cored, seeded, and cut into matchsticks

1 cucumber, peeled, seeded, and cut into matchsticks

½ cup unsalted peanuts, toasted in a dry skill over medium heat, shaken frequently, until fragrant, 3 to 5 minutes, and chopped

COOK ONCE, EAT TWICE

If by chance you have any leftover meat, use it in a steak sandwich. If you have both salad and meat, stuff it all inside a pita pocket for a great lunch.

1. Light a fire in your grill.

2. In a shallow dish, combine the soy sauce, coriander, and white pepper and mix well. Put the steak in the dish and turn to coat it well.

3. When the fire has died down and the coals are hot (you can hold your hand 5 inches above the grill surface for 1 to 2 seconds), place the steak on the grill and cook until well seared on one side, about 4 minutes. Turn and continue to cook to desired doneness, about 6 minutes total cooking time for rare. To check for doneness, nick, peek, and cheat: Make a ¼-inch cut in the thickest part of the meat; it should be slightly less done than you like it. Remove the steak from the grill, cover it loosely with foil, and allow it to rest while you make the dressing.

4. In a medium bowl, whisk the dressing ingredients together until well combined. Place the arugula, herbs, carrot, bell pepper, and cucumber in a large bowl, add as much of the dressing as you like, and toss well.

5. Thinly slice the steak on the bias, against the grain. Place a serving of greens on each plate, top with a few slices of steak, and garnish with the peanuts.

THE CUT

See Southeast Asian–Style Grilled Skirt Steak (page 110) for details on skirt steak and how to buy it.

OTHER CUTS YOU CAN USE

Flank steak is great here and hanger steak would also be fine. Any of the top round steaks or the chuck blade steak are also good options. If you use the chuck blade, though, remember to remove the line of gristle that runs down the center.

Lime-Soaked, Cumin-Crusted Grilled Skirt Steak with Green Olive–Chile Relish

SERVES 4

Although we don't often marinate, the unique striated texture of the skirt steak makes it a good candidate for this technique. The lime juice actually works it way into the fibers of the meat, giving it some citrus flavor. But don't let the meat sit in the juice for more than an hour, or the acid may start to make the surface of the meat unpleasantly mushy.

Chilean influences figure heavily in this dish, with its green olives, cumin, chiles, and lime juice. Serve this with grilled pita, Simple Rice Pilaf (page 417), and a green salad.

2 pounds skirt steak

1 cup fresh lime juice (about 8 limes)

FOR THE RUB

3 tablespoons cumin seeds (or 1½ tablespoons ground cumin)

2 tablespoons minced garlic

⅓ cup roughly chopped fresh cilantro

Kosher salt and freshly cracked black pepper to taste

FOR THE RELISH

½ cup finely chopped pitted green olives

1 teaspoon chopped dried red chile peppers of your choice, or to taste

¼ cup olive oil

2 tablespoons freshly cracked black pepper

1. Place the steak in a shallow dish and pour the lime juice over it. Cover the dish and let it sit in the refrigerator for 30 minutes to 1 hour, turning occasionally.

2. Light a fire in your grill.

3. In a small bowl, combine all the rub ingredients and mix well. Remove the steak from the marinade, pat dry with paper towels, and rub it all over with the spice rub, pressing gently to be sure it adheres.

4. When the fire has died down and the coals are hot (you can hold your hand 5 inches from the grill surface for 1 to 2 seconds), place the steak on the grill and cook until well seared on one side, about 4 minutes. Turn and continue to cook to the desired doneness, about 4 minutes more for rare. To check for doneness, nick, peek, and cheat: Make a ¼-inch cut in the thickest part of the meat and take a peek; it should be slightly less done than you like it. Remove the steak from the heat, cover it loosely with foil, and allow it to rest for 5 minutes while you make the relish.

5. In a medium bowl, combine all the relish ingredients and mix well.

6. Slice the steak as thin as possible against the grain and serve with the relish.

Sliced Grilled Skirt Steak on Greek Salad

SERVES 4 TO 6

This is another example of steak served on top of greens, which for some reason we find particularly appealing. Maybe it's because, particularly with a rich cut of beef like skirt steak, the freshness of the greens and the acid of the dressing balance out the meat so nicely.

Serve this with grilled pita, rough red wine, and an ouzo chaser.

2 tablespoons olive oil

2 tablespoons minced garlic

1 teaspoon red pepper flakes

Kosher salt and freshly cracked black pepper to taste

2 pounds skirt steak

FOR THE DRESSING

½ cup extra virgin olive oil

¼ cup fresh lemon juice (about 1 lemon)

3 tablespoons roughly chopped fresh oregano (or substitute 1½ tablespoons dried)

Kosher salt and freshly cracked black pepper to taste

FOR THE SALAD

2 small heads romaine lettuce, washed, dried, and torn into bite-sized pieces

½ cup good-quality black olives, pitted

1 medium cucumber, peeled, seeded, and diced medium

1 large tomato (about the size of a baseball), cored and diced large

½ cup crumbled feta cheese

COOK ONCE, EAT TWICE

Leftover steak from this dish is great in a simple salad of Romaine lettuce, olives, and tomatoes. If you have any relish left, toss that into the salad too.

THE CUT

See the description in Southeast Asian–Style Grilled Skirt Steak (page 110) for details on skirt steak and how to buy it.

OTHER CUTS YOU CAN USE

Flank steak is an obvious, and excellent, substitute here, and hanger steak is also fine.

1. Light a fire in your grill.

2. In a small bowl, combine the olive oil, garlic, red pepper flakes, and salt and pepper and mix well. Dry the skirt steak with paper towels, then rub it generously with this mixture, pressing gently to be sure it adheres.

3. When the fire has died down and the coals are covered with white ash, check the temperature: you want a hot fire here (you can hold your hand 5 inches above the grill surface for 1 to 2 seconds). Place the steak on the grill and sear well on one side, about 4 minutes. Turn and continue cooking to the desired doneness, about 6 minutes more for rare. To check for doneness, nick, peek, and cheat: Make a ¼-inch cut in the thickest part of the meat and take a peek; it should be slightly less done than you like it. Remove the meat from the grill, cover it loosely with foil, and let it rest while you prepare the dressing.

4. In a large bowl, whisk together the olive oil, lemon juice, oregano, and salt and pepper until well combined. Add the lettuce, olives, cucumber, and tomato and toss well to thoroughly coat with the dressing, then crumble the feta cheese on top.

5. Slice the steak very thin on the bias against the grain. Place the salad on a serving platter or individual plates, top with the slices of steak, and serve.

Fennel-Crusted Flank Steak with Orange–Black Olive Relish and Spicy Mint Honey

SERVES 4

Here we find a collection of flavors from one of the great culinary regions of the world, North Africa. Oranges and black olives are a classic Moroccan combination, and mint and honey are both widely used throughout the region. Fennel, which is also popular in North Africa, is a great spice that is not used often enough in our country. In this dish, each of these components plays off the other: The relish is very citrusy, which sets up the flavor of the beef nicely; the honey glaze subdues the acid in the relish; and the fennel seeds provide crunch and a subtle, licoricey sweetness to balance everything out.

To segment the oranges, peel them with a sharp knife, removing the white pith entirely. Cut between the membranes and remove each section whole, taking care to remove the seeds.

Try serving this with grilled pita bread, a carrot and raisin salad, and couscous or Simple Rice Pilaf (page 417).

THE CUT

Flank steak, which comes from the lower rear side of the beast, is a long, relatively thin steak with a distinctive longitudinal grain. It can be tough if not properly prepared, but if cooked quickly to rare or medium-rare and then sliced very thin on the bias, against the grain, it is perfectly tender. That's good, because it lets you fully enjoy this cut's very rich, deep, beefy flavor. (It can also be cooked very slowly and comes out great; see Puerto Rican Vinegar-Braised Flank Steak, page 77.) Flank steak is easily recognizable by its longitudinal grain, and it is readily available in most supermarkets.

FOR THE RELISH

1/2 small red onion, peeled and diced small

1/2 cup orange segments (see headnote)

1/4 cup roughly chopped pitted black olives

1/4 cup fresh orange juice

1/4 cup extra virgin olive oil

1 teaspoon minced garlic

1/4 cup roughly chopped fresh parsley

1 tablespoon freshly cracked black pepper

FOR THE HONEY

1/3 cup roughly chopped fresh mint

2 tablespoons cumin seeds (or 1 tablespoon ground cumin)

1 teaspoon red pepper flakes

1/4 cup honey

2 tablespoons olive oil

1/2 cup crushed fennel seeds

Kosher salt and freshly cracked black pepper to taste

One 2 1/2-pound flank steak, about 1 inch thick

1. Light a fire in your grill.

2. In a medium bowl, combine all the relish ingredients and mix well; set aside.

3. Make the honey: In a small bowl, combine the mint, cumin, red pepper flakes, and honey and mix well. Set this aside too.

4. In another small bowl, combine the olive oil, fennel seeds, and salt and pepper and mix well. Dry the steak with paper towels, then rub it generously with this mixture, pressing to make sure it adheres.

5. When the fire dies down and the coals are covered with white ash, check the temperature: you want a hot fire here (you can hold your hand 5 inches above the grill surface for 1 to 2 seconds). Place the steak on the grill and sear well on one side, about 4 minutes. Turn and continue to cook to the desired doneness, about 4 minutes more for rare. To check for doneness nick, peek, and cheat: Make a 1/4-inch cut in the thickest part of the meat; it should be slightly less done than you like it. Remove the steak from the grill, cover it loosely with foil, and allow it to sit for about 5 minutes.

6. Slice the steak thin against the grain, on the bias, and serve accompanied by the relish and the honey.

OTHER NAMES

London broil, jiffy steak.

OTHER CUTS YOU CAN USE

Skirt steak is a good substitute here. You could even go with a sirloin steak.

COOK ONCE, EAT TWICE

Stuff any leftover steak into a pita along with the leftover relish and some fresh cucumber slices, and your lunch is ready.

THE THREE FLAT STEAKS

Most beef steaks are cut from thick muscles, particularly those of the short loin and sirloin. But there are three steaks that don't fit this mold, because they are actually relatively flat pieces of meat. All three of them—flank steak, skirt steak, and hanger steak—have recently undergone a transformation from neglected to fashionable, as people have discovered that flavor can be more important than texture, even when you're talking about steaks.

These three newly popular steaks share the distinction of coming from the chest and side of the animal. Hanger and flank both come from the rear of the side, while skirt comes from the area between the abdomen and the chest cavity. In addition to location, these steaks share certain other basic qualities: All are long, relatively thin, quite tough and grainy, but with rich, deep, beefy flavor. In other words, they are embodiments of the inverse relationship between toughness and flavor in meat: The tougher the meat, the more flavor it tends to have.

Of course, there are also differences between these flavorful steaks. Hanger, a thick muscle that is attached to the diaphragm, derives its name from the fact that when a cow is butchered, this steak hangs down into the center of the carcass. It used to be called "butcher's steak" because butchers tended to take it home and eat it themselves. Because it is a classic French bistro dish, though, this cut is highly prized by restaurants and therefore difficult to find in butcher shops. To our mind, this is no great loss, since hangers have the toughest texture and least rich, beefy flavor of these three cuts.

Fortunately, flank steak is quite easy to find in any butcher shop or supermarket. Easily recognizable from its longitudinal grain, flank has excellent beef flavor and is quite tender if cooked to rare or medium-rare and sliced thin against the grain. Unfortunately, largely because of the popularity of fajitas and London broil, flank has become a relatively expensive cut.

The skirt steak, which was the cut originally used in fajitas, can also be hard to locate in supermarkets or butcher shops. This is a real pity, because the skirt steak is a beef eater's dream come true. It has more fat than the hanger or flank, which makes it juicier and richer; at the same time, it also has a deep, full beefy flavor that outdoes either the flank or the hanger. If you can get your hands on a skirt steak, by all means do so. We promise you won't be sorry.

Korean-Style Grilled Short Ribs with Ginger, Chiles, and Quick Kimchee

SERVES 4

We've enjoyed this dish many times at Jae's, a Korean restaurant right next door to the East Coast Grill, where they do a great job with this preparation. For this dish, you need a special cut, the flanken-style short rib, which can be cut thinner than English-style. This is very important, because if the butcher cuts the ribs more than three quarters of an inch thick, they will not cook through before burning on the outside. This meat has some chew to it, but we enjoy that. Plus, the typical Korean combination of sweet, hot, and pungent makes them fantastic.

This makes a great lunch served with brown rice and some seared greens with ginger.

FOR THE KIMCHEE

¼ cup soy sauce

¼ cup rice vinegar

1 tablespoon minced fresh ginger

1 teaspoon minced garlic

1 tablespoon minced fresh chile peppers of your choice

1 tablespoon sugar

½ cup Napa cabbage (Tianjin bok choy), sliced ¼ inch thick

1 cucumber, peeled, seeded, and thinly sliced

½ red bell pepper, cored, seeded, and thinly sliced

1 medium carrot, peeled and very thinly sliced

2½ pounds flanken-style beef short ribs, ½ to ¾ inch thick

FOR THE MARINADE

⅓ cup soy sauce

½ cup fresh lime juice (about 4 limes)

1 tablespoon minced garlic

2 tablespoons minced fresh ginger

¼ cup roughly chopped fresh cilantro

2 tablespoons minced fresh chile peppers of your choice

3 tablespoons freshly cracked white pepper (or substitute black pepper)

1 teaspoon ground coriander

THE CUT

See Black Pepper–Crusted Wine-Braised Short Ribs (page 75) for details on short ribs. For this rather unusual approach, in which we cook the short ribs briefly over high dry heat instead of for a long time using slow moist heat, you need flanken-style ribs, which are much thinner than English-style. You will most likely have to go to the butcher to get these, since the supermarket will probably only have English-style. You may find both chuck and plate short ribs in the flanken style, but not the slightly more tender rib section short ribs.

OTHER NAMES

Barbecue ribs, kosher ribs.

OTHER CUTS YOU CAN USE

This dish works very well with any of the very tender steaks from the short loin (New York strip, tenderloin, porterhouse, or T-bone), but for economy's sake, we would recommend a skirt steak, flank steak, or even a boneless chuck or top round steak here.

1. Make the kimchee: In a small bowl, combine the soy sauce, rice vinegar, ginger, garlic, chile peppers, and sugar and whisk together well. In a medium bowl, toss the cabbage, cucumber, red pepper, and carrot together. Add just enough of the dressing to moisten the vegetables and mix well; refrigerate.

2. Place the short ribs in a large bowl. Combine all the marinade ingredients in a small bowl and pour the mixture over the short ribs. Cover and refrigerate for at least 1 hour and up to 3 hours.

3. Meanwhile, light a fire in your grill.

4. Remove the meat from the marinade and pat it dry with paper towels; discard the marinade. When the fire has died down and the coals are very hot (you can hold your hand 5 inches above the heat source for only 1 to 2 seconds), place the meat on the grill and sear well on one side, about 3 minutes. Turn and continue cooking to the desired doneness, about 3 minutes more for rare. Remove the meat from the grill, cover loosely with foil, and allow to rest for 5 minutes.

5. Serve the ribs hot, accompanied by the kimchee.

RECIPES FOR
SMALL TOUGH CUTS OF BEEF

Orange-and-Chile-Stewed Bottom Round Steaks with Butternut Squash and Oregano

Old-Style Chunky Beef and Beer Stew with Onions, Peppers, and Tomatoes and Crunchy Parsley–Bread Crumb Shake

Beef and Black Bean Stew with Brazilian Flavors and Fried Plantains

K.L.–Style Gingered Beef Stew with Red Onion–Lime Sambal

African-Style Beef and Tuber Stew with Toasted Spices

Old-School Southern-Style Beef Stew with Corn, Tomatoes, and Bacon

The World's Hottest Chili, with Scotch Bonnet Peppers, Yucca, and a Cucumber-Mango Coolant

Señor Sanchez's Salvadoran Soup of Kings with Short Ribs, Corn, and Plantains

Steak Bomb—Fully Loaded with Mushrooms, Onions, and Peppers

Aromatic Ginger and Beef Broth with Hoisin and Traditional Southeast Asian Garnishes

Texas-Style Ground Beef Casserole with Sweet Potato Crust and A-1 Parsley Butter

Indian-Spiced Beef-Stuffed Red Onions with Fresh Coconut-Ginger Chutney and Simple Yogurt Sauce

Red Wine–Braised Oxtails over Spaghetti with Garlic and Spinach

Basil-Crusted Meat Loaf with Brandy, Walnuts, and Spicy Tomato Sauce

---

10 STEPS TO GREAT BEEF STEWS

1. Dry the meat cubes.

2. Season the meat cubes generously.

3. Brown the meat cubes well, in batches if necessary.

4. Remove the meat from the pot, adjust the amount of fat in the pot, and sauté the aromatics and vegetables.

5. Deglaze the pot with some of the liquid.

6. Return the meat to the pot along with enough liquid to cover.

7. Bring to a simmer and skim off any film, then reduce the heat to low and simmer gently.

8. Check for doneness early and often; just take out a cube of meat and try it.

9. Skim any film and fat from the liquid.

10. Add any final seasonings, season again to taste with salt and pepper, and serve.

This steak comes from the bottom part of the round, which is basically the rear leg of the animal from the butt down to the shank. While we usually prefer to use meat from the chunk when stewing, in this case, the round works better because you get a smoother slab of meat, with fewer breaks in it from sinews or cartilage. That way, you get a more uniform steak to cook. You can easily find this cut in the supermarket, no special knowledge required.

OTHER CUTS YOU CAN USE

You can substitute any steak cut from the round in this recipe, or a chuck steak if you prefer.

Orange-and-Chile-Stewed Bottom Round Steaks with Butternut Squash and Oregano

SERVES 4

Here you have what is basically a Swiss steak with Latin American flavors. You could definitely braise this cut of beef, but we like the flavor of the liquid so much that we decided the beef should swim in it rather than just wade in it. After spending an hour and a half or so in this situation, this tough cut of meat becomes amazingly tender. It's a really good example of how the proper cooking method can convert what may seem an unpalatable cut of meat into something you want to make again and again.

Serve this over white rice to absorb the flavorful liquid; for another touch of Latin authenticity, mix the rice with cooked black beans.

½ cup coarsely ground cornmeal

2 tablespoons ground cumin

1 teaspoon kosher salt, plus more to taste

1 teaspoon freshly cracked black pepper, plus more to taste

Four 12-ounce bottom round steaks, about 1 inch thick

¼ cup vegetable oil

3 onions, peeled and diced small

¼ cup minced garlic

1 tomato, cored and diced small

1 to 2 tablespoons minced canned chipotle chiles in adobo or fresh chile peppers of your choice

3 cups peeled and cubed butternut squash (or substitute any other hard winter squash)

About 2 cups beef stock (or see Stock Options, page 32)

1 cup fresh orange juice (about 2 juice oranges)

2 cinnamon sticks (or 2 teaspoons ground cinnamon)

½ cup chopped fresh oregano

1. In a small bowl, combine the cornmeal, cumin, salt, and pepper and mix well. Dry the steaks with paper towels, then dredge them in this mixture, shaking off the excess.

2. In a 5-inch-deep Dutch oven or other large heavy pot with a lid, heat the oil over medium-high heat until very hot but not smoking. Add the steaks and sear well, about 3 minutes per side. Remove the steaks from the pot and set aside on a platter.

3. Drain all but 2 tablespoons of the oil from the pot. Reduce the heat to medium, add the onions, and cook, stirring occasionally and scraping up any browned bits from the bottom of the pot, until lightly browned, 11 to 13 minutes. Add the garlic, tomato, and chiles and cook, stirring, for 1 minute.

4. Return the steaks to the pot, along with any juices that have accumulated on the platter, then add the squash, stock, orange juice, and cinnamon. (If the liquid does not cover the ingredients, add enough stock so that it does.) Bring to a boil and skim any scum off the top of the liquid. Reduce the heat to low, season with salt and pepper, cover, and cook until fork-tender, 1 hour and 10 minutes to 1½ hours. To check for doneness, plunge a fork straight down into the meat and try to pull the fork out. If the fork slides out easily, the meat is done; if the meat hangs on to the fork, give it more time. When the steaks are done, transfer them to a platter and cover them loosely with foil.

5. Skim any fat from the sauce and remove the cinnamon sticks if you used them. If the sauce is not as thick as you like, place the pot over high heat and reduce to the desired consistency. Stir in the oregano, season to taste, and serve the steaks accompanied by liquid.

COOK ONCE, EAT TWICE

Like all stews, this is fantastic reheated next day. Or you can heat it up, transfer it to a bun with a slotted spoon, and have a Mexican-style Sloppy Joe. Try it for a lunch on a cool fall day.

Chuck is a richly flavorful part of the cow, and for some reason it seems to match up perfectly with beer. The easiest way to get chuck stew meat is to simply buy any roast or steak from the chuck and cube it up yourself. Chuck arm or shoulder steaks are good choices; in fact, anything with "chuck" in it is OK, except for the chuck mock tender.

OTHER CUTS YOU CAN USE

If chuck is not available, you can use top or bottom round here.

Old-Style Chunky Beef and Beer Stew with Onions, Peppers, and Tomatoes and Crunchy Parsley–Bread Crumb Shake

SERVES 6 TO 8

A few winters ago I (Chris) really got into stews, so I spent a lot of time playing around with different liquids to use in them. I found that beer was actually the top contender for the role. So people would see me cooking in the kitchen, drinking beer and dumping beer into everything I was cooking, and they would think it was pretty funny. But it actually works really well. Beer has a lot of body and a lot of flavor, and somehow it works out perfectly as a vehicle to soak up other flavors. When you use a dark beer, as we do here, it adds a lot of character.

In some ways, this particular dish is chili without the chili. The crunchy parsley–bread crumb shake adds a nice fresh flavor and texture dynamic right at the end of the cooking. Since the shake contains a good amount of salt and pepper, it's best to underseason the stew, then add more salt and pepper after the shake if you think it is needed.

Serve this with some buttered crusty bread for dunking into the stew and a crisp Romaine salad with some grated hard cheese and a vinegary dressing.

> 3 tablespoons vegetable oil, or more if needed
>
> 3 pounds boneless beef chuck, such as chuck arm or chuck shoulder steak, cut into 2-inch cubes
>
> Kosher salt and freshly cracked black pepper to taste
>
> 2 large onions, peeled and diced small
>
> 3 red bell peppers (or a mix of red and green), cored, seeded, and diced large
>
> 3 tablespoons minced garlic
>
> 1½ cups beef stock (or see Stock Options, page 32)
>
> One 16-ounce can dark beer, or more if needed
>
> 2 cups whole canned tomatoes, drained and roughly chopped
>
> 1 tablespoon dark brown sugar
>
> 2 teaspoons dried thyme
>
> 1 bay leaf
>
> 2 whole cloves, crushed

1 cup toasted bread crumbs

$\frac{1}{2}$ cup roughly chopped fresh parsley

1 tablespoon minced garlic

1 tablespoon kosher salt

2 tablespoons freshly cracked black pepper

1. In a 5-inch-deep Dutch oven or other large heavy pot with a lid, heat the oil over medium-high heat until very hot but not smoking. Dry the meat well with paper towels and sprinkle it generously with salt and pepper. Place it in the pot in a single layer, in batches if necessary to avoid crowding, and brown well on all sides, about 10 minutes total; transfer the pieces to a platter as they are done.

2. Pour off the fat or add oil to the pot as needed so you have a total of about 2 tablespoons in the pot. Add the onions and bell peppers and cook, stirring occasionally, until the onions are translucent, 7 to 9 minutes. Add the garlic and cook, stirring, for 1 minute.

3. Return the meat to the pot along with any juices that have accumulated on the platter, then add the stock, beer, tomatoes, brown sugar, thyme, bay leaf, and cloves and stir well to combine. (If the ingredients are not completely covered, add enough extra beer to cover them.) Bring to a simmer over medium heat and skim any scum off the top of the liquid. Cover the pot, reduce the heat to low, and simmer gently until the meat is tender, 1½ to 2 hours. To check for doneness, take a piece of meat out of the stew, cut into it to check for color, and taste for tenderness. When the stew is done, skim off any scum from the top of the liquid.

4. While the stew is cooking, combine the bread crumb shake ingredients in a small bowl and mix well.

5. Top each bowl of stew with a shake of the shake and serve.

THE CUT

See African-Style Beef and Tuber Stew (page 128) for information about beef chuck cuts to use for stew beef. In addition to the cuts suggested there, beef chuck under blade pot roast or beef chuck eye roast are also good choices.

Beef and Black Bean Stew with Brazilian Flavors and Fried Plantains

SERVES 6 TO 8

Feijoada is a black bean stew that is practically the national dish of Brazil. It usually includes not only beef and sausage, but pig's ears and tongue as well. This is the WASP version, in which we use only one type of meat, good stew beef from the chuck. You can certainly get away with using canned beans here; add them after the meat has been cooking about 1 hour.

As for all stews, don't be tempted to skip the final adjustment of seasoning. This can make a huge difference in the taste. In fact, it's best to add less salt and pepper than you think you'll need in the initial stages, then balance them at the end when the stew is just ready to come off the stove.

Serve this with white rice, a hearts of palm salad, and some juicy oranges or more exotic fruit, and you've got yourself a great tropical dinner.

¼ cup olive oil

2 pounds boneless beef chuck, cut into 1-inch cubes

Kosher salt and freshly cracked black pepper to taste

2 large onions, peeled and diced medium

¼ cup cumin seeds (or 2 tablespoons ground cumin)

¼ cup cracked coriander seeds (or 2 tablespoons ground coriander)

¼ cup minced garlic

¼ cup minced canned chipotle peppers in adobo, with their sauce

2 cups dried black beans, picked over and rinsed

6 cups water

FOR THE SALSA

2 small red onions, peeled and diced small

½ cup roughly chopped fresh cilantro

¼ cup extra virgin olive oil

¼ cup fresh lime juice (about 2 limes)

1 tablespoon minced garlic

1 tablespoon red pepper flakes, or to taste

Kosher salt and freshly cracked black pepper to taste

FOR THE PLANTAINS

2 cups vegetable oil

3 green plantains, peeled and sliced into rounds about ¼ inch thick

Kosher salt and freshly cracked black pepper to taste

1. In a 5-inch-deep Dutch oven or other large heavy pot with a lid, heat the oil over medium-high heat until very hot but not smoking. Dry the beef with paper towels and sprinkle it generously with salt and pepper. Add the beef to the pot in a single layer, in batches if necessary to avoid crowding, and brown well on all sides, about 10 minutes; transfer the pieces to a platter as they are done.

2. Pour off the fat or add oil to the pot as needed, so you have about 2 tablespoons. Add the onions and cook, stirring occasionally, until translucent, 7 to 9 minutes. Add the cumin, coriander, garlic, and chipotles and cook, stirring, for 2 minutes more.

3. Return the meat to the pot, add the beans and water, and bring to a simmer. Skim any scum from the surface of the liquid, then reduce the heat to low, cover, and cook gently until the meat is tender, 1½ to 2 hours. To check for doneness, take a piece of meat out of the stew, cut into it to check for color, and taste for tenderness. When the meat is done, skim any scum off the surface, taste the liquid, and adjust the seasoning with salt and pepper if necessary.

4. Meanwhile, make the salsa: In a medium bowl, combine all the ingredients and mix well. Set aside.

5. Make the plantains: In a small saucepan, heat the oil until very hot but not smoking. Drop the plantain rounds into the oil 3 at a time and cook until well browned, 2 to 3 minutes. Remove them from the oil and drain on paper towels or a brown paper bag. Using a heavy object such as a small cutting board or sauté pan, mash each fried round down as flat as a pancake, applying steady pressure. Put the mashed plantain sections back into the hot oil, 2 or 3 at a time, and cook for 2 minutes or so until the entire surface is golden brown. Remove, drain on paper towels or a brown paper bag, and season liberally with salt and pepper.

6. Serve the stew over rice, passing the fried plantains and the salsa on the side for dipping.

We like to use chuck or even cubes from top sirloin here, because we're calling for relatively large chunks of meat and we don't want them to be too terribly tough. If you can't find packages of cubed beef labeled either "chuck" or "sirloin," buy a chuck steak or roast and cut it into cubes yourself. It doesn't take long, and you'll get better meat. This is a price-conscious supermarket item, no particular need to go to the butcher.

OTHER NAMES

Stew beef.

OTHER CUTS YOU CAN USE

Top round is an acceptable substitute here.

K.L.–Style Gingered Beef Stew with Red Onion–Lime Sambal

SERVES 6 TO 8

We ate various versions of this rather thick stew many times at the amazing hawker stalls of Singapore and Malaysia, where you can get top-quality versions of street food from all over Asia. Our favorite rendition was one from a stall not far from the Arabian Nights–style train station in Kuala Lumpur, which is why we call this "K.L.-Style."

Although it's a stew, this is a good dish for a hot summer night, thanks to its many spices. To get the proper flavor dynamic, it's important that the curry powder be well cooked in the sauté stage. This is a technique often used by Indian cooks, the acknowledged masters of spice cookery. The sambal—which is basically a Southeast Asian or East Asian version of the type of flavorful relish that is elsewhere called a chutney or a salsa—is simplicity itself to make, but it adds a giant burst of fresh flavor to the stew.

Serve this with rice and a green vegetable such as broccoli or string beans.

½ cup all-purpose flour

1 teaspoon cayenne pepper

Pinch of ground cinnamon

Pinch of ground cloves

Kosher salt and freshly cracked black pepper to taste

2 pounds beef stew meat (preferably chuck or top sirloin), cut into 2-inch cubes

¼ cup vegetable oil, or more if needed

2 large onions, peeled and thinly sliced

3 tablespoons minced fresh ginger

2 tablespoons minced garlic

¼ cup curry powder

2 tablespoons minced fresh chile peppers of your choice

About 2½ cups beef stock (or see Stock Options, page 32)

3 medium sweet potatoes, peeled and cut into large chunks

FOR THE SAMBAL

1 red onion, peeled and diced small

2 to 4 tablespoons minced chile peppers of your choice, or to taste

⅓ cup fresh lime juice (about 2 limes)

⅓ cup roughly chopped fresh mint

Kosher salt and freshly cracked black pepper to taste

1 cup canned unsweetened coconut milk

¼ cup roughly chopped fresh cilantro

½ cup roughly chopped peanuts, toasted in a dry skillet over medium heat, shaken frequently, until fragrant, 3 to 5 minutes

COOK ONCE, EAT TWICE
If you have some of this stew left, try putting it in a small baking pan, covering it with a layer of mashed sweet or white potatoes, and making yourself a kind of Malaysian shepherd's pie. (We never saw any shepherds when we were in Malaysia, but the dish tastes great anyway.)

1. In a small bowl, combine the flour, cayenne, cinnamon, cloves, and salt and pepper and mix well. Dry the meat cubes with paper towels, then dredge them in the spiced flour, shaking off any excess.

2. In a 5-inch-deep Dutch oven or large heavy pot with a lid, heat the oil over medium-high heat until very hot but not smoking. Add the meat in a single layer, in batches if necessary to avoid crowding, and brown well on all sides about 10 minutes; transfer the pieces to a platter as they are done.

3. Pour off the fat or add oil to the pot as needed so you have a total of about 2 tablespoons in the pot. Reduce the heat to medium, add the onions, and cook, stirring occasionally, until they just begin to color, 9 to 11 minutes. Add the ginger, garlic, curry powder, and chiles and cook, stirring, for 3 minutes.

4. Return the meat to the pot, add the stock, and bring to a simmer. Skim any scum from the surface, then reduce the heat to low, cover, and cook for 30 minutes. Add the sweet potatoes and, if there is not enough liquid to cover all the ingredients, enough stock, water, pineapple juice, or (our favorite) beer to cover. Continue to cook until the meat is tender, 45 minutes to 1 hour more. To check for doneness, take a piece of meat out of the stew, cut into it to check for color, and taste for tenderness.

5. While the stew is cooking, make the sambal: In a medium bowl, combine the onion, chiles, lime juice, and mint and mix well. Season with salt and pepper.

6. When the meat is tender, skim any scum from the surface of the liquid, add the coconut milk, and continue to cook for 1 minute. Remove from the heat, adjust the seasoning with salt and pepper if needed, and stir in the cilantro. Garnish with the peanuts and serve, passing the sambal separately.

As usual, we like meat from the chuck section of the cow best for stew because it has great flavor and isn't too tough. If you can't get stew beef that you know comes from the chuck, buy a piece of chuck and cube it yourself. For this stew, we like the chuck blade roast or chuck 7-bone blade pot roast.

OTHER CUTS YOU CAN USE

Cubes of top round, rump, or even brisket would be just fine in this dish.

African-Style Beef and Tuber Stew with Toasted Spices

SERVES 6 TO 8

In this country, we are used to pretty straightforward stews. But if you travel around the world—particularly in the tropics—you will find that stews often feature a lot of spices. This makes sense to us, since when you make stews, you are typically working with the more flavorful cuts of beef that can stand up to the intense flavors of spices. It also makes for very lively eating. This particular dish starts with a deep level of garlic, ginger, and chile peppers, then we finish it off with a toasted spice mixture that adds a whole other flavor dimension.

We see eating this with some sautéed leafy greens and a big chunk of melon.

2 pounds boneless beef chuck, cut into 2-inch cubes

Kosher salt and freshly cracked black pepper to taste

4 slices bacon, diced large

3 large onions, peeled and diced small

3 tablespoons minced garlic

1/3 cup peeled and roughly chopped fresh ginger

3 tablespoons minced fresh chile peppers of your choice, or to taste

1 medium tomato, cored and roughly chopped

About 6 cups beef stock (or see Stock Options, page 32)

1 medium white potato, peeled and cut into 1-inch cubes

1 medium sweet potato, cut into 1-inch cubes

1 pound yucca, peeled and cut into 1-inch cubes (or substitute acorn squash)

3 tablespoons cumin seeds (or 1½ tablespoons ground cumin)

1 tablespoon black mustard seeds (or 1½ teaspoons dry mustard)

3 tablespoons coriander seeds (or 1½ tablespoons ground coriander)

1. Dry the beef with paper towels and sprinkle it generously with salt and pepper. In a 5-inch-deep Dutch oven or other large heavy pot with a lid, sauté the bacon over medium heat until it is crisp and has rendered much of its fat, about 6 minutes. Use tongs or a slotted spoon to transfer the bacon to a medium bowl, leaving the fat in the pot.

2. Add the beef to the pot in a single layer, in batches if necessary to avoid crowding, and cook until well browned on all sides, about 10 minutes; transfer the pieces to the bowl with the bacon as they are done.

3. Pour off all but 2 tablespoons of the fat from the pot, add the onions, and cook, stirring occasionally, until they are golden brown, 11 to 13 minutes. Add the garlic, ginger, chiles, and tomato and cook for 3 minutes more, stirring constantly to keep the garlic from burning.

4. Return the beef and bacon to the pot and add the stock and a big pinch each of salt and pepper. (If there is not enough liquid to cover the solid ingredients, add enough stock, water, or beer to cover.) Bring to a simmer and skim any scum from the surface, then cover, reduce the heat to low, and cook very gently for 1 hour. Add the potato, sweet potato, and yucca and cook until the meat and vegetables are tender, about 45 minutes more. To check for doneness, take a piece of meat out of the stew, cut into it to check for color, and taste for tenderness. Skim any scum from the surface of the stew, taste, and add more salt and/or pepper if necessary.

5. While the stew is cooking, toast the spices in a small heavy sauté pan over medium heat, shaking frequently, until they darken and become fragrant, about 2 minutes; be careful not to burn the spices.

6. Serve the stew steaming hot, strewn with the toasted spices.

COOK ONCE, EAT TWICE

The spices and root vegetables in this stew make it a natural for other uses, because it has such a dynamic flavor mixture going for it. If you have leftovers, drain off the liquid, chop all the solids pretty small, form them into patties, and fry them in a little butter. The yucca will do the work of holding the patties together, and they will taste incredible.

To get 2-inch cubes of chuck, you are going to have to buy a chuck steak or roast and cut it up yourself. But that's fine, because it's the easiest way to be sure that you are getting chuck meat rather than the mixture of anonymous cuts that is often contained in precut "beef stew meat." Just about any portion of the chuck will do. Chuck eye roasts or steaks are very nice here, if you want to spend a few extra pennies. Chuck is a supermarket item, no particular need to go to the butcher.

OTHER CUTS YOU CAN USE

Top sirloin or top round are also good in this dish.

Old-School Southern-Style Beef Stew with Corn, Tomatoes, and Bacon

SERVES 6 TO 8

While it is made with beef rather than squirrel, this stew has its roots in that classic of the American South, Brunswick stew. As usual, we prefer to use chuck because it has more flavor than other cuts often used for stew. Here we cut the meat into large two-inch cubes rather than the smaller cubes often called for in stew recipes. This both keeps the meat somewhat more tender and makes it a bigger, more dominant presence in the stew.

Serve this with buttered corn bread and a simple green salad or coleslaw.

6 strips bacon

2 pounds boneless beef stew meat, preferably chuck, cut into 2-inch cubes

Kosher salt and freshly cracked black pepper to taste

¼ cup all-purpose flour

2 large red onions, peeled and diced medium

3 tablespoons minced garlic

2 cups fresh corn kernels (about 4 ears)

4 plum tomatoes, cored and diced medium

2 large carrots, peeled and diced medium

About 4 cups beef stock (or see Stock Options, page 32)

1 cup roughly chopped fresh parsley

1. In a 5-inch-deep Dutch oven or other large heavy pot with a lid, cook the bacon over medium-high heat until crisp, about 6 to 8 minutes. Remove and drain on paper towels.

2. Pour off all but 3 tablespoons of fat from the pot. Dry the beef with paper towels, sprinkle generously with salt and pepper, and toss with the flour. Add the beef to the pot in a single layer, in batches if necessary to avoid crowding, and brown it well on all sides, about 10 minutes; transfer the pieces to a platter as they are done.

3. Meanwhile, coarsely chop the bacon; set it aside.

4. When all the beef has been browned, add the onions to the pot and cook, stirring occasionally, until golden brown, 11 to 13 minutes. Add the garlic, corn, tomatoes, and carrots and cook, stirring, for 3 minutes.

5. Return the meat to the pot, add enough stock to cover, and bring to a simmer, stirring to dissolve the brown crusty stuff in the bottom of the pot. Skim any scum off the top, then cover, reduce the heat to low, and cook gently until the meat is tender, 1½ to 2 hours. To check for doneness, take a piece of meat out of the stew, cut into it to check for color, and taste for tenderness. When the meat is tender, skim any scum off the surface, taste the liquid, and adjust the seasoning with salt and pepper if necessary.

6. Serve the stew in bowls, garnished with the parsley and reserved bacon.

The World's Hottest Chili, with Scotch Bonnet Peppers, Yucca, and a Cucumber-Mango Coolant

SERVES 6 TO 8

If you are not a total chili-head—if you don't enjoy feeling sweat running down your face as your head starts to tingle and your whole body begins to go numb—don't go any farther. This is ground that only crazed chili fanatics will want to tread on.

This is not traditional chili, but a Caribbean variation, with yucca as the starch, ginger as a dominant flavor, and Scotch bonnet as the fuel. Now, many people will tell you that the habanero and the Scotch bonnet are the same. I (Chris) disagree. To my taste buds, the Scotch bonnet, which basically grows in the Caribbean, has a much more fruity flavor than the basically Mexican-grown habanero. So if there is a Caribbean market in your town, it might be worth making a trip there to get the real thing.

Of course, the recipe is also a total winner even without the chiles, so you can eliminate them—in which case, if you're in a hurry, you can forget the coolant too.

We like to serve this over plain white rice, accompanied by a really fresh green vegetable—sautéed broccoli rabe (page 430), for example, or simple steamed green beans would be nice.

THE CUT
Almost any cut from the top or bottom round will work in this dish, so long as it is cut into 1½-inch cubes. The best option is probably the rump roast, while the cut to avoid is the eye round, which is simply too lean for this approach. We're in the cheap cuts here, so just go to the supermarket and pick the meat up.

OTHER CUTS YOU CAN USE
Chuck is fine here too, but it's probably not worth the extra pennies.

¼ cup olive oil, or more if needed

1½ pounds top or bottom beef round, cut into 1½-inch cubes

Kosher salt and freshly cracked black pepper to taste

2 large red onions, peeled and diced medium

2 red bell peppers, cored, seeded, and diced medium

3 tablespoons minced garlic

3 tablespoons minced fresh ginger

2 to 6 tablespoons minced Scotch bonnet or habanero chiles, depending
    on your taste for heat (if you don't really like heat, substitute
    2 teaspoons red pepper flakes)

¼ cup ground cumin

¼ cup ground coriander

¼ cup paprika

1 tablespoon ground cinnamon

2 tablespoons curry powder

1 cup canned mango juice (or substitute pineapple juice)

1 cup beef stock (or see Stock Options, page 32)

One 12-ounce can beer, or more if needed

2 cups yucca, peeled, fibrous core removed, and diced small (about 1 large)
    (or substitute potatoes)

FOR THE COOLANT

3 mangoes, peeled, pitted, and diced medium

2 cucumbers, peeled, seeded, and diced medium

½ cup fresh lime juice (about 4 limes)

1 tablespoon sugar

1 cup roughly chopped fresh cilantro

1. In a 5-inch-deep Dutch oven or other large heavy pot with a lid, heat the oil over medium-high heat until very hot but not smoking. Dry the meat with paper towels and sprinkle it generously with salt and pepper. Add to the pot in a single layer, in batches if necessary to avoid crowding, and cook until well browned on all sides, about 10 minutes; transfer the pieces to a platter as they are done.

2. Pour off the fat or add oil to the pot as needed so you have a total of about 2 tablespoons in the pot. Reduce the heat to medium, add the onions and red peppers, and cook, stirring occasionally, until they just begin to color, 9 to 11 minutes. Add the garlic, ginger, and chiles and cook, stirring constantly, for 2 minutes. Add the remaining spices and cook, stirring, for 3 minutes more.

3. Return the meat to the pot, then add the mango juice, stock, and beer. (If there is not enough liquid to cover the ingredients, top the stew off with some more beer.) Bring to a simmer and skim any scum off the top, then cover, reduce the heat to low, and cook for 30 minutes. Add the yucca and continue to cook, covered, until the meat and yucca are tender, about 1 hour more. To check for doneness, take a piece of meat out of the stew, cut into it, and taste it for tenderness. When the chili is done, skim off any scum from the top of the liquid and adjust the seasoning with salt and pepper.

4. While the chili is cooking, make the coolant: In a medium bowl, combine the mangoes, cucumbers, lime juice, and sugar and toss to combine.

5. Serve the chili in big bowls over rice, topped with the cilantro, with the coolant on the side.

Señor Sanchez's Salvadoran Soup of Kings with Short Ribs, Corn, and Plantains

SERVES 6 TO 8

This soup is a tradition at the East Coast Grill. The head day chef, Elmer Sanchez, has worked there for eight years and runs a dedicated crew of prep cooks. It's a lucky day for his crew when they arrive for work and find Elmer making his *sopa del rey*. This is not for the customers, but a special lunch for the prep chefs, and it's become one of my (Chris's) favorite meals. It's a little effort to eat this—you've got the bone-in ribs and the corn on the cob to deal with—but its rough-and-ready nature appeals to me. It's a sublime Central American eating experience, and my very favorite part is the broth.

Elmer serves this with Latin-Style Black Beans and Rice (page 422), a bottle of Tabasco sauce, and, if we're having a good day and we're on top of the prep list, a cold beer. I recommend you do just the same.

COOK ONCE, EAT TWICE

This is a great leftover stew, but when you put it in the refrigerator, make sure to put a huge label on it saying "For Knuckleheads Only" or something like that; if an unsuspecting guest eats this, he or she will be in some serious trouble.

THE CUT

See Black Pepper–Crusted Wine-Braised Short Ribs (page 74) for more details on short ribs and how to get what you want when buying them.

OTHER CUTS YOU CAN USE

You could make this with beef shins, veal shanks, or even lamb shanks.

1½ pounds English-style beef short ribs, cut into 2-inch lengths

Kosher salt and freshly cracked black pepper to taste

¼ cup olive oil

2 large onions, peeled and thinly sliced

3 tablespoons minced garlic

3 tablespoons ground cumin

2 tablespoons chili powder

2 tablespoons minced fresh chile peppers of your choice

3 green plantains, peeled and each cut into 5 pieces (or substitute yucca, malanga, taro, or boniato)

2 sweet potatoes, peeled and cut into chunks the same size as the plantain

About 6 cups chicken stock (or see Stock Options, page 32)

3 ears corn, husked and each cut crosswise into 5 pieces

½ cup roughly chopped fresh cilantro

1 large red onion, peeled and diced small

4 limes, quartered

1. Dry the ribs with paper towels and sprinkle them generously with salt and pepper. In the largest Dutch oven or large heavy pot that you have, heat the oil over medium-high heat until hot but not smoking. Add only enough ribs to cover the bottom of the pan in a single layer without touching and brown well, 10 to 12 minutes per side. Remove and set aside. Repeat until all the ribs are browned.

2. Pour out all but about 3 tablespoons of fat from the pot. Add the onions to the pot and cook, stirring occasionally, until just translucent, 7 to 9 minutes. Add the garlic, cumin, chili powder, and chiles and cook, stirring, for 2 minutes. Add the browned ribs, the plantains, and sweet potatoes, along with enough stock to cover, bring to a boil, and skim off any film from the top. Reduce the heat to low and simmer, uncovered, for 1 hour.

3. Add the corn and continue to cook until the ribs are tender, 30 minutes to 1 hour more.

4. Season the stew with salt and pepper and stir in the cilantro. Transfer to serving bowls. Sprinkle the red onion over the top and serve with the lime quarters for squeezing.

Steak Bomb—Fully Loaded with Mushrooms, Onions, and Peppers

SERVES 4

Also known as a grinder, hero, or hoagie, the "bomb" is a classic American sandwich, a Dagwood-style creation loaded up with whatever strikes the creator's fancy. My (Chris's) grandmother was particularly fond of this version, which features shaved steak, relatively tough but very flavorful beef cut very, very thin so it is not so chewy.

This is a Sunday afternoon classic, best served in front of the television with a big bottle of your favorite soda and a bag of chips. If you're a fan of Philly cheese steak, grate some Parmesan or Asiago on top of this and you'll have an upscale version of your favorite.

3 tablespoons extra virgin olive oil

2 red onions, peeled and thinly sliced

1 red bell pepper, cored, seeded, and thinly sliced

1 pound white mushrooms, stemmed and thinly sliced

1 tablespoon minced garlic

¼ cup roughly chopped fresh parsley

1 pound shaved steak (see The Cut, right)

Kosher salt and freshly cracked black pepper to taste

1 tablespoon balsamic vinegar

1 to 3 teaspoons Tabasco sauce

2 tablespoons catsup

4 sub rolls, split and toasted

1. In a very large sauté pan, heat 1 tablespoon of the oil over medium-high heat until hot but not smoking. Add the onions and red pepper and cook, stirring occasionally, until golden brown, 11 to 13 minutes. Transfer the onions and peppers to a medium bowl and set aside.

2. Add 1 tablespoon of the remaining oil to the pan. When the oil is very hot, add the mushrooms and cook, stirring occasionally, for 5 minutes. Add the garlic and cook, stirring, for 1 minute more. Remove from the heat, stir in the parsley, and add to the bowl of peppers and onions; set aside.

3. Wipe out the pan with paper towels. Add the remaining 1 tablespoon oil and heat over medium-high heat until very hot but not smoking. Dry the meat with paper towels and sprinkle it generously with salt and pepper. Add it to the pan, in batches if necessary to avoid crowding, and

THE CUT

Like London broil, shaven steak is not a particular cut of meat but an approach to butchering. Basically, the butcher takes meat from the tougher sections of the cow such as the round and shaves it very thin. This tenderizes the meat by cutting the strands of connective tissue, so when you cook the meat, it seems a bit chewy but not tough. It's a smart way to get all the flavor out of these tougher cuts.

OTHER CUTS YOU CAN USE

Thinly sliced flank steak or skirt steak are both delicious in this recipe.

cook, stirring, until nicely browned, 2 to 3 minutes. Remove from the heat, add the vinegar, Tabasco, and catsup, and stir to coat.

4. Divide the steak among the toasted sub rolls, then load them up with the onions, peppers, and mushrooms and eat.

Aromatic Ginger and Beef Broth with Hoisin and Traditional Southeast Asian Garnishes

SERVES 4 TO 6 AS AN APPETIZER

This is our version of the fantastic meat broths of Southeast Asia, of which Vietnamese *pho* is probably the best known in the United States. We really enjoy the flavor dynamics of these soups. Instead of creating broths that have lots of heavy flavors, the way Western stews often do, Southeast Asian cooks tend to concentrate on making broths that are light and aromatic, almost perfumey. They pour the broth over the other ingredients, which have been cooked separately. Here we feature cellophane noodles and strips of sautéed beef round flavored with sesame and hoisin. What really makes the dish, though, is the platter of garnishes, or "add-ins," that you pass around so everyone can add what he or she chooses.

This dish seems a little complicated, but it really goes together quickly. It's a meal all by itself and, as you might expect from its heritage, it's particularly welcome in hot weather.

One 1¼- to 1½-pound top round steak, about 1 inch thick
Kosher salt and freshly cracked black pepper to taste
2 tablespoons sesame oil, or more if needed
1 large yellow onion, peeled and thinly sliced
3 tablespoons minced garlic
3 tablespoons roughly chopped fresh ginger (unpeeled is OK)
4 stalks lemongrass, roughly chopped (or substitute 2 tablespoons grated lemon zest)
6 cups water
¼ cup fish sauce (*nam pla*)
2 plum tomatoes, cored and diced small
2 tablespoons sugar
¼ cup cracked coriander seeds (or 2 tablespoons ground coriander)
Freshly cracked white (or black) pepper to taste
¼ cup hoisin sauce
4 ounces cellophane noodles, soaked in 4 cups warm water for 1 hour

The round, which is the upper leg of the cow, has three muscles: top round, eye round, and bottom round. All are lean and rather tough. Here we are looking for something from the top round, which is the most tender of the three. Since we only want a small quantity of meat, the best choice is a top round steak. You could also use the beef round tip steak, also known as the top sirloin steak, which comes from a small section of the round that is nearest the sirloin.

OTHER CUTS YOU CAN USE
Beef brisket is great here, and a small flank steak would also work well.

BUTCHERSPEAK
Top round is a supermarket item. If you want to go for the authentic Southeast Asian touch, though, go to your butcher and ask if he can cut you a small piece (about 1½ pounds) off the tail end of a brisket. Use that in the soup and you'll think you're in downtown Ho Chi Minh City.

5 scallions (white and green parts), thinly sliced

1 bunch mint, leaves only

1/2 cup fresh cilantro leaves

1/3 cup chili paste or 5 fresh chile peppers of your choice, thinly sliced

4 limes, halved

1 cup coarsely chopped unsalted roasted peanuts

1 cup bean sprouts of your choice (optional)

1. Dry the meat with paper towels and sprinkle it generously with salt and pepper. In a 5-inch-deep Dutch oven or other large heavy pot with a lid, heat the oil over medium-high heat until very hot but not smoking. Place the meat in the pot and brown well on both sides, about 10 minutes total. (The sesame oil will be very aromatic; don't worry, it is supposed to be.) Transfer the meat to a platter.

2. Pour off the fat or add oil to the pot as needed so you have a total of about 2 tablespoons in the pot. Heat the oil until hot but not smoking, then add the onion and cook, stirring occasionally, until translucent, 7 to 9 minutes. Add the garlic, ginger, and lemongrass and cook, stirring, for 3 minutes more.

3. Return the meat to the pot, add the water, fish sauce, tomatoes, sugar, and coriander, and bring to a simmer. Skim any scum off the surface, then cover, reduce the heat to low, and simmer gently (a few bubbles rather than continuous bubbling), occasionally skimming any film that forms on the surface with a large spoon, until the meat is tender, 1 to 1½ hours. To check for doneness, plunge a fork straight down into the meat and try to pull the fork out. If the fork slides out very easily, the meat is done; if the meat hangs on to the fork, give it more time.

4. Meanwhile, preheat the oven to 325°F.

5. When the meat is done, remove it from the pot and, as soon as it is cool enough to handle, slice it very thin against the grain. Place in a medium bowl, season with salt and white pepper, and toss with the hoisin to coat. Spread the meat on a baking sheet and place in the oven for 15 minutes.

6. While the meat is in the oven, strain the broth, return it to the pot, and set over low heat. Skim any scum from the broth, taste, and adjust the seasoning with salt and pepper if necessary.

7. Drain the cellophane noodles and divide them evenly among individual soup bowls. Ladle the hot broth over the noodles and top with the meat slices. Arrange the garnishes in bowls or on a large platter and allow your guests to add what they like.

We prefer ground chuck for
its combination of great
beef flavor and good value.
For more information,
see About Ground Beef
(page 140).

OTHER CUTS YOU CAN USE

Ground round, ground sir-
loin.

Texas-Style Ground Beef Casserole with Sweet Potato Crust and A-1 Parsley Butter

SERVES 6 TO 8

Here is a famous staff meal from the East Coast Grill, as prepared by chef Owen Tilley. Owen is from Texas, and he claims that his mother used to make this dish for him all the time. Although we're sure that Texans would say they invented the concept, it's actually a variation on shepherd's pie, in which you basically stew up a bunch of lamb, cover it with potatoes, and throw it in the oven. To pep it up a bit, we have added a bit of spice in the form of cumin, coriander, and curry powder, and exchanged sweet potatoes for the white potatoes.

To save time, make the flavored butter ahead of time and freeze it. That way, you can just pull it out, slice as much as you want, and return the rest to the freezer for next time.

Kids love this dish, but it's sophisticated enough for adult tastes too. Serve it with corn bread, coleslaw, and baked beans.

FOR THE BUTTER

$1/2$ pound (2 sticks) unsalted butter, at room temperature

$1/4$ cup A-1 sauce

$1/4$ cup roughly chopped fresh parsley

Kosher salt and freshly cracked black pepper to taste

3 large sweet potatoes, peeled and diced large

$3/4$ cup half-and-half

Kosher salt and freshly cracked black pepper to taste

3 tablespoons olive oil

2 large red onions, peeled and thinly sliced

1 red bell pepper, cored, seeded, and diced small

1 green bell pepper, cored, seeded, and diced small

2 tablespoons minced garlic

1 tablespoon minced fresh chile peppers of your choice, or to taste

2 tablespoons cumin seeds (or 1 tablespoon ground cumin)

2 tablespoons cracked coriander seeds (or 1 tablespoon ground coriander)

Pinch of ground cinnamon

$2^1/2$ pounds ground beef

2 tablespoons molasses

$1/4$ cup catsup

1. Make the butter: In a small bowl, combine the butter, A-1, parsley, and salt and pepper and mix well. Place on a piece of waxed paper or plastic wrap and roll it into a cylinder, then refrigerate until firm.

2. In a large saucepan, bring 2 quarts of water and a pinch of salt to a boil over medium-high heat. Add the sweet potatoes and cook for about 10 minutes, or until they are easily pierced by a fork but still offer some resistance. Drain the potatoes and place them in a medium bowl.

3. Heat the half-and-half in a small saucepan until hot but not quite simmering, add to the potatoes, and mash until the potatoes are smooth; the mixture should be fairly loose. Season with salt and pepper and set aside.

4. Preheat the oven to 350°F.

5. In a large sauté pan, heat the oil over medium-high heat until hot but not smoking. Add the onions and bell peppers and cook, stirring occasionally, until golden brown, 11 to 13 minutes. Add the garlic, chiles, and spices and cook, stirring, for 1 minute. Add the ground beef and continue to cook, stirring, until browned and crumbled, about 10 minutes more. Drain off the excess fat in the pan and add the molasses, catsup, and salt and pepper to taste.

6. Spread the meat mixture in a 2-quart casserole dish. Cover with the sweet potatoes. Bake until the sweet potatoes are crusty and brown and the filling is bubbly, about 40 minutes.

7. Remove the casserole from the oven. Unwrap the butter and slice thin, then put one third of it on top of the casserole, letting it melt. Serve the rest of the butter on the side, for your guests' discretionary use.

COOK ONCE, EAT TWICE
This is an excellent dish for making ahead of time and refrigerating, then heating up for 30 minutes at 350°F just before serving. If you have leftover butter, it's fantastic on steaks or chops of any description.

ABOUT GROUND BEEF

As the name implies, ground beef is simply muscle meat (as opposed to offal) that has been ground up or chopped very fine in a meat grinder. "Hamburger" is a specific type of ground meat in that it is allowed by federal regulation to contain added fat and/or seasonings. All other ground beef, however, is nothing but that: ground-up beef.

But that doesn't mean that all ground beef is the same. Not at all. Any particular package has two defining characteristics: the part of the cow that it comes from and the percentage of fat that it contains. Unfortunately, while you can be sure of the second, you can't always be sure of the first.

Let's explain. Meat labeled as just plain "ground beef" is made from cheap cuts such as brisket and may contain up to 30 percent fat. Next step up the price scale is ground chuck, which has 15 to 20 percent fat, is still relatively cheap, and has wonderful beefy flavor. Because of this favorable intersection of taste and cost, it is our first choice for ground beef. Ground round and ground sirloin, both of which are more expensive, are also leaner. Ground sirloin usually has around 15 percent fat, while ground round may have as little as 11 percent. For our taste, these last two are a bit too expensive and, particularly when it comes to ground round, slightly too lean, with a tendency to become dry.

Unfortunately, though, this is one of those cases where a label can be misleading. The percentage of fat in ground beef is checked and enforced at the retail level, so that something labeled "80% lean" ground beef can only contain 20 percent fat. But there is no comparable regulation governing labeling of what cut the beef comes from. Since few butchers actually segregate meat trimmings, there is no guarantee that something labeled "ground chuck" actually all comes from the chuck. All that such a label guarantees is that the meat has about 15 to 20 percent fat.

So, if you really, really care about having the very best ground beef, we recommend the same course of action that we advocate for stew beef: Buy a piece of chuck and ask the butcher to grind it for you. But if you're not that fanatical, just look for a package labeled "ground chuck"; at least you know you're getting the right mix of meat and fat.

THE CUT

As with other ground beef dishes, we prefer using ground chuck here for its combination of flavor and value. See About Ground Beef, above.

OTHER CUTS YOU CAN USE

Ground round, ground sirloin.

Indian-Spiced Beef-Stuffed Red Onions with Fresh Coconut-Ginger Chutney and Simple Yogurt Sauce

SERVES 4

To our minds, this is among the most dynamic ground beef dishes in the world. That's largely because it is inspired by the spice cookery of India, where just about every home cook is remarkably sophisticated in the myriad uses of spices. Proper preparation and roasting of the onions are also key to this dish. Trim off a little bit of the bottom of each one so that it sits flat in the pan, then roast them, let them cool for a few minutes, carve out the centers, stuff with the spicy beef, and roast them again. It's a little complicated, but the flavor combinations and the unusual presentation are worth it.

If you think of it, you can make the chutney up to 3 days ahead, then cover and refrigerate it, so you have less to do at the last minute.

Serve this with Crispy Fried Okra (page 429) and a simple salad.

8 medium red onions (about the size of baseballs), unpeeled

FOR THE CHUTNEY

1 cup finely chopped fresh coconut (or substitute ⅔ cup unsweetened dried grated coconut)

¼ cup minced fresh ginger

½ cup roughly chopped fresh cilantro

2 tablespoons dark brown sugar

6 tablespoons fresh lime juice (about 3 limes)

2 teaspoons red pepper flakes

FOR THE SAUCE

1 cup plain yogurt

¼ cup roughly chopped fresh mint

1 tablespoon ground cumin

1 to 2 tablespoons vegetable oil

1 pound ground beef, preferably chuck

Kosher salt to taste

1 small yellow onion, peeled and diced small

2 teaspoons cumin seeds (or 1 teaspoon ground cumin)

2 teaspoons coriander seeds (or 1 teaspoon ground coriander)

5 whole cloves (or 1 teaspoon ground cloves)

2 tablespoons minced garlic

2 tablespoons minced fresh chile peppers of your choice, preferably green

2 tablespoons curry powder

Freshly cracked black pepper to taste

1. Preheat the oven to 350°F. Lightly grease a small roasting pan.

2. Cut a thin slice off the root end of each onion so that it will stand upright. Cut off the top one quarter or so of each onion. Place the onions root side down in the roasting pan and roast until they are tender enough so you can easily stick a fork all the way into the center, about 45 minutes. Remove from the oven, leaving the oven on, and set the onions aside to cool.

3. While the onions are roasting, make the chutney and the sauce: Combine all the chutney ingredients in a small bowl, mix well, and set aside. (If you're using a fresh coconut, try adding a couple of tablespoons of the water from the inside of the coconut to the chutney.) Combine the yogurt, mint, and cumin in another small bowl, mix well, cover, and refrigerate until ready to use.

4. When the onions are cool enough to handle, remove the skin and any outer layers that have become leathery. Then, one at a time, holding each onion with both hands, gently push the inner layers out from the bottom, leaving a shell of 2 or 3 layers. Set aside while you make the filling.

5. In a large sauté pan, heat 1 tablespoon of the oil over medium-high heat until hot but not smoking. Add the ground beef, breaking it up with a fork, and cook, stirring, until just browned, about 8 to 10 minutes. Season with salt and transfer to a medium bowl.

6. If there is less than about 2 tablespoons of fat in the pan from the ground beef, add the remaining 1 tablespoon oil and heat until hot but not smoking. Add the onion and cook, stirring occasionally, until golden brown, 11 to 13 minutes. (If you are using whole spices, use the time while the onion is sautéing to grind the cumin, coriander, and cloves in a spice grinder or coffee grinder or crush in a mortar and pestle.)

7. When the meat is browned, add the garlic and chiles and cook, stirring, for 1 minute. Add the curry powder, cumin, coriander, and cloves and cook, stirring constantly, for another 2 minutes. Reduce the heat to low, return the meat and any accumulated juices to the pan, season with salt and pepper, and mix very well.

8. Arrange the hollowed-out onions in the same roasting pan you used for the initial roasting and heap the hot filling into the onions, mounding the tops. Place in the oven and roast until hot throughout, 15 to 20 minutes. Drizzle generously with the yogurt sauce and serve, passing the chutney and the remaining yogurt sauce on the side.

Red Wine–Braised Oxtails over Spaghetti with Garlic and Spinach

SERVES 4 TO 6

Like many traditional pasta sauces from Italy, this one spends a long time cooking. But most of that is unattended oven time, so it's not really that much work. And it's definitely worth it for the rich, full, deep flavors of the finished sauce. It's a good bet that you'll end up not only using it on pasta, but doing as we've done and dipping little pieces of crusty bread into it for snacks.

Because the oxtails render quite a lot of fat into the sauce as they cook, you may want to make the sauce a day ahead, then refrigerate it overnight; much of the fat will rise to the top and congeal, and you can simply skim it off. Then reheat the sauce, cook the spaghetti, and you're ready to go.

FOR THE SAUCE

5 to 6 pounds oxtails

¼ cup olive oil

Kosher salt and freshly cracked black pepper to taste

1 large red onion, peeled and diced small

1 medium carrot, peeled and diced small

2 tablespoons minced garlic

3 cups beef stock (or see Stock Options, page 32)

1 cup dry red wine

½ cup balsamic vinegar

1 cup canned tomatoes, diced medium (including juice)

FOR THE SPAGHETTI

2 tablespoons kosher salt

1 pound spaghetti

2 tablespoons olive oil

½ pound spinach, stemmed, well washed, and dried

3 tablespoons minced garlic

Kosher salt and freshly cracked black pepper to taste

¼ cup roughly chopped fresh oregano, for garnish

¼ cup freshly grated Parmesan cheese, for garnish

1. Preheat the oven to 500°F.

2. In a large bowl, combine the oxtails, olive oil, and salt and pepper and toss to coat. Place the oxtails in a roasting pan large enough to hold

Oxtails sometimes actually are the tails of oxen, which are castrated bulls used for work such as pulling wagons. But more often they are tails of standard beef cattle. Our guess is that they are still called oxtails because it just doesn't sound as enticing to say that you are serving "cow tail stew." In any case, they are a prime example of the inverse relationship between flavor and tenderness. Full of cartilage, they need to be cooked for a very long time to get tender, but once they have reached that stage, they are incredibly flavorful and rich. A good butcher will certainly have this cut, and you can often find it in the supermarket as well.

COOK ONCE, EAT TWICE

This is an excellent sauce to make in advance and freeze, then pull out and thaw when you want a sauce with deep, rich beef flavor in very little time.

them all without touching and roast until they are well browned, about 20 minutes. Transfer the oxtails to a platter and reduce the oven temperature to 300°F.

3. Pour off all but about 2 tablespoons of fat from the roasting pan and place it over two burners on medium-high heat. Add the onion and carrot to the pan and sauté, stirring occasionally, until the onion is golden brown, 11 to 13 minutes. Add the garlic and continue to sauté, stirring, for 1 minute. Add the stock, wine, and vinegar and bring to a simmer, stirring to dissolve the brown crusty stuff in the bottom of the pan. Add the tomatoes and oxtails, season with salt and pepper, and cover with a tight-fitting lid or heavy-duty aluminum foil.

4. Place in the oven and cook until the oxtails are very tender and almost falling off the bone, 2 to 3 hours.

5. When the oxtails are done, transfer them to a platter and skim the fat from the braising liquid. Taste the liquid and reduce it if necessary to give it more flavor. For a thicker sauce, reduce it until it coats the back of a spoon.

6. As soon as the oxtails are cool enough, remove the meat from the bones and add it to the sauce in the roasting pan. At this point, you can either refrigerate the sauce for several hours or overnight, skim off the congealed fat, and then reheat it, or you can skim the fat from the top of the sauce again and simply keep it warm while you prepare the spaghetti and spinach.

7. Bring 4 quarts water and the salt to a boil in a large pot. Add the spaghetti and cook until tender but not mushy, 8 to 10 minutes. Drain and keep warm.

8. While the spaghetti is cooking, heat the olive oil in a large sauté pan over medium-high heat until hot but not smoking. Add the spinach and sear, tossing madly, for 1 minute. Add the garlic and toss to combine. Remove the pan from the heat, add the hot pasta, season with salt and pepper, and toss well.

9. Divide the spaghetti and spinach among large pasta bowls. Top each with the oxtail sauce and garnish with the oregano and cheese.

Basil-Crusted Meat Loaf with Brandy, Walnuts, and Spicy Tomato Sauce

SERVES 4 TO 6

Any meat loaf worth the name should reward the cook with great sandwich material, and this one is no exception. Spread a little tomato sauce on the bread of your choice and run it under the broiler, then load the toasted bread up with sliced meat loaf and shredded iceberg lettuce and dig in. This particular meat loaf is also wonderful when eaten cold or at room temperature, so it's perfect for picnics.

FOR THE CRUST

1 bunch basil, leaves only, roughly chopped

3 tablespoons olive oil

4 garlic cloves, peeled

Kosher salt and freshly cracked black pepper to taste

2 pounds ground beef, preferably chuck

2 teaspoons minced garlic

1 small onion, peeled and grated

$1/2$ cup walnuts, toasted in a skillet over medium heat, shaking frequently, until aromatic, about 3 minutes, and coarsely chopped

$1/2$ cup prunes, pitted and roughly chopped

2 large eggs

1 cup fresh bread crumbs

$1/4$ cup brandy

$1/2$ teaspoon ground allspice

2 tablespoons kosher salt

1 tablespoon freshly cracked black pepper

FOR THE SAUCE

$1/4$ cup olive oil

2 medium onions, peeled and diced small

2 tablespoons minced garlic

1 tablespoon ground coriander

$1/2$ teaspoon ground cinnamon

2 teaspoons red pepper flakes, or to taste

1 cup dry red wine

THE CUT

As with other ground beef dishes, we prefer using ground chuck here for its combination of value and flavor. See About Ground Beef (page 140) for more information.

OTHER CUTS YOU CAN USE

Ground round, ground sirloin.

2 cups canned crushed Italian tomatoes (with their juice)

1 bay leaf

1 cup freshly grated Parmesan cheese, for garnish

1. Preheat the oven to 350°F.

2. Make the crust: With the food processor running, feed the basil, olive oil, garlic, and salt and pepper through the feed tube in that order. Process until everything just comes together to form a paste; do not overblend. Transfer to a small bowl, cover with plastic wrap pressed directly against the surface, and set aside.

3. In a large bowl, combine the ground beef, garlic, onion, walnuts, prunes, eggs, bread crumbs, brandy, allspice, salt, and pepper. Mix well and shape into a loaf in a shallow baking dish. Spread the basil paste evenly over the meat.

4. Bake until the juices run clear when you poke a knife into the loaf, about 1 hour.

5. While the meat loaf is baking, make the sauce: In a large sauté pan, heat the oil over medium-high heat until hot but not smoking. Add the onions and cook, stirring occasionally, until golden brown, 11 to 13 minutes. Add the garlic, coriander, cinnamon, and red pepper flakes and cook, stirring, for 2 minutes more. Pour in the wine, stir once or twice, and simmer gently for 4 minutes. Add the tomatoes and bay leaf and simmer, stirring frequently, until the sauce has thickened to your liking, about 45 minutes for a medium-thick sauce.

6. Cut the meat loaf into thick slabs and serve topped with the tomato sauce and Parmesan cheese.

RECIPES FOR
BEEF ODD CUTS: OFFAL ET AL.

Corned Beef and Sweet Potato Hash with Red Wine–
Caramelized Onions

You Gotta Have (Grilled Beef) Heart, Peruvian-Style

Hangover-Style Tripe Stew

Marrow Hobo Packs on Toast

Grilled Beef Liver and Slab Bacon Kebab on Cornmeal Mush
with Smoky Tomato-Bacon Relish

A Severe Tongue Hashing with Turnips and Swiss Chard

Head Cheese Reuben

Corned beef is basically beef that has been cured in a seasoned salt brine. Originally this was done for preservation, but now it is done for flavor, which means the cured meat has to be cooked. The term "corned" derives from the fact that in the sixteenth century, the English word *corn* referred to any small particles, including the grains of salt that were used in preserving beef. Brisket is the cut most often corned, although cuts from the round are also sometimes used. Brisket is a better bet, since it is more flavorful.

Corned beef brisket is available in many super-markets, but butcher shops are likely to have the best quality. Also, commercial packaged corned beef makes no distinction between the two cuts of brisket; at the butcher shop, you can ask for corned beef from the flat cut, which is less fatty than the point cut.

Corned Beef and Sweet Potato Hash with Red Wine–Caramelized Onions

SERVES 4 TO 5

If you are one of those people who has always found traditional corned beef hash to be delicious but too salty, try this version; the sweet potatoes have a way of countering the saltiness of the corned beef. Since hash is basically a creative use of leftovers, this dish starts out with two items that have already been cooked, the corned beef and the sweet potatoes. If you don't feel like cooking the corned beef, you can use canned, which is really pretty good. You can also make the onions ahead of time—in fact, you may want to make a double recipe, since they are fantastic on sandwiches or crostini or served with grilled meats.

This hash makes a great brunch dish for company or a simple supper dish for the family. Do not rush its cooking: It needs some time in the skillet to develop its crust.

1½ pounds corned beef (or substitute about 5 cups canned corned beef)
2 large sweet potatoes

FOR THE ONIONS
⅓ cup olive oil
3 medium red onions, peeled, halved, and very thinly sliced
½ cup sugar
1 cup dry red wine
½ cup balsamic vinegar
Kosher salt and freshly cracked black pepper to taste
½ cup currants (or substitute ¼ cup dark raisins)

Kosher salt and freshly cracked black pepper to taste
2 tablespoons olive oil

1. If using fresh corned beef, do the advance prep: Place the corned beef in a large pot, add water to cover, and bring to a boil, then reduce the heat to low and cook at a bare simmer until a sharp knife will pass all the way through without much resistance, about 2½ hours. Drain well, then, as soon as the meat is cool enough to handle, chop it fine. Set aside.

2. Meanwhile, preheat the oven to 350°F. Pierce the sweet potatoes in a few places with a fork and bake until just tender, about 50 minutes. As soon as they are cool enough to handle, peel and dice small. Set aside.

3. Make the onions: In a large sauté pan, heat the oil over medium-high heat until hot but not smoking. Add the onions, sugar, wine, and vinegar and cook, stirring occasionally, until most of the liquid has evaporated and the onions are golden brown, 30 to 40 minutes. Season well with salt and pepper, stir in the currants, and set aside.

4. In a large bowl, combine the corned beef, sweet potatoes, and salt and pepper (use plenty). In a large sauté pan, heat the olive oil over medium-high heat until very hot but not smoking. Add the meat mixture, spreading it out to cover the entire bottom of the pan. Press the hash down evenly with a large metal spatula, reduce the heat to medium, cover the pan, and let the hash cook undisturbed for 15 minutes. Uncover the pan, turn the hash over in sections with the spatula, and raise the heat to high. Cook for 5 more minutes, turning the hash every once in a while with the spatula.

5. Serve the hash hot, covering each portion with a generous layer of the caramelized onions.

You Gotta Have (Grilled Beef) Heart, Peruvian-Style

SERVES 6 TO 8 AS AN APPETIZER

This may seem strange, but beef heart is a classic Peruvian street food, usually eaten with grilled corn and boiled sweet potatoes. It's not as if you're actually going to sit down to a big heart; the meat is cut into cubes and grilled, then tossed with a simple spicy vinaigrette-style dressing. It has a good, slightly liver-like flavor and plenty of chew.

This is a good appetizer to serve before a vegetable entrée or a simple grilled fish.

THE CUT

While not often used in the United States, beef heart is popular in many other countries, particularly Peru, because it is very cheap but cooks up nicely. We have seldom seen this in a supermarket; you are probably going to have to go to a quality butcher for it.

OTHER CUTS YOU CAN USE

Any relatively tough cut of beef will work fine in this recipe. Top and bottom round, for example, make very good substitutes.

1 small beef heart, about 2 pounds

¼ cup olive oil

2 tablespoons minced garlic

1 tablespoon ground cumin

1 to 3 teaspoons red pepper flakes

Kosher salt and freshly cracked black pepper to taste

FOR THE DRESSING

¼ cup red wine vinegar

¼ cup olive oil

1 to 3 teaspoons minced fresh chile peppers of your choice

¼ cup roughly chopped fresh parsley

¼ cup fresh lemon juice (about 1 lemon)

1. Build a fire in your grill.

2. Trim any fat from the beef heart, dry the meat with paper towels, and cut it into 1-inch cubes. In a small bowl, combine the oil, garlic, cumin, red pepper flakes, and salt and pepper and mix well. Add the meat and toss to coat well.

3. Thread the meat onto skewers. When the fire has died down and the coals are very hot (you can hold your hand 5 inches above the grill surface for 1 second), place the skewers on the grill and sear well on one side, about 4 minutes. Turn and continue cooking to the desired doneness, about 6 minutes total for rare. To check for doneness, make a ¼-inch cut in the thickest part of the meat; it should be slightly less done than you like it. Remove the meat from the grill and allow to rest for 5 minutes while you make the dressing.

4. In a medium bowl, whisk the vinegar, oil, chiles, parsley, lemon juice, and salt and pepper to taste together well. Slide the meat off the skewers and toss with the dressing before serving.

Hangover-Style Tripe Stew

SERVES 8

Although it is not to everybody's taste, we love tripe. It not only has some real flavor, it also is rich in vitamin B, which is suggested as a cure for a hangover. Tripe is also a bedrock food of the people in many parts of the world, one of those cast-off parts of the animal that cooks who couldn't afford the more desirable cuts have managed to turn into something very tasty. Of course, dealing with tripe takes some time, so you should do much of the prep work for this dish the day before you plan to have that hangover.

Serve this brothy soup, a variation on Mexican *menudo*, with corn bread and the hair of whatever dog bit you.

1 cup kosher salt

1 cup white vinegar

2 pounds honeycomb tripe

Kosher salt and freshly cracked black pepper to taste

¼ cup peanut or vegetable oil

3 large onions, peeled and diced small

2 tablespoons dried oregano

3 tablespoons minced garlic

2 quarts chicken stock (or see Stock Options, page 32)

1 small ham hock, about 8 to 10 ounces

One 16-ounce can hominy

¼ cup finely chopped fresh chile peppers of your choice

FOR THE GARNISH

8 limes, halved

1 cup fresh cilantro leaves

1 cup shredded green cabbage

1 medium red onion, peeled and diced small

¼ cup cumin seeds, toasted in a skillet over medium heat, shaken
frequently, until fragrant, about 2 minutes

1. Prepare the tripe: Mix the salt and vinegar together well. Pour one third of the mixture into a large bowl and scrub the tripe in the mixture vigorously for 5 minutes with a clean brush, as if laundering a dirty shirt. Rinse in cold water and repeat two more times. Place the tripe in a bowl of cold water to cover, cover the bowl, and refrigerate for at least 12 hours and up to 36 hours, changing the water once or twice.

THE CUT

Tripe is stomach lining, which makes it sound less tasty than it actually is. There are three types of tripe, but by far the most flavorful and tender is honeycomb tripe, the inner side of which has a honeycomb pattern. You can find honeycomb tripe in most supermarkets, although, as with most offal, a quality butcher is likely to have the freshest. Even "fresh" tripe is actually partially cooked.

OTHER CUTS YOU CAN USE

Are you kidding? What could you substitute for a stomach lining?

2. Remove the tripe from the water and place it in a large pot with fresh water to cover. Bring it to a boil and simmer for 1 hour. Drain well.

3. Light a very low fire in your grill.

4. Sprinkle the tripe with salt and pepper. When the fire dies down (you can hold your hand 5 inches above the grill surface for about 6 seconds), place the tripe on the grill and cook for 10 to 15 minutes, or until the exterior is an even crusty golden brown. Remove the tripe from the grill and, as soon as it is cool enough to handle comfortably, slice very thin and set aside.

5. Make the stew: In a 5-inch-deep Dutch oven or large heavy pot, heat the oil over medium-high heat until it is very hot but not smoking. Add the onions and cook, stirring frequently, until translucent, 7 to 9 minutes. Add the oregano and garlic and cook, stirring, for 2 minutes. Add the chicken stock and bring to a simmer, then add the ham hock, hominy, and grilled tripe. Reduce the heat to low and simmer, uncovered, for 2 hours.

6. Just before serving, stir in the chile peppers. Squeeze the juice of half a lime into each individual bowl of tripe. Garnish with the remaining lime halves, the cilantro, cabbage, onion, and cumin seeds.

Marrow Hobo Packs on Toast

SERVES 4 AS AN APPETIZER

We love fat, and marrow is very fatty. But it is also very light and digestible, not qualities you usually associate with fat. This is one of my (Chris's) favorite items to serve when I have a bunch of chefs over to the house, because chefs are always big fat eaters. It couldn't be easier to do, either. You just salt and pepper the bones, wrap them up in foil, and cook them in the oven or in the coals of a charcoal fire, then knock the marrow out onto toast. Now, that's some good eating.

Try serving these as an appetizer in front of an entrée salad.

Eight 2- to 3-inch-long beef shin bones

3 tablespoons olive oil

Kosher salt and freshly cracked black pepper to taste

⅓ cup roughly chopped fresh parsley

12 slices French bread, toasted

1. Preheat the oven to 400°F, or build a fire in your charcoal grill.

2. In a large bowl, toss the marrow bones with the oil and salt and pepper so that they are thoroughly coated. Tear off eight sheets of heavy-duty foil, each about 2 feet long, and stack them one on top of the other. Arrange half the bones in the center of the top sheet. Fold up the top four of the sheets of foil around the bones, one after the other, turning the package one quarter turn between each sheet and making sure that each sheet is well sealed. Repeat this process with the remaining bones.

3. Cook the hobo packs in the oven for 35 to 45 minutes. Or when the fire has died down and the coals are medium-hot (you can hold your hand 5 inches above the grill surface for 2 to 3 seconds), place the packs on the bottom of the grill, pile the coals up on all sides of them, and cook for 40 to 50 minutes, depending upon the intensity of the coals. The marrow should be soft throughout.

4. Remove the bones from the foil and sprinkle them with the parsley and more salt and pepper. Serve with long spoons for scooping the marrow out onto the toasted French bread.

THE CUT

Marrow bones are the shin bones of the steer, which are large enough to have substantial marrow in the center. Marrow has long been considered a delicacy in Europe, and it is now gaining some acceptance in the United States due to the recent popularity of osso buco, braised veal shanks that contain marrow.

OTHER NAMES

Clear bones.

BUTCHERSPEAK

You can sometimes find marrow bones in the supermarket, but be sure that you don't get regular "soup bones" instead; they don't have enough marrow in them for this approach. Tell the butcher that you want shin bones, rather than knuckle bones.

Beef liver, which can be distinguished from calf's liver by its reddish-brown color, is very dense, rich, and a bit tough.

OTHER CUTS YOU CAN USE

Calf's liver is, of course, fine here. Just cook it for slightly less time. This kebab is also excellent when made with any tender cut of beef; try tenderloin tips or sirloin tips in place of the liver.

Grilled Beef Liver and Slab Bacon Kebab on Cornmeal Mush with Smoky Tomato-Bacon Relish

SERVES 4

There was a period in my (Doc's) youth when, on the advice of a nutritionist, my mother would get up every morning and cook herself liver for breakfast. It probably *was* very good for her health, but waking up every day to that smell put me off liver for a long time. Over the past few years, though, I have come to like its dense texture and its rich flavor.

In fact, despite its bad reputation, liver can be really delicious if cooked right and served with the right complementary ingredients. Here's a perfect example. The straightforward corn flavor of the mush and the very smoky, rich taste of the relish are perfect accompaniments to the liver, and since we're grilling the meat, it does not get overcooked, which liver so often is.

With a simple green salad, this is a meal in itself. Of course, you can also go ahead and serve the kebabs very simply, without the mush or the relish. But in that case, make the relish another time, because it is very versatile and very delicious.

FOR THE RELISH

4 large garlic cloves, unpeeled

1 large red bell pepper, cored, seeded, and halved

6 ripe plum tomatoes, cored

2 small red onions, peeled and halved

2 tablespoons minced canned chipotle peppers in adobo

1/2 cup olive oil

3 tablespoons roughly chopped fresh parsley

2 to 3 tablespoons fresh lime juice (1 to 2 limes)

Kosher salt and freshly cracked black pepper to taste

8 ounces slab bacon (or substitute sliced bacon)

One 2-pound piece beef liver, peeled, cleaned, and cut into twenty 1 1/2-inch cubes

1/4 cup olive oil

FOR THE CORNMEAL MUSH

4 tablespoons (1/2 stick) unsalted butter

1 small yellow onion, peeled and diced small

4 cups chicken stock (or see Stock Options, page 32)

1 cup yellow cornmeal

Kosher salt and freshly cracked black pepper to taste

1. Light a fire in your grill.

2. Double-wrap the garlic cloves in heavy-duty aluminum foil. When the fire dies down and the coals are medium-hot (you can hold your hand 5 inches above the grill surface for 3 to 4 seconds), place the garlic package in the coals to roast for 15 minutes. Place the red pepper, tomatoes, and onions on the grill grid and cook the pepper and tomatoes, turning occasionally, until the skins are charred on all sides, 5 to 6 minutes; remove them from the grill and place them in a paper bag to cool. Leave the onions on the grill and cook, turning occasionally, until they are tender all the way through, about 10 minutes. Remove from the grill.

3. When they are cool enough to handle, coarsely chop the onions and place them in a medium bowl. Pull the skins off the tomatoes, coarsely chop them, and add them to the bowl with the onions. Unwrap the garlic and squeeze the cloves out of their skins into a food processor. Remove the skin from the bell pepper, add to the food processor, along with the chipotles, and process until finely chopped. With the machine running, slowly add the olive oil. Process until smooth, stopping to scrape down the sides of the work bowl. Scrape the pepper paste into the tomato and onion mixture, then stir in the parsley, lime juice, and salt and pepper. Set aside.

4. In a small sauté pan, cook the bacon over medium-high heat until it is cooked through but not crisp, about 5 minutes. Drain on paper towels or a brown paper bag, then cut into twenty 1-inch pieces.

5. Dry the liver pieces with paper towels and thread them alternately with the bacon onto four long skewers, using 4 pieces of liver and 5 pieces of bacon on each. Brush lightly with olive oil, then set aside while you make the mush.

6. Melt the butter in a medium sauté pan over medium-high heat. Add the onion and cook, stirring occasionally, until golden brown, 11 to 13 minutes. Pour in the chicken stock, then whisk in the cornmeal. Bring the mixture to a simmer, whisking to breaking up any lumps, then reduce the heat to low and cook, stirring often, until the mush is thick and creamy without any lumps—this may take from 10 to 30 minutes. Season with salt and pepper. Cover and keep the mush warm off the heat while you grill the skewers.

7. Beef up the fire so it's very hot (you can hold your hand 5 inches above the grill surface for 1 second). Season the skewers with salt and pepper and grill until well seared on one side, about 4 minutes. Turn and continue cooking to the desired doneness, about 6 minutes total cooking time for rare. To check for doneness, nick, peek, and cheat: Make a ¼-inch cut in the thickest part of the meat; it should be slightly less done than you like it.

8. To serve, scoop some cornmeal mush onto each plate (thin it with a little hot water if it seems too thick), then top with a kebab and a hefty spoonful of relish.

A Severe Tongue Hashing with Turnips and Swiss Chard

SERVES 6

Okay, so you might not think the pun is so funny, but it has a purpose—we're trying to get your attention so you will try this dish, even if you're not a big fan of tongue. When you think about it, tongue is really no weirder than many other parts of the animal. Well, maybe you don't want to think about it. Instead, just go to the market, get some fresh tongue, and make this hash. It has plenty of earthy flavors to match the beef, and once you have tried it, we're pretty sure you will feel differently about tongue, unless you liked it to begin with.

Serve this with crusty bread and a salad of mixed greens, and you've got a wonderful Sunday supper for a cold winter night.

2 pounds fresh beef tongue, trimmed of the fatty meat at its base

1 large onion, peeled and diced large

2 bay leaves

2 whole cloves

1 teaspoon black peppercorns

3 tablespoons unsalted butter

2 medium onions, peeled and diced small

1 pound white turnips, diced large, blanched in boiling salted water until fork-tender (about 15 minutes), and drained

2 tablespoons olive oil

1 pound red chard leaves, cleaned and roughly chopped

1 tablespoon minced garlic

¼ cup lemon juice (about 1 lemon)

½ cup roughly chopped fresh parsley

Kosker salt and freshly cracked black pepper to taste

½ cup dried bread crumbs

4 tablespoons (½ stick) unsalted butter, melted

1. Place the tongue, onion, bay leaves, cloves, and peppercorns in a 5-inch-deep Dutch oven or other large heavy pot, add water to cover, and bring to a simmer over high heat. Reduce the heat to low and simmer gently until the meat is fork-tender, about 1½ to 2 hours, periodically skimming off any fat that rises to the surface. To check for doneness, plunge a fork straight down into the meat and try to pull the fork out. If the fork slides out easily, the meat is done; if the meat hangs on to the fork, give it more time. Set the cooked tongue aside to cool slightly.

2. Preheat the oven to 350°F.

3. When the tongue is cool enough to handle, peel it and dice the meat into ½-inch cubes.

4. In a large sauté pan, melt the butter over medium heat. Add the onions and cook, stirring occasionally, until translucent, 7 to 9 minutes. Transfer to a really large bowl. Add the blanched turnips to the sauté pan and cook, stirring occasionally, until heated through, about 4 minutes. Add the turnips to the bowl with the onions.

5. Return the sauté pan to the stovetop over medium-high heat, add the olive oil, and heat until hot but not smoking. Add the diced tongue and cook, stirring frequently, until lightly browned, about 6 to 8 minutes. Remove the tongue from the pan and add it to the bowl. Add the chard to the pan and cook until it is wilted and tender, about 3 minutes. Add the chard to the bowl, along with the garlic, lemon juice, parsley, and salt and pepper, and mix well.

6. Turn the hash into a buttered casserole dish. Toss the bread crumbs with the melted butter and sprinkle over the top of the hash. Bake for 15 minutes to blend the flavors. Serve hot.

OTHER CUTS YOU CAN USE

Cooked corned beef is the traditional meat here, so of course it makes a good substitute for head cheese. Or try using pastrami or thinly sliced roast beef.

Head Cheese Reuben

SERVES 4

Our friends Ihsan and Valerie Gurdal, proprietors of Formaggio Kitchen in Cambridge, Massachusetts, are adventurous eaters who know a tremendous amount about food. They feature this sandwich, which is an excellent way to eat head cheese, at their store. This is a deli meat that we particularly admire because it uses parts of the animal that might otherwise be thrown out and is quite tasty. Don't be put off by the name; if it helps, just think of it as beef pâté or sausage, which is what it actually is.

Instead of using prepared Russian dressing, it's easy to make your own. Combine equal parts ketchup and mayonnaise, a spoonful of minced sweet pickles, a dash of Worcestershire sauce, and fresh lemon juice to taste.

Serve this sandwich with napkins and a good stout or porter.

4 tablespoons (½ stick) unsalted butter, at room temperature

8 slices light rye bread

1 pound head cheese, cut into 4 thick slices

⅓ cup prepared or homemade Russian dressing

8 large, thin slices Gruyère or other Swiss cheese

One 8-ounce can sauerkraut, drained, refreshed under cold water, and drained again

1. Spread the butter over one side of each slice of bread.

2. Heat a large cast-iron skillet or heavy sauté pan over medium-high heat until quite hot. Add the head cheese, 1 slice at a time, and sear on both sides for about 1 minute, then transfer to a platter and cover with foil to keep warm.

3. Place 4 slices of the bread in the pan, buttered side down, and top each slice with a spoonful of dressing and 2 slices of cheese, followed by a generous amount of sauerkraut and then a slice of the seared head cheese. Add a bit more dressing if desired and top with the remaining 4 slices of bread, buttered side up.

4. When the bottom slices of bread are golden brown, 4 to 5 minutes, carefully turn the sandwiches over, using a large metal spatula. Cover the pan and cook over medium-low heat until the second slices of bread are golden brown, the cheese has melted, and the Reubens are heated through, 4 to 5 minutes. Remove from the pan and serve hot.

VEAL: GUESS WHO'S COMING *to* DINNER?

Veal can be a tough hombre for the home cook. By that, we don't mean that it's tough to cut or chew. Just the opposite. Veal, which is the meat of young calves, is the most tender of all red meats.

What we do mean is that veal can be tough to find, and pricey as well. Many cuts are available only in butcher shops, and some are difficult to locate outside of restaurants, period. But we've also found that, if you're willing to spend a little effort getting your hands on the various cuts of veal, you'll discover that it is a versatile and very tasty meat. Plus it has the advantage that people really don't expect you to serve it to them at home. In other words, it's so "out" that it's actually cool.

That's not to say that veal's grandiose reputation comes out of nowhere. This tender, delicate meat has occupied a rarefied culinary position for thousands of years. It was popular among the wealthy nobles of ancient Sumeria and Babylonia, and feasting on an orphaned calf was considered the ultimate extravagance among the early nomadic tribes of Central Asia. In Biblical times, the image of killing and eating a "fatted calf" (read "veal") conveyed an air of luxurious indulgence meant to mark a momentous occasion.

But when it comes to veal enthusiasm, no one can match the ancient Romans, who had a tendency to take all things culinary just a bit too far. Around the third century B.C., Roman epicures became so inordinately fond of eating veal that the emperor himself had to issue an edict forbidding the practice to avoid the depletion of the empire's herds.

Although the demand for veal never reached such near-hysterical heights again, this tender meat has continued to be popular throughout Europe. In the United States, on the other hand, veal was all but nonexistent until about forty years ago. While European farmers were pampering male calves of dairy cattle, feeding them on milk and then eggs until they were two or three months old and then slaughtering them for their pale, delicate meat, American dairy farmers were taking a different path. In this country male calves were considered nothing but a liability, since they would never grow up to give milk. So they were usually slaughtered not long after birth. The meat from these calves, known as "bob veal," was so tasteless and uninteresting that there was little demand for it.

This situation changed in the early 1960s, when Americans were introduced to the concept of formula-raised veal, an idea developed in Holland. Farmers there had found that if they fed calves on a formula comprising of skim milk, other dairy by-products, and sometimes antibiotics, they could bring larger veal to market with better-looking, more flavorful, and even more tender meat. When this technology was imported into the United States, veal became much more widely available here as well. But it has never really caught on with the majority of American cooks. Pale in color, delicate in flavor, and very expensive, veal is still perceived by most home cooks here as the prima donna of red meat, a restaurant dish intimately connected with the grand cuisines of Europe. As a result, it is the meat that we eat the least of, consuming less than one pound per person per year.

It is true that veal has largely been a restaurant item here, but that does not need to continue to be the case. To change this perception, we can look to the home cooks of Europe, who have long incorporated veal into their repertoire as a luxury item.

Food historian Waverly Root suggests that Italians are particularly fond of veal because, like pasta, it has a subtlety of flavor that allows the cook to demonstrate his or her dexterity with sauces without having the taste of the meat interfere. Whatever the strength of that hypothesis, it is true that many of the best-known dishes of the Italian classic repertoire, from saltimbocca to veal piccata to osso buco, take advantage of the delicate flavor of this young meat. The German contribution to classic veal dishes is the wide range of schnitzels, while Eastern European cooking features wonderful veal stews, and classic French cuisine contains numerous veal dishes from veal Cordon Bleu to the stew known as *blanquette de veau*.

We enjoy the dishes of this classical repertoire, in which veal tends to be combined with other subtle and often expensive ingredients, and there are quite a few incarnations of that flavor dynamic here. But we also like to push the veal envelope a bit in terms of flavor combinations, matching this delicate meat with ingredients that are a bit more robust. It works surprisingly well, particularly when the dishes in question are braises and stews.

In fact, as we widened the range of veal cuts that we were cooking, we were amazed at how well this aristocrat of meats worked in homey, rough-and-tumble dishes. It's just not the way most of us think of veal. So we did some investigating, and came up with an explanation.

Veal's surprising affinity for stews and braises derives from the same characteristic as its pale delicacy–its youth. Since veal calves do not live long enough to develop any appreciable amount of intramuscular fat, their meat is quite lean. This is generally not a great quality for meat that you want to cook long and slow, because fat helps keep meat moist and flavorful during the extended cooking process. But veal also contains a hidden advantage in the form of collagen, the structural protein that holds together muscle segments in the flesh of animals and binds the muscles to the bones. The fine muscle fibers of young animals contain a very high proportion of this connective tissue, and veal is particularly high in it. In fact, veal has about twice as much collagen, pound for pound, as even a year-old calf.

Now, it is true that collagen can make meat very tough. But when the meat is cooked slowly in the presence of moisture, the collagen melts into tender, slightly viscous gelatin. This transformation takes place far more quickly and easily in meat from young animals than from older animals. And because veal contains so much collagen, as the meat stews or braises, the gelatin that is quickly formed from the collagen almost magically transforms the cooking liquid into a sauce, imparting to it a luxuriously suave, silken texture.

So don't be intimidated by veal's haughty reputation. Get on the phone to your butcher and order up a special roast, or bring home a veal breast and braise it in some flavorful liquid, or try using veal the next time you feel like making a hearty, warming stew. We think you'll find that, despite its famed delicacy, veal doesn't have to be such a prima donna after all.

ABOUT CUTS OF VEAL

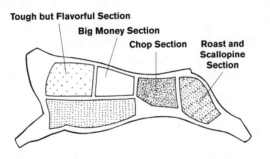

Tough but Flavorful Section
Big Money Section
Chop Section
Roast and Scallopine Section

The key to enjoying veal is finding a butcher who is willing to get the various cuts for you, because there's a lot more to veal cookery than just osso buco and wiener schnitzel, delicious as they are.

To gain an understanding of the cuts of veal, you have to face one primary fact: like it or not, a veal is a baby cow. This means that cuts of veal are basically the same as cuts of beef, but smaller and more tender.

As with the cow, we try to understand the veal calf by dividing it into four parts. Starting from the front of the animal, they are: the shoulder, which is the equivalent of the beef chuck, the Tough but Flavorful Section; next comes the rib, known by us as the Big Money Section; then there's the loin, which we call the Steak Section in the cow but will name the Chop Section in the calf; and finally the round or leg, which we called the Roast Section in the cow. Here we add a second designation, calling it the Roast and Scallopine Section.

The shoulder area provides us with one of our favorite cuts of veal, the shank, as well as a shoulder roast for braising and a shoulder blade steak, often labeled as a shoulder chop in the supermarket, which is great for grilling. The shoulder is also what we consider the best source for veal stew meat.

From the rib we get what may well be the single most expensive cut in the meat world, the rack of veal, which can be formed into the regal crown roast of veal. Any questions about why this is the Big Money Section? If you cut the rib roast into smaller cuts, it becomes the world famous veal rib chops, which would be rib-eye steaks if this were a cow. The ends of the ribs, which some people call riblets and others call short ribs, are excellent for moist cooking.

Next up is the loin, which in its entirety is the loin roast. But it is more frequently cut into loin chops, which is why we call it the Chop Section. Veal chops from the loin are the equivalent of the T-bone and porterhouse steaks. Take the bones out of these chops, and you are left with the top loin and tenderloin muscles, which may in turn be cut into strip steaks as well as veal medallions, which are the equivalent of the beef filet mignon. The loin is also the home of the veal flank; if you can find this in the butcher store, it is a very unique and interesting cut of meat, well worth searching out.

The round, or the Roast and Scallopine Section in our lexicography, is the best source for those small, flat pieces of meat known variously as scallopine, cutlets, birdies, or schnitzel. It is also home to the rump roast and, if the whole leg is cooked as a single roast, the steamship round.

Let's look at these various cuts in terms of the methods that you use to cook them.

Roasting is a great technique for veal. Because of its tenderness, basically most large cuts of veal are appropriate for roasting. Veal roasts are splendid for big gatherings or celebratory events. Our favorite is the rack of veal, otherwise known as the rib roast, which is one of the nicest restaurant cuts that you can prepare at home when you want to serve something really special. Veal loin is also exquisite, as is the rump roast, which is considerably more tender than its beef counterpart.

A cut that has recently caught the imagination of many American cooks is the veal chop, the best known of the veal cuts that are cooked by dry, high-heat methods. We're along for the ride on this one, because chops are our #1 favorite cut of veal, probably because they take so well to grilling and we love to grill. And, as we mentioned already, all those cuts that are steaks in beef are chops in veal. So, for example, the equivalent of the New York strip is the veal top loin chop. That means that veal chops, whether from the rib, the loin, or even the shoulder, are very delicious cuts indeed.

If you can get your hands on them, the über-tender tenderloin and the flavorful flank steak are also superb cuts for dry cooking. Then there is perhaps the most familiar small and tender version of veal, best known as scallopini. These are basically thin slices of veal, usually from the leg, that are cooked quickly, usually sautéed, often in breading. They are traditionally served with a pan sauce; they can also be stuffed, at which point they become known as birdies, roulades, or paupiettes. These little guys are quick-cooking, rather impressive, and a good vehicle for combining veal with other luxe ingredients from crabmeat to pancetta to Cognac.

The recent popularity of osso buco has done a lot to help popularize the braising approach to veal among American cooks. Along with the veal breast and certain cuts taken from the shoulder, the shank has a particularly high level of collagen, even for veal. All three of these create beautifully rich, silken sauces as they braise.

Veal is also perfectly suited for stews and kebabs. Fortunately, since veal is so tender, it is not as crucial as with other meats to know which cut is the source of your stew or kebab meat. So, unlike pork or beef, when you buy prepackaged "veal stew meat"—one of the few cuts of veal that is readily available in most grocery stores—it will almost always be tender enough to make good stew or tasty skewers. But if you have a choice, get cuts from the shoulder and cut them into cubes yourself, which will ensure that you get the very best flavor.

In addition to making for great stews and braises, the high collagen content of veal also makes ground veal an excellent choice for meat loaf. The same dynamic that creates a silky stewing or braising liquid makes for a meat loaf with the dense texture and rich mouth feel of a pâté.

Veal is also the best source for organ meats of all varieties, which are perfect for the "green eggs and ham" approach to cooking. You might want to reserve brains for your most adventurous friends, but sweetbreads are awesome when grilled and calf's liver, with its delicate, rich flavor and silky texture, is a surprise to anyone who has eaten only beef liver before. This is your chance to really widen your meat horizons and get a reputation as a bold and daring cook while you're at it.

OUR TOP 5 FAVORITE CUTS OF VEAL

1. **Breast**

2. **Loin chop**

3. **Shank**

4. **Sweetbreads**

5. **Flank steak**

BUYING VEAL

When it comes to choosing veal, the first choice is basically a political one, because veal is the most controversial of all red meats.

Traditionally, calves intended for veal have been raised in tight confinement, because exercise causes their muscles to develop, which in turn makes their meat less tender. They have also been fed a diet consisting largely of milk, so that their meat will be so pale as to be almost colorless. The modern version of this milk diet is the formula we talked about above, developed by Dutch farmers and introduced to the United States in the 1960s.

Veal raised in this manner is referred to as "milk-fed" or "formula-fed." It is preferred by those who value extreme tenderness and very pale meat. Some argue that only this type of veal is acceptable for use in traditional recipes.

There are others, however, who believe that raising veal in this manner is inhumane. They favor what is called "grass-fed" or "range-fed" veal. As the name implies, these calves are allowed more movement, and their diet is at least partially composed of grass. This type of veal may also be called "natural" or "humanely raised" veal. According to the USDA, it must be labeled "calf."

The meat from grass-fed veal is, as you might expect, slightly less tender than that of milk-fed veal, and it is also a darker color, a dark rosy pink. It also has a more pronounced (some would say less bland) flavor.

As more people have opted for humanely raised veal, which was once obtainable only by mail-order, it has become more readily available in butcher shops and natural food stores. There is no doubt that the raising of grass-fed veal is more humane. (We have to add, though, that no animals raised for food are really treated that well. Have you ever been to a chicken farm? So this all seems a difference of degree.) You may wish to promote this more humane approach to raising calves, or you may agree with traditionalists who maintain that meat from calves that are not raised in confinement is not really veal. The choice is up to you. As for flavor and texture of the meat, it is definitely a matter of degree; either type is going to be mild in flavor and very tender.

Other than bob veal, the meat you buy may be from calves between eight and twelve weeks of age and typically weighing between a hundred and fifty and two hundred and fifty pounds, or it may come from calves as old as sixteen weeks, with a weight of up to four hundred pounds. As with other meats, the older, the tougher, but in this case, it is just not that much of an issue. Since veal is hard to locate to begin with, we wouldn't spend a whole lot of time worrying about its exact age.

Veal is rarely graded, because all veal is tender and because marbling, the intramuscular fat that is a virtue in beef, is (or should be) all but absent from veal. So grading is not an issue. But color is. Traditionally raised veal should be a pale grayish pink, while natural veal, or calf, should be a deep rosy pink. The meat of either type should have a very fine grained texture, the fat should be firm and very white, and the marrow should be reddish.

Veal does not keep as well as other red meats. It should be stored in the refrigerator, well wrapped (see page 27), for only one or two days before you cook it. It will keep in the freezer, again well wrapped, for as long as six months, but it's really best to use it within a month or two.

Veal's moist nature also makes it particularly important that you dry it very well before you brown it. If you don't, the liquid will not only make the oil splatter all over the place, it will also cause the meat to steam rather than brown.

Because veal can be difficult to find, and because it would be a shame to miss out on the recipes in this chapter because you don't have a good source of veal, wherever it is appropriate, we have listed cuts of beef, lamb, or (most often) pork that can be substituted for the veal cut that we call for. You will also notice that in most of the recipes that follow we haven't given suggestions for using leftovers. That's not an oversight; it's because in our experience, almost no one ever buys more veal than they are planning to eat. You might think that's only because it's so expensive, but try a few of these recipes and we think you'll find another reason—it's really delicious.

RECIPES FOR
LARGE TENDER CUTS OF VEAL

Rack of Veal with Roast Chestnut Stuffing, Brandied Oranges, and Light Basil Jus

Rosemary-Crusted Roasted Rack of Veal with Exotic Mushrooms, White Wine, and Lemon

Honey-and-Bourbon-Glazed Roasted Loin of Veal with Crusty Sweet Potatoes and Smithfield Ham–Raisin Jus

Simple Veal Rump Roast with Stilton-Stuffed Apples

Veal Steamship Round with Green Olives and Oven-Dried Tomatoes

10 STEPS TO GREAT ROASTED VEAL

1. Preheat the oven.

2. Dry the meat.

3. Season the meat well.

4. Put the roast on a rack in a roasting pan, set on the middle shelf of the preheated oven, and sear it.

5. Turn down the oven temperature.

6. Add the vegetables, if any.

7. Check for doneness early and often.

8. Transfer the meat to a platter, cover loosely with foil, and allow to rest for 10 to 20 minutes, depending on size.

9. Pour off the excess fat from the pan, add stock, deglaze, and simmer to reduce the liquid.

10. Carve and serve, passing the jus separately.

There are many cuts of veal that are tender enough to dry-roast, but this is the one with the most flavor. It's a pretty fancy cut, so you will definitely be heading to your butcher for this. As always with cuts that are somewhat unusual, it pays to call a couple of days in advance to be sure the butcher can get it for you.

OTHER NAMES

Hotel rack, veal rib roast.

OTHER CUTS YOU CAN USE

A loin roast of veal, either boneless or bone-in, would work very well in this recipe. You could also substitute a pork loin or rib roast.

BUTCHERSPEAK

This cut is known in the trade as a "hotel rack," probably because it was often served in fancy hotel dining rooms in days past. If you go to any butcher who supplies meat to high-end restaurants and ask him for a hotel rack, you will get exactly what you want: a 7-bone veal roast with the bones frenched.

Rack of Veal with Roast Chestnut Stuffing, Brandied Oranges, and Light Basil Jus

SERVES 6 TO 7

If you're looking for a very impressive dish to serve for a holiday dinner, you've just found it. The rib rack has all the best attributes of veal: It is tender, it has some rich flavor, and it makes a nice foil for other somewhat subtle ingredients. Here we just sprinkle it with salt and pepper and roast it very simply, then dress it up with a chestnut stuffing, brandied oranges, and a light jus flavored with basil.

The key to making this dish, with its various components that come together at the end, is to make everything in the right order: Get the veal in the oven to brown, then make the stuffing so it can go into the oven when you turn the heat down, then brandy the oranges, and then, when the meat comes out of the oven, set it aside to rest and make the quick jus.

When you have this dish coming to the table, all you need to complete your holiday dinner is some applesauce and the green vegetable of your choice, or, if you're feeling really ambitious or have another cook who wants to chip into the effort, maybe a cheese soufflé.

One 7-bone rack of veal, frenched, about 5 pounds
Kosher salt and freshly cracked black pepper to taste

FOR THE STUFFING

3 tablespoons unsalted butter

1 red onion, peeled and diced small

1 cup celery diced small

1 tablespoon minced garlic

2 tablespoons fresh thyme leaves (or 1 tablespoon dried thyme)

5 cups 1-inch cubes country-style bread

1 cup veal or chicken stock (or see Stock Options, page 32)

One 10-ounce can chestnuts, rinsed

1/2 cup roughly chopped fresh parsley

Kosher salt and freshly cracked black pepper to taste

FOR THE ORANGES

2 tablespoons unsalted butter

5 navel oranges, peeled and pulled apart into segments

1/3 cup sugar

⅓ cup brandy or Cognac

Pinch of salt

FOR THE GRAVY

½ cup dry red wine

½ cup veal or chicken stock (or see Stock Options, page 32)

⅓ cup roughly chopped fresh basil

Kosher salt and freshly cracked black pepper to taste

1. Preheat the oven to 500°F.

2. Dry the veal and sprinkle it generously with salt and pepper. Place it on a rack in a roasting pan and roast until well browned, about 20 minutes. Reduce the oven temperature to 300°F and cook until the meat is done to your liking, 30 to 40 minutes for medium-rare. To check for doneness, insert a meat thermometer into the dead center of the roast and let it sit for 5 seconds, then read the temperature: 126°F is medium-rare, 134°F is medium, 150°F is medium-well, and 160°F is well-done; we like to pull it at 132°F.

3. Once the veal has gone into the oven, make the stuffing: In a very large sauté pan, melt the butter over medium heat. Add the onion and celery and cook, stirring occasionally, until the onion is translucent, 7 to 9 minutes. Add the garlic and thyme and sauté, stirring, for 1 minute. Add the bread cubes, stir to coat well with the butter, and sauté, stirring occasionally, until lightly toasted, 3 to 4 minutes. Turn the heat to medium-high, add the stock, and stir gently to distribute it evenly. Add the chestnuts and parsley, stir gently to mix, and season with salt and pepper. Turn the stuffing into a lightly buttered casserole dish or other ovenproof dish and cover (with aluminum foil if the dish doesn't have a cover). When you turn the oven down to 300°F for the veal, place the stuffing in the oven and cook for 30 minutes.

4. After the stuffing has gone into the oven, make the oranges: In a large sauté pan, melt the butter over medium heat. Add the orange segments and stir gently to coat with the butter. Sprinkle the sugar over the oranges, add the brandy and salt, and cook, stirring occasionally, until the oranges are well glazed, about 20 minutes. Remove from the heat and set aside.

5. When the veal is done, transfer it to a platter, tent it loosely with foil, and let it rest for 20 minutes or so.

6. Tilt the roasting pan to skim off and discard the fat that has collected in the pan, leaving the drippings behind. Place the roasting pan on the stove over medium-high heat and add the red wine and stock. Bring to a simmer, stirring to dissolve the brown crusty stuff in the bottom of the pan, and continue to simmer until the liquid is reduced by about half, about 15 minutes. Stir in the basil and season with salt and pepper.

7. Carve the rack between the bones into individual chops. Place a small serving of stuffing on each plate, place a chop on top, drizzle the basil jus over the top, put several orange segments alongside, and serve.

Rosemary-Crusted Roasted Rack of Veal with Exotic Mushrooms, White Wine, and Lemon

SERVES 7 TO 8

THE CUT
See Rack of Veal with Chestnut Stuffing (page 166) for details about rack of veal, also known as veal rib roast.

OTHER CUTS YOU CAN USE
Any veal loin roast would work great here, as would a pork loin roast.

BUTCHERSPEAK
Ask the guy behind the counter to cut through the chine bone so that you can easily slice through the roast when it's done.

We love roasts because they don't take much effort or preparation time but the end result is fantastic. The roast in question here is a rack of veal, which is what veal rib chops are before they are cut apart. So when you slice the roast, you end up serving each person a luscious veal chop. This particular preparation features the classic veal-lemon-mushroom combination, which to our minds is hard to beat. To make it easy and to really get the flavors working together, we roast the mushrooms right along with the veal, then make a sauce with them while the roast is resting after coming out of the oven.

Serve this with risotto or Hash Browns (page 412), depending on your mood, and, of course, a green salad.

3 tablespoons kosher salt, plus more to taste

3 tablespoons freshly cracked black pepper, plus more to taste

3 tablespoons fresh rosemary needles (or 1½ tablespoons dried rosemary)

2 tablespoons minced garlic

½ cup olive oil

One 7-bone rack of veal, frenched, about 5 pounds

3 pounds mushrooms of your choice (portobello, shiitake, cremini, chanterelles, enoki, etc., or even white mushrooms), trimmed and left whole if small, cut into thick slices if large

2 tablespoons vegetable oil

1 tablespoon unsalted butter

1 red onion, peeled and diced small

1 cup dry white wine

2 cups veal or chicken stock (or see Stock Options, page 32)

¼ cup roughly chopped fresh parsley

¼ cup fresh lemon juice (about 1 lemon)

1. Preheat the oven to 500°F.

2. In a small bowl, combine the salt, pepper, rosemary, garlic, and one quarter cup of the olive oil and mix well. Pat the rack of veal dry with paper towels and rub it thoroughly with this mixture, pressing lightly to be sure it adheres. Place the veal on a rack in a roasting pan (use one that will be big enough for the mushrooms to fit around the meat) and roast until well browned, about 20 minutes.

3. While the veal is browning, toss the mushrooms gently in a large bowl with the remaining ¼ cup olive oil and salt and pepper to taste.

4. When the veal is browned, add the mushrooms to the roasting pan, reduce the oven temperature to 300°F, and roast until the veal is done to your liking, 20 to 40 minutes longer for medium-rare. To check for doneness, insert a meat thermometer into the dead center of the roast and let it sit for 5 seconds, then read the temperature: 126°F is medium-rare, 134°F is medium, 150°F is medium-well, and 160°F is well-done; we like to pull it at 132°F. When the roast is done to your liking, remove it from the oven, cover it loosely with foil, and let it rest for 20 minutes or so. Remove the mushrooms from the roasting pan and set them aside.

5. In a large sauté pan, heat the vegetable oil and butter over medium-high heat until hot but not smoking. Add the onion and sauté, stirring occasionally, until translucent, 7 to 9 minutes. Add the wine and stock, bring to a simmer, and continue to simmer until reduced by two thirds, about 20 minutes. Add the mushrooms, with their accumulated juices, and cook, stirring gently, for 2 minutes more. Remove from the heat and stir in the parsley, lemon juice, and salt and pepper to taste.

6. Carve the rack into chops and serve, topped with the mushroom sauce.

The loin runs a close second to the rack of veal as top veal roast. It is very tender, of course, but it also has a good amount of flavor. That should come as no surprise, given the fact that if this were beef, it would be the section that contains those most excellent steaks, the T-bone and the porterhouse. This cut is also slightly less fatty than the rack. As with most large veal cuts, this is one you'll need to special-order from your butcher.

OTHER CUTS YOU CAN USE

Rack of veal is the natural substitute in this recipe; a pork loin roast would also be very nice.

Honey-and-Bourbon-Glazed Roasted Loin of Veal with Crusty Sweet Potatoes and Smithfield Ham–Raisin Jus

SERVES 6

Anytime you cook a big veal roast, it's an occasion. It may be a holiday, it may be a celebration of an important event in someone's life, or it may just be that you feel like cooking something special for a group of friends. That doesn't mean, though, that you can't have some fun with the dish. Here we take a very luxe piece of meat, the veal loin, and pair it with some down-home Southern flavors—bourbon, sweet potatoes, and the justly famed Smithfield ham that I (Chris) grew up with in tidewater Virginia. If you can't get your hands on a Smithfield, you can use prosciutto or any American country ham.

In keeping with the Southern slant of this dish, serve it with corn bread or grits and a big green salad.

One 3-pound boneless veal loin, fat trimmed to ¼ inch
Kosher salt and freshly cracked black pepper to taste
4 sweet potatoes, peeled and halved
2 tablespoons olive oil
½ cup honey
¼ cup bourbon

FOR THE JUS

1 cup dry red wine
1 tablespoon unsalted butter
1 red onion, peeled and diced small
2 cups veal or chicken stock (or see Stock Options, page 32)
¼ pound thinly sliced Smithfield ham, diced small (or substitute prosciutto or any American country ham)
¼ cup dark raisins
3 tablespoons roughly chopped fresh sage
Kosher salt and freshly cracked black pepper to taste

1. Preheat the oven to 350°F.

2. Dry the veal loin with paper towels, sprinkle it generously with salt and pepper, and place it on a rack in a large roasting pan. Rub the sweet potatoes with the oil and sprinkle with salt and pepper. Place the sweet potatoes around the meat. In a small bowl, combine the honey and bourbon, mix well, and brush both the veal and potatoes with the mixture.

3. Place the roasting pan in the oven and roast, basting a couple of times with the honey mixture, until the potatoes are crusty and the veal is done to your liking, 40 to 50 minutes for medium-rare. To check for doneness, insert a meat thermometer into the dead center of the roast and let it sit for 5 seconds, then read the temperature: 126°F is medium-rare, 134°F is medium, 150°F is medium-well, and 150°F is well-done; we like to pull it at 132°F. When the roast is done to your liking, remove it from the oven, cover it loosely with foil, and let it rest for 20 minutes or so.

4. Tilt the roasting pan and spoon off any accumulated fat from the pan juices. Place the pan on the stove over medium-high heat, add the wine, and cook, stirring to dissolve the brown crusty stuff in the bottom of the pan, about 4 minutes. Remove from the heat and set aside.

5. In a large sauté pan, melt the butter over medium heat. Add the onion and cook, stirring occasionally, until translucent, 7 to 9 minutes. Raise the heat to medium-high, add the stock, and simmer until the sauce is reduced by two thirds and thick enough to coat the back of a spoon, 10 to 15 minutes. Add the wine and crusty bits from the roasting pan, the ham, and raisins and cook, stirring, for 2 minutes more. Remove from the heat, stir in the sage, and season with salt and pepper.

6. Cut the veal into slices about 1 inch thick, drizzle it and the potatoes with the jus, and serve.

Like the beef rump roast, this is what its name says: the rump of the beast. While some people feel that the beef rump roast is a little tough for dry-roasting, there are no such qualms about the veal rump. Like most veal roasts, this is one you're going to have to call ahead and reserve at your butcher shop.

Rump of veal.

Any veal roast will work very well with this recipe. You can also use any tender roast of pork.

Simple Veal Rump Roast with Stilton-Stuffed Apples

SERVES 4

This is a pretty straight-ahead French-derived preparation, which works well with the veal rump roast. As with many French dishes, its flavor base is a trio of everyday vegetables—onions, carrots, and celery—that, when chopped and sautéed together in a little fat, are called a *mirepoix*.

Not being French, we had to add some cheese-stuffed apples to give the dish an American feel. Put the apples in the oven when you reduce the heat after browning the veal; they need to spend longer in the low-temperature oven than the meat does, but that just means that the meat has a chance to rest and get its juices redistributed before you carve it.

This is a grand dish for that fall evening when you want to feel as if you're ready for the winter to come. And since it's veal, it has a certain air of luxury about it too.

One 3-pound boneless veal rump roast

Kosher salt and freshly cracked black pepper to taste

2 onions, peeled and diced medium

1 carrot, peeled and diced medium

1 stalk celery, diced medium

1/3 cup olive oil

FOR THE APPLES

3 tablespoons unsalted butter, at room temperature

4 Golden Delicious, Rome, Cortland, Baldwin, or Northern Spy apples, peeled and cored

1/4 cup honey

1/4 cup dry red wine

1/2 cinnamon stick (or 1/2 teaspoon ground cinnamon)

2 cardamom pods, crushed (or a pinch of ground cardamom)

8 ounces Stilton or other blue cheese of your choice

1 cup dry red wine

2 teaspoons dried thyme

1 whole clove

1 cup veal or chicken stock (or see Stock Options, page 32)

2 tablespoons roughly chopped fresh parsley

1. Preheat the oven to 500°F.

2. Dry the veal with paper towels and sprinkle it generously with salt and pepper. Place it on a rack in a roasting pan and roast until well browned, about 20 minutes.

3. While the veal is browning, prepare the vegetables and the apples: For the vegetables, combine the onions, carrot, celery, and olive oil in a large bowl, toss well to coat, and set aside. For the apples, using the 3 tablespoons of butter, butter a casserole dish just big enough to hold the apples comfortably and arrange the apples upright in it. In a small saucepan, combine the honey, wine, cinnamon, and cardamom and simmer for about 5 minutes. Brush the apples generously with this mixture and set them aside.

4. When the veal has browned, reduce the oven temperature to 300°F and add the vegetables to the roasting pan. Roast, stirring the vegetables around once or twice, until the meat is done to your liking, about 40 minutes more for medium-rare. To check for doneness, insert a meat thermometer into the dead center of the roast and let it sit for 5 seconds, then read the temperature: 126°F is medium-rare, 134°F is medium, 150°F is medium-well, and 160°F is well-done; we like to pull it at 126°F.

5. Meanwhile when you add the vegetables to the roasting pan, place the apples in the oven on a separate rack. Bake the apples, basting frequently with more of the wine mixture, for 30 minutes. Remove the apples from the oven, crumble the cheese, and push a quarter of it into the center of each apple. Return the apples to the oven and bake until quite soft, about 30 minutes more.

6. When the roast is done to your liking, remove it from the oven, cover it loosely with foil, and let it rest for 20 minutes while you make the sauce.

7. Tilt the roasting pan and spoon off any accumulated fat from the pan juices. Place the pan on the stove over medium-high heat, add the wine, and cook, stirring to dissolve the brown crusty stuff in the bottom of the pan, about 2 minutes. Add the thyme, clove, and stock, bring to a simmer, and skim any scum off the surface of the meat, then simmer until the liquid is slightly reduced, about 5 minutes. Stir in the parsley and remove from the heat.

8. Carve the roast into thin slices. Put an apple on each plate, arrange some of the meat around it, drizzle with the sauce, and serve.

A "steamship round" is the name that professional chefs give to a whole leg of beef. As nearly as we can tell, it got its name because it used to be the main attraction of the "carving tables" on steamships. In any case, a steamship round of beef is so big that it requires professional-size cooking equipment. But here we take advantage of the smaller size of veal cuts, and basically call for a whole leg of veal cut in the manner of a steamship round. You'll really have to talk to your butcher about this, because it is a very odd request. But we are willing to lay odds that he will be happy and impressed that you are even attempting something like this. Obviously, this is a cut for a very special occasion, but it's got great flavor and that incredible smooth, tight veal texture, so your guests will love it.

Veal Steamship Round with Green Olives and Oven-Dried Tomatoes

SERVES 30 OR MORE

What the heck is this, you might ask? Well, it's a whole leg of veal. This is a real carnivore's feast, the kind of thing that comes to mind when they talk about "a haunch of meat" in old English novels. At first it might seem a little daunting, but when all is said and done, it's really just a large roast. You rub it, you put it in the oven, you brown it at 500°F, and then you turn down the heat and cook it for a long time, checking with your trusty thermometer to be sure you don't overcook it. Because of the size of the roast (which may not fit in your oven—check first to be sure), there is a margin of error here of about an hour, so you need to keep checking doneness over quite a long period of time. But, assuming you've got a large enough roasting pan, it's really no harder to cook than any other roast, which means not hard at all.

And it is worth it, because this is a cut of meat that will get you a lot of distance with friends and family. This is what I (Chris) served when my wife, Marcy Jackson, and I had our "families meet and greet" event at my house shortly after we got engaged. I chose to prepare this for my fiancée's friends and family in the hope that they might like me, and it worked. I'm still very popular with my in-laws to this day as a result of cooking this for them, despite all the things I have done to them since then. In fact, it worked so well that Marcy and I also served it at our wedding. If you cook this and serve it the way that I did, you will have some happy guests. (Also, it's a perfect excuse to have all your friends over at the same time and repay all those social debts in one fell swoop.)

We call for oven-dried tomatoes here, which you need to prepare in advance, since they require even more time in the oven than the steamship round. But you can literally do this in your sleep—just put the tomatoes in a low oven and leave them overnight. You will be surprised at the luscious texture and deep flavors of tomatoes you have dried yourself. If you run out of time, though, you can substitute store-bought sun-dried tomatoes (not the oil-marinated kind) that you have soaked in warm water for a couple of hours.

I served this to my future in-laws with some nice crusty bread, some eggplant chutney, and some mango chutney and had people make roast veal sandwiches. I recommend you try it that way too.

FOR THE TOMATOES

12 plum tomatoes

3 tablespoons extra virgin olive oil

Kosher salt and freshly cracked black pepper to taste

1 tablespoon minced fresh rosemary (optional)

1 veal steamship round, about 25 pounds

2 cups kosher salt

2 cups freshly cracked black pepper

4 onions, peeled and diced small

6 stalks celery, diced small

4 carrots, peeled and diced small

2 heads garlic, halved

1 bottle dry white wine

4 cups veal or chicken stock (or see Stock Options, page 32)

2 cups brine-cured green olives, pitted

1 cup fresh thyme leaves (or 6 tablespoons dried)

1. Prepare the tomatoes: Cut the tomatoes lengthwise in half, rub them with the oil, and sprinkle them with salt and pepper and the rosemary if desired. Place the tomatoes cut side up in a single layer on a wire rack set on a cookie sheet and place the sheet on the middle rack of the oven. Turn the oven to 200°F and let the tomatoes dry for about 8 hours; they should be reduced in size by about one quarter and shriveled on the outside but still tender and juicy on the inside. Remove from the oven and set aside. (They can be covered and refrigerated for 4 to 5 days.)

2. Preheat the oven to 500°F.

3. Rub the veal all over with the salt and pepper, pressing gently to be sure they adhere. Place the meat on a rack in a very large roasting pan and roast until well browned, about 30 minutes. Reduce the heat to 300°F and add the onions, celery, carrots, and garlic to the pan. Cook, stirring the vegetables around every 30 minutes or so, until the veal is done to your liking, 3 to 4 hours for medium-rare. To check for doneness, insert a meat thermometer into the dead center of the roast and let it sit for 5 seconds, then read the temperature: 126°F is medium-rare, 134°F is medium, 140°F is medium-well, and 160°F is well-done; we like to pull it at 132°F. When the roast is done, remove it from the oven, cover it loosely with foil, and let it rest for at least 20 and up to 40 minutes.

4. Place the roasting pan over 2 burners on the stove over medium-high heat and add the wine and stock. Bring to a simmer, stirring to dissolve any brown crusty stuff in the bottom of the pan. Strain the liquid into a large saucepan, discarding the solids. Skim the fat off the surface of the liquid, then add the olives and tomatoes, bring to a simmer, and simmer until the liquid is reduced by about half, 15 to 20 minutes. Remove from the heat and stir in the thyme.

5. Carve the veal into thin slices and serve, moistening with the pan sauce and passing the remaining sauce separately.

RECIPES FOR
LARGE TOUGH CUTS OF VEAL

10 STEPS TO GREAT BRAISED VEAL

1. Dry the meat.

2. Season the meat well.

3. Sear the meat.

4. Remove the meat from the pot, adjust the amount of fat in the pot, and sauté the aromatics and vegetables.

5. Deglaze the pot with some of the liquid.

6. Return the meat to the pot, along with enough liquid to cover it about halfway.

7. Bring to a simmer, skim the film, cover the pot, and place in a 300°F oven.

8. Check for doneness early and often: Look for "fork-tender."

9. Skim the fat and any film from the liquid and, if you want, remove the meat and reduce the liquid; season to taste.

10. Carve the meat and serve with the braising liquid on the side.

This cut is just what the name says: the breast of the veal. It is quite cheap for veal, because it has a lot of fat and bones. But if cooked long and slow, it becomes very tender, and it is perhaps the most flavorful veal cut of all. You will have to order this in advance from your butcher, but it's not that unusual a cut for him, and when you place the order, the butcher's estimation of your meat knowledge will definitely go up a notch.

OTHER CUTS YOU CAN USE

A great substitute here would be a bone-in pork belly, a.k.a. bone-in rack of pork ribs.

BUTCHERSPEAK

The veal breast is very often stuffed before it's cooked, so butchers are used to cutting it with a pocket for the stuffing. But stuffing the breast is a tedious task, and the stuffing often leaks out anyway, so we prefer to cook it straight on. Make sure your butcher knows you don't want a pocket in the breast. But do ask him to nick the chine bone so you can get between the ribs to serve the meat. Some people say that the middle section of the breast is the best, but in our experience, there is more variation in quality from breast to breast than within a single breast.

Latin-Style Barbecued Veal Breast with Sour Orange–Chipotle Barbecue Sauce

SERVES 6 TO 8

This is one of our absolute favorite cuts of veal. It is filled with bones and fat, but if you cook it up over the slow heat and smoke of a low fire, you will have one of the finest eating experiences of your life. What we're talking about here is basically veal bacon; it is tender, juicy, and full of flavor, and this is definitely one place where the mild nature of veal becomes a real advantage.

So we're going bold with this cut. First we rub it with a flavorful paste and let it sit over the fire for 4 hours, then coat it with a barbecue sauce with the flavors of Latin America. (If you have access to sour oranges, use them in place of regular juice oranges in the barbecue sauce, and reduce the lime juice by half.)

If you take the time to order this from your butcher and prepare this recipe, I guarantee that you will be a hero to your cooking friends. Try serving with sweet corn, a sweet potato salad, or maybe a Sweet Potato–Raisin Hobo Pack (page 441).

FOR THE SAUCE

2 cups fresh orange juice (about 4 oranges)

1 cup dry red wine

1 to 2 tablespoons minced canned chipotle chiles in adobo

1/3 cup molasses

1/4 cup fresh lime juice (about 2 limes)

1/2 cup roughly chopped fresh cilantro

1/4 cup olive oil

1/3 cup fresh lemon juice (about 1 1/2 lemons)

1/4 cup minced garlic

1/4 cup cumin seeds (or 2 tablespoons ground cumin)

1/4 cup kosher salt

1/4 cup freshly cracked black pepper

1/2 cup roughly chopped fresh oregano

10 to 15 dashes Tabasco sauce

1 small veal breast or a portion of a larger breast, 6 to 8 pounds (with no pockets)

1. Make the sauce: In a small saucepan, bring the orange juice, wine, and chipotles to a boil over high heat. Reduce the heat to medium-low and simmer vigorously until the liquid is reduced to 1½ cups, about 30 minutes. Remove from the heat, stir in the molasses, lime juice, and cilantro, and set aside.

2. Light a fire well over to one side of a kettle grill, using enough charcoal to fill half a shoe box.

3. In a small bowl, combine the oil, lemon juice, garlic, cumin, salt, pepper, oregano, and Tabasco sauce and mix well. Dry the meat with paper towels, then rub it all over with this mixture, pressing to be sure it adheres. When the fire dies down and the coals are very hot, place the meat on the side of the grill away from the coals, being careful that none of the meat is directly over the coals. Put the lid on the grill, open the vents one quarter of the way, and cook until the meat is super-tender, about 3 hours, adding a handful of fresh charcoal about every 30 minutes. To check for doneness, stick a fork straight down into the meat and try to pull the fork out. If the fork slides out easily, the meat is done; if the meat hangs on to the fork, give it more time.

4. When the meat is cool enough to handle, slice it between the bones. Add enough of the barbecue sauce to moisten the meat well, then serve, passing the remaining barbecue sauce on the side.

See Latin-Style Barbecued
Veal Breast (page 178) for
details on veal breast and
how to get what you want
when buying it. You'll most
likely have to call your
butcher in advance to get
this cut.

Beer-Braised Veal Breast with Macumber Turnips and Greens

SERVES 6 TO 8

Here's another dish featuring our #1 favorite cut of veal, the bone-in breast. As befits this homely piece of meat, this is a real country-style dish with a lot of root vegetables, including both parts of the turnip, root and greens. When you dip your spoon into the broth of this dish, with the rich meat and earthy turnips balanced by the slight bitterness of the greens and beer, you're going to be one happy eater.

We like to use the Macumber turnip, a local variety grown only in the region around Westport, Massachusetts. It's particularly sweet, since it is actually a cross between a rutabaga and a radish. In other parts of the country, you can use regular turnips (preferably whatever is grown closest to you) or rutabagas. If you don't have access to turnip greens, substitute some other slightly bitter green such as collards, kale, or (our favorite) mustard greens.

Like many other flavorful cuts, the veal breast is quite fatty, so be sure that you skim a lot of fat off the braising liquid at the end of the cooking process.

3 tablespoons olive oil, or more if needed

One 5- to 6-pound veal breast (with no pocket)

Kosher salt and freshly cracked black pepper to taste

2 onions, peeled, halved, and thinly sliced

2 carrots, peeled and cut into 1-inch chunks

2 tablespoons minced garlic

8 ounces cooked ham, diced small

1 cup balsamic vinegar

Two 12-ounce bottles dark beer of your choice

2 tablespoons dark brown sugar

1 bay leaf

3 allspice berries (or substitute 1 whole clove)

1 pound turnip greens or other cooking greens of your choice, trimmed, washed, and roughly chopped

1½ pounds Macumber turnips (or substitute rutabagas or small, young turnips), peeled and cut into chunks about the size of a golf ball

About 1 cup veal or chicken stock (or see Stock Options, page 32)

1. Preheat the oven to 300°F.

2. In a large roasting pan or Dutch oven wide enough to hold the veal breast comfortably, heat the oil over medium-high heat until very hot but not smoking. Dry the veal with the paper towels, sprinkle it generously with salt and pepper, and brown it well on all sides, 8 to 10 minutes total. Transfer the veal to a platter.

3. Pour off the fat or add oil to the pan as needed so you have a total of about 2 tablespoons in the pan. Add the onions and carrots to the pan and cook, stirring occasionally, until the onions are golden brown, 10 to 12 minutes. Add the garlic and ham and cook, stirring, for 2 minutes. Add the vinegar and beer and bring to a simmer, scraping up any browned bits from the bottom of the pan.

4. Return the veal to the pan along with the brown sugar, bay leaf, allspice, greens, turnips, and enough stock so the liquid comes to about halfway up the sides of the meat. Bring to a simmer and skim any scum off the surface, then cover (foil works well if using a roasting pan), place in the oven, and cook until the meat is very tender, about 3 hours. To check for doneness, plunge a fork straight down into the meat and try to pick up the meat. If the fork slides out, the meat is done; if the meat hangs on to the fork, give it more time.

5. When the meat is done, remove it from the pan, cover it loosely with foil, and set it aside.

6. Skim the fat from the cooking liquid, then taste the liquid. If it needs more flavor, remove the greens and turnips with a slotted spoon, place the roasting pan on the stove over two burners set at medium-high, and simmer to reduce the liquid. Replace the greens and turnips. Season to taste with salt and pepper.

7. To serve, slice the meat and spoon the sauce, greens, and turnips over and around it.

Veal shanks can come either from the front (fore) leg of the animal or the rear leg. Either one of them will work perfectly well in this dish, but we have a slight preference for the foreshank, which is just a bit more tender. The hind shank, on the other hand, tends to be a little meatier. You can very often find this cut in the supermarket, and any good butcher will have them.

OTHER CUTS YOU CAN USE

You can substitute lamb shanks or pork osso buco for the veal shanks, but then you might want to use red wine instead of white in the braising liquid.

BUTCHERSPEAK

Since a lot of flavor comes from the marrow in the center of the shanks, you want to get shanks with nice, soft, creamy marrow. If they're not packaged in cellophane, press the centers to be sure they are soft.

Tomato-Braised Veal Shanks with Pumpkin Risotto and Lemon-Pistachio Power Pack

SERVES 6

Due to the Italian dish called osso buco (literally, "bone with hole"), veal shanks have become quite popular in the United States. This is good because it has made them more readily available, but bad because they are also much more expensive than they used to be. They do deserve their new-found place of honor, though. When cooked slowly, they create a very rich flavorful, silken-textured sauce that is fantastic—and the meat itself is delicious too.

This is a classic osso buco–style dish, complete with risotto and our takeoff on gremolata, both of which are traditionally served with osso buco. Of course, you can also serve the shanks over pasta or plain rice if you don't feel like making the risotto—but it's really good.

All you need with this is a green salad, maybe with a bit of cheese, and you've got a fantastic meal.

3 tablespoons olive oil, or more if needed

Six 8- to 12-ounce veal foreshanks (or substitute hind shanks)

Kosher salt and freshly cracked black pepper to taste

2 large onions, peeled and diced large

6 ripe plum tomatoes, peeled, quartered, and seeded

1 head garlic, peeled and minced

2 cups dry white wine

About 1 cup veal or chicken stock (or see Stock Options, page 32)

FOR THE POWER PACK

2 teaspoons minced garlic

2 teaspoons finely grated orange zest

1 teaspoon finely grated lemon zest

2 teaspoons finely chopped anchovy fillets (optional)

1/3 cup roughly chopped fresh parsley

1/3 cup roughly chopped salted pistachios

FOR THE RISOTTO

5 cups chicken stock (or see Stock Options, page 32)

6 tablespoons (3/4 stick) unsalted butter

2 small onions, peeled and diced small

1 pound pumpkin or other winter squash, peeled, seeded, and diced medium (about 4 cups)

2 teaspoons minced garlic

2 cups arborio rice

1 cup dry white wine or dry vermouth

$\frac{1}{2}$ cup freshly grated Parmesan cheese

Kosher salt and freshly cracked black pepper to taste

1. Preheat the oven to 300°F.

2. In a 5-inch-deep Dutch oven or other heavy ovenproof pot with a lid, heat the oil over medium-high heat until very hot but not smoking. Dry the shanks with paper towels and sprinkle generously with salt and pepper. Add them to the pot in a single layer, in batches if necessary to avoid crowding, and cook until well browned on all sides, about 15 minutes total; transfer the shanks to a platter as they are done.

3. Pour off the fat or add oil to the pot as needed so you have a total of about 3 tablespoons in the pot. Add the onions and cook, stirring occasionally, until golden brown, 11 to 13 minutes. Add the tomatoes and garlic and cook, stirring, for 5 minutes more. Pour in the wine and bring to a simmer, stirring to dissolve the brown crusty stuff in the bottom of the pot.

4. Return the shanks to the pot and add enough stock to come halfway up the sides of the shanks. Bring to a simmer and skim any scum off the surface, then cover the pot, place it in the oven, and cook until the meat is tender and comes easily off the bone, about 2 hours.

5. While the shanks are cooking, combine the power pack ingredients in a small bowl and mix well, then cover and refrigerate until serving time.

6. When the shanks have been cooking for about 1½ hours, begin making the risotto: In a small saucepan, bring the stock to a boil over medium-high heat, then reduce the heat to low and keep at a simmer. In a large sauté pan, melt the butter over medium heat. Add the onions and pumpkin and cook, stirring occasionally, until the onions are translucent, 7 to 9 minutes. Add the garlic and cook, stirring, for 1 minute. Add the rice, stirring to coat with the butter, and cook until the rice just begins to color, 3 to 4 minutes. Add the wine and then the simmering stock ½ cup at a time, stirring very frequently until all the liquid is absorbed each time before adding more. It should take 25 to 30 minutes to add all of the liquid. Remove the pan from the heat and stir in the Parmesan cheese. Season with salt and pepper.

7. When the shanks are done, remove them from the pot, cover loosely with foil, and set aside. Skim the fat from the cooking liquid. Taste the liquid and, if you think it needs more flavor, place the pot on the stove over medium-high heat and simmer to reduce the liquid. Season with salt and pepper.

8. To serve, place a serving of risotto on each plate, top with a shank, drizzle with the sauce, and sprinkle with the power pack.

THE CUT

See Tomato-Braised Veal Shanks (page 182) for details about veal shanks.

OTHER CUTS YOU CAN USE

You can substitute lamb shanks, and we actually like this recipe made with beef short ribs too.

EZ–Style Sherry-Braised Veal Shank with Raisins and Parsley

SERVES 4

This is a simple approach to shanks, which works well because it is a very favorable cut in and of itself. To us, the best part of a veal shank is sucking the marrow out of the bones, so make sure you do this. The classic way is to use small-bowled, long-handled spoons that are made just for this purpose and are called (oddly enough) marrow spoons. If you have ice tea spoons, they usually work pretty well–or you can just use a narrow-bladed knife.

Serve this with a side of risotto or pasta and a salad of arugula with blue cheese and olives.

Four 12- to 14-ounce veal hind shanks
Kosher salt and freshly cracked black pepper to taste
Flour for dredging
1/4 cup olive oil, or more if needed
1 large red onion, peeled and diced small
2 carrots, peeled and diced small
2 stalks celery, diced small
1 tablespoon minced garlic
2 plum tomatoes, cored and diced medium
1/2 cup dark raisins
1 cup sherry
2 tablespoons minced anchovies (optional)
About 2 cups veal or chicken stock (or see Stock Options, page 32)
1/4 cup roughly chopped fresh parsley

1. Preheat the oven to 300°F.

2. Dry the shanks with paper towels, sprinkle them generously with salt and pepper, and dredge them lightly with the flour, shaking off any excess. In a 5-inch-deep Dutch oven or a large ovenproof pot with a lid, heat the oil over medium-high heat until hot but not smoking. Add the shanks in a single layer, in batches if necessary to avoid crowding, and brown well on all sides, about 15 minutes total. Transfer the shanks to a platter as they are done and set aside.

3. Pour off the fat or add oil to the pot as needed so you have a total of about 2 tablespoons in the pot. Add the onion, carrots, and celery and cook, stirring occasionally, until the onions are translucent, 7 to 9 minutes. Add the garlic and tomatoes and cook, stirring, for 1 minute. Add the raisins and sherry and bring to a simmer, stirring to dissolve the brown crusty stuff on the bottom of the pan.

4. Add the veal shanks, along with the anchovies, if using, and enough stock to come halfway up the sides of the shanks. Bring to a simmer and skim any scum from the surface of the liquid, then place in the oven and cook until the shanks are tender, 1½ to 2 hours. To check for doneness, plunge a fork straight down into the meat and try to pull the fork out. If the fork slides out easily, the meat is done; if the meat hangs on to the fork, give it more time.

5. When the shanks are done, remove them from the pot, cover loosely with foil, and set aside. Skim the fat from the cooking liquid. Taste the liquid, and if you think it needs more flavor, place the pot on the stove over two burners set at medium-high heat and simmer to reduce the liquid. Stir in the parsley and season with salt and pepper.

6. Serve the shanks splashed with a generous amount of the braising liquid, passing any remaining liquid separately.

You can use either the arm roast or the blade roast of veal here. The arm is a thicker cut, but since this is veal, it will still be tender. You might be able to pick up a veal shoulder roast in a supermarket, but you're likely to get a better-quality roast at your butcher.

OTHER NAMES

For arm roast, veal round bone roast.

OTHER CUTS YOU CAN USE

Shoulder roasts of lamb, pork, or beef will work perfectly well in this recipe. Or you can substitute veal shoulder steaks. If you do, use a roasting pan rather than a Dutch oven so you have more surface area. That way, the same amount of liquid will still only come halfway up the sides of the meat.

Orange-Braised Veal Shoulder with Sweet-and-Sour Braised Cabbage and Fennel Slaw

SERVES 6

The shoulder of veal is a perfect illustration of a paradox about this meat: Although it is younger and therefore more tender than beef, veal has more collagen, the connective tissue that can make older meat tough. This means that, when cooked long and slow by a moist-heat method such as braising, veal creates a particularly rich, silky liquid.

Here we use a roast from the shoulder for a dish with Alsatian overtones that would be great on a cold fall or winter afternoon. Notice that the cabbage goes in the oven after the veal has been cooking for about half an hour and comes out after one hour even if the veal is not quite done yet.

Serve this with Mashed Potatoes (page 413) or buttered noodles and a nice Alsatian wine.

2 tablespoons olive oil, or more if needed

One 4-pound veal shoulder roast

Kosher salt and freshly cracked black pepper to taste

2 red onions, peeled and diced small

1 cup dry red wine

2 cups orange juice

1/2 cup red wine vinegar

FOR THE CABBAGE

2 tablespoons olive oil

1 medium head red cabbage, cored and thinly sliced

1/2 cup red wine vinegar

1/4 cup sugar

1/4 cup dark raisins

2 tablespoons caraway seeds

Kosher salt and freshly cracked black pepper to taste

FOR THE SLAW

1 cup thinly sliced fennel

1/4 cup fresh lemon juice (about 1 lemon)

1/4 cup roughly chopped fresh parsley

1. Preheat the oven to 300°F.

2. In a 5-inch-deep Dutch oven or other large ovenproof pot with a lid, heat the oil over medium-high heat until very hot but not smoking. Dry the veal roast with paper towels and sprinkle it generously with salt and pepper. Place it in the Dutch oven and brown well on all sides, about 8 minutes per side. Transfer the meat to a platter and set aside.

3. Pour off the fat or add oil to the pot as needed so you have a total of about 2 tablespoons in the pot. Add the onions and cook, stirring occasionally, until translucent, 7 to 9 minutes. Add the red wine and bring to a simmer, stirring to dissolve the brown crusty stuff in the bottom of the pot, then continue to simmer until the wine is reduced by half, about 10 minutes.

4. Return the meat to the pot, add the orange juice and vinegar, and bring to a simmer again. Skim any scum from the surface of the liquid, then cover the pot, place it in the oven, and braise until the meat is very tender, 1½ to 2 hours. To check for doneness, plunge a fork straight down into the meat and try to pull the fork out. If the fork slides out easily, the meat is done; if the meat hangs on to the fork, give it more time.

5. Meanwhile, make the cabbage: In another Dutch oven or large ovenproof pot, heat the oil over medium-high heat until hot but not smoking. Add the cabbage and cook, stirring occasionally, until softened, 5 to 7 minutes. Add the vinegar, sugar, raisins, and caraway seeds, season with salt and pepper, and mix well. Cover and braise along with the meat for its last hour of cooking. (Be sure to take the cabbage out of the oven after 1 hour even if the meat is not quite done yet.)

6. While the cabbage and meat are cooking, make the slaw: In a medium bowl, combine the fennel, lemon juice, and parsley and mix well.

7. When the meat is done, remove it from the pot, cover it loosely with foil, and set it aside. Skim the fat from the braising liquid, then taste it. If it needs more flavor, place the pot on the stove over medium-high heat and simmer to reduce the liquid. Season with salt and pepper.

8. To serve, slice the veal into slices about 1 inch thick. Place a bed of braised cabbage on each plate, top with several slices of veal, and drizzle generously with the braising liquid; pass the remaining braising liquid and the slaw separately.

RECIPES FOR
SMALL TENDER CUTS OF VEAL

10 STEPS TO GREAT GRILLED VEAL

1. Build a two-level fire using hardwood charcoal.

2. Wait for the flames to die down and the coals to be covered with gray ash.

3. Check the temperature of the fire.

4. Dry the meat well.

5. Season the meat well.

6. Sear the meat over a hot fire.

7. Move the meat to the cooler part of the fire if it needs to cook more slowly (don't use the cover).

8. Flip the meat only once during cooking.

9. Check for doneness early and often (nick, peek, and cheat).

10. Remove the meat from the heat, cover with foil and allow it to rest, then serve it up.

Seared Veal Tenderloins over Watercress and Walnuts with Blue Cheese–Madeira Sauce

Hazelnut-Crusted Veal Tenderloin with Roasted Grapes and Port

Broiled Veal Loin Chop with Exotic Mushrooms, Bacon, and Sherry

Grilled Veal Loin Chops with Spicy Green Olive and Sun-Dried Tomato Relish

Simple Grilled Veal Rib Chops with Smoky Portobello Relish

Grilled Veal Shoulder Chops with Nectarine-Ginger Chutney and Cucumbers with Mint and Yogurt

Grilled Veal T-Bones with a Hobo Pack of Fig, Prosciutto, and Spinach

Sautéed Medallions of Veal with Artichoke Hearts, Lemon, and Thyme

Paillard of Veal with Pancetta, White Mushrooms, and Madeira

Spicy Pan-Seared Veal Loin Medallions with Anchovies and Green Olives

Panfried Veal Cutlets in the German Style

Veal Birdies Tidewater-Style, with Smithfield Ham, Backfin Crab, and Lemon-Caper Sauce

Mango-Stuffed Veal Birdies with Cognac–Green
Peppercorn Sauce

Veal Stir-fry on Big Fried Polenta Croutons

Grilled Veal, Sweet Potato, and Red Onion Kebabs in the
Piccata Style

Grilled Veal Flank Steak on Texas Toast with Yellow Tomato
Chutney and Balsamic Raisins

**10 STEPS TO GREAT SAUTÉED
VEAL**

1. Use a big heavy sauté
   pan.

2. Dry the meat well.

3. Season the meat well.

4. Use only a small
   amount of oil.

5. Get the pan and the
   oil hot.

6. Don't overcrowd the
   meat in the pan.

7. Sear the meat.

8. Flip the meat only once
   while cooking.

9. Check for doneness
   early and often (nick,
   peek, and cheat).

10. Remove the meat from
    the heat, cover with
    foil, and allow to rest,
    then serve.

**10 STEPS TO GREAT BROILED
VEAL**

Check out sautéing:
The steps are the same
except you use a
broiler pan instead of a
sauté pan, preheat the
broiler instead of get-
ting the oil hot, and
skip the searing step.

See Hazelnut-Crusted Veal
Tenderloin (page 192) for
details on the veal tenderloin and how to buy it. For
this cut, you probably need
to call your butcher and
have him order it for you.

OTHER CUTS YOU CAN USE

You can substitute bone-
less veal chops in this
recipe, or you can go with
pork tenderloins.

Seared Veal Tenderloins over Watercress and Walnuts with Blue Cheese–Madeira Sauce

SERVES 4

This dish is all about richness. You've got the rich veal, the rich blue cheese, and the rich, sweet Madeira wine. But don't be put off—it is a fantastic combination.

A key to this dish is lightly browning the veal tenderloin in a sauté pan, then transferring it to the oven to finish cooking. This is actually very similar to a classic grilling technique in which you sear meat over a hot fire, then move it to a slow fire to finish cooking. That way, you get good flavor on the outside of the meat but don't overcook the inside.

We like this dish as a high-class lunch, served with simple steamed green beans and roasted sweet potatoes or squash.

2 veal tenderloins, about 1 pound each

Kosher salt and freshly cracked black pepper to taste

3 tablespoons olive oil

1/2 red onion, peeled and diced small

1/2 cup semi-dry Madeira (or substitute dry red wine)

1 cup veal or chicken stock (or see Stock Options, page 32)

1/4 cup crumbled blue cheese of your choice

1/4 cup roughly chopped fresh parsley

FOR THE WATERCRESS

1/3 cup extra virgin olive oil

2 tablespoons fresh lemon juice (about 1 lemon)

Kosher salt and freshly cracked black pepper to taste

2 small bunches watercress, trimmed, washed, and dried

1/4 cup chopped walnuts, toasted in a dry skillet over medium heat, shaking frequently, until fragrant, 3 to 5 minutes

1. Preheat the oven to 300°F.

2. Dry the tenderloins with paper towels and sprinkle generously with salt and pepper. In a sauté pan large enough to hold the two tenderloins comfortably, heat 2 tablespoons of the oil over medium-high heat until hot but not smoking. Add the tenderloins to the pan and brown well on all sides, 12 to 15 minutes total.

3. Transfer the meat to a small roasting pan, place in the oven, and roast to an internal temperature of 130°F for medium-rare, 12 to 15 minutes. (Or nick, peek, and cheat: Make a ¼-inch cut in the thickest part of the meat; it should be slightly less done than you like it.) Remove from the pan, cover loosely with foil, and allow to rest for 10 minutes before slicing.

4. Meanwhile, return the sauté pan to medium-high heat, add the remaining 1 tablespoon oil, and heat until hot but not smoking. Add the onion and cook, stirring occasionally, until translucent, 7 to 9 minutes. Add the Madeira and cook, stirring, for 1 minute. Add the stock, bring to a simmer, and simmer until it is reduced by about half, 10 to 15 minutes. Remove the sauce from the heat, skim any scum off the surface, and stir in the blue cheese, parsley, and salt and pepper to taste. Set aside, covered to keep the sauce warm.

5. In a small bowl, whisk together the extra virgin olive oil, lemon juice, and salt and pepper. Toss the watercress and walnuts with the dressing and divide the salad among four plates.

6. Slice the veal on the bias into slices about 1 inch thick. Place a few slices on top of each serving of watercress, drizzle generously with the sauce, and serve.

COOK ONCE, EAT TWICE

On the unlikely chance that you have any of this dish left over, put the veal on thin slices of bread, add some of the sauce, and you've got some very classy open-faced veal sandwiches.

With veal, as with beef, the tenderloin is a unique cut, the most tender part of the animal. Since veal is all about tenderness, you might say that this is the quintessential cut of veal, probably the single most tender cut of meat in the world. This is definitely a butcher shop item, and he will probably have to order it for you in advance, so give him a call a couple of days before you plan to cook.

OTHER CUTS YOU CAN USE

You can use boneless veal chops in this recipe. The best substitute, though, is pork tenderloin.

Hazelnut-Crusted Veal Tenderloin with Roasted Grapes and Port

SERVES 4

As we often do with veal, we are playing rich with rich here, avoiding intense flavors that might overpower the delicate meat. But that doesn't mean this dish is meek or mild. With the discreet bite of mustard, the richness of the hazelnuts, the herby thyme, and the sweetness of the roasted grapes, there is plenty going on here.

You can roast the grapes well ahead of time, then cover and refrigerate them until you're ready to cook the dish. But beware—they are like little pieces of soft grape candy, and you run the risk of eating them all before you make the dish. Also, be careful not to overbrown this dish, because you may burn the nut crust.

We might serve this with Parsleyed New Potatoes (page 412) and some sautéed mushrooms or broccoli.

2 cups seedless red grapes

2 veal tenderloins, about 1 pound each

Kosher salt and freshly cracked black pepper to taste

1/3 cup grainy mustard

1/3 cup hazelnuts, lightly toasted in a dry skillet over medium heat, shaken frequently, until fragrant, 3 to 5 minutes, and ground (or substitute pecans)

3 tablespoons fresh thyme leaves (or 1 1/2 tablespoons dried thyme)

2 tablespoons unsalted butter

1 tablespoon olive oil

1/2 red onion, peeled and diced small

1/2 cup port wine

1 cup veal or chicken stock (or see Stock Options, page 32)

1/4 cup balsamic vinegar

1. Preheat the oven to 300°F.

2. Place the grapes on a very lightly greased small rimmed baking sheet and roast until shrunken and caramelized but not burned, 45 minutes to 1 hour. Remove from the oven and set aside. (Leave the oven on.)

3. Meanwhile, dry the tenderloins with paper towels, sprinkle them generously with salt and pepper, and rub them all over with the mustard. In a small bowl, combine the hazelnuts and thyme and mix well, then coat the tenderloins with this mixture. In an ovenproof sauté pan large enough to hold the 2 tenderloins comfortably, melt the butter over medium heat. Add the tenderloins and brown on all sides, about 10 minutes total. (You are looking for a golden brown here, not a dark brown, because of the nut-herb coating.)

4. Place the pan in the oven and cook the veal to an internal temperature of 130°F for medium-rare, 13 to 18 minutes. (Or nick, peek, and cheat: Make a ¼-inch cut in the thickest part of the meat; it should be slightly less done than you like it.) Transfer the tenderloins to a platter and cover loosely with foil.

5. Pour any drippings out of the pan and wipe it clean with paper towels. Return the pan to the stove over medium-high heat, add the olive oil, and heat until hot but not smoking. Add the onion and cook, stirring occasionally, until translucent, 7 to 9 minutes. Add the port and cook, stirring frequently, for 1 minute. Add the veal stock and vinegar, bring to a simmer, and continue to simmer until the sauce is reduced enough to lightly coat the back of a spoon, 10 to 15 minutes. Season with salt and pepper and add the grapes, tossing to coat them with the sauce.

6. Slice the tenderloin on the bias into slices about 1 inch thick and serve topped with the grape-port sauce.

Broiled Veal Loin Chop with Exotic Mushrooms, Bacon, and Sherry

SERVES 4

You're never going to go wrong with mushrooms and veal. In fact, if you were to research what other food veal has been most combined with in the history of human eating, we would take any bets that it would be mushrooms. Whenever we have veal and mushrooms together, we think of our friend Gordon Hamersley and his combination of mushrooms, bacon, and sherry in the justly famed mushroom sandwich he serves at Hamersley's Bistro in Boston. So this dish is our tribute to Gordon. With no cream and not too much butter, this is actually a little less heavy and rich than many veal dishes.

We like this with orzo or buttered fettuccine and Brussels Sprouts in Brown Butter (page 428).

FOR THE MUSHROOMS

4 slices bacon, diced small

1 red onion, peeled and diced small

3 tablespoons unsalted butter

2 pounds assorted exotic mushrooms of your choice (portobello, shiitake, cremini, chanterelles, enoki, etc., or substitute white mushrooms), trimmed and thinly sliced

1/3 cup dry sherry

1/3 cup roughly chopped fresh parsley

Kosher salt and freshly cracked black pepper to taste

1 tablespoon minced garlic

1/4 cup roughly chopped fresh oregano (or substitute 2 tablespoons dried)

3 tablespoons olive oil

Four 10- to 12-ounce veal loin chops, 1 to 1 1/2 inches thick

1. Preheat the broiler on the highest setting.

2. In a large sauté pan, cook the bacon over medium-high heat until crisp, 6 to 8 minutes. Transfer the bacon to a small bowl and pour off all but 2 tablespoons fat from the pan.

3. Add the onion to the pan and cook, stirring occasionally, until golden brown, 11 to 13 minutes. Add the onions to the bacon and set aside.

4. Pour any remaining bacon grease out of the pan, then melt the butter in the pan over medium heat. Add the mushrooms and cook, stirring occasionally, until they are moist throughout, 10 to 13 minutes (peek inside one to check). Add the sherry, bacon, and onions and continue cooking for 1 minute. Remove from the heat and toss with the parsley and salt and pepper.

5. In a small bowl, combine the garlic, oregano, and olive oil and mix well. Dry the chops with paper towels, coat them well with this mixture, and season them generously with salt and pepper. Place on a broiling pan and broil 3 inches from the heat source until well seared on one side, 5 to 6 minutes. Turn and continue cooking to the desired doneness, 5 to 6 minutes more for medium-rare. To check for doneness, nick, peek, and cheat: Make a ¼-inch cut in the thickest part of the meat; it should be slightly less done than you like it.

6. Allow the chops to rest for 5 to 10 minutes, then top with the mushroom sauce and serve.

See Broiled Veal Loin Chop
(page 194) for details
about veal loin chops and
how to get what you want
when you buy them.

Any veal chop, including
the shoulder chop, would
be great here. Thick pork
chops would also do the
trick.

Grilled Veal Loin Chops with Spicy Green Olive and Sun-Dried Tomato Relish

SERVES 4

The spicy relish we use here is a bit of a challenge to the veal, but these chops do have the texture to stand up to it. As always, remember that when grilling tender, subtle veal, you want to use a somewhat cooler fire and grill for less time than when you are cooking beef, lamb, or even pork.

If you don't have any sun-dried tomatoes, you can substitute a couple of ripe plum tomatoes in the relish. To get a bit deeper flavor, though, try grilling them for 3 to 4 minutes along the edge of the fire before you chop them and add them to the relish.

This dish is great with buttered pasta or risotto as a starch and an Autumn Vegetable Hobo Pack (page 443).

FOR THE RELISH

½ cup roughly chopped pitted green olives

5 oil-packed sun-dried tomatoes, roughly chopped

¼ cup golden raisins

1 to 3 teaspoons red pepper flakes

¼ cup extra virgin olive oil

¼ cup roughly chopped fresh basil

¼ cup pine nuts, toasted in a dry skillet over medium heat, shaken frequently, until just fragrant, 5 to 7 minutes

Kosher salt and freshly cracked black pepper to taste

Four 10- to 12-ounce veal loin chops, 1 to 1½ inches thick

Kosher salt and freshly cracked black pepper to taste

1. Light a fire in your grill.

2. Make the relish: In a medium bowl, combine all the relish ingredients and mix well; set aside.

3. Dry the veal loins well with paper towels, then sprinkle them generously with salt and pepper. When the fire has died down and the coals are medium-hot (you can hold your hand 5 inches above the grill surface for 2 to 3 seconds), place the veal on the grill and cook until well seared on one side, 4 to 5 minutes. Turn and continue cooking to the desired doneness, 8 to 10 minutes total cooking time for medium-rare. To check for doneness, nick, peek, and cheat: Make a ¼-inch cut in the thickest part of the meat; it should be slightly less done than you like it. Remove the meat from the grill and allow it to rest for about 5 minutes.

4. To serve, top each chop with a tablespoon or two of the relish and serve, passing the remaining relish on the side.

Simple Grilled Veal Rib Chops with Smoky Portobello Relish

SERVES 4

Veal chops are meaty, flavorful, and tender, making them perhaps the single most popular cut of veal right now. We like them for all those reasons, plus the fact that they are hearty enough to stand up to grilling, unlike many other cuts of veal. Portobello mushrooms also are particularly nice on the grill, because their size makes them easy to maneuver and because they really go well with the smoky flavor that grilling imparts. In fact, grilled portobellos almost taste like meat themselves. So we grill them up and make them into a simple but tasty relish to go with the classic grilled veal chop.

Again, you don't want to brown veal as deeply as you would beef. You are looking to get a nice sear on it, but it doesn't require the overall deep, dark brown surface that is needed to bring out the flavors of a piece of beef.

Serve this with Butternut Squash Hobo Packs (page 442) and Mashed Potatoes (page 413) or Hash Browns (page 412).

Four 12-ounce veal rib chops, about 1 inch thick
Kosher salt and freshly cracked black pepper to taste

FOR THE RELISH

1 pound portobello mushroom caps
⅓ cup olive oil
1 tablespoon minced garlic
Kosher salt and freshly cracked black pepper to taste
1 large tomato (the size of a baseball), diced medium
⅓ cup balsamic vinegar
¼ cup roughly chopped fresh marjoram (or substitute oregano)

THE CUT

The veal rib chop, a very tender cut that also has wonderful flavor, comes from the same place in the veal calf as the Delmonico or rib-eye steak in a cow. Because it is presently undergoing a bout of popularity in restaurants around the country, you should be able to find this chop in most supermarkets.

OTHER CUTS YOU CAN USE

Any veal loin chop would work well here, as would pork loin chops.

1. Light a fire in your grill.

2. Dry the chops with paper towels and sprinkle them generously with salt and pepper. When the fire has died down and the coals are medium-hot (you can hold your hand 5 inches above the grill surface for 3 to 4 seconds), place the chops on the grill and cook until well seared on one side, about 5 minutes. Turn and continue cooking to the desired doneness, 5 to 7 minutes more for medium-rare. To check for doneness, nick, peek and cheat: Make a ¼-inch cut in the thickest part of the meat; it should be slightly less done than you like it. Remove from the heat, cover loosely with foil, and allow to rest for 5 minutes.

3. Meanwhile, as soon as the chops go on the grill, coat the mushroom caps with the olive oil and garlic, sprinkle with salt and pepper, and place on the grill around the edges of the fire, where the heat is medium. Grill for 5 to 7 minutes per side, until the mushrooms are tender but not mushy, and moist throughout. Remove from the grill, dice medium, and place in a medium bowl. Add the tomato, vinegar, and marjoram, mix well, and season with salt and pepper.

4. Serve the chops accompanied by the relish.

Grilled Veal Shoulder Chops with Nectarine-Ginger Chutney and Cucumbers with Mint and Yogurt

SERVES 4

Here we're pushing the limits of the subtle flavor of veal. But pushing limits usually ends up being a lot of fun, so why not? In this dish, we use some relatively strong flavors from the Indian flavor footprint, so we match them with veal shoulder chops, which have a little bolder flavor than the loin and rib chops. The sweet and pungent chutney is a wonderful contrast to the veal, while the slightly tangy yogurt sauce adds another level of flavor.

Try serving this with grilled eggplant and the rice of your choice.

FOR THE CHUTNEY

2 tablespoons olive oil

1 red onion, peeled and diced medium

1 red bell pepper, cored, seeded, and diced medium

2 tablespoons minced fresh ginger

4 nectarines, pitted and cut into eighths (or substitute peaches or plums)

1 cup cider vinegar

½ cup packed brown sugar

Pinch of ground allspice

Kosher salt and freshly cracked black pepper to taste

FOR THE CUCUMBER

1 cucumber, peeled, seeded, and diced large

½ cup plain yogurt

½ cup roughly chopped fresh mint

Four 10-ounce veal shoulder chops, about ¾ inch thick

Kosher salt and freshly cracked black pepper to taste

3 tablespoons cracked coriander seeds

1. Light a fire in your grill.

2. Make the chutney: In a large sauté pan, heat the oil over medium-high heat until hot but not smoking. Add the onion and bell pepper and cook, stirring occasionally, until the onion is translucent, 7 to 9 minutes. Add the ginger and nectarines and cook, stirring frequently, for another 3 minutes. Add the vinegar, brown sugar, allspice, and salt and pepper and bring to a simmer. Reduce the heat to medium-low and simmer until the chutney begins to thicken, 15 to 20 minutes. Remove from the heat and set aside.

3. Meanwhile, in a medium bowl, combine the cucumber, yogurt, and mint and mix well; cover and refrigerate until ready to serve.

4. Dry the chops with paper towels, sprinkle them generously with salt and pepper, and rub them all over with the cracked coriander seeds, pressing gently to be sure they adhere.

5. When the fire has died down and the coals are medium-hot (you can hold your hand 5 inches above the grill surface for 3 to 4 seconds), place the chops on the grill and cook until well seared on one side, 4 to 5 minutes. Turn and continue cooking to the desired doneness, 4 to 5 minutes more for medium. To check for doneness, nick, peek, and cheat: Make a ¼-inch cut in the thickest part of the meat; it should be slightly less done than you like it. Remove the chops from the grill and allow to rest for about 5 minutes.

6. To serve, top each chop with a couple of tablespoons of the chutney and pass the cucumbers on the side.

OTHER NAMES

Veal shoulder blade steak.

OTHER CUTS YOU CAN USE

Veal shoulder arm steak is a perfect substitute here. Since this dish has some strong flavors, you could also substitute pork chops or even lamb shoulder chops.

When it comes to beef, we love T-bones and porter-houses. So it just makes sense that when it comes to veal, we love the loin chops, which correspond to those two cuts of beef. Just as with beef, the advantage is that you get part of the loin muscle and part of the tenderloin muscle in each chop. You can probably find these chops in some better supermarkets, but to get them this thick, you may well have to go to the butcher.

OTHER CUTS YOU CAN USE

You can easily substitute the veal top loin chop, which is the same piece of meat without the portion of tenderloin. If you can find it, the veal kidney chop, which is a loin chop with a section of the kidney left attached to it, is also excellent. Veal rib chops are also fine for this treatment, but they may not need to cook as long. If veal chops are not around, pork loin chops also work well here.

Grilled Veal T-Bones with a Hobo Pack of Fig, Prosciutto, and Spinach

SERVES 4

Italian cooks are even more fond of veal than the French are, and over the centuries they have come up with plenty of excellent flavor combinations for this tender meat. In this Italian-style dish, we use fresh figs, sage, and prosciutto with the veal. We're not Italian, though, so we put all these accompaniments in a hobo pack, then add some spinach and just a bit of coriander, a light, perfumey spice that doesn't overpower the delicate meat.

If it's winter and you don't feel like grilling, you can also sauté or broil this T-bone.

Serve this with risotto and you're all set.

FOR THE HOBO PACK

2 cups trimmed, well washed, and dried spinach

4 ounces thinly sliced prosciutto

6 fresh figs, halved

1 large tomato (about the size of a baseball), cored and diced medium

1 tablespoon minced garlic

1/3 cup extra virgin olive oil

15 fresh sage leaves

Kosher salt and freshly cracked black pepper to taste

Four 12-ounce veal loin chops, about 1 1/2 inches thick

Kosher salt and freshly cracked black pepper to taste

3 tablespoons cracked coriander seeds (or 1 teaspoon ground coriander)

1. Light a fire in your grill.

2. Make the hobo pack: Tear off four sheets of heavy-duty foil, each about 2 feet long, and stack them one on top of the other. In a large bowl, combine all the hobo pack ingredients and toss gently to combine. Place this mixture in the center of the top sheet of foil, then fold up the sheets of foil around the ingredients, one after the other, turning the package one quarter turn between each sheet and making sure that each sheet is well sealed.

3. When the fire has died down and the coals are medium-hot (you can hold your hand 5 inches above the grill surface for 3 to 4 seconds), place the hobo pack on the outside periphery of the coals, where the fire is less intense. Pile the coals around them and cook for about 20 minutes.

4. Meanwhile, dry the veal chops with paper towels, sprinkle them generously with salt and pepper, and coat them well with the coriander, pressing gently so it adheres. Place the chops on the grill and cook until well seared on one side, 5 to 7 minutes. Turn and continue cooking to the desired doneness, 5 to 7 minutes more for medium-rare. To check for doneness, nick, peek, and cheat: Make a ¼-inch cut in the thickest part of the meat; it should be slightly less done than you like it.

5. Allow the chops to rest for about 5 minutes while you open the hobo pack and divide the contents among four plates. Top each plate with a veal chop and serve.

Sautéed Medallions of Veal with Artichoke Hearts, Lemon, and Thyme

SERVES 4

A medallion of veal is one of those cuts for which sautéing was invented. Tender enough to cook through quickly, it responds perfectly to this high-heat approach. So we feature them in this very simple, straightforward dish full of flavors from the northern shores of the Mediterranean. If you want to make a fancy dinner in a hurry, make this recipe using the canned artichoke heart option. And don't be afraid of the pan sauce in this or any of the other veal recipes. Making the sauce is actually very simple—just taste and reduce, taste and reduce, and add a bit of salt and pepper at the end. Once you get the hang of it, you'll be a regular French chef.

We might serve this with Simple Rice Pilaf (page 417) and Quick-Sautéed Spinach with Garlic (page 427).

THE CUT

Generally, veal medallions come from the leg, which is called the round, and there are a lot of choices for the particular cut. (You can also get medallions from the loin, but to us that seems somewhat of a waste; you might as well save that more expensive cut for thicker pieces.) The best choices for medallions are any cuts from the top, bottom, or tip sections of the round.

You can make medallions
from the boneless veal sirloin steak, which will be
slightly tougher but also a
bit more flavorful. If you
want to be really bold (and
spend more money), you
can pound veal tenderloin
steak into medallions. Or
try pork tenderloin in this
application.

BUTCHERSPEAK

Just ask your butcher for
medallions from the top,
bottom, or tip of the veal
leg and you'll be getting
the right meat.

8 baby artichokes (or substitute 12 canned artichoke hearts)

1 lemon, halved and seeded

2 tablespoons olive oil, or more if needed

1½ pounds boneless veal leg, cut into 8 medallions about ½ inch thick

Kosher salt and freshly cracked black pepper to taste

½ red onion, peeled and finely chopped

1 teaspoon minced garlic

1 cup veal or chicken stock (or see Stock Options, page 32)

½ cup dry white wine or white vermouth

2 tablespoons cold unsalted butter, cut into pieces (optional)

2 tablespoons fresh thyme (or 1 tablespoon dried thyme)

2 tablespoons roughly chopped fresh parsley

1. Prepare the artichokes (if using canned artichoke hearts, skip to Step 3): Trim the stems and snap off the coarse outer leaves, then cut 1 inch off the tops of each one; rub the cut areas immediately with one of the lemon halves. Quarter each artichoke and remove the hairy-looking choke from each quarter. Transfer to a bowl of water, along with the used lemon half.

2. Bring a large pot of salted water to a boil over high heat. Add the artichokes, reduce the heat to low, and simmer until they are tender, 15 to 20 minutes. Drain, cool in a bowl of ice water, and drain again. Set aside.

3. In a large sauté pan, heat the olive oil over medium-high heat until it is hot but not smoking. Dry the veal medallions with paper towels and sprinkle generously with salt and pepper. Add the medallions to the pan, in batches if necessary to avoid crowding, and sauté until they are just nicely browned, 3 to 4 minutes per side; transfer the medallions to a platter as they are done.

4. When all the medallions have been cooked, pour off the fat or add oil to the pan as needed so you have a total of about 2 tablespoons in the pan. Add the onion and cook over medium-high heat, stirring occasionally, until translucent, 7 to 9 minutes. Add the garlic and cook, stirring, for 1 minute more. Add the stock and wine, squeeze the juice from the remaining lemon half into the pan, turn the heat to high, and bring to a boil. Skim any scum from the surface of the liquid and simmer vigorously until reduced by half, 10 to 12 minutes. Reduce the heat and, if using the butter, swirl it into the sauce bit by bit, keeping the sauce at a gentle simmer.

5. Add the veal medallions, along with any accumulated juices, thyme, parsley, and artichokes to the sauce and season to taste. Leave on the heat for just 1 minute, then serve the veal topped with the sauce and artichokes.

Paillard of Veal with Pancetta, White Mushrooms, and Madeira

THE CUT

See Sautéed Medallions of Veal (page 201) for details on the veal leg, which is called the round, and how to choose cuts from this section of the animal.

SERVES 4

A paillard is essentially a slightly bigger version of a cutlet. We're using the term here just so you can make your guests feel that you're serving them a fancy dish, even though it's really quite easy to make.

Sometimes we think that the flavor of veal is a little too subtle, so we like to add some deeper tastes to it with ingredients such as bacon. In this case, we use pancetta, a very tasty Italian bacon that is cured with salt and spices but not smoked. It gives you some great pan drippings to use in making a sauce that adds an extra layer of subtle but enriched flavor to the veal.

Serve this with buttered noodles and some seared greens from the slightly bitter camp, such as beet greens or chard; the edge of bitterness cuts through the richness of this dish nicely.

6 ounces pancetta, diced small (or substitute bacon)

8 ounces small white mushrooms, trimmed and quartered

1 teaspoon minced garlic

Kosher salt and freshly cracked black pepper to taste

1/4 cup dry white wine

2 pounds veal top round, cut into 8 large slices and lightly pounded to a 1/4-inch thickness

Flour for dredging

Olive oil as needed

1/2 cup dry Madeira

1/2 cup veal or chicken stock (or see Stock Options, page 32)

2 tablespoons fresh lemon juice (about 1/2 lemon)

3 tablespoons roughly chopped fresh parsley

1. In a large sauté pan, cook the pancetta over medium-low heat, stirring frequently, until it is crisp and brown, about 7 minutes. Transfer the pancetta to paper towels to drain and pour all but 2 tablespoons of the rendered fat into a small bowl.

2. Increase the heat to medium-high, add the mushrooms to the pan, and cook, stirring occasionally, until the juices have evaporated and the mushrooms are golden brown, 8 to 10 minutes. Add the garlic and cook, stirring, for 1 minute more. Season with salt and pepper and transfer the mushrooms to a bowl. Add the pancetta and cover to keep warm.

3. Add the wine to the pan and bring to a simmer, stirring to dissolve the brown crusty stuff in the bottom of the pan. Pour this liquid into the bowl with the mushrooms and pancetta, then wipe out the skillet with a paper towel.

4. Dry the veal slices well with paper towels and sprinkle them generously with salt and pepper. Dredge each slice lightly in flour, shaking off the excess. In the same sauté pan, heat the reserved pancetta fat with enough olive oil to reach a depth of ¼ inch over medium-high heat. When the fat is very hot but not smoking, add the veal to the pan in a single layer, in batches if necessary to avoid crowding, and cook until golden brown, 1 to 2 minutes per side: transfer the pieces to a platter as they are done. Cover the veal to keep warm while you prepare the sauce.

5. In the same sauté pan, bring the Madeira and stock to a boil over high heat, stirring and scraping up any brown bits in the bottom of the pan. Reduce the heat to medium-low and simmer until the liquid is reduced by half, 10 to 12 minutes. Skim any scum from the surface, then add the lemon juice along with the sautéed pancetta and mushrooms, and any juices that have accumulated on the veal platter. Cook for 1 minute more. Remove the sauce from the heat, add the parsley, and season with salt and pepper.

6. Spoon the sauce over the veal and serve immediately.

Spicy Pan-Seared Veal Loin Medallions with Anchovies and Green Olives

SERVES 4

Now, some of you may be asking, "How come this recipe is in the 'Small Tender' section, when we start out with a two-and-a-half-pound hunk of veal loin?" We have an answer: Because in this case, you're going to be the butcher. You start out with a nice piece of boneless veal loin, spike it with a flavorful spice mixture, and then cut it into medallions and pan-sear it. We think this actually makes it a bit more fun, plus it's a good way to make sure that your medallions are from the loin, not the leg, and that they are nice and thick.

Serve this with noodles or Spanish Rice (page 419) and a green salad.

2 teaspoons fennel seeds

2 teaspoons coriander seeds

1 tablespoon black peppercorns

1 tablespoon red pepper flakes

2 teaspoons kosher salt, plus more to taste

1 cup packed fresh basil leaves, plus 2 tablespoons roughly chopped fresh basil

1/2 cup packed fresh oregano leaves

3 cloves garlic, peeled

1 teaspoon grated orange zest (orange part only)

1/4 cup olive oil

One 2- to 2 1/2-pound boneless veal loin

2 tablespoons vegetable oil

1/2 cup red vermouth (or substitute dry red wine)

1 cup veal or chicken stock (or see Stock Options, page 32)

1/2 cup brine-cured green olives, pitted and quartered

3 anchovy fillets, roughly chopped

2 tablespoons cold unsalted butter, cut into pieces

Freshly cracked black pepper to taste

1. In a small dry sauté pan, toast the fennel, coriander, and peppercorns over medium heat, shaking the pan frequently to keep them from scorching, until fragrant, about 3 minutes. In a food processor fitted with a steel blade, combine the toasted spices, red pepper flakes, salt, the cup of

THE CUT
See Honey-and-Bourbon-Glazed Roasted Loin of Veal (page 170) for details on the veal loin and how to get what you want when you buy it.

OTHER CUTS YOU CAN USE
You can easily make this recipe using medallions from the veal leg. Just rub the spice mixture over the the medallions. Pork loin will also work perfectly well.

basil, the oregano, garlic, orange zest, and olive oil and process until slightly chunky but of a uniform consistency.

2. Dry the veal well with paper towels. Using a paring knife, make 20 or so small slits in the surface of the veal and push some of the spice mixture into each one. Rub any remaining mixture on the surface of the meat. Cut the loin into 12 medallions about 1 inch thick.

3. In a large sauté pan, heat the vegetable oil over medium-high heat until very hot but not smoking. Add the medallions, in batches if necessary to avoid crowding, and sauté until deep golden brown on each side, 2 to 3 minutes per side; transfer the medallions to a platter as they are done and cover loosely with foil. To check for doneness, nick, peek, and cheat: Make a ¼-inch cut in a medallion; it should be slightly less done than you like it.

4. When all the medallions are browned, add the vermouth and stock to the pan and bring to a simmer, stirring to dissolve the brown crusty stuff in the bottom of the pan. Continue to simmer until the liquid is reduced by half, about 10 minutes. Add the olives and anchovies, then stir in the butter piece by piece to incorporate it well. Season with salt and pepper, remove from the heat, and stir in the chopped basil.

5. Pour the sauce over the medallions and serve immediately.

Panfried Veal Cutlets in the German Style

SERVES 4

A lot of the veal consumed in this world is prepared very much like this, and there's a good reason for that: It's delicious. This is the classic schnitzel, also known as Veal Française, which we felt we had to include in this book or it simply would not be complete.

Putting the breading on the cutlet is not complicated, but it does require that you be organized and systematic so you get an even coat and don't make a mess. Lots of waxed paper on the counter is a good idea. Also, notice that breaded meat requires more fat than plain sautéed meat; the fat should come almost halfway up the sides of the cutlets. And, finally, be sure you get the butter nice and brown, but don't let it go over the end into burned territory.

Serve this with buttered noodles and applesauce for a real Germanic experience.

12 veal leg cutlets (about 1½ pounds)

Kosher salt and freshly cracked black pepper to taste

Flour for dredging (about 1½ cups)

4 large eggs, lightly beaten with 2 tablespoons milk

2 cups fine dry bread crumbs

½ cup olive oil

4 tablespoons (½ stick) unsalted butter

1 lemon, quartered and seeded

2 tablespoons roughly chopped fresh parsley

OTHER NAME

Veal leg cutlets.

OTHER CUTS YOU CAN USE

You can buy any cut from the leg (see Sautéed Medallions of Veal, page 201, for details) and form the cutlets yourself. Cutlets of pork tenderloin are also fine.

1. Place each cutlet between two pieces of waxed paper and pound with a meat mallet or other heavy blunt object such as a small frying pan to a ½-inch thickness. Dry the cutlets well with paper towels and season them generously with salt and pepper. Dredge each cutlet lightly with the flour, then dip in the egg mixture and then in the bread crumbs to coat. Place the breaded cutlets on a cake rack set over waxed paper and let them dry at room temperature for 15 minutes.

2. In a large heavy sauté pan, heat the oil over medium-high heat until hot but not smoking. Add the veal in a single layer, in batches if necessary to avoid crowding, and sauté just until nicely browned, 2 to 3 minutes per side; transfer the cutlets to a paper towel–lined platter as they are done and cover to keep warm.

3. Pour the fat out of the pan, wipe out the pan with paper towels, then place it back over medium-high heat. Add the butter, swirling the pan so that it melts evenly. When the butter has reached a nutty golden brown color, immediately squeeze the lemon juice into the pan. Add the parsley and season with salt and pepper.

4. Remove the pan from the heat and pour the brown butter over the cutlets. Serve immediately.

Here we are using the veal leg, or round, and just about any cut from that part of the animal will do. See Sautéed Medallions of Veal (page 201) for more details on these cuts.

You can buy any cut from the leg (see Sautéed Medallions of Veal, page 201, for more details) and slice the cutlets yourself. Cutlets of pork tenderloin are also fine.

Veal Birdies Tidewater-Style, with Smithfield Ham, Backfin Crab, and Lemon-Caper Sauce

SERVES 4

This is a wonderful dish that looks (and tastes) very fancy but is not really that hard to make. If you've got some guests coming over who you suspect think you're not that great a cook, serve this and you'll have them in awe. (If you're wondering about the name of this dish, *birdie* is a term for a stuffed and rolled veal scallopine. If you want to get fancy, they are also known as roulades or paupiettes.)

To make this, we take scallopini from the leg of the veal, pound it thin, and wrap up some crab and Smithfield ham inside it, then sauté it in butter and finish up with a lemon-caper sauce. Anyone from the South might recognize this as a Norfolk-style dish, since backfin crab and Smithfield ham are a very common combination in that neck of the woods. This dish also owes somewhat of a debt to Veal Oscar, a classic in which veal cutlets are topped with crab and Hollandaise sauce.

Serve this with Hash Browns (page 412), sautéed spinach, and a green salad with blue cheese dressing.

½ pound backfin crabmeat, picked over for shells and cartilage

2 tablespoons roughly chopped fresh chervil (or substitute parsley)

Eight 4-ounce slices veal leg

Kosher salt and freshly cracked black pepper to taste

8 very thin slices Smithfield ham (or substitute prosciutto)

4 tablespoons (½ stick) unsalted butter

3 tablespoons capers, rinsed well

½ lemon

¼ cup roughly chopped fresh parsley

1. Preheat the oven to 300°F.

2. In a small bowl, combine the crabmeat and chervil and toss gently. Cover and refrigerate.

3. Dry the veal with paper towels, then place each slice between two pieces of waxed paper and, using a meat mallet or other blunt instrument like a small sauté pan, pound to about a ¼-inch thickness. Sprinkle the veal slices generously with salt and pepper, then lay 1 slice of ham on top of each slice. Top each piece of ham with one eighth of the crab mixture. Roll up each veal slice into a fat tube and secure with one or more toothpicks. If you have time, place the birdies in the refrigerator for 20 minutes; this will help keep them sealed as they cook.

4. In a large sauté pan, melt 2 tablespoons of the butter over medium heat. Add the veal, in batches if necessary to avoid crowding, and cook until browned on all sides, 3 to 4 minutes per side; transfer the birdies to an ovenproof platter as they are done. When all the birdies are browned, turn off the oven and place the platter in the oven while you prepare the sauce.

5. Add the capers to the pan and cook, stirring, for 3 minutes. Drain off the darkened butter, leaving the capers in the pan. Add the remaining 2 tablespoons butter to the pan. When the butter has melted, squeeze the lemon juice over the capers. Add the parsley and stir to combine. Season with salt and pepper, pour the sauce over the platter of veal birds, and serve right away.

Both the cutlets and the veal cubes for the stuffing in this dish come from the veal leg, which may well be the most useful section of the animal. You can either buy 2½ pounds of the round (leg) and cut the appropriate amounts into cutlets and cubes, or you can buy 8 cutlets and 1 pound of the round for cubes. It depends on what's available where you are shopping. For details on veal cutlets and how to get what you want when buying them, see Panfried Veal Cutlets in the German Style (page 206).

As for many other veal recipes, cutlets and cubes of pork tenderloin would perform very well here.

Mango-Stuffed Veal Birdies with Cognac–Green Peppercorn Sauce

SERVES 6 TO 8

We're getting a little radical with veal here, letting it step out a bit from its usual role. It's unlikely that this preparation has been seen in either France or Italy, the main haunts of veal dishes. But the mellow tropical flavor of mango and the distinctive bite of green peppercorn really enliven this dish, and it all works great together. The Cognac–green peppercorn combination used to be called a Madagascar sauce, and it is wonderful not only with this stuffed veal dish but with any steak. Just be careful that you are not standing over the sauté pan when you add the Cognac, in case it flames up.

This goes great with Rice Pilaf with Almonds and Currants (page 417) and the green vegetable of your choice.

FOR THE STUFFING

1 large onion, peeled and quartered

1 clove garlic, peeled

1 pound top or bottom veal round, cut into 1-inch cubes

1 cup dried bread crumbs

1 large egg, lightly beaten

3 ounces dried mango, chopped (or substitute 14 small or 8 large dried apricots, chopped)

1 tablespoon roughly chopped fresh parsley

2 teaspoons roughly chopped fresh sage (or 1 teaspoon dried sage)

2 teaspoons kosher salt

1 teaspoon freshly cracked black pepper

8 veal cutlets, about 1½ pounds total

Kosher salt and freshly cracked black pepper to taste

Flour for dredging

3 tablespoons olive oil

1 large shallot, minced

½ cup Cognac, warmed

1 cup veal or chicken stock (or see Stock Options, page 32)

2 tablespoons green peppercorns in brine, well rinsed

2 tablespoons cold unsalted butter, cut into pieces

2 tablespoons roughly chopped fresh parsley

1. Preheat the oven to 300°F.

2. Make the stuffing: In a food processor fitted with a steel blade, process the onion and garlic until fine. Add the veal, bread crumbs, and egg and pulse repeatedly until the mixture is firm and smooth. Add the mango, herbs, salt, and pepper and pulse a few times, until the mixture is of an even consistency. Cover and refrigerate until ready to use.

3. Dry the veal cutlets with paper towels, then place them one by one between two pieces of waxed paper and, using a meat pounder or other blunt object like a small sauté pan, pound to about a ¼-inch thickness. Arrange the pounded veal slices on a work surface and sprinkle generously with salt and pepper. Divide the stuffing among the veal slices, placing it in the center of each. Roll the slices up, securing each with one or more toothpicks. If you have time, cover and refrigerate the stuffed birdies for 20 minutes; this will help keep the birdies sealed during cooking.

4. Dredge the veal birdies lightly with flour, dusting off the excess. In a large sauté pan, heat the oil over medium heat until hot but not smoking. Add the veal, in batches if necessary to avoid crowding, and cook until browned on all sides, 3 to 4 minutes per side; transfer the birdies to a small roasting pan as they are done. When all the birdies are browned, turn off the oven and place the roasting pan in the oven while you prepare the sauce.

5. Increase the heat under the sauté pan to medium-high, add the shallot, and cook, stirring, for 3 minutes. Add the Cognac, stock, and green peppercorns (be very careful when adding the Cognac—watch for flames! If the Cognac catches fire, take the pan off the heat and let the flames burn out on their own before you continue) and bring to a simmer, stirring to dissolve the brown crusty stuff in the bottom of the pan. Simmer until the liquid is reduced by one third, about 10 minutes. Add the cold butter a little at a time, stirring constantly to incorporate it into the sauce. Remove from the heat, stir in the parsley, and season with salt and pepper.

6. Arrange the veal birds on a platter, spoon the sauce over them, and serve right away.

COOK ONCE, EAT TWICE

If you have any of the green peppercorn sauce left over, it is fantastic on steak of any kind. In fact, it's a very good idea to make a double quantity so you *will* have some left over.

The best option here would be tips from the veal tenderloin. As with beef, the thin end of this tapered muscle is often too small to be used in roasts or steaks and is therefore cut into tips. However, veal is so tender that tips from any part of the loin or even the leg would be fine. Ask your butcher for guidance here.

OTHER CUTS YOU CAN USE

Cubes or strips of pork tenderloin or pork loin roast would work very well in this recipe.

Veal Stir-fry on Big Fried Polenta Croutons

SERVES 4

Veal is most widely used in France and Italy, so it seems to have a particular affinity for the flavors of those regions. But because it's so tender, it is also perfectly suited to stir-frying, the quick high-heat cooking technique of China and Southeast Asia. So here we bring the two together for a stir-fry with Mediterranean flavors.

FOR THE POLENTA

3½ cups cold water

1 cup coarse yellow cornmeal

½ cup freshly grated Parmesan cheese

Kosher salt and freshly cracked black pepper to taste

2 tablespoons unsalted butter, at room temperature

Kosher salt

¼ cup olive oil

2 small onions, peeled and sliced ¼ inch thick

1 red bell pepper, cored, seeded, and cut into 2-inch squares

1 yellow bell pepper, cored, seeded, and cut into 2-inch squares

2 teaspoons minced garlic

Freshly cracked black pepper to taste

1 tablespoon roughly chopped fresh marjoram or oregano

2 pounds veal tips

1 cup veal or chicken stock (or see Stock Options, page 32)

½ cup dry red wine

2 tablespoons roughly chopped fresh basil

2 tablespoons fresh lemon juice

Flour for dredging

Vegetable oil for frying

1. Make the polenta squares: In a medium saucepan, bring the water to a boil over medium-high heat. Very slowly whisk in the cornmeal. Bring the polenta back to a simmer, whisking to break up any lumps, and cook, stirring every few minutes, until thick and creamy, about 30 minutes. The polenta should be thick enough so a wooden spoon can stand up by itself in the pot. Stir in the cheese, season with salt and pepper, and remove from the heat.

2. Grease a rimmed baking sheet with the butter and pour in the polenta, smoothing the surface with a metal spatula. Cool completely, then cut the polenta into 4-inch squares. (The polenta can be made several hours ahead or even the day before; cover and refrigerate.)

3. In a large sauté pan, heat 2 tablespoons of the olive oil over medium-high heat until hot but not smoking. Add the onions and cook, stirring occasionally, until translucent, 7 to 9 minutes. Add the peppers and cook, stirring frequently, until they are soft, about 7 minutes. Add the garlic and cook, stirring, for 1 minute more. Season with salt and pepper and stir in the marjoram. Transfer to a bowl.

4. In the same pan, heat the remaining 2 tablespoons olive oil over medium-high heat until hot but not smoking. Dry the veal well with paper towels and season it with salt and pepper. Add to the sauté pan and stir-fry, moving the meat around very frequently so it cooks relatively evenly, until well browned, 3 to 4 minutes. Add the veal to the bowl of onions and peppers.

5. Pour the stock and wine into the pan, stirring to dissolve the brown crusty stuff in the bottom. Bring to a boil and cook until reduced by half, 3 to 5 minutes. Add to the onions, peppers, and veal and toss well to coat. Add the basil and lemon juice and adjust the seasoning with salt and pepper, then cover to keep warm and set aside. (You can put the bowl in an oven set on the lowest setting if you want.)

6. Dredge the polenta squares lightly in flour. In a large sauté pan, heat ½ inch oil over medium-high heat until it is hot but not smoking. Add the polenta squares in batches to the oil and fry them until they are a deep golden brown on both sides, about 2 minutes. Drain on paper towels.

7. To serve, place a polenta crouton on each plate and spoon the veal and sauce over.

See Sautéed Medallions of Veal (page 201) for details on the veal leg, which is called the round, and how to choose cuts from this section of the animal. You can buy a cut of round and cube it yourself, or you can often find veal cubes in the supermarket or butcher store.

OTHER CUTS YOU CAN USE

Since these cubes are going onto the grill, any cut from the veal round (leg) can be used. But if you can't find veal in your store when you go to buy the ingredients for this dish, you can also substitute cubes of pork tenderloin.

Grilled Veal, Sweet Potato, and Red Onion Kebabs in the Piccata Style

SERVES 4

Veal piccata, which is basically sautéed veal cutlets served with a lemon-garlic-parsley sauce, is a classic Italian dish. Here we update this traditional approach by cutting the veal into chunks, threading them onto skewers with some red onions and sweet potatoes, and then basting with a lemon-garlic vinaigrette as the meat grills. "But what about the parsley?" you may ask. Well, to give the finished dish an added textural dimension, we roll the kebabs in parsleyed bread crumbs when they're done.

You could serve this with a cold pasta salad or a spinach salad. We might even serve it on top of some pesto pasta.

FOR THE VINAIGRETTE

1 tablespoon minced garlic

Minced zest of 1 lemon (yellow part only)

2 tablespoons fresh lemon juice

$1/3$ cup extra virgin olive oil

Kosher salt and freshly ground black pepper to taste

1 cup fresh bread crumbs

$1/4$ cup roughly chopped fresh parsley

$1/2$ teaspoon minced garlic

3 tablespoons unsalted butter, melted

Kosher salt and freshly ground black pepper to taste

2 pounds boneless veal leg, cut into sixteen 1-inch cubes

$1/4$ cup roughly chopped fresh sage

2 large sweet potatoes, peeled, halved, boiled for 5 minutes, drained, and cut into 16 chunks

2 large red onions, peeled and cut into 16 chunks

1. Light a fire in your grill. Preheat the oven to 300°F.

2. Make the vinaigrette: In a small bowl, whisk together the garlic, lemon zest and juice, olive oil, and salt and pepper. Set aside.

3. Toss the bread crumbs, parsley, garlic, melted butter, and salt and pepper together in a small bowl. Spread out on a small baking sheet, place in the oven, and toast, stirring frequently, until golden, about 7 minutes.

4. Dry the veal cubes with paper towels, sprinkle them generously with salt and pepper, and rub them with the sage. Thread them onto skewers alternately with the sweet potatoes and onions. Brush the kebabs with the vinaigrette.

5. When the fire has died down and the coals are medium-hot (you can hold your hands 5 inches above the grill surface for 3 to 4 seconds), place the kebabs on the grill and cook for 5 to 6 minutes per side for medium-rare, basting two or three times with the vinaigrette. To check for doneness, nick, peek, and cheat: Cut into the center of one of the veal cubes; it should be slightly less done than you like it.

6. When the kebabs are done, brush them lightly with the vinaigrette, roll them in the toasted crumbs, and serve.

It's going to take some advance work to get hold of this cut; call your favorite butcher and see if he can get it for you. As the name indicates, it comes from the flank of the animal, and, because we're talking a small animal here, the flank steak itself is also small.

All of these flavors also go very well with beef flank steak, which is of course a lot easier to find. And, again, pork tenderloin works very well in this recipe too.

Grilled Veal Flank Steak on Texas Toast with Yellow Tomato Chutney and Balsamic Raisins

SERVES 4 TO 6

This is a unique cut, which you are only going to find at the butcher's. But it does exist, and if you can get your hands on it and grill it up, people will go nuts over it. It has a pleasingly soft, tender texture because it's veal, but it comes from a well-exercised part of the animal, so it's also got some real flavor on it. That means we can pair it with garlicky Texas toast and a mild all-purpose yellow tomato chutney, then add some vinegar-soaked raisins for an extra burst of flavor. (If you happen to forget to soak the raisins, though, they are not essential. We know this because it's happened to us once or twice.)

Serve this with a Spicy Yellow Squash Hobo Pack (page 441) and some simple grilled peaches for a very luxe outdoor dinner.

FOR THE CHUTNEY

2 tablespoons olive oil

1 red onion, peeled and diced small

2 large or 3 small yellow tomatoes, cored and diced small

½ cup tomato juice

¾ cup cider vinegar

⅓ cup packed brown sugar

Pinch of ground allspice

Kosher salt and freshly cracked black pepper to taste

FOR THE TOAST

5 tablespoons olive oil

2 tablespoons minced garlic

Four to six 1-inch-thick slices Italian bread (1 per serving)

2 tablespoons minced garlic

¼ cup roughly chopped fresh parsley

¼ cup olive oil

Two 1½-pound veal flank steaks, about 1 inch thick

Kosher salt and freshly cracked black pepper to taste

½ cup dark raisins, soaked in ¼ cup balsamic vinegar for 4 hours

1. Light a fire in your grill.

2. Make the chutney: In a large sauté pan, heat the oil over medium-high heat until hot but not smoking. Add the onions and cook, stirring occasionally, until translucent, 7 to 9 minutes. Add the tomatoes, tomato juice, vinegar, brown sugar, and allspice and bring to a simmer, then reduce the heat to low and simmer until the mixture begins to thicken nicely, 30 to 45 minutes. Season with salt and pepper and set aside.

3. Preheat the oven to 300°F.

4. In a small bowl, combine the oil and 2 tablespoons of the minced garlic and mix well. Coat the bread lightly with this mixture, place on a baking sheet, and toast in the oven until hard and crispy, 5 to 10 minutes. Set aside.

5. In a small bowl, combine the remaining 2 tablespoons garlic with the parsley and olive oil and mix well. Dry the steaks with paper towels, coat them thoroughly with this mixture, and sprinkle generously with salt and pepper.

6. When the fire has died down and the coals are medium-hot (you can hold your hand 5 inches above the grill surface for 3 to 4 seconds), place the steaks on the grill and cook until well seared on one side, 3 to 4 minutes. Turn and continue cooking to the desired doneness, 4 to 5 minutes more for medium-rare. To check for doneness, nick, peek, and cheat: Make a ¼-inch cut in the thickest part of the meat; it should be slightly less done than you like it. When the meat is done to your liking, remove it from the grill, cover loosely with foil, and allow to rest for about 5 minutes.

7. Thinly slice the steaks across the grain. Top the garlic toasts with the veal, sprinkle with the balsamic-soaked raisins, and serve, passing the chutney on the side.

RECIPES FOR
SMALL TOUGH CUTS OF VEAL

10 STEPS TO GREAT VEAL STEWS

1. Dry the meat cubes.

2. Season the meat cubes generously.

3. Brown the meat cubes, in batches if necessary.

4. Remove the meat from the pot, adjust the amount of fat in the pot, and sauté the aromatics and vegetables.

5. Deglaze the pot with some of the liquid.

6. Return the meat to the pot along with enough liquid to cover.

7. Bring to a simmer and skim off any film, then reduce the heat to low and simmer gently.

8. Check for doneness early and often.

9. Skim the film and fat from the liquid.

10. Add any final seasonings, season to taste with salt and pepper again, and serve.

Stewed Veal Riblets with Beer, Bacon, and Beans

Pepper-Crusted Veal Riblets Braised with Red Onions over Mushroom Risotto

Southeast Asian–Style Veal Cakes with Aromatic Herbs and Two Dipping Sauces

A Hot Open-Faced Veal Meat Loaf Sandwich with Arugula and Blue Cheese–Tomato Relish

White Veal Stew with Mushrooms, Corn, and Sherry

Simple Brown Veal Stew with Tomatoes, Peppers, and Capers

Spring Veal and Vegetable Stew with Bacon and Chervil

Veal, Sausage, and Fava Bean Stew with Lemony Greens

Stewed Veal Riblets with Beer, Bacon, and Beans

SERVES 4

If you liked beans and bacon when you were a kid, you are going to go out of your mind over this dish. It is basically a high-tone version of that classic down-home dish, with veal ribs adding a particularly flavorsome component. You can use either boneless or bone-in riblets here; the bone-in tend to add a bit more flavor, but the boneless ones make for easier eating.

To make this quicker, you can use good-quality canned beans but add them at the end.

All you need to add for a fantastic meal is a salad of arugula or romaine.

2 tablespoons olive oil

3 pounds veal riblets

Kosher salt and freshly cracked black pepper to taste

4 slices bacon, diced large

1 onion, peeled and diced small

Two 12-ounce bottles beer of your choice

2 plum tomatoes, cored and diced small

¼ cup grainy mustard

¼ cup catsup

¼ cup molasses

½ cup balsamic vinegar

1 pound (about 2 cups) dried white beans, picked over, rinsed, soaked in water to cover for 2 hours, and drained (or substitute two 15½-ounce cans white beans, rinsed and drained)

½ cup roughly chopped fresh parsley

1. In a 5-inch-deep Dutch oven or other large heavy pot with a lid, heat the oil over medium-high heat until very hot but not smoking. Dry the veal riblets with paper towels and sprinkle them generously with salt and pepper. Add them to the pot in a single layer, in batches if necessary to avoid crowding, and brown well on all sides, 10 to 12 minutes total; transfer the pieces to a platter as they are done.

2. When all the veal is browned, pour the fat out of the pot, then add the bacon to the pot and cook until it is crisp, 6 to 8 minutes. Transfer the bacon to the platter of ribs.

Unlike beef short ribs, which can come from three separate sections of the animal, veal riblets come only from the breast. These guys are small, but they are very flavorful and, after long cooking, incredibly tender. You will probably have to go to a butcher shop to get them.

OTHER CUTS YOU CAN USE

You can substitute veal stew meat for the riblets, or you can use 1-inch cubes of beef chuck stew meat.

3. Pour off all but about 2 tablespoons of fat from the pot, add the onion and cook, stirring occasionally, until golden brown, 11 to 13 minutes. Add the beer and bring to a simmer, stirring to dissolve the brown crusty stuff in the bottom of the pan. Add the tomatoes, mustard, catsup, molasses, vinegar, beans, and the bacon, stirring well to combine. Bring just to a boil, then reduce the heat to low, cover, and simmer gently for 1 hour if using soaked white beans, 10 minutes if using canned beans.

4. Return the ribs and bacon to the pot and continue cooking until both beans and meat are tender, 1½ to 2 hours more. Season with salt and pepper, garnish with the parsley, and serve.

THE CUT

See Stewed Veal Riblets (page 219) for more information about veal riblets.

OTHER CUTS YOU CAN USE

It's fine to substitute veal stew meat for the riblets in this recipe, or you can substitute 1-inch cubes of beef chuck or lamb leg.

Pepper-Crusted Veal Riblets Braised with Red Onions over Mushroom Risotto

SERVES 4

Deeply flavored braised meats seem to match up perfectly with risotto. In this simple recipe, we braise veal riblets in red wine and stock along with a lot of red onions, then serve them on top of a risotto flavored with white mushrooms. You can substitute any kind of wild or exotic mushrooms if you want, but the standard supermarket "button" mushrooms actually have more meaty flavor than they get credit for.

3 tablespoons vegetable oil, or more if needed

2 pounds veal riblets

Kosher salt to taste

⅓ cup freshly cracked black pepper, plus more to taste

4 red onions, peeled and diced small

1 cup dry red wine

2 cups veal stock (or see Stock Options, page 32)

FOR THE RISOTTO

4 to 6 cups veal or chicken stock (or see Stock Options, page 32)

3 tablespoons unsalted butter

1 small onion, peeled and diced small

1 pound white mushrooms, trimmed and thinly sliced

1½ cups arborio rice

¼ cup freshly grated Parmesan cheese

¼ cup roughly chopped fresh parsley

Kosher salt and freshly cracked black pepper to taste

1. In a 5-inch-deep Dutch oven or other heavy pot with a lid, heat the oil over medium-high heat until very hot but not smoking. Dry the veal riblets with paper towels and sprinkle them generously with salt and with the pepper. Add them to the pot in a single layer, in batches if necessary to avoid crowding, and brown well on all sides, 10 to 12 minutes total; transfer the pieces to a platter as they are done.

2. When all the riblets are browned, pour off the oil or add more to the pot as needed so that you have about 3 tablespoons of oil. Add the onions and cook, stirring occasionally, until light brown, 11 to 13 minutes. Pour in the wine and cook for 2 more minutes, stirring to dissolve the brown crusty stuff in the bottom of the pan.

3. Return the veal to the pot, add the stock, and season with salt and pepper. Bring to a boil and skim any film from the surface, then reduce the heat, cover, and simmer gently until the riblets are tender, 1½ to 2 hours.

4. When the riblets have been cooking for 1 hour, start the risotto: In a medium saucepan, bring the stock to a boil, then reduce the heat to low and keep at a simmer. In a large sauté pan, melt the butter over medium heat. Add the onion and mushrooms and cook, stirring occasionally, until the onion is translucent, 7 to 9 minutes. Add the rice, stirring to coat with the butter, and cook until the rice just begins to color, 3 to 4 minutes. Add the simmering stock ½ cup at a time, stirring constantly until all the liquid is absorbed each time before adding more. It should take 25 to 30 minutes to add all of the liquid. Remove the pan from the heat, stir in the Parmesan cheese and parsley, and season with salt and pepper.

5. Serve the risotto with the riblets arranged on top.

Ground veal, which may come from trimmings from just about any part of the animal but the shank, is perhaps the second most readily available type of veal, coming in right after cutlets. You can often find it in the supermarkets; if you don't see it, ask the butcher if he has any trimmings or the odd piece of veal shoulder that he can grind up for you.

OTHER CUTS YOU CAN USE

Ground pork is also very good in this dish; you just might want to cook it a little longer.

Southeast Asian–Style Veal Cakes with Aromatic Herbs and Two Dipping Sauces

SERVES 8 AS AN APPETIZER

This is a kind of Southeast Asian veal burger. Cooks in that part of the world, especially in Vietnam, where beef and veal are most readily available, tend to treat this subtly flavored meat as they do fish: They use plenty of spices with it. Rather than covering up the flavor, the aromatic spices actually tend to complement it.

After the burgers are browned, you pile on whole fresh herbs, wrap them up in lettuce leaves, and dip them into the slightly spicy sauces. They are very light, very aromatic, and very delicious.

These make a wonderful appetizer served in front of any Asian-style entrée.

FOR DIPPING SAUCE #1

¼ cup fresh lime juice (about 2 limes)

¼ cup fish sauce (*nam pla*)

3 tablespoons sugar

FOR DIPPING SAUCE #2

¼ cup roasted unsalted peanuts, finely chopped

2 tablespoons minced fresh ginger

2 tablespoons sesame oil

¼ cup soy sauce

2 tablespoons white vinegar

¼ cup finely chopped scallions (white and green parts)

2 pounds ground veal

3 tablespoon minced fresh ginger

1 tablespoon minced garlic

1 tablespoon minced fresh chile peppers of your choice

¼ cup roughly chopped fresh cilantro

Kosher salt and freshly ground white pepper to taste

¼ cup cracked coriander seeds (or 2 tablespoons ground coriander)

3 tablespoons vegetable oil

16 large lettuce leaves

½ cup fresh mint leaves

½ cup fresh basil leaves

½ cup sprigs fresh cilantro

1. Make the dipping sauces: In a small bowl, combine the lime juice, fish sauce, and sugar and stir well to combine and dissolve the sugar; set aside. In another small bowl, combine the peanuts, ginger, sesame oil, soy sauce, vinegar, and scallions. Mix well to combine and set aside.

2. Make the veal cakes: In a large bowl, combine the ground veal, ginger, garlic, chiles, cilantro, and salt and white pepper and mix until it forms a uniform consistency. Form into 16 small meatballs. Sprinkle them generously with salt and white pepper, roll in the coriander, and flatten each one to make a 1-inch-thick patty.

3. In a large sauté pan, heat the oil over medium-high heat until hot but not smoking. Add the veal cakes in a single layer, in batches to avoid crowding, and cook until lightly browned, about 3 minutes on each side; transfer them to paper towels to drain as they are done. To check for doneness, nick, peek, and cheat: Make a ¼-inch cut in a veal cake; it should be slightly less done than you like it.

4. To serve, arrange the veal cakes on a serving platter. Arrange the lettuce, mint, basil, and cilantro and the dipping sauces on another large platter. Pass the veal cakes so that guests can "wrap their own" in lettuce leaves, garnishing with the fresh herbs and dipping sauces.

See Southeast Asian–Style Veal Cakes (page 222) for more information on ground veal.

Ground lamb, pork, or even beef also works just fine in this recipe; we like a combination of lamb and pork.

A Hot Open-Faced Veal Meat Loaf Sandwich with Arugula and Blue Cheese–Tomato Relish

MAKES 6 SANDWICHES

We think it's worth cooking meat loaf just to be able to have sandwiches made from it. This version is pretty straightforward and, because it is made from veal, it's lighter than many others. The tomato relish is simple but full of flavor, and when you put it all together on some thick, crusty bread with a little arugula, you've got a great hot sandwich.

Serve this with some deviled eggs on the side and you'll have a lunch to dream about.

FOR THE MEAT LOAF
2 tablespoons olive oil
1 red onion, peeled and diced small
2 stalks celery, diced small
1 tablespoon minced garlic
2 tablespoons tomato puree (or substitute catsup)
¼ cup roughly chopped fresh basil
2 large eggs
Kosher salt and freshly cracked black pepper to taste
2 pounds ground veal

FOR THE RELISH
2 tomatoes (about the size of baseballs), cored and diced small
½ cup crumbled blue cheese of your choice
¼ cup roughly chopped fresh parsley
2 tablespoons balsamic or red wine vinegar

⅓ cup olive oil
2 tablespoons fresh lemon juice (about ½ lemon)
Kosher salt and freshly cracked black pepper to taste
2 bunches arugula, trimmed, washed, and dried
6 thick slices of your favorite bread

1. Preheat the oven to 300°F. Lightly oil a small roasting pan.

2. Make the meat loaf: In a large sauté pan, heat the oil over medium-high heat until hot but not smoking. Add the onion and celery and cook, stirring occasionally, until the onion is translucent, 7 to 9 minutes. Add the garlic and cook, stirring, for 1 minute. Add the tomato puree and continue to cook, stirring frequently, for 2 minutes more. Remove from the heat and allow to cool almost to room temperature (in the refrigerator if you're in a hurry).

3. In a large bowl, combine the eggs, salt and pepper, and veal. Add the cooled onion mixture and mix well. Shape into a loaf about the size of a loaf of bread, place in the oiled roasting pan, and bake for 45 minutes to 1 hour, until the juice that comes out when you stick a fork into the center of the loaf is clear rather than red or pink. Remove from the oven, cover loosely with foil, and allow to rest for 10 to 20 minutes before slicing.

4. While the meat loaf is baking, make the relish and the salad: In a small bowl, combine the tomatoes, blue cheese, parsley, and vinegar and mix well. In a large bowl, combine the olive oil, lemon juice, and salt and pepper and whisk to combine. Add the arugula and toss well to coat.

5. When the meat loaf has rested, toast the bread and cut the meat loaf into thick slices. Place a piece of toast on each plate, top it with a portion of the salad and a slice of loaf, then spoon some of the relish on top and serve.

White Veal Stew with Mushrooms, Corn, and Sherry

SERVES 4 TO 6

There is a very famous French dish called *blanquette de veau,* a light-colored stew of veal, mushrooms, and baby onions in a sauce of cream and white wine. Its name comes from the word *blanc,* French for "white." It's too rich a dish for our palates, but we still like the idea of taking advantage of veal's lightness—both in color and flavor—to make a stew that is not as heavy as most of the genre. So here we brown the veal lightly, just until it is golden brown, then combine it with the traditional onions and mushrooms, add some fresh corn for an American touch, and use sherry instead of white wine. Because it is a fortified wine, it gives the stew plenty of richness without all that cream.

This light stew is great on a cool fall day, with a French baguette and a "chopped salad" of cucumbers, tomatoes, green beans, and blue cheese with just a bit of leaf lettuce.

COOK ONCE, EAT TWICE

Meat loaf is one of those dishes that is just as good cold as hot. If you've got any of this left over, just make cold sandwiches. If you run out of the tomato relish, this is also great with—what else?—catsup.

THE CUT

You should not have much of a problem finding stew meat in any supermarket that sells veal. Stew meat can come from many cuts of veal, basically any place where the butcher trims a larger piece of meat and has some decent-sized chunks of trim left over. Because veal is so tender, it is not as crucial as with other meats to know which cut is the source of your stew meat. If might be difficult, though, finding cubes as large as we call for here. In that case, you can, of course, use smaller cubes and brown them for a shorter time, or you can get hold of a piece of boneless veal, preferably from the shoulder or round, and cube it up yourself.

2 tablespoons unsalted butter

2 tablespoons vegetable oil, or more if needed

2 pounds veal stew meat, trimmed and cut into 1½-inch cubes

Kosher salt and freshly cracked white pepper to taste

Flour for dredging

2 onions, peeled and diced small

1 tablespoon minced garlic

1 pound white mushrooms, trimmed and quartered

1 cup dry sherry

1 cup fresh corn kernels (1 to 2 ears)

2 cups veal or chicken stock (or see Stock Options, page 32)

3 tablespoons fresh thyme leaves

1. In a 5-inch-deep Dutch oven or other large heavy pot with a lid, heat 1 tablespoon each of the butter and oil over medium heat until the butter has just melted. Dry the veal with paper towels, sprinkle it generously with salt and white pepper, and dredge it lightly in the flour, shaking off any excess. Add half of the veal to the pot, in a single layer, and brown lightly on all sides, 8 to 10 minutes; transfer the pieces to a platter as they are done. Add the remaining 1 tablespoon each butter and oil to the pot and, as soon as the butter has melted, add the remaining veal and brown in the same manner, transferring the pieces to the platter as they are done.

2. Pour off the fat or add more oil to the pot as needed so you have about 2 tablespoons of fat in the pot. Add the onions and cook, stirring occasionally, until translucent, 7 to 9 minutes. Add the garlic and cook, stirring, for 1 minute. Add the mushrooms and cook, stirring frequently, for 5 minutes. Pour in the sherry and continue to cook for 2 more minutes, stirring to dissolve any brown crusty stuff in the bottom of the pot.

3. Return the veal to the pot, add the corn and stock, and season with salt and white pepper. Bring to a boil, reduce the heat to low, cover, and simmer gently until the veal is fork-tender, 1 to 1½ hours. To check for doneness, take a piece of meat out of the stew, cut into it to check for color, and taste it for tenderness.

4. When the stew is done, remove it from the heat, stir in the fresh thyme, and serve.

Simple Brown Veal Stew with Tomatoes, Peppers, and Capers

SERVES 6

THE CUT

See White Veal Stew (page 225) for information on veal stew meat.

This classic veal stew has some kinship with the famous Hungarian goulash, which is really just a meat-and-vegetable stew flavored with paprika. Somehow we think of bell peppers as being an important part of that dish, though, so this reminds us of it. To finish off the stew, we top it with some crisp-fried capers, which add a fresh salty-tart taste to the final dish.

Be sure that you don't overbrown the veal cubes, which would make them a little tough; you are just looking for a golden brown on the outside of the meat here.

¼ cup olive oil, or more if needed

2 pounds veal stew meat, trimmed and cut into 1-inch cubes

Kosher salt and freshly cracked black pepper to taste

All-purpose flour for dredging

2 onions, peeled and diced medium

1 red bell pepper, cored, seeded, and diced medium

1 green bell pepper, cored, seeded, and diced medium

2 tablespoons minced garlic

1 cup dry white wine

3 plum tomatoes, cored and diced small

1 cup veal or chicken stock (or see Stock Options, page 32)

3 tablespoons unsalted butter

½ cup small capers, rinsed

⅓ cup roughly chopped fresh parsley

1. In a 5-inch-deep Dutch oven or other large heavy pot with a lid, heat 2 tablespoons of the oil over medium-high heat until hot but not smoking. Dry the veal with paper towels, sprinkle it generously with salt and pepper, and dredge it lightly in the flour, shaking off any excess. Add half the veal to the pot, in a single layer, and brown lightly on all sides, 8 to 10 minutes total; transfer the pieces to a platter as they are done. Add the remaining 2 tablespoons oil to the pot and brown the second half of the veal in the same manner, transferring the pieces to the platter as they are done.

2. Add oil to the pot or pour off the fat as needed so that you end up with about 2 tablespoons fat in the pot. Add the onions and cook, stirring occasionally, until golden brown, 11 to 13 minutes. Add the bell peppers and garlic and cook, stirring, for 2 minutes more. Pour in the wine and cook for 2 minutes, stirring to dissolve any brown crusty stuff on the bottom of the pot.

3. Return the veal to the pot, add the tomatoes and stock, and season with salt and pepper. Bring to a boil and skim any film off the surface. Then reduce the heat to low, cover, and simmer gently until the veal is very tender, 1 to 1½ hours. To check for doneness, take a piece of meat out of the stew, cut into it to check for color, and taste it for tenderness.

4. When the stew is almost done, cook the capers: In a medium sauté pan, melt the butter over medium heat. Add the capers and cook, stirring occasionally, until crisp, 4 to 5 minutes.

5. Place a generous helping of the stew in each bowl and sprinkle with the parsley. Top with the capers, drizzle with any leftover butter from the caper pan, and serve.

THE CUT
See White Veal Stew (page 225) for information on veal stew meat.

Spring Veal and Vegetable Stew with Bacon and Chervil

SERVES 6

This stew features some of the same root vegetables that you see in heartier dishes—carrots, onions, and turnips—but because veal has such light flavor for a red meat, the result is lighter than you might think. For a fresh spring flavor, we add some peas, then finish up the dish by sprinkling a crunchy, flavorful combination of bread crumbs, crumbled bacon, and chervil over the top for some flavor contrast. Chervil is a very nice, mild spring herb; since it is in the parsley family, though, you can always substitute parsley.

6 slices bacon, diced small
2 pounds veal stew meat, trimmed and cut into 1-inch cubes

Kosher salt and freshly cracked black pepper to taste

All-purpose flour for dredging

12 small pearl onions, peeled

2 carrots, peeled and diced small

1 small turnip, peeled and diced small (about 1 cup)

1 cup dry white wine

1 cup veal or chicken stock (or see Stock Options, page 32)

1 cup fresh peas, blanched in boiling water for 30 seconds and drained

¼ cup roughly chopped fresh chervil (or substitute parsley)

¼ cup fresh bread crumbs, toasted

1. In a 5-inch-deep Dutch oven or other heavy pot with a lid, cook the bacon over medium-high heat until crisp, 6 to 8 minutes. Remove and drain on paper towels.

2. Pour off all but about 2 tablespoons of fat from the pot. Dry the veal with paper towels, sprinkle it generously with salt and pepper, and dredge it lightly in the flour, shaking off any excess. Add the veal to the pot in a single layer, in batches if necessary to avoid crowding, and brown well on all sides, about 10 minutes total; transfer the pieces to a platter as they are done.

3. Add the onions, carrots, and turnip to the pot and cook, stirring occasionally, just until the onions begin to turn translucent, 4 to 5 minutes. Return the veal to the pot, add the white wine and stock, and season with salt and pepper. Bring to a boil and skim any scum off the surface, then cover, reduce the heat to low, and simmer gently until the veal is tender, 1 to 1½ hours. To check for doneness, take a piece of meat out of the stew, cut into it to check for color, and taste it for tenderness. When the veal is done, add the peas and taste to adjust the seasoning.

4. While the stew is cooking, crumble the bacon and place it in a small bowl with the chervil and bread crumbs. Mix well to combine.

5. Place a generous serving of stew in each bowl, sprinkle with the bacon mixture, and serve hot.

THE CUT

See White Veal Stew
(page 225) for details
about veal stew meat.

OTHER CUTS YOU CAN USE

Cubes of beef chuck or
lamb leg are also good in
this dish.

Veal, Sausage, and Fava Bean Stew with Lemony Greens

SERVES 6

Veal works very well in stews, which is fortunate, because stew meat is one of the few cuts of this meat that is very readily available. In this recipe, we combine the veal with fava beans, one of the world's most flavorful beans, and a staple of Mediterranean cooking. We love favas, maybe because we were introduced to them in Tunis, where you can stop on the street and buy little cones of roasted fava beans the way you buy peanuts in New York or chestnuts in Hong Kong. Fresh favas are unbeatable, but they are hard to locate and difficult to prepare, so here we used the dried version. If you can't find them, you can always substitute lima beans. (You can also use canned beans, but add them just 15 minutes before the stew is done.) With a little sausage for some underlying oomph and lemony greens to add a little tart and a little bitter, this is a stew with a lot of great flavors going on.

All you'll need to make a meal of this is a loaf of good bread, but Minted Fresh Peas (page 428) make a nice light accompaniment.

1 pound dried fava beans (or substitute dried lima beans)

2 tablespoons vegetable oil, or more if needed

1 pound veal stew meat, trimmed and cut into 1-inch cubes

Kosher salt and freshly cracked black pepper to taste

1 pound Italian hot or sweet sausage links, cut into 1-inch cubes

2 large onions, peeled and diced small

2 tablespoons minced garlic

1 cup canned whole tomatoes, diced small (with their juice)

2 cups dry white wine

FOR THE GREENS

3 tablespoons olive oil

2 tablespoons minced garlic

1 pound spinach (or substitute other dark leafy greens such as Swiss chard, beet greens, or young kale), trimmed, well washed, and dried

1 lemon, halved

Kosher salt and freshly cracked black pepper to taste

1. If using dried beans, soak them overnight in cold water; drain.

2. Place the soaked beans in a saucepan, cover with 2 inches of water, and simmer, partially covered, over medium heat for 15 minutes. Drain, reserving 1 cup of the cooking liquid, then slip outer skins off the beans and set the beans aside. (If using frozen beans, thaw according to the package directions.)

3. In a 5-inch-deep Dutch oven or other large heavy pot with a lid, heat the oil over medium-high heat until very hot but not smoking. Dry the veal with paper towels and sprinkle it generously with salt and pepper. Add the veal to the pot in a single layer, in batches if necessary to avoid crowding, and brown lightly on all sides, 8 to 10 minutes total; transfer to a platter as they are done. In the same pot, cook the sausages, in batches if necessary, until well browned, about 10 minutes.

4. Pour off all but 2 tablespoons of the fat. Add the onions and cook, stirring occasionally, until translucent, 7 to 9 minutes. Add the garlic and cook, stirring, for 1 minute more.

5. Return the veal and sausage to the pot and add the drained beans, the reserved liquid (or 1 cup water or veal or chicken stock if using frozen beans), the tomatoes, and white wine. Bring to a boil and skim any film off the surface, then reduce the heat to low, cover, and simmer gently until the meat and beans are tender, 1 to 1½ hours. To check for doneness, take a piece of meat out of the stew, cut into it to check for color, and taste it for tenderness.

6. When the stew is almost done, make the greens: In the largest sauté pan you have, heat the oil over medium-high heat until hot but not smoking. Add the garlic and cook, stirring, for just 10 seconds. Add the spinach and cook, stirring vigorously, until wilted, about 1 minute more. Remove the pan from the heat, squeeze both lemon halves over the spinach, and toss to coat. Season with salt and pepper.

7. Spoon a generous serving of stew into each bowl, top with the sautéed greens, and serve hot.

RECIPES FOR
ODD CUTS OF VEAL: OFFAL ET AL.

Scrambled Eggs on Toast with Calf's Brains and Truffle Oil

Calf's Brains Meunière

Grilled Sweetbreads over Wilted Spinach with Sweet-and-Sour Bacon Dressing

Seared Calf's Liver with Bacon, Onions, and Sweet-and-Sour Madeira Sauce

Seared Veal Kidneys with Roasted Pears and Horseradish-Mustard Sauce

Scrambled Eggs on Toast with Calf's Brains and Truffle Oil

SERVES 4

OK, so this is not a dish for everybody. But if you can get past your squeamishness (and if you can find a butcher who still sells them), calf's brains are really a great dish. You do have to put a fair amount of work into it, though, because brains are very perishable and need to be subjected to multiple rinsings, then simmered, then pressed down to firm them up, then sautéed. But if you have adventurous friends who are looking for some food that they have not had before, this luxe version of the ultimate comfort food, scrambled eggs on toast, might just fit the bill.

In fact, I (Chris) would like to dedicate this dish to Saul Garlic, a close personal friend who also happens to be a trusted business adviser. Over the years Saul's guidance through the treacherous waters of the restaurant business has proven indispensable. So acute is his acumen that to a small group of colleagues he is known as "the Brain." Nearly as impressive as his business skills is his ability to recall the smallest details of meals that he consumed twenty years ago. His appetite and his appreciation of food has always been inspiring. So, Brain, this is for you, because I know that if you were ever to actually eat brains you would definitely want them fried.

½ pound calf's brains

¼ cup white vinegar

2 teaspoons kosher salt, plus more to taste

White pepper to taste

All-purpose flour for dredging

5 tablespoons unsalted butter

2 tablespoons vegetable oil

½ cup minced shallots

2 tablespoons light cream

8 large eggs, lightly beaten

2 tablespoons chopped fresh chives

6 slices toast, buttered

White truffle oil to taste

1. Place the brains in a stainless steel or enamel saucepan, add enough water to cover, and allow to sit for 5 minutes, then drain; repeat this process three times. Remove the membranes and trim the white bits

---

THE CUT

Like other parts of the animal that we Americans tend to find offputting, brains are a delicacy in many parts of the world. They have a wonderful creamy texture and a very rich, delicate flavor. And besides, cooking with them is a kind of a testament to the historical importance of making use of every part of the animal. So you not only get some delicious food, you can feel virtuous about it at the same time.

from the brains. Place the brains in the saucepan again, add water to cover and 2 tablespoons of the vinegar, and allow to sit for 2 hours.

2. Drain the brains once again, then return to the saucepan. Pour enough boiling water into the pan to just cover the brains, add the salt and the remaining 2 tablespoons of vinegar, and bring just to a simmer over medium-high heat. Reduce the heat to low and simmer gently for 20 minutes. Remove the pan from the heat and let the brains cool in the pan.

3. When the brains are cool, remove them from the liquid and place them on a parchment-lined baking sheet. Cover them with another sheet of parchment, then cover with another baking sheet. Weight down the top baking sheet with a phone book or some heavy cans and refrigerate the brains for 1 hour. (Pressing the brains will firm them up so they will slice and sauté more easily.)

4. Cut the brains into ½-inch slices and dry them with paper towels. Sprinkle them generously with salt and pepper and dredge them lightly in the flour. In a large sauté pan, melt 3 tablespoons of the butter with the oil over medium-high heat. Add the brains and brown lightly, about 3 minutes per side. Transfer to a platter.

5. In another large sauté pan, melt the remaining butter over medium-high heat. Add the shallots and sauté until very soft, about 3 minutes. Whisk the cream into the eggs, add the eggs to the pan, and scramble them gently, stirring frequently, until they are just set. Season them with salt and white pepper and add the chives. Fold the hot brains into the eggs, spoon over the hot buttered toast, drizzle with truffle oil, and serve immediately.

THE CUT

See Scrambled Eggs on Toast with Calf's Brains (page 233) for more information on brains.

Calf's Brains Meunière

SERVES 6 AS AN APPETIZER

This dish, which is a variation on the traditional French *meunière* approach to brains, is a tribute to our friend James Burke. Many people think that Jimmy is known as "a brain" because of his uncanny ability to serve fantastic Italian food at his Waltham, Massachusetts, restaurant, Tuscan Grill, while simultaneously vacationing in Florida. But we know that it's because he loves to cook and serve brains.

Try this as an appetizer when you plan to serve a straightforward grilled or roasted entrée.

1½ pounds calf's brains

¼ cup white vinegar

2 teaspoons kosher salt, plus more to taste

Freshly cracked black pepper to taste

All-purpose flour for dredging

2 tablespoons unsalted butter

2 tablespoons vegetable oil

3 tablespoons roughly chopped fresh parsley

FOR THE SAUCE

3 tablespoons unsalted butter, cut into pieces

1 lemon, halved

2 tablespoons capers, rinsed and drained

1. Place the brains in a stainless steel or enamel saucepan, add enough water to cover, and allow to sit for 5 minutes, then drain; repeat this process three times. Remove the membranes and trim the white bits from the brains. Place the brains in the saucepan again, add water to cover and 2 tablespoons of the vinegar, and allow to sit for 2 hours.

2. Drain the brains once again, then return to the saucepan. Pour enough boiling water into the pan to just cover the brains, add the salt and the remaining 2 tablespoons vinegar, and bring just to a simmer over medium-high heat. Reduce the heat to low and simmer gently for 20 minutes. Remove the pan from the heat and let the brains cool in the pan.

3. When the brains are cool, remove them from the liquid and place them on a parchment-lined baking sheet. Cover them with another sheet of parchment, then cover with another baking sheet. Weight down the top baking sheet with a phone book or some heavy cans and refrigerate the brains for 1 hour. (Pressing the brains will firm them up so they will slice and sauté more easily.)

4. Cut the brains into ½-inch slices and dry them with paper towels. Sprinkle them generously with salt and pepper and dredge them lightly in the flour. In a large sauté pan, melt the butter with the oil over medium-high heat. Add the brains and brown lightly, about 3 minutes per side. Transfer to a platter and sprinkle with the parsley.

5. Make the sauce: Add the butter to the sauté pan, swirling the pan so that the butter melts evenly. When the butter has reached a nutty golden brown color, immediately squeeze the lemon juice into the pan and add the capers. Pour the browned butter sauce over the brains and serve immediately.

Veal sweetbreads are usually the thymus gland of the calf, although they may also be the pancreas. It might be hard to find fresh sweetbreads, but they are worth looking for, so try your local high-quality butcher. As with all organ meats, be sure they are very fresh.

Grilled Sweetbreads over Wilted Spinach with Sweet-and-Sour Bacon Dressing

SERVES 4 TO 6 AS AN APPETIZER

This is the famous "green eggs and ham" dish. Sweetbreads are great, and if you introduce people to them cooked this way, most of them will think you're a culinary genius because you've given them an appreciation for something they thought they would hate.

Classically, sweetbreads are poached whole, then sliced and sautéed. But we prefer to poach them only briefly, then separate the "nuggets" and grill them. This not only minimizes their sometimes mealy consistency, it also provides a crispy crust to contrast with the creamy, tender interior.

Try this as an appetizer in front of a simple grilled steak dinner.

¼ cup white vinegar

1 bay leaf

1½ pounds veal sweetbreads

Kosher salt and freshly cracked black pepper to taste

½ cup olive oil

1 pound spinach, trimmed, well washed, and dried

4 slices bacon, diced small

1 teaspoon sugar

3 tablespoons balsamic vinegar

1. Build a fire in your grill.

2. In a large saucepan, bring the white vinegar, bay leaf, and enough water to cover the sweetbreads to a boil over high heat. Add the sweetbreads and salt and pepper, lower the heat so that the water just barely simmers, and poach gently for 10 minutes; drain and place the sweetbreads in a bowl of ice water to cool.

3. When the sweetbreads are completely cooled, drain them, dry them with paper towels, and remove as much of the membrane as possible. Separate the meat into nuggets, toss them gently with ¼ cup of the olive oil, and sprinkle generously with salt and pepper. Thread the sweetbreads onto four to six skewers (one per serving) and refrigerate.

4. Place the spinach in a large bowl. In a large sauté pan, cook the bacon slowly over medium heat until it is crisp and golden brown, 8 to 10 minutes. Drain off and discard all but 3 tablespoons of the fat, leaving the bacon in the pan. Add the sugar, the remaining ¼ cup olive oil, and the balsamic vinegar to the pan and bring to a boil. Pour the hot dressing over the spinach, tossing to wilt the spinach and coat it with the dressing. Season with salt and pepper and set aside.

5. When the fire has died down and the coals are medium-hot (you can hold your hand 5 inches above the surface of the grill for 3 to 4 seconds), place the skewers on the grill and cook until well seared and crisp on the outside, 4 to 5 minutes per side. To check for doneness, nick, peek, and cheat: Make a ¼-inch cut in the thickest part of one of the nuggets; it should be warm throughout with no red, only the faintest trace of pink. When the sweetbreads are fully cooked, remove them from the heat and let them rest for 5 minutes.

6. To serve, place some spinach on each plate and top with a sweetbread skewer.

Seared Calf's Liver With Bacon, Onions, and Sweet-and-Sour Madeira Sauce

SERVES 4

If you have never had calf's liver, it is going to change your mind about liver forever. It is a favorite of butchers as well as restaurant chefs, so it can be hard to locate, but it is well worth the search. Delicate and rich in flavor, it also has a wonderful texture. The mistake that most cooks make with this organ meat is to overcook it, which changes its texture from silky smooth to dry and chalky. We recommend that you cook it just to medium-rare, still pink in the center.

Some combinations can't be beat, and one of those is liver, bacon, and onions. So here we stick to that favorite, adding a sweet-and-sour sauce flavored with Madeira, a fortified wine originally from Portugal that makes an excellent complement to veal of any kind.

THE CUT

Smaller than beef liver, calf's liver is also lighter in color, pale red or pink to yellow brown. It is usually sold presliced, but if you do buy your liver whole, it may still have an outer membrane on it. If so, remove it, since it gets tough as it cooks.

OTHER NAME

Veal liver.

BUTCHERSPEAK

You are probably only going to find true calf's liver at a pretty high-level butcher shop. Make sure that you are not fooled into buying "young beef liver," which is merely beef liver by another name, and quite a different item.

8 slices bacon, diced small

2 red onions, peeled and thinly sliced

Kosher salt and freshly cracked black pepper to taste

3 tablespoons unsalted butter

Four 8-ounce slices calf's liver, about ½ inch thick (outer membrane removed if still present)

All-purpose flour for dredging

1 cup dry Madeira

¼ cup apricot preserves

¼ cup balsamic vinegar

¼ cup roughly chopped fresh parsley

1. In a large sauté pan, cook the bacon slowly over medium heat until it is crisp and golden brown, 8 to 10 minutes. Transfer the bacon to a small bowl and discard all but 3 tablespoons of the fat from the pan. Add the onions to the pan and cook, stirring frequently, until well browned, about 13 minutes. Season with salt and pepper and transfer to another small bowl.

2. Discard the bacon fat, return the pan to medium heat, and add the butter. Season the liver with salt and pepper and dredge it lightly in the flour. When the butter is melted, add the liver to the pan and sear for 2 to 3 minutes per side for medium-rare, transferring the pieces to a platter as they are done. To check for doneness, nick, peek, and cheat: Make a ¼-inch cut in a piece of the liver; it should be slightly less done than you like it. Cover the liver to keep it warm while you make the sauce.

3. Pour off any remaining fat and return the pan to medium-high heat. Add the Madeira and bring to a simmer, stirring to dissolve the brown crusty stuff in the bottom of the pan. Continue to simmer until the liquid is reduced by half, 5 to 10 minutes. Add the preserves and cook, stirring, for 1 minute. Stir in the vinegar, remove the pan from the heat, and season the sauce with salt and pepper.

4. To serve, scatter the onions over the liver on the serving platter. Pour the sauce over the onions and sprinkle the bacon bits and parsley over the top.

Seared Veal Kidneys with Roasted Pears and Horseradish-Mustard Sauce

SERVES 4

For years, I (Doc) thought of kidneys as a faintly ridiculous English breakfast dish. This came, no doubt, from reading lots of English mystery novels in which the obligatory country house weekend always included a breakfast with a silver salver of kidneys on the sideboard. But calf's kidneys are actually a very tasty dish. Like most organ meats, they respond poorly to overcooking, so keep an eye on them.

Here we serve the kidneys with roasted pears, for several years my favorite breakfast dish, and add the horseradish-mustard sauce that Jim Burke always served with kidneys when Chris worked for him at the Harvest Restaurant in Cambridge, Massachusetts, many years ago.

Even though we are big fans of browning meat in general, kidneys are too delicate for this treatment, so if they are not done enough for your liking after 3 to 4 minutes in the sauté pan, finish them up in the oven.

2 ripe but firm Bosc pears, halved and cored

2 tablespoons olive oil

Kosher salt and freshly cracked black pepper to taste

5 tablespoons unsalted butter

3 calf's kidneys, trimmed

½ red onion, peeled and diced small

1 cup dry white wine

½ cup heavy cream

¼ cup grainy mustard

2 tablespoons grated fresh horseradish

⅓ cup roughly chopped fresh parsley

1. Preheat the oven to 350°F.

2. Rub the pears with the olive oil, sprinkle with salt and pepper, and arrange cut side up in a roasting pan. Roast until they are well browned and tender when pierced with a fork, about 45 minutes.

3. In a large sauté pan, melt 3 tablespoons of the butter over medium heat. Add the kidneys, turn the heat to medium-high, and sear for 3 to 5 minutes per side; transfer to an ovenproof platter as they are done. To check for doneness, nick, peek, and cheat: Make a ¼-inch cut in one of the kidneys and take a peek; it should be slightly pink inside. If they are less done than you like, place the platter of kidneys in the hot oven while you make the sauce.

4. Pour off any remaining fat and return the pan to medium heat. Add the remaining 2 tablespoons butter and, when it is melted, add the onion and cook, stirring occasionally, until translucent, 7 to 9 minutes. Turn the heat up to medium-high, add the wine, and bring to a simmer, stirring to dissolve the brown crusty stuff in the bottom of the pan. Continue to simmer until the wine is reduced by two thirds, 5 to 10 minutes. Add the cream, mustard, and horseradish and simmer for 3 more minutes, then remove from the heat. Season with salt and pepper and stir in the parsley.

5. Drizzle the kidneys generously with the sauce and serve.

LAMB: IT MIGHT as WELL be SPRING

We are big fans of lamb, mainly because this is meat with some real flavor to it. Earthy and rich with a faint, almost aromatic, sweet-ness, it can stand up to strong flavorings from chile peppers to garlic to cilantro. On the other hand, the taste of lamb is also refined enough for just about anyone.

Certainly this meat has a long and honorable history as a friend of humanity. Sheep were domesticated long before cattle or pigs, in about 9000 B.C., in northern Iraq. From that time on, humans in much of the world were shepherds, and the meat they knew best was lamb. Sheep became an almost universal symbol for purity and redemption in the ancient world, the prime choice of ancient religions for sacrifices to the gods. Even today lamb is the only universally accepted meat. Hindus are forbidden to eat beef, Muslims shun pork, but no culture or religion outlaws lamb.

Oddly enough, though, in America lamb has always been the least-consumed of the big three red meats. In 1998, for example, the average American ate just over one pound of lamb, compared to almost fifty-three pounds of pork and some sixty-eight pounds of beef.

Lamb's lack of popularity among American cooks is particularly puzzling given its prominence in other cuisines. From the shores of North Africa and Italy to the steppes of Mongolia, and nearly all the lands in between, this meat is a staple. In the Middle East, it is so dominant that when you say "meat," it is virtually understood you are talking about lamb.

It's not surprising, then, that both of us acquired our fondness for lamb while traveling in other countries. When I (Chris) was about ten years old, my parents took my sister and me to Europe. During the first part of the trip, my specialty was keeping track of the currencies in the different countries, but when we arrived in Greece, I became a specialist in lamb. I clearly remember driving back from Delphi to Athens one day eating lamb skewers in the back seat of the car, throwing the skewer sticks on the floor in my haste to start eating another little set of those juicy, flavorful lamb cubes. On another day, we stopped at a taverna where a boy not much older than I was sat turning a whole baby lamb on a spit. I was impressed with the fact that he was given this responsibility, and even more impressed when his father invited me to choose the particular portion of the lamb I wanted, then sliced it off and handed it to me. My father and I sat down at a rough-hewn table, sprinkled the rosy pink meat with lemon juice and salt and pepper, and ate with our fingers.

Inspired by these experiences, when we got back to the United States, I convinced my father to let me grill lamb chops, which were just about his favorite meal. They were the first thing I had ever grilled and, predictably, I charred them beyond recognition. But we ate them anyway, and my father claimed they were the best he'd ever had. That was the beginning of the cooking career that brought me to the point where I could be writing this book, so to this day I still have a special fondness for lamb chops.

I (Doc) was introduced to the pleasures of lamb later in life. Back in the late 1970s, I sold my car, gave up my apartment, and flew to London with my friend Rick to embark on what turned out to be a four-month cross-continent trip to Istanbul, including a three-week sojourn in Morocco. In the back alleys of Tangier and at the *souks* in Fez, we ate tiny lamb skewers that had been squirted with lemon juice and rolled in fresh mint before being grilled on charcoal-fueled braziers. In a campground in a desert oasis near Quarzazate, a newfound Moroccan friend cooked us an incredible *tagine* of lamb and green olives, and when we splurged by eating at a "real" restaurant in Marrakech, I was lucky enough to choose a classic braised lamb dish, spoon-tender and flavored with almonds, saffron, and cumin. More such treats awaited us in Algeria, Tunisia, and Greece, so by the time we arrived in Istanbul and began sampling the lamb and eggplant dishes in the inexpensive restaurants of the European part of that amazing city, I had become a confirmed lamb devotee.

Since then, we've both continued to enjoy lamb in places from Malaysia to China to Peru. But there is no need to travel the world to find out how fantastic lamb can be; there is great lamb as close as your supermarket. That's why it is so perplexing that most American home cooks continue to think of lamb only when Easter or Passover rolls around.

History can best explain this prejudice. At the time the Europeans came to America, the farms in much of the rest of the world (think the entire Mediterranean, just for starters) were small, pasture land was scarce, and the weather was dry. It made most sense to raise sheep, which, unlike cows, can subsist on little pasture and, unlike pigs, give not only meat but also milk. In land-rich America, on the other hand, cattle were not only easier to raise, but also more profitable, at least partially due to the British prohibition against the manufacture of woolen goods. So, since colonial times, there has been a widespread feeling that lamb is somehow "un-American," the food of people from other, less fortunate lands. The early prejudice against lamb was reinforced by the fact that, unlike beef and pork, it could not be converted into the colonial version of fast food by salting or smoking. This negative attitude was solidified by the range wars between sheepherders and cattle ranchers that flared up in the American West during the late 1800s. Cattle ranchers managed to successfully characterize sheep, which will eat grass right down to the roots, as little better than four-legged locusts, and the American antipathy toward lamb became even more ingrained.

But it is not only history that is to blame for lamb's relative obscurity in this country. This meat also has somewhat of a reputation for being gamy, with too strong a flavor for many diners. This preconception seems to have originated with mutton, which is the name given to meat from sheep that are over a year old. It is true that mutton does have quite a strong and gamy flavor. But that has little relevance today, since mutton is no longer sold commercially in the United States except in some halal (Orthodox Muslim) butchers. In other words, it won't be foisted on you; you have to seek it out.

There is another factor in lamb's lack of acceptance, though, that's actually based in scientific reality. Many people associate the taste of lamb with the smell of burning lamb fat, which does have a very "lamby" odor. This is because it is what is known as a hard fat, meaning it has a higher melting point than the fat of beef or pork. This not only imparts an intense aroma to the molten fat, but also gives the solid fat a kind of waxy property that makes it less inviting than, say, beef or pork fat.

Whatever the reasons for it, this neglect of lamb is a shame. And it's one of those phenomena that feeds on itself. Cooks who recognize half a dozen steaks and several roasts of beef are familiar with only the leg of lamb, the loin chop, and maybe the rib chop. As a result, there is little demand for other cuts. Since there is little demand, butchers and supermarkets don't display them, so consumers don't know about them. And round and round it goes.

We want to help break this circle by encouraging as many of you as possible to eat all kinds of cuts of lamb. Fortunately, this is a particularly good time to start exploring the virtues of lamb, because the quality that you find in the stores has improved markedly over the past decade or two. Although the lamb industry has lagged behind the pork and beef industries in using genetics to produce the type of meat that consumers want, it is now playing a good game of catch-up. Simply put, the cuts of lamb available today are considerably larger than those that our parents bought, with a higher proportion of meat to bone. In fact, since the 1940s, the average weight of a sheep at slaughter has increased by about 60 percent. As a result, you can easily find an eight- or ten-pound leg of lamb in a market, whereas in the old days, a leg that large would have come from older (and tougher) mutton. Best of all, this increase in size has been achieved by carefully selective breeding, without sacrificing tenderness or increasing the ratio of fat to lean meat.

ABOUT CUTS OF LAMB

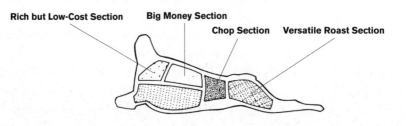

So what are options for cooking lamb? Well, there are plenty.

As with beef and veal, the easiest way to understand lamb is to divide it into four parts. Let's be logical again and start with the front of the animal, the shoulder, which we like to call the Rich but Low-Cost Section; next comes the rib or rack, which like its counterpart in the steer or calf is the Big Money Section; this is followed by the loin, which we are naming the Chop Section; and finally the leg, or Versatile Roast Section. (To simplify things, we are including the foreleg with the shoulder and the breast with the rib section.)

Like the chuck portion of the steer, the shoulder of the lamb is tougher than many other cuts but also has very deep flavor. As a roast, it is one of those dual-purpose cuts: just tender enough to be roasted, but also tough enough to respond to the long, slow moist heat of braising. Chops from the shoulder are particularly nice; somewhat chewy but full of flavor, they are ideal for grilling.

The rib area of the lamb is, like prime rib in beef, very tender and quite flavorful. This portion of the lamb is either cut into flavorful little rib chops or left as lamb racks. A single rack makes a sophisticated and intimate dinner for two, while two racks can be specially cut and formed into a crown roast of lamb.

The lamb loin is also very tender. It is usually cut into butter-soft loin chops, which resemble tiny T-bone steaks. It can also be divided into the ultra-tender tenderloin and flavorful top loin chops. The saddle, which is basically both loins of the lamb, provides a particularly elegant roast.

We don't try to dictate to people the degree to which they should cook their meat. After all, we figure that you bought the meat and that means you get to decide how done you want it. But we like to cook these tender cuts of lamb to rare/medium-rare, so the times in our recipes are for that degree of doneness.

Another important factor when cooking these tender cuts is thickness. We generally prefer thick cuts, and we think they are worth seeking out because they allow you to get a good sear on the outside of the meat without overcooking the interior. We realize, though, that it may not be possible for everyone to get hold of these thick cuts. If you can't, by all means go ahead and buy the thinner version and make the recipe anyway. Just be sure you shorten the cooking times and check even more carefully than you usually do to be sure you don't cook the lamb past the point you want it to be.

Since lamb is brought to market very young, cuts that can be tough in, say, beef, are actually quite tender in lamb. The primary example of this is the leg, which is not only the best known cut of lamb but also the most versatile. It makes a wonderful roast, but it can

Grill-Roasted Rib Roast (Prime Rib) with Potato
Garlic Hobo Pack, Sour Cream

Balsamic-Braised Pot Roast with Tomatoes, Lemons,
Raisins, and Black Olive–Pine Nut Relish
(page 66)

Puerto Rican Vinegar–Braised Flank Steak
with a Cabbage, Corn, and Yucca Salad
(page 77)

Mr. Perfect Steak for Two
(page 89)

Laotian-Style Aromatic Beef Salad
(page 102)

**Sliced Grilled Skirt Steak
on Greek Salad
(page 113)**

**Korean-Style
Grilled Short Ribs
with Ginger,
Chiles, and Quick
Kimchee
(page 117)**

The World's
Hottest Chili,
with Scotch
Bonnet Peppers
and Yucca and
a Cucumber-
Mango Coolant
(page 131)

Señor
Sanchez's
Salvadoran
Soup of Kings
with Short
Ribs, Corn,
and Plantains
(page 133)

Corned Beef and Sweet Potato Hash
with Red Wine–Caramelized Onions
(page 148)

Rack of Veal with Roast Chestnut Stuffing,
Brandied Oranges, and Light Basil Jus
(page 166)

**Tomato-Braised Veal Shanks with Pumpkin
Risotto and Lemon-Pistachio Power Pack
(page 182)**

Grilled Veal Shoulder Chops with Nectarine-Ginger
Chutney and Cucumbers with Mint and Yogurt
(page 198)

**Veal Birdies Tidewater-Style with Smithfield Ham,
Backfin Crab, and Lemon-Caper Sauce
(page 208)**

Grilled Veal, Sweet Potato, and Red Onion Kebabs in the Piccata Style (page 214)

A Hot Open-Faced Veal Meat Loaf Sandwich with Arugula and Blue Cheese–Tomato Relish (page 224)

**Grilled Sweetbreads over Wilted Spinach with
Sweet-and-Sour Bacon Dressing (page 236)**

Grill-Roasted Bone-In Leg of Lamb with Grilled
Peaches and Red Onion–Cilantro Salsa
(page 258)

Grilled Peppered
Lamb Leg Top
on Arugula, Fennel,
and Oranges with
White Bean–Roasted
Red Pepper Relish
(page 260)

Broiled Double-
Thick Lamb Rib
Chops with Slicked-
Up Store-bought
Mint Jelly Sauce
(page 284)

**Broiled Sherried Lamb Skewers with Dried
Apricots and Green Olive Dressing
(page 294)**

Lamb, Leek, and White Bean Stew
with Oregano, Walnuts, and Hard Cheese
(page 305)

Grill-Roasted Rum-Brined Fresh Ham with Mango
Salsa and Grilled Pineapples and Bananas
(page 328)

Roast Pork Loin
with Spicy Hoisin Sauce,
"Peking Duck Style"
(page 332)

Ginger-Rubbed Rack
of Pork with Chile-
Lychee Sambal
(page 337)

Molasses-Glazed Pork Tenderloin with Seared Sweet and
Sour Red Onions and Sage-Date Power Pack
(page 376)

Grilled Pork Loin Fillets on Latin-Style
Salad with Sour Orange–Oregano Dressing
(page 366)

**Grilled Thin Pork Chops
with Avocado-Corn Salsa
(page 374)**

Grilled Baby Back Ribs,
Buffalo Style
(page 380)

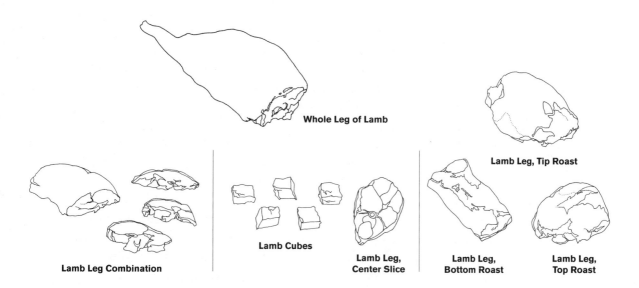

Whole Leg of Lamb

Lamb Leg Combination

Lamb Cubes

Lamb Leg, Center Slice

Lamb Leg, Tip Roast

Lamb Leg, Bottom Roast

Lamb Leg, Top Roast

also be used in a more dynamic fashion, yielding chops and a smaller roast, lamb steaks and a good amount of kebab meat, or even three "subprimal" boneless mini-roasts. (See Getting a Leg Up, page 257, for more details.) When it comes to stews, lamb shines. Meat from either the shoulder or the leg is perfectly suited to stews, and this is one of those places where lamb's affinity for strong flavors comes to the fore.

And then, of course, there are lamb shanks. Served up one per person with the bone sticking out of them, they have the same kind of visceral appeal as veal shanks, but since they are larger they have an even more immediate resonance for the cave person within.

OUR TOP 5 FAVORITE CUTS OF LAMB

1. **Shoulder lamb chop**

2. **Lamb leg top roast**

3. **Center-cut lamb leg steak**

4. **Denver ribs**

5. **Lamb kebab meat from the shoulder**

BUYING LAMB

Shopping for lamb is relatively easy. For one thing, there is no need to spend time looking for a "spring lamb," the one descriptive term that most of us are vaguely familiar with when it comes to this meat. In earlier times, this term denoted an animal that was born in February or March, fed on milk in early spring and grass throughout the summer, and then slaughtered in the fall. Because it was young, it was tender and therefore highly prized. The description was also a nice, catchy phrase that people latched on to because it was easy to understand. But today this term has meaning only as a marketing tool. Lambs may be born any time throughout the year, but almost all are brought to market before they are a year old, most of them between five and seven months. So virtually any lamb you buy today will have the tenderness that the seasonal label used to guarantee.

There is, however, one situation in which "spring lamb" does have some meaning, although it is one that few of us will encounter. Lamb that is 100 percent pasture-fed will have subtle differences in flavor from season to season, because different plants are available for foraging. For instance, in the early spring, there is a lot of wild garlic and onion grass growing in the pastures of rural Pennsylvania, so the free-range lambs raised there by Jamison Farms will pick up those flavors.

But in the United States, well over 80 percent of sheep raised for meat spend some time in feed lots before being slaughtered. This final grain feeding makes the flavor of the fat a bit more mild than what you get with strictly grass-fed lambs, which have a little gamier flavor.

In very high-end butcher shops, you may also occasionally see baby lamb, also known as milk-fed lamb. Under two months old, this is the lamb equivalent of veal, with an extraordinarily tender texture and very mild flavor.

The basic rule of thumb, though, is that almost all the lamb you find will be from sheep under a year old, and therefore very tender. Still, it makes sense to take a look at the lamb you buy to be sure it is in fact what you want. So, when you go to the meat counter, look for lamb that is pinkish red rather than dark purplish red, since the darker the color, the older the lamb. The meat should also look moist and bright, rather than sticky, and the fat should look waxy-white. Another good way to be sure you aren't getting old lamb is to look at the ends of the bones. They should be moist, red in color, and rather porous; if they are white and dry, look somewhere else.

That's about all there is to it. Like beef, lamb is graded Prime, Choice, or Select. However, this ranking is far less important with sheep than with cattle. Over 90 percent of lambs sold in the United States are graded Prime or Choice, largely because they are very efficient converters of grain to meat. As a result, you don't see lamb labeled by grade in markets, because it's just not that much of an issue. Even if it were, choosing the grade you want would not be obvious. Some cooks prefer Prime because it is silkier in texture than Choice, while others find it too fatty.

These days, you see quite a lot of lamb from Australia, New Zealand, and even Iceland in the stores. Like all natural products, lamb differs widely from sample to sample. On the whole, though, imported lamb tends to be smaller and somewhat less fatty than American lamb. This is not, as you might suspect, because the lambs are younger when slaughtered, but simply because they are smaller breeds than those commonly raised in the United States. We encourage you to check out imported lamb for yourself, but in our opinion, American-raised lamb is superior for several reasons: It generally has a higher proportion of meat to bone, it tends to have more robust flavor, and (most important) it doesn't need to be frozen to get to your supermarket.

One final word about buying lamb. Most of us at some point or the other have heard mention of something called "fell" in relation to lamb. Fell is actually a thin membrane that covers the fat of the lamb. It is inedible and needs to be trimmed off before you cook the lamb, but it is really a nonissue. Almost any lamb you buy, whether from a butcher or in a supermarket, will already be trimmed of fell.

Along with beef, lamb is one of the red meats that keeps relatively well. It is generally fine to keep it in the refrigerator, well wrapped, for three to five days. It will freeze, again well wrapped (see page 27), for as long as nine months, although we recommend using it within a month or two.

RECIPES FOR
LARGE TENDER CUTS OF LAMB

Crown Roast of Lamb with Saffron Rice and Apricot-Mint Sauce

Crusty Rack of Lamb with Raisin-Parsley Vinaigrette

Straight-Up Roasted Whole Leg of Lamb over Potatoes and Onions with Lemon, Garlic, and Oregano

Crusty Grilled Butterflied Leg of Lamb with Smoky Eggplant-Fig Relish

Grill-Roasted Bone-in Leg of Lamb with Grilled Peaches and Red Onion–Cilantro Salsa

Grilled Peppered Lamb Leg Top on Arugula, Fennel, and Oranges with White Bean–Roasted Red Pepper Relish

Very Impressive Roasted Lamb Saddle with Peach-Pomegranate Sauce and Garlic-Roasted Tomatoes

Couscous-Stuffed Lamb Loin with Smooth Apricot-Lemon Chutney

Garlic-Studded, Mustard-Crusted Roasted Shoulder of Lamb with Cherry Tomato–Ginger Confit and Rosemary Jus

10 STEPS TO GREAT ROASTED LAMB

1. Preheat the oven.

2. Dry the meat.

3. Season the meat well.

4. Put the roast on a rack in a roasting pan, set on the middle shelf of the preheated oven, and sear it.

5. Turn down the oven temperature.

6. Add the vegetables, if any.

7. Check for doneness early and often.

8. Transfer the meat to a platter, cover loosely with foil, and allow to rest for 10 to 20 minutes, depending on size.

9. Pour off the excess fat from the pan, add stock, deglaze, and simmer to reduce the liquid.

10. Carve the meat and serve, passing the jus separately.

Crown Roast of Lamb with Saffron Rice and Apricot-Mint Sauce

SERVES 4 TO 6

You've probably seen some version of this dish in a movie, or at least in a fancy "lifestyle" magazine. It's so showy—and so expensive—that it's become a kind of shorthand for luxury and a certain style of elegance. It also tastes great when properly cooked.

Basically, the crown roast consists of two racks of lamb that have been cut through the backbone and the chine bone so that they can be fashioned into a circle that resembles a crown. Forming the crown is not all that easy, so you'll want to have the butcher do it for you. He will also "french" the bones, a term that simply means scraping the meat away from the ends of the bones so they look neat and pretty. (If you want to go the whole nine yards, you can even buy those little French white paper hats to put on the ends of the bones after the roast comes out of the oven.)

There are three components to our version of this soigné dish, so there's a little coordination element to the cooking. Since the sauce can easily be reheated, we think it works best to get the sauce started, then make the rice, then put the lamb in the oven. Of course, you could save a little time by making the sauce while the lamb is in the oven, which is certainly a fine way to go. But there is one good reason to get the sauce out of the way first: You're working with a very expensive cut of meat here, so you want to take a lot of care with it. Make sure you have a meat thermometer on hand, for example, because that's the only way to tell when the lamb is cooked to your liking, and start checking for doneness right after you reduce the oven heat to 300°F. Overcooking is the surest way to ruin this piece of meat.

Of course, how you treat this cut really depends on how fancy you want the final dish to look. If you aren't intensely concerned with presentation and want to save time, you can simply prop the two racks up against each other like hands forming a steeple with the fingers interlocking and roast them like that. This is known in the trade as an "honor guard."

Either way, rack of lamb is very easy to serve—just cut between the ribs with a knife, and you'll have rib chops. They're small, so we like to serve four per person.

For a really bang-up sumptuous feast, serve this with sautéed water-cress, Potatoes Anna (page 409) or Au Gratin Potatoes (page 410), and a lettuce salad with homemade blue cheese dressing.

FOR THE SAUCE

1 teaspoon unsalted butter

1 small red onion, peeled and diced small

¾ cup dry red wine

¾ cup red wine vinegar

⅓ cup apricot preserves

⅓ cup roughly chopped fresh mint

Kosher salt and freshly cracked black pepper to taste

FOR THE RICE

1 tablespoon unsalted butter

Large pinch of saffron (20 threads)

1 tablespoon ground coriander

1 small red onion, peeled, halved, and thinly sliced

1½ cups long-grain white rice

3 cups water or chicken stock (or see Stock Options, page 32)

¼ cup sliced almonds, toasted in a dry skillet over medium heat, shaken frequently, until fragrant, 3 to 5 minutes

3 tablespoons roughly chopped fresh parsley

Kosher salt and freshly cracked black pepper to taste

1 lamb rib crown roast (2 racks of lamb, about 1½ pounds each, frenched and tied in a crown shape)

2 tablespoons olive oil

Kosher salt and freshly cracked black pepper to taste

2 tablespoons minced garlic

2 tablespoons freshly cracked coriander seeds (or 1 tablespoon ground coriander)

½ cup roughly chopped fresh parsley

1. Make the sauce: In a medium sauté pan, melt the butter over medium-high heat. Add the onion and cook, stirring occasionally, until translucent, 7 to 9 minutes. Add the wine, vinegar, and preserves and simmer until the sauce is reduced to about 1 cup, 35 to 40 minutes. Remove the pan from the heat, add the mint, and season with salt and pepper.

2. Preheat the oven to 500°F.

3. Make the rice: In a medium sauté pan, melt the butter over medium heat. Add the saffron, coriander, and onion and cook, stirring occasionally, until the onion is translucent, 7 to 9 minutes. Add the rice and stir to coat with the oil, then add the water. Bring to a simmer, cover, reduce the heat to low, and cook until all the liquid has been absorbed, 15 to 18 minutes. Stir in the almonds and parsley and season with salt and pepper. Cover the pan with a tea towel, put the lid on, and set aside.

4. While the rice is cooking, dry the lamb with paper towels, then rub it with the olive oil and sprinkle it generously with salt and pepper. In a small bowl, combine the garlic, coriander, and parsley and mix well, then rub this mixture all over the meat, pressing gently to be sure it adheres. Place the lamb on a rack in a roasting pan and roast for 20 minutes. Reduce the heat to 300°F and continue to cook 5 to 15 minutes more for medium-rare, which is how we like it, or longer if you like it more well-done. To check for doneness, insert a meat thermometer into the dead center of the roast and let it sit for 5 seconds, then read the temperature: 120°F is rare, 126°F is medium-rare, 134°F is medium, 150°F is medium-well, and 160°F is well-done.

5. When the lamb is done, transfer it to a serving platter and pile the saffron rice in the center. Cover with aluminum foil and allow the meat to rest for 10 to 20 minutes. (While it is resting, you may want to reheat the sauce.)

6. To serve, spoon out the rice onto the plates. Cut the butcher's twine and slice the racks into individual chops. Top the rice with the chops and pass the sauce separately.

Crusty Rack of Lamb with Raisin-Parsley Vinaigrette

THE CUT
See Crown Roast of Lamb (page 248) for details on rack of lamb.

SERVES 2

We can't think of a nicer, more intimate, more celebratory meal for two people than this little mini-roast, the rack of lamb. Because the rack is so small, we sear it on top of the stove in a sauté pan rather than searing in the oven as we would a larger roast. We then coat it with a simple mustard sauce and some flavored crumbs and finish cooking it in the oven.

We serve the rack with a simple raisin-parsley vinaigrette, which speaks to us of the Middle Eastern expertise in combining different flavors with lamb.

Serve this with couscous, a Romaine or arugula salad, and perhaps Creamed Spinach (page 431).

OTHER CUTS YOU CAN USE
Lamb leg top roast, known in the restaurant business as a "lamb top," makes an excellent substitute here if you can get it.

1 tablespoon grated lemon zest (yellow part only)

1 teaspoon minced garlic

1 tablespoon cracked coriander seeds (or 1½ teaspoons ground coriander)

¼ cup fresh bread crumbs

2 tablespoons roughly chopped fresh thyme or oregano

2 tablespoons olive oil

Kosher salt and freshly cracked black pepper to taste

1 tablespoon balsamic vinegar

¼ cup grainy mustard

1 rack of lamb, about 1 pound

FOR THE VINAIGRETTE

⅓ cup extra virgin olive oil

2 tablespoons fresh lemon juice

1 tablespoon dry sherry

¼ cup dark raisins

¼ cup roughly chopped fresh parsley

Kosher salt and freshly cracked black pepper to taste

1. Preheat the oven to 350°F.

2. In a small bowl, combine the lemon zest, garlic, coriander, bread crumbs, thyme, 1 tablespoon of the oil, and salt and pepper. Mix well and set aside. In another small bowl, combine the balsamic vinegar and mustard and mix well; set aside.

3. Dry the rack of lamb with paper towels and sprinkle it generously with salt and pepper. In a large ovenproof sauté pan, heat the remaining 1 tablespoon oil over high heat until hot but not smoking. Add the lamb and sear until well browned on both sides, about 5 minutes per side. Remove the lamb from the pan. Paint the top and sides of the meat with the mustard mixture and then pat the bread crumb mixture all over so it adheres to the lamb.

4. Put the lamb back in the sauté pan, place in the oven, and roast for about 20 minutes for rare, or about 25 minutes for medium-rare, which is how we like it, or longer if you like it more well-done. To check for doneness, insert a meat thermometer into the dead center of the meat and let it sit for 5 seconds, then read the temperature: 120°F is rare, 126°F is medium-rare, 134°F is medium, 150°F is medium-well, and 160°F is well-done. When the lamb is done to your liking, remove it from the oven, cover it loosely with aluminum foil, and allow it to rest, for 10 to 20 minutes before carving.

5. Meanwhile, make the vinaigrette: In a medium bowl, combine the olive oil, lemon juice, sherry, raisins, parsley, and salt and pepper and whisk to mix well.

6. Cut the rack into single or double chops, as you wish, and serve, passing the vinaigrette separately.

Straight-Up Roasted Whole Leg of Lamb over Potatoes and Onions with Lemon, Garlic, and Oregano

SERVES 8 TO 10

Leg is among our favorite cuts of lamb, for its near-ideal combination of flavor and tenderness. Like other roasts, it's also an easy way to feed a crowd. A lot of people must agree with our assessment, because the leg is the second most popular and readily available cut of lamb, after loin chops.

Here we roast a whole lamb leg on a bed of potatoes and onions so the juice from the lamb drips down onto the vegetables as it roasts. Some of the potatoes and onions will stick to the pan as the roast cooks, but to us those are the very best, slightly blackened and permeated with lamb juices. We

THE CUT

The name says it all: This is the rear leg of the lamb. Since lambs are small and young, the whole leg is not too big to fit in your oven. For the same reasons, the leg is quite tender, even though it is used to move the animal around and, therefore, has a good deal of connective tissue. In other words, the leg of lamb provides an excellent combination of flavor and tenderness. Half legs are also readily available for those occasions when you're not feeding a large also throw some lemons into the mix; they become a little sweet as they roast and give the vegetables a wonderful flavor.

The general rule with a bone-in leg of lamb is that you get about a 50 percent yield. So if you are looking to serve each person about half a pound of meat, you need to allow a pound per person.

Serve this with a good loaf of crusty bread and a salad of spinach and red onion.

½ cup minced garlic

1 cup chopped fresh oregano

¼ cup olive oil

¼ cup kosher salt, plus more to taste

¼ cup freshly cracked black pepper, plus more to taste

One 10-pound bone-in leg of lamb

8 medium potatoes, peeled and thinly sliced

2 large red onions, peeled, halved, and thinly sliced

3 whole lemons, very thinly sliced and seeded

¼ cup olive oil

1. Preheat the oven to 500°F.

2. In a small bowl, combine the garlic, oregano, olive oil, salt, and pepper and mix well. Dry the lamb well with paper towels. With the point of a paring knife, cut 8 or 10 slits about 2 inches deep in the roast. Push some of the oregano mixture into these slits and into any gaps between the bone and the meat on the ends of the roast, then rub the rest all over the outside of the roast.

3. In a large roasting pan, combine the potatoes, onions, and lemons. Drizzle with the olive oil, sprinkle generously with salt and pepper, and toss to coat.

4. Place the lamb on a rack, place it in the roasting pan with the potato mixture, and roast until well seared, about 20 minutes. Stir the potato-onion mixture around, reduce the oven temperature to 300°F, and continue to cook until the lamb is done the way you like it. To check for doneness, insert a meat thermometer into the dead center of the roast and let it sit for 5 seconds, then read the temperature: 120°F is rare, 126°F is medium-rare, which is how we like it, 134°F is medium, 150°F is medium-well, and 160°F is well-done. Transfer the roast to a cutting board, cover loosely with foil, and allow to rest for 10 to 20 minutes.

5. Carve the lamb into thin slices and serve, accompanied by the potatoes and onions.

crowd. We prefer the sirloin half, nearer the hip, because it is both more tender and meatier than the shank end. See Getting a Leg Up (page 257) for ways to get the most out of a leg of lamb.

OTHER CUTS YOU CAN USE
Any bone-in lamb roast works great in this recipe.

COOK ONCE, EAT TWICE
Any leftover lamb is a great addition to a white bean salad.

Crusty Grilled Butterflied Leg of Lamb with Smoky Eggplant-Fig Relish

SERVES 6 TO 8

Grilled lamb is the absolute rock-solid classic entrée of the Middle East and Greece, and for good reason. The smoky flavor and crusty sear that lamb picks up from a grilling fire work perfectly with the pronounced flavor of the meat.

Here we are using a boned and butterflied leg of lamb, which is pretty easy to cook and carve. This is a big piece of lamb, though, so we are building a two-level fire for the "sear and move" technique. Make sure that you get the meat seared really well, then move it off to the other side of the grill to finish cooking. A big grill is very handy here, because lamb has plenty of fat, so to avoid flare-ups, you may have to move the meat back and forth a couple of times from the hot to the cool part of the grill as it sears. But you can minimize the need for this by only flipping the meat over once while it's searing, no matter how often you have to slide it back and forth.

The relish here may sound a little offbeat, but it is out of this world. You might want to make a double or triple batch, because people will be eating it by the spoonful. To save a little time, you can put the eggplant and onions for the relish on the hotter side of the grill (it will have cooled down to medium-hot by this time) while the lamb finishes cooking on the cooler side.

Serve this with a Spicy Yellow Squash Hobo Pack (page 441) and a pasta salad or spinach salad.

3 tablespoons cumin seeds (or 1½ tablespoons ground cumin)

3 tablespoons coriander seeds (or 1½ tablespoons ground coriander)

¼ cup black peppercorns (or 2 tablespoons freshly cracked black pepper)

¼ cup dried oregano, crumbled

3 tablespoons kosher salt

One 4- to 5-pound boned and butterflied leg of lamb, 2 to 2½ inches thick

10 large garlic cloves, peeled and halved lengthwise

¼ cup olive oil

FOR THE RELISH

2 cups dry red wine

2 tablespoons sugar

2 tablespoons honey

½ cinnamon stick (or 1 teaspoon ground cinnamon)

Minced zest of ½ lemon (yellow part only; about 2 tablespoons)

8 ounces dried figs, quartered (about 1½ cups)

1 large eggplant, cut into ½-inch slices

1 large onion, peeled and quartered

3 tablespoons olive oil

1 tablespoon minced garlic

Kosher salt and freshly cracked black pepper to taste

¼ cup fresh lemon juice (about 1 lemon)

¼ cup roughly chopped fresh parsley

1. Light a two-level fire in your grill.

2. If using whole spices, put the cumin, coriander, and peppercorns in a small heavy sauté pan and toast over medium heat, shaking the pan frequently, until the spices are fragrant, 2 to 3 minutes. Cool, then coarsely grind the spices in a coffee grinder, spice grinder, or mortar and pestle. Stir in the crumbled oregano and salt and set aside. (If using ground spices, simply combine and mix well.)

3. With a paring knife, make 20 small slits in the surface of the lamb and push a piece of garlic into each one. Rub the lamb with the oil, then rub it all over with the spice mixture, pressing lightly to be sure it adheres.

4. When the flames have died down and the coals are covered with white ash, shove about three quarters of the coals to one side of the grill, for a hot fire (you can hold your hand 5 inches above the grill surface for 1 to 2 seconds) and about one quarter to the other side, for a medium fire (you can hold your hand 5 inches above the grill surface for 3 to 4 seconds). Place the lamb directly over the hot section of the fire, fat side up, and sear well, about 10 minutes. Turn and sear the second side, about 10 minutes more. Move to the medium-hot side of the grill and cook, turning once, for 5 to 10 minutes more, until the meat is done to your liking. To check for doneness, insert a meat thermometer into the dead center of the roast, let it sit for 5 seconds, then read the temperature: 120°F is rare, 126°F is medium-rare, which is how we like it, 134°F is medium, 150°F is medium-well, and 160°F is well-done. If you don't want to use a thermometer, check for doneness by the nick, peek, and cheat method: Make a ¼-inch cut in the thickest part of the meat; it should be slightly less done than you like it. When the lamb is done, remove it from the grill, cover it loosely with foil, and let it rest for 10 to 20 minutes.

COOK ONCE, EAT TWICE
If you have any leftover lamb, it is a fantastic addition to a lentil or couscous salad.

5. Meanwhile, make the relish: In a small saucepan, combine the wine, sugar, honey, cinnamon, lemon zest, and figs, stir, and bring just to a simmer over medium-high heat. Reduce the heat and simmer gently for 12 minutes. Remove from the heat and set aside.

6. Rub the eggplant slices and onion quarters with the olive oil and season with the garlic and salt and pepper. Grill the vegetables over the medium-hot fire until they are well browned and the eggplant slices are moist all the way through, 5 to 6 minutes per side. Let cool slightly, then chop the vegetables and add them to the fig sauce. Add the lemon juice and parsley, stir well to combine, and season with salt and pepper.

7. Cut the lamb into thin slices against the grain and serve with the relish.

GETTING A LEG UP

Well known as an excellent roast, leg of lamb can also be used in a more dynamic fashion. Buy a leg, spend a few minutes talking to your butcher, and you can walk away from the meat counter with some very nice chops as well as a user-friendly roast, or with meaty steaks and enough tender cubes for several meals of kebabs.

The first option is to have the butcher cut four or five thick chops from the sirloin or butt end of the leg. These chops have the advantage of being cheaper than chops from the rib and more tender than those from the shoulder. As a point of comparison, they are identical in bone and muscle structure to the steaks from the sirloin of the cow. Some butchers actually call them steaks to distinguish them from chops from other parts of the lamb.

One note of caution: It is a good idea to check out the first chop taken from the end before the butcher wraps up the meat. This chop sometimes has a large knot of white fat in it. If that is the case, ask the butcher to make that meat into cubes for skewers or stew and cut another chop. Fortunately, lamb freezes well, so you can keep the cubes to add to another batch in the future.

With the chops removed, what remains is a four- to five-pound roast. This is the perfect size for many cooks, who find a whole leg not only too large for most meals but too large for their roasting pans as well. This smaller roast will also be of a more uniform thickness, which translates to more even cooking.

A second option for dividing the leg is to cut about half a dozen thick steaks from the center. These substantial but tender center-cut steaks, which resemble ham steaks, can be cooked in the same way as leg chops. Once the steaks are cut from the center, the remaining two portions of the leg can be cut into cubes for skewers.

Yet another approach is to ask the butcher to divide the leg into the three boneless "subprimal" roasts, the top roast, bottom roast, and tip roast. While our favorite among these is the top, all three are very nice little roasts. This will leave you with a nice big shank, plus some scraps that can be turned into ground lamb.

Of course, if you prefer, you can also roast the entire leg in traditional fashion.

THE CUT

See Straight-Up Roasted Whole Leg of Lamb (page 252) for details on leg of lamb.

Grill-Roasted Bone-in Leg of Lamb with Grilled Peaches and Red Onion–Cilantro Salsa

SERVES 8 TO 10

To our taste buds, bone-in meat has a rich, deep taste that can't be matched by anything else in the known world. Here we start with a bone-in leg of lamb, which already has great flavor, then add a barbecue-style spice rub, a sweet-sour glaze, and the unbeatable flavor that comes from slow cooking over the smoke and heat of a live fire. Throw in some grilled peaches and a simple onion salsa, and you've got a pretty astounding combination of tastes and textures.

Of course, if you're in a rush, you can skip the peaches or the salsa or even the glaze, but when you've got a little time, it's definitely worth making the whole shebang.

To carve a bone-in leg of lamb, what you want to do is first take a couple of slices off the thick end and set them aside. Next, grab the leg from the shank (thin) end, hold it up at an angle, and cut as many long horizontal slices off the top of it as you can, continuing until you hit the bone. Turn the leg over and do the same on the opposite side. Finally, cut away any meat that is still attached to the bone. Don't throw the bone away, though; keep it for making an intensely flavorful white bean soup.

Serve this with Latin-Style Black Beans and Rice (page 422) or just plain steamed white rice, some tortillas or crusty bread, and a simple green salad, and you've got one fine feast.

FOR THE SALSA

1 large red onion, peeled and diced small

$1/2$ cup roughly chopped fresh cilantro

$1/3$ cup fresh lime juice (about 2 limes)

5 to 10 dashes Tabasco sauce, or to taste

Kosher salt and freshly cracked black pepper to taste

FOR THE GLAZE

$1/4$ cup red wine vinegar

$1/4$ cup molasses

$1/4$ cup pineapple juice (or substitute orange juice)

$1/4$ cup catsup

2 tablespoons minced canned chipotle peppers in adobo

½ cup cumin seeds (or ¼ cup ground cumin)

½ cup coriander seeds (or ¼ cup ground coriander)

¼ cup kosher salt

¼ cup freshly cracked black pepper

¼ cup paprika

¼ cup packed dark brown sugar

One 10-pound bone-in leg of lamb, trimmed of all but ¼ inch of surface fat

5 ripe peaches, halved and pitted

3 tablespoons olive oil

Kosher salt and freshly cracked black pepper to taste

COOK ONCE, EAT TWICE

If you have any lamb left over, use it as a substitute for ground lamb in New School Shepherd's Pie (page 311).

1. Start a fire well over to one side of a large kettle grill, using enough coals to fill half a shoe box.

2. Make the salsa: In a small bowl, combine the onion, cilantro, lime juice, Tabasco, and salt and pepper and mix well; set aside.

3. Make the glaze: In another small bowl, combine the vinegar, molasses, pineapple juice, catsup, and chipotles and mix well; set aside.

4. In a third small bowl, combine the cumin, coriander, salt, pepper, paprika, and sugar and mix well. Dry the lamb with paper towels and rub it all over with this mixture, pressing gently to be sure it adheres.

5. When the fire has died down and the coals are covered with white ash, place the lamb on the grill on the side away from the coals, being careful that none of the meat is directly over the coals. Put the lid on the grill with the vents open one quarter of the way. Cook, adding a handful of fresh charcoal about every 30 minutes, until the meat reaches the internal temperature you like, 1½ to 2 hours for medium-rare. To check for doneness, insert a meat thermometer into the dead center of the roast, let it sit for 5 seconds, then read the temperature: 120°F is rare, 126°F is medium-rare, which is how we like it, 134°F is medium, 150°F is medium-well, and 160°F is well-done. During the last 2 minutes of cooking, brush the lamb all over with the glaze. Remove the lamb from the grill, cover it loosely with foil, and let it rest for 10 to 15 minutes.

6. While the lamb is cooking, grill the peaches: Brush the peaches with the olive oil, sprinkle them with salt and pepper, and place on the grill right over the hot coals. Cook until nicely browned, 5 to 7 minutes. During the last minute of cooking, brush the peach halves with the glaze.

7. Carve the lamb and serve it with the peaches and salsa, passing any remaining glaze on the side.

The lamb leg top roast is the equivalent of the beef top round, but smaller and more tender. It is what is known as a "subprimal," which is to say a smaller cut fashioned from one of the primals, the larger cuts into which animals are butchered for the whole-sale market. Shaped almost like a large softball, the top roast is one of three boneless subprimals that can be cut from the lamb leg. (The other two are the lamb leg bottom and lamb leg tip.) Like other cuts with the label "top," its name is derived not from its position on the animal but from its position on the butcher's table, where it faces up when the butcher does the carving.

OTHER CUTS YOU CAN USE

You can use any small boneless lamb roast in this recipe, but it should be no larger than 1½ pounds.

Grilled Peppered Lamb Leg Top on Arugula, Fennel, and Oranges with White Bean–Roasted Red Pepper Relish

SERVES 2

Right here is one of my (Chris's) very favorite cuts of lamb. You won't find this in a supermarket, but if you go to a butcher, he will most likely have it, espe-cially if he does any food service business. In the restaurant business, we call this a "lamb top." It weighs about a pound or a little more and although it looks almost like a giant filet mignon, it is actually a mini-roast, which is about my favorite type of cut. I use lamb top all the time at the East Coast Grill. Rela-tively free of connective tissue, it's not only the largest single muscle in the leg of lamb but also the most tender. It is ideal for grilling, it makes a beautiful contiguous slice, and people go wild for it.

Here we use the classic "sear and move" grilling technique, then thinly slice the lamb and serve it on top of a Mediterranean-style salad with a little white bean relish. To segment the oranges, peel them with a sharp knife, removing the white pith entirely, then cut between the membranes and remove each section whole, taking care to remove the seeds.

You've got meat, you've got salad, you've got relish—all you need with this is some good bread and maybe Roasted Garlic Mashed Potatoes (page 413).

FOR THE RELISH

1 teaspoon minced garlic

3 tablespoons balsamic vinegar

3 tablespoons olive oil

¼ cup roughly chopped fresh basil

2 roasted red bell peppers, peeled and seeded, diced small

½ cup cooked or drained canned white beans

¼ cup chopped pitted Kalamata olives (or substitute any briny black olive)

5 scallions, thinly sliced (white and green parts)

Kosher salt and freshly cracked black pepper to taste

One 1-pound lamb top round roast

2 tablespoons kosher salt

3 tablespoons freshly cracked black pepper

FOR THE SALAD

1 small bunch arugula, trimmed, washed, and dried

½ small red onion, peeled and thinly sliced

1 orange, peeled and cut into segments (see headnote above)

½ small fennel bulb, tough outer layer removed and very thinly sliced

⅓ cup extra virgin olive oil

¼ cup fresh lemon juice (about 1 lemon)

Kosher salt and freshly cracked black pepper to taste

COOK ONCE, EAT TWICE

If by chance you have any lamb left over, slice it very thin and put it between two slices of bread with grainy mustard and arugula for a very classy lamb sandwich.

1. Light a two-level fire in your grill, putting about three quarters of the charcoal on one side of the grill bed and one quarter on the other side.

2. Make the relish: In a medium bowl, whisk together the garlic, vinegar, olive oil, and basil. Add the red peppers, beans, olives, and scallions and mix well. Season with salt and pepper; set aside.

3. Dry the lamb with paper towels and rub it all over with the salt and pepper. When the fire has died down and the coals are covered with ash, place the lamb over the hot section. Sear very well on both sides, about 10 minutes per side. Move to the medium-hot side of the grill and continue to cook until the meat reaches the internal temperature you like, 4 to 6 minutes per side for medium-rare. To check for doneness, insert a meat thermometer into the dead center of the roast, let it sit for 5 seconds, then read the temperature: 120°F is rare, 126°F is medium-rare, which is how we like it, 134°F is medium, 150°F is medium-well, and 160°F is well-done. Remove from the grill, cover loosely with foil, and allow to rest for 10 minutes.

4. Make the salad: In a large bowl, combine the arugula, onion, orange segments, and fennel. Drizzle with the olive oil and lemon juice and season with salt and pepper. Toss well and divide between two dinner plates.

5. Slice the lamb against the grain into ¼- to ½-inch slices. Fan the slices over the salads and top each with a spoonful of the relish, passing the remaining relish on the side.

As our friend Mark Bittman
says, "You'll know a saddle
of lamb when you see
it–it's where you would sit
if you were trying to ride
the lamb." To be a bit more
technical, the saddle is the
loin area of the lamb,
extending from the last rib
to the sirloin area. As such,
it contains the most tender
muscles, so it is a very
deluxe piece of meat. While
a whole saddle is going to
set you back a fair amount,
it is not as expensive as it
would be if it were divided
up and sold as, for exam-
ple, double loin chops. To
get this cut, you're definitely going to have to call
your butcher in advance.

Very Impressive Roasted Lamb Saddle with Peach-Pomegranate Sauce and Garlic-Roasted Tomatoes

SERVES 4 TO 5

Okay, let's be honest. To attack this recipe, you are going to have to be a seri-ous lamb fan, and you'll need a cooperative butcher to boot. But as is often the case, when you take the risk, you will be fully rewarded. If you don't already have a butcher who considers you a particularly worthy customer, you will after you ask him to create this cut for you. Because in asking for this cut, you are honoring meat.

What you are going to do is have the butcher take a full lamb loin and bone it out for you. But make sure he leaves the "flaps" on and gives you the spine bone, because what you are going to do then is to put one rub on the inside of the saddle and another on the outside, wrap the meat back up around the bone, and roast it. After it's roasted, you take the bone out and carve it up. It's definitely some work, but the inside-rub/outside-rub effect is amazing, and when you serve this up, you're going to feel like a bona fide lamb genius.

If there is any part of the world that has specialized in lamb cookery over the centuries, it would have to be the Middle East. To honor that, we are making a simple sauce flavored with peaches and pomegranate molasses for this lamb feast.

Serve this with Rice Pilaf with Lime Zest, Pine Nuts, and Aromatic Spices (page 417) and Minted Fresh Peas (page 428).

FOR RUB #1

¼ cup olive oil

1 tablespoon minced garlic

½ cup roughly chopped fresh parsley

Kosher salt and freshly cracked black pepper to taste

FOR RUB #2

¼ cup cracked coriander seeds (or 2 tablespoons ground coriander)

¼ cup kosher salt

¼ cup freshly cracked black pepper

One 6-pound lamb saddle, spine boned out and put back into place, flap
    left on

FOR THE TOMATOES

1 tablespoon extra virgin olive oil

⅓ cup fresh bread crumbs

1 tablespoon minced garlic

3 tablespoons roughly chopped fresh parsley

4 plum tomatoes, cored and halved

Kosher salt and freshly cracked black pepper to taste

2 medium red onions, peeled and diced small

1 peach, pitted and diced small

1 cup dry red wine

¼ cup pomegranate molasses

1. Preheat the oven to 500°F.

2. Make the rubs: Combine the olive oil, garlic, parsley, and salt and pepper in a small bowl and mix well. Combine the coriander, salt, and pepper in a second small bowl and mix well.

3. Remove the spine bone that the butcher has cut away from the rest of the saddle and generously rub the garlic-parsley mixture all over the inside saddle. Replace the bone and re-form the roast, placing the tenderloins under the loin and above the bone. Tie the roast firmly in several places with kitchen twine. Rub the outside of the saddle with the coriander rub. Place the lamb on a rack in a roasting pan and roast until well browned, about 20 minutes.

4. While the roast is browning, prepare the garlic tomatoes: In a small bowl, combine the oil, bread crumbs, garlic, and parsley and mix well. Place the tomato halves on a foil-lined baking sheet, place one eighth of the garlic mixture on each one, and season with salt and pepper. Meanwhile, put the tomatoes on the shelf below the lamb and cook until the bread crumbs are crisp and golden brown, about 30 minutes.

5. Reduce the oven temperature to 300°F, add the onions and peaches to the roasting pan, and roast until the lamb reaches the internal temperature you like, about 20 minutes more for medium-rare. To check for doneness, insert a meat thermometer into the dead center of the roast, let it sit for 5 seconds, then read the temperature: 120°F is rare, 126°F is medium-rare, which is how we like it, 134°F is medium, 150°F is medium-well, and 160°F is well-done.

6. When the lamb is done, remove it from the roasting pan, leaving the onions and peaches in the pan. Cover the lamb loosely with foil and let it rest for 10 minutes.

7. Meanwhile, make the sauce: Remove the excess fat from the roasting pan and place the pan on the stove over two burners on medium-high heat. Add the wine, stirring to dissolve the brown crusty stuff stuck to the bottom of the pan, bring to a simmer, and simmer until the liquid is reduced by one quarter, about 5 minutes. Add the pomegranate molasses, season with salt and pepper, and cover over low heat to keep warm.

8. Cut the twine from the lamb, remove the spine bone, and cut the meat in thick slices against the grain. Drizzle generously with the peach-pomegranate sauce and serve, accompanied by the roasted tomatoes.

THE CUT

This is a boned saddle of lamb, which is the two loins of the animal. In other words, it's basically a double boned lamb loin roast. See Very Impressive Roasted Lamb Saddle (page 262) for more details on this cut, which you will definitely have to get from a butcher.

OTHER CUTS YOU CAN USE

You can apply the flavor principles of this recipe to a roast leg of lamb. Just follow the general directions in Straight-Up Roasted Whole Leg of Lamb (page 252) for roasting the leg, then make the couscous separately and serve the lamb with the couscous and chutney on the side.

Couscous-Stuffed Lamb Loin with Smooth Apricot-Lemon Chutney

SERVES 5

Years ago, a roasted saddle of lamb was a classic "high elegant" dish, served on special occasions in grand homes where the cook, not the owner, did the cooking. Now it has gone out of favor, and the loins (which make up the saddle) are usually cut into chops. But for a really spectacular dinner, it is worth calling your butcher and asking him to bone out a saddle of lamb for you so you can make this dish.

Basically what you do here is lay the lamb loins out flat, spread the couscous stuffing out on top of them, lay the tenderloin over the stuffing, then roll the loins up around it, and tie them securely with string. After that, it's just a matter of browning in a high oven and finishing in a medium-low oven as usual. Stuffing the lamb with the couscous brings the grains into direct contact with the lamb juices, which makes for a much more flavorful side dish.

The chutney here is one of our favorites, with intense spikes of sweet, tart, and hot that get your mouth excited with each bite. Don't worry about the peels on the lemons; they get nice and soft during the half hour of simmering.

Serve this with pita bread, a Romaine lettuce salad with a simple lemon vinaigrette, and Roasted Asparagus (page 427).

FOR THE CHUTNEY

¼ cup roughly chopped fresh ginger

1 tablespoon minced garlic

1 medium red onion, peeled and cut into eighths

1 tablespoon minced fresh chile peppers of your choice, or to taste

1 cup cider vinegar

1½ cups dried apricots diced small (about 8 ounces)

2 lemons, quartered lengthwise, seeded, and quarters cut crosswise into thin slices

1 cup sugar

½ cup fresh pomegranate seeds (or substitute ½ cup currants)

Kosher salt to taste

2 cups instant couscous

1 cup boiling water

2 tablespoons fresh thyme (or 1 tablespoon dried thyme)

1 to 2 teaspoons red pepper flakes, or more to taste

3 tablespoons olive oil

1 medium onion, peeled and diced small

1 tablespoon minced garlic

Kosher salt and freshly cracked black pepper to taste

1 boneless lamb saddle with tenderloin, flaps left on

1. Make the chutney: In a blender, puree the ginger, garlic, onion, and chiles with the cider vinegar. Transfer to a medium nonreactive saucepan and add the apricots, lemons, and sugar. Bring to a boil over medium heat, then reduce the heat to low and simmer until the fruit is very soft and the chutney has thickened, about 30 minutes. Stir in the pomegranate seeds and season with salt. Cover and refrigerate.

2. Preheat the oven to 500°F.

3. Prepare the couscous: In a medium bowl, combine the couscous with the water and allow it to sit for 5 minutes, then fluff it with a fork. Stir in the thyme and pepper flakes. In a large sauté pan, heat the oil over medium-high heat until hot but not smoking. Add the onion and cook, stirring occasionally, until golden brown, 11 to 13 minutes. Add the garlic and cook, stirring, for 1 minute more. Add the onion and garlic to the couscous, mixing well. Season with salt and pepper.

4. Dry the lamb with paper towels, sprinkle the inner surface generously with salt and pepper, and spread it evenly with the couscous filling, leaving about a 1-inch border around the edges. Place the trimmed tenderloin lengthwise across the center of the filling, roll the lamb saddle up around it, and tie firmly at several locations with kitchen twine.

5. Place the roast on a rack in a large roasting pan and roast for 20 minutes to brown. Reduce the oven temperature to 300°F and continue to cook until the meat reaches the internal temperature you like, about 25 minutes for medium-rare. To check for doneness, insert a meat thermometer into the dead center of the roast and let it sit for 5 seconds, then read the temperature: 120°F is rare, 126°F is medium-rare, which is how we like it, 134°F is medium, 150°F is medium-well, and 160°F is well-done. When the roast is done, remove it from the oven, cover it loosely with foil, and let it rest for 10 minutes.

6. Slice the lamb into 1-inch-thick slices and serve, passing the chutney on the side.

Garlic-Studded, Mustard-Crusted Roasted Shoulder of Lamb with Cherry Tomato–Ginger Confit and Rosemary Jus

SERVES 6

THE CUT
See Mango-Braised Lamb Shoulder (page 275) for more information on this cut. You'll probably need to go to the butcher for it.

OTHER CUTS YOU CAN USE
A bone-in half leg of lamb is an excellent substitute for the shoulder roast in this recipe.

BUTCHERSPEAK
Ask the butcher if he can give you the rib side of the shoulder; it's the more tender portion, so a little better for roasting.

When roasting, we generally prefer bone-in meat. We like the heft of the bone, we like the meat that is close to the bone, and, although we have never found anyone who has a fully satisfactory scientific explanation for it, we just think meat cooked bone-in tastes a little bit better. Every butcher and meat aficionado we have talked to agrees, so there must be something to it.

Here we are roasting a bone-in shoulder of lamb, which is very flavorful, if a little bit chewier than other lamb roasts such as the leg or the loin. We push half cloves of garlic into the meat and coat it with grainy mustard before it goes into the oven, then serve it with a tomato-ginger confit and flavor the pan sauce with rosemary, another great lamb accompaniment. So, all in all, there are going to be a lot of rich flavors going on when you bring this to the table.

Serve this with Roasted Potatoes with Black Olives (page 414) and a salad of arugula and blue cheese.

One 5- to 6-pound bone-in lamb shoulder roast

10 cloves garlic, peeled and halved lengthwise

½ cup grainy mustard

¼ cup kosher salt, plus more to taste

¼ cup freshly cracked white pepper (or substitute black pepper), plus more to taste

2 medium carrots, peeled and diced small

2 stalks celery, diced small

1 medium onion, peeled and diced small

FOR THE CONFIT

1 medium red onion, peeled and diced small

1 pint cherry tomatoes, stemmed

3 tablespoons minced fresh ginger

2 tablespoons extra virgin olive oil

2 tablespoons fresh lemon juice (about 1/2 lemon)

2 tablespoons brown sugar

Kosher salt and freshly cracked black pepper to taste

1 cup lamb or chicken stock (or see Stock Options, page 32)

1 cup dry red wine

1/2 cup balsamic vinegar

1/4 cup fresh rosemary needles

1. Preheat the oven to 350°F.

2. With a paring knife, make 20 small slits in the surface of the lamb and push a half garlic clove into each one. In a small bowl, combine the mustard, salt, and white pepper and mix well. Rub this mixture generously over the meat, place the meat in a roasting pan, and surround with it the carrots, celery, and onion.

3. Place the lamb in the oven and roast until it is done the way you like it, 1 hour to 1 hour and 10 minutes for medium-rare. To check for doneness, insert a meat thermometer into the dead center of the roast and let it sit for 5 seconds, then read the temperature: 120° is rare, 126°F is medium-rare, which is how we like it, 134°F is medium, 150°F is medium-well, and 160°F is well-done.

4. While the lamb is roasting, make the confit: In a small roasting pan, combine the onion, tomatoes, ginger, and olive oil and toss to mix. Place in the oven and roast until the tomatoes are shrunken and wrinkled and the onions are slightly caramelized, about 45 minutes. Transfer to a small bowl, add the lemon juice, brown sugar, and salt and pepper and stir gently to mix well. Set aside.

5. When the roast is done to your liking, transfer it to a platter, cover it loosely with foil, and let it rest for 20 minutes.

6. Meanwhile, make the sauce: Pour off any excess fat from the roasting pan and place the pan on the stove over two burners at medium-high heat. Add the stock, wine, and vinegar, stirring to dissolve the brown crusty stuff stuck to the bottom of the pan. Bring to a simmer and let simmer until the liquid is reduced by half, about 15 minutes. Strain the sauce, add the rosemary, and season with salt and white pepper.

7. Cut the lamb into thick slices, drizzle it with some of the jus, and serve, accompanied by the confit and the remaining jus.

RECIPES FOR
LARGE TOUGH CUTS OF LAMB

10 STEPS TO GREAT BRAISED LAMB

1. Dry the meat.

2. Season the meat well.

3. Sear the meat hard.

4. Remove the meat from the pot, adjust the amount of fat in the pot, and sauté the aromatics and vegetables.

5. Deglaze the pot with some of the liquid.

6. Return the meat to the pot along with enough liquid to cover it about halfway.

7. Bring to a simmer, skim the film, cover the pot, and place in a 300°F oven.

8. Check for doneness early and often: Look for "fork-tender."

9. Skim the fat and any film from the liquid and, if you want, remove the meat and reduce the liquid; season to taste.

10. Carve the meat and serve with the braising liquid on the side.

North African–Style Braised Lamb Shanks with Lemons, Tomatoes, and Green Olives

THE CUT

See Chianti-and-Balsamic-Braised Lamb Shanks (page 270) for details on lamb shanks.

SERVES 6

Lemons, tomatoes, and green olives are typical flavors of North African cooking, and together they give this dish a bold, tangy flavor. We particularly like the strong jolt the dish gets from the whole lemon segments.

To segment the lemons, peel them with a sharp knife, removing the white pith entirely, then cut between the membranes and remove each section whole, being careful to take out all the seeds.

You might serve this over couscous and accompany it with a salad of oranges and red onions or a green salad with feta cheese. Or try it with Horseradish Mashed Potatoes (page 413).

- 6 lamb shanks, about 1 pound each, well trimmed
- Kosher salt and freshly cracked black pepper to taste
- 2 tablespoons olive oil, or more if needed
- 2 onions, peeled, halved, and thinly sliced
- 2 tablespoons minced garlic
- 2 stalks celery, diced small
- About 2 cups dry white wine
- 2 cups lamb or chicken stock (or see Stock Options, page 32)
- 6 large sprigs fresh thyme, plus 2 tablespoons fresh thyme leaves (or 1 tablespoon dried thyme)
- 1 bay leaf
- 2 whole cloves
- 3 lemons, peeled and cut into segments (see headnote above)
- 2 large tomatoes, cored and diced large
- ¾ cup green olives in brine, rinsed, pitted, and halved
- ½ cup roughly chopped fresh parsley

1. Preheat the oven to 300°F.

2. Dry the shanks with paper towels and sprinkle them generously with salt and pepper. In a 5-inch-deep Dutch oven or other large ovenproof pot with a lid, heat the oil over medium-high heat until very hot but not smoking. Add the shanks in a single layer, in batches if necessary to avoid crowding, and brown well on all sides, about 15 minutes total cooking time. Transfer the shanks to a platter as they are done.

3. Pour off the fat or add oil to the pot as needed so you have a total of about 2 tablespoons in the pot. Add the onions and cook, stirring occasionally, until translucent, 7 to 9 minutes. Add the garlic and celery and cook, stirring occasionally, for 5 minutes. Add the wine and stock and bring to a simmer, scraping to dissolve any browned bits on the bottom of the pan.

4. Add the shanks, along with the thyme sprigs, bay leaf, and cloves. (The liquid should come about halfway up the shanks; if it does not, add more wine or water.) Season with salt and pepper, bring to a simmer, and skim any film from the surface. Cover, place in the oven, and cook until the meat is tender, 2 to 2½ hours. To check for doneness, plunge a fork straight down into the meat and try to pull the fork out. If the fork slides right out, the meat is done; if the meat hangs on to the fork, give it more time.

5. When the shanks are done, transfer them to a platter and cover them loosely with foil to keep warm. Skim the fat from the braising liquid and reduce it until it has thickened slightly, then season with salt and pepper and strain into a clean pot. Add the cooked shanks, the lemon segments, tomatoes, and green olives and cook, stirring frequently, for 5 minutes. Remove from the heat, stir in the thyme leaves and parsley, season with salt and pepper, and serve, preferably over couscous.

THE CUT

The shank is basically the lower part of the leg of the lamb. It is very tough, with lots of connective tissue, but it becomes very tender and creates an elegant, silky liquid when braised. Foreshanks (known as trotters) or hind shanks both work perfectly well, but we prefer the hind shanks. They are larger and meatier, and because lamb is slaughtered so young, they are not all that much tougher.

Chianti-and-Balsamic-Braised Lamb Shanks over Creamy Parmesan Polenta with Roasted Tomato–Garlic Relish

SERVES 6

Over the past few years, lamb shanks have become popular in the restaurant world. The lamb equivalent of the highly fashionable osso buco, they are relatively inexpensive but have a tremendous amount of flavor, and if cooked slowly in moist heat, they become very tender. They are also nearly impossible to screw up, an advantage in any kitchen.

This recipe demonstrates some of the reasons for the popularity of lamb shanks. The lamb is amazingly easy to make, and when it comes out of the oven after that long, slow cooking in flavorful liquid, it tastes fantastic.

Creamy polenta makes a great base for these shanks, but if you don't want to take the time to make it, you can simply serve the shanks and the flavorful braising liquid over egg noodles or Mashed Potatoes (page 413). By the same token, you can make the polenta and skip the relish if you like. But we recommend you go ahead and make all three components. It's not really that much work (the relish can be made several days ahead) and together they make for a very impressive and full-flavored Italian-style meal.

We would serve this with a salad of tomatoes and arugula and Quick-Sauteed Spinach with Garlic (page 427).

OTHER CUTS YOU CAN USE
You can make this recipe with meaty beef short ribs if you like.

6 lamb shanks, about 1 pound each, trimmed

Kosher salt and freshly cracked black pepper to taste

3 tablespoons vegetable oil, or more if needed

2 onions, peeled and thinly sliced

2 carrots, peeled and diced medium

2 stalks celery, diced medium

2 tablespoons minced garlic

4 sprigs fresh thyme (or 2 teaspoons dried thyme)

2 whole cloves

1 bay leaf

About 2 cups Chianti or other dry red wine

1 cup balsamic vinegar

About 1½ cups lamb or chicken stock (or see Stock Options, page 32)

FOR THE RELISH

¼ cup olive oil

6 plum tomatoes, cored, peeled, seeded, and cut into eighths

1 head garlic, separated into individual cloves and peeled

½ teaspoon ground allspice

1 tablespoon dark brown sugar

Kosher salt and freshly cracked black pepper to taste

Splash of red vermouth (optional)

FOR THE POLENTA

2 tablespoons unsalted butter

1 medium yellow onion, peeled and diced small

3½ cups milk

3½ cups chicken stock

1½ cups medium-grind yellow cornmeal

1 cup freshly grated Parmesan cheese

Kosher salt and freshly cracked black pepper to taste

1. Preheat the oven to 300°F.

2. Dry the lamb shanks with paper towels and sprinkle them generously with salt and pepper. In a 5-inch-deep Dutch oven or other large ovenproof pot with a lid, heat the oil over medium-high heat until very hot but not smoking. Add the shanks in a single layer, in batches if necessary to avoid crowding, and cook until well browned on all sides, 10 to 15 minutes total; transfer the shanks to a platter as they are done.

3. Pour off all but about 2 tablespoons of fat from the pot. Add the onions and cook, stirring occasionally, until translucent, 7 to 9 minutes. Add the carrots and celery and cook, stirring occasionally, for 5 minutes. Add the garlic, thyme, cloves, and bay leaf and cook, stirring, for 1 minute more.

4. Return the lamb to the pot and pour in the wine, vinegar, and stock. (The liquid should come about halfway up the sides of the shanks; if it does not, add more wine or stock.) Bring to a simmer, stirring to incorporate any brown crusty stuff in the bottom of the pot, and skim any film from the surface. Cover, place in the oven, and cook until the lamb is very tender, 1½ to 2 hours. To check for doneness, plunge a fork straight down into the meat and try to pull the fork out. If the fork slides right out, the meat is done; if the meat hangs on to the fork, give it more time.

5. While the shanks are braising, make the relish: Combine all the ingredients in a shallow baking dish, cover with aluminum foil, and place in the oven beside the shanks. Cook until tender, stirring occasionally, 2 to 2½ hours.

6. When the shanks are done, transfer them to a platter and cover with foil to keep warm. Skim the fat from the braising liquid, taste the liquid, and reduce it if necessary to give it more flavor. For a thicker sauce, reduce it until it coats the back of a spoon. Strain the sauce into a clean pot, add the cooked shanks, cover, and keep warm.

7. About 20 minutes before you think the lamb will be done, start making the polenta. In a medium sauté pan, melt the butter over medium heat. Add the onion and cook, stirring occasionally, until golden brown, 11 to 13 minutes. Add the milk and chicken stock and bring to a boil, then slowly add the cornmeal in a steady stream, whisking constantly. Bring back to a simmer, whisking to break up any lumps, and cook, stirring frequently, until the polenta is thick and creamy but not so thick that a wooden spoon stands up by itself, 20 to 25 minutes. Stir in the cheese, season with salt and pepper, and serve immediately, topped with the shanks and lots of sauce.

Barbecued Lamb Shoulder Kentucky-Style, with Chile-Vinegar Sauce and Sweet-and-Sour Slaw

SERVES 4 TO 5

While this dish may surprise even a lot of die-hard barbecue fans, it is actually in the fine old Kentucky tradition of barbecued mutton. Barbecuing is essentially a smoke braise, in which the meat is cooked through long exposure to indirect heat and smoke. It works perfectly for relatively tough cuts of meat such as shoulder. In fact, you can feel free to use some of the tougher (and even cheaper) lamb shoulder cuts, like the blade roast, in this treatment. After all, if a few hours in the barbecue pit can make mutton tender, a slightly gnarly lamb shoulder should present no problems whatsoever.

The deep, rich, smoky flavor of this lamb goes great with Grilled Corn on the Cob (page 433) and sweet potato salad.

¼ cup kosher salt

¼ cup paprika

2 tablespoons ground cumin

2 tablespoons ground coriander

2 tablespoons cayenne pepper

1 teaspoon ground cinnamon

¼ cup packed dark brown sugar

One 5-pound boneless lamb shoulder roast

FOR THE SLAW

3 cups shredded green cabbage

1 carrot, peeled and grated

¼ cup dried apricots, diced small

¼ cup granulated sugar

½ cup cider vinegar

2 tablespoons celery seeds

Kosher salt and freshly cracked black pepper to taste

FOR THE SAUCE

1 cup white vinegar

2 tablespoons Tabasco sauce

Kosher salt and freshly cracked black pepper to taste

THE CUT

What we are using here is the boneless lamb shoulder roast, which is the square-cut shoulder roast (see Mango-Braised Lamb Shoulder, page 275) with the bones removed. Using the boneless version not only makes it easier to carve, but brings the roast down to about the 5-pound range. Of course, the bone-in version is also excellent here. If you like, you could also use what is called the shoulder cushion roast; this is another boneless version of the same roast, but instead of being rolled up, it is laid out flat.

OTHER CUTS YOU CAN USE

A lamb shoulder eye roast, sometimes called a Saratoga roast, is also fine for this treatment, as is a lamb shoulder blade roast. You could even use a leg of lamb, but in that case, leave at least ¼ inch of fat on the exterior so that it stays moist as it cooks.

COOK ONCE, EAT TWICE

Like shredded pork barbe-
cue, lamb barbecue keeps
a long time and freezes
well. Or you can substitute
leftover barbecued lamb
for the ground lamb in New
School Shepherd's Pie
(page 311).

1. Light a fire well over to one side of a large kettle grill, using enough coals to fill half a shoe box.

2. In a small bowl, combine the salt, paprika, cumin, coriander, cayenne, cinnamon, and brown sugar. Rub the lamb all over with this mixture, pressing gently to be sure it adheres.

3. When the fire has died down and the coals are covered in white ash, place the meat on the side of the grill away from the coals, being careful that none of the meat is directly over the coals. Put the lid on the grill with the vents open one quarter of the way. Cook, adding a handful of fresh charcoal about every 30 minutes, until the meat is super-tender, 3 to 4 hours. To check for doneness, plunge a fork straight down into the meat and try to pull the fork out. If the fork slides out easily, the meat is done; if the meat hangs on to the fork, give it more time.

4. While the lamb is cooking, make the slaw: In a medium bowl, combine the cabbage, carrot, and dried apricots and toss well. In a small bowl, combine the granulated sugar, vinegar, and celery seeds and mix very well. Pour the dressing over the cabbage, toss to combine, and season with salt and pepper. Cover and refrigerate.

5. Make the sauce: In a small bowl, whisk together the vinegar, Tabasco sauce, and salt and pepper.

6. When the lamb is done, remove it from the grill and chop or shred the meat. Mix with the vinegar-Tabasco sauce to taste and serve, accompanied by the slaw.

Mango-Braised Lamb Shoulder with Sweet Toasted Spices and Tomato-Cucumber Relish

SERVES 4 TO 6

One of the great things about braising is that because of the long cooking time and the strong character of the cuts of meat that are best for braising, you can add plenty of intense flavors and still not overpower the dish.

Here we take advantage of that dynamic to make an Indian-inspired dish from a large shoulder lamb roast. Slow-cooking the lamb in mango juice, wine, and vinegar along with some sautéed garlic, ginger, and chile peppers gives both lamb and liquid a range of deep, compelling flavors. We then finish the dish by toasting a mixture of sweet spices, grinding them up together, and passing them around for people to sprinkle on their meat like high-powered salt and pepper. It's similar to the way Indian cooks add the spice mix known as *garam masala* to dishes at the end of cooking. For a little coolant, we also add a simple but tasty tomato-cucumber relish.

We would serve this with basmati or plain long-grain rice, some *chapatis* or other flatbread, and a simple green salad.

> One 5- to 6-pound lamb square-cut shoulder roast, trimmed of most external fat
>
> Kosher salt and freshly cracked black pepper to taste
>
> 2 tablespoons olive oil
>
> 1 onion, peeled and diced small
>
> 1 red bell pepper, cored, seeded, and diced small
>
> 1 green bell pepper, cored, seeded, and diced small
>
> 2 tablespoons minced garlic
>
> 2 tablespoons minced fresh ginger
>
> 1 to 2 tablespoons minced fresh chile peppers of your choice, or to taste
>
> 2 cups mango juice (or substitute orange juice)
>
> ½ cup balsamic vinegar
>
> About 1 cup dry red wine
>
> 5 cardamom pods
>
> 1 star anise

THE CUT

Shoulder is the lamb equivalent of beef chuck. Like chuck, it comes from a part of the animal that does a lot of work, so it has plenty of connective tissue. It also has quite a few bones and a fair amount of fat. But it has excellent flavor and when cooked properly, which is to say long and low with some liquid, it becomes quite tender. As an added selling point, it is usually quite cheap.

Our first choice for this recipe is the bone-in lamb square-cut shoulder roast, often simply referred to as a lamb shoulder roast. This is basically the whole shoulder and upper arm, so it is often as large as 8 pounds. If you can't find one in the 5- to 6-pound neighborhood, go ahead and buy the larger one, then ask your butcher to slice off a few arm chops; you can toss them in the freezer for another day.

Those of you who don't like carving around a variety of bones might opt for the boneless shoulder roast, which is the same cut with the bones removed. It's a little bit less flavorful, but it's certainly less work. The choice is yours.

OTHER CUTS YOU CAN USE

Lamb shoulder roasts can be hard to locate, so really you should feel free to use any roast from the shoulder in this recipe. The outside shoulder roast and shoulder blade roast are good choices, as is a shoulder arm roast.

2 tablespoons coriander seeds

1 tablespoon cumin seeds

½ cinnamom stick

2 tablespoons white peppercorns

FOR THE RELISH

4 plum tomatoes, cored and diced small

1 cucumber, peeled, seeded, and diced small

⅓ cup fresh lemon juice (about 1½ lemons)

2 tablespoons yellow mustard seeds

1 tablespoon fennel seeds

Kosher salt and freshly cracked black pepper to taste

1. Preheat the oven to 300°F.

2. Dry the lamb with paper towels and rub it generously all over with salt and pepper. In a 5-inch-deep Dutch oven or other large ovenproof pot with a lid, heat the oil over medium-high heat until very hot but not smoking. Add the lamb and brown well on all sides, about 15 minutes total. Transfer the meat to a platter.

3. Pour off all but about 2 tablespoons of fat from the pot. Add the onion and peppers and cook, stirring occasionally, until the onion is golden brown, 11 to 13 minutes. Add the garlic, ginger, and chiles and cook, stirring, for 2 minutes more. Add the mango juice and vinegar and bring to a simmer, scraping up any browned bits from the bottom of the pot.

4. Return the meat to the pot and add the wine. (The liquid should come about halfway up the side of the lamb; if it does not, add water or more wine.) Bring to a simmer again and skim any scum from the surface. Cover, place in the oven, and cook until the meat is very tender, 1½ to 2 hours. To check for doneness, plunge a fork straight down into the meat and try to pull the fork out. If the fork slides out easily, the meat is done; if the meat hangs on to the fork, give it more time.

5. While the meat is cooking, place the cardamom, anise, coriander, cumin, cinnamon, and white peppercorns in a small heavy sauté pan and toast over medium heat, shaking the pan frequently to prevent scorching, until they darken and become fragrant, 2 to 3 minutes. Grind together in a spice mill or coffee grinder and set aside.

6. Make the relish: In a medium bowl, combine the tomatoes, cucumber, lemon juice, mustard seeds, fennel seeds, and salt and pepper and mix well.

7. When the meat is done, remove it from the pot and cover it loosely with foil to keep warm. Skim the fat from the braising liquid. Taste the liquid, and if it needs more flavor, place the pot on the stove over medium-high heat and simmer to reduce the liquid. For a thicker sauce, reduce it until it coats the back of a spoon. Season with salt and pepper.

8. Cut the meat into thick slices, drizzle with the braising liquid, and serve, passing the relish and toasted spices separately.

COOK ONCE, EAT TWICE

As with other braised meats, leftover lamb from this dish is great cut into cubes, mixed with rice and enough of the braising liquid to moisten, and then heated up like a casserole. If you have any leftover relish, serve it alongside. If not, try some mango pickles.

RECIPES FOR
SMALL TENDER CUTS OF LAMB

10 STEPS TO GREAT GRILLED LAMB

1. Build a two-level fire using hardwood charcoal.

2. Wait for the flames to die down and the coals to be covered with gray ash.

3. Check the temperature of the fire.

4. Dry the meat well.

5. Season the meat well.

6. Sear the meat hard over a hot fire.

7. Move the meat to the cooler part of the fire if it needs to cook more slowly (don't use the cover).

8. Flip the meat only once during cooking.

9. Check for doneness early and often (nick, peek, and cheat).

10. Remove the meat from the fire, cover with foil, allow to rest, then serve it up.

Grilled Peppered Lamb Loin Chops with Green Grape–Parsley Relish

Grilled Double-Thick Lamb Loin Chops with Roasted Peppers and Onions and Creamy Braised Garlic-Parmesan Vinaigrette

Broiled Double-Thick Lamb Rib Chops with Slicked-Up Store-bought Mint Jelly Sauce

Grilled Lamb Tenderloins on Greek Salad with Grilled Pita

Grilled Lamb Shoulder Chops Greek-Style

Parsley-Coated Grilled Lamb Loin with Smoky Eggplant Planks and Tomato-Fig Hobo Pack

Sautéed Lamb Medallions with Red Wine–Pomegranate Sauce and Minted Vegetables

Indobob: Spice-Rubbed Grilled Lamb Skewers with Peanut-Herb Power Pack

Grilled Lamb and Peach Skewers with Cumin-Raisin Vinaigrette

Broiled Sherried Lamb Skewers with Dried Apricots and Green Olive Dressing

Grilled Lamb Leg Steaks on Eggplant Planks with Mint-Yogurt Sauce and Cucumber–Red Onion Relish

Denver Lamb Ribs Adobo with Fresh Pineapple-Chipotle Glaze

Stir-fried Lamb with Green Beans, Eggplant, and Peppers in Hoisin-Ginger Sauce

10 STEPS TO GREAT SAUTÉED LAMB

1. Use a big heavy sauté pan.

2. Dry the meat well.

3. Season the meat well.

4. Use only a small amount of oil.

5. Get the pan and the oil hot.

6. Don't overcrowd the meat in the pan.

7. Sear the meat hard.

8. Flip the meat only once while cooking.

9. Check for doneness early and often (nick, peek, and cheat).

10. Remove the meat from the heat, cover with foil, and allow to rest, then serve.

10 STEPS TO GREAT BROILED LAMB

Check out sautéing: The steps are the same except you use a broiler pan instead of a sauté pan, preheat the broiler instead of getting the oil hot, and skip the searing step.

As their name states, lamb loin chops come from the loin, which is a very tender part of the animal. They are like little baby T-bones, each one containing a small piece of the ultra-tender tenderloin muscle and a larger piece of the top loin muscle, divided by a T-shaped bone. They are the most expensive type of lamb chops, which means they cost a pretty penny indeed. But they are worth it for many cooks, because they are extremely tender and have a delicate lamb flavor that is appreciated even by people who are not always that fond of lamb.

Top loin chops, which do not have the tenderloin portion, are also excellent in this recipe. Shoulder chops and leg chops are fine too, but they should be cooked over a hot rather than medium-hot fire, for a minute or so less per side.

Grilled Peppered Lamb Loin Chops with Green Grape–Parsley Relish

SERVES 4

You have to be careful when cooking lamb chops over live fire because they contain a fair amount of fat that can drip into the fire and cause flare-ups. (When you are cooking loin chops, which sometimes have little tails, you also have to watch that these thin tails don't burn.) So make sure you leave a portion of the grill with no coals so you can move the chops there to let any flare-ups die down.

If you have cooked from our other books, you may well have seen this relish before, because it's one of our bedrock favorites. It's a little unusual, but the sweetness of the grapes perfectly balances out the strong vinegar and garlic flavors, and it's a breeze to make. It will keep, covered and refrigerated, for 3 to 4 days.

Serve this with grilled pita bread, Green Beans with Mushrooms and Almonds (page 429), and a spinach or cucumber and tomato salad.

FOR THE RELISH
1 cup seedless green grapes, halved
¼ cup red wine vinegar
¼ cup virgin olive oil
1 teaspoon minced garlic
¼ cup roughly chopped fresh parsley
Kosher salt and freshly cracked black pepper to taste

Eight 6-ounce lamb loin chops, 1½ inches thick
¼ cup kosher salt
⅓ cup freshly cracked black pepper
2 tablespoons minced garlic
2 tablespoons olive oil

1. Light a fire in your grill, making sure to leave part of the grill free of coals.

2. Make the relish: In a small bowl, combine the grapes, vinegar, olive oil, garlic, parsley, and salt and pepper. Mix well and set aside.

3. Dry the lamb chops with paper towels and rub them on all sides with the salt, pepper, minced garlic, and olive oil. When the fire has died down and the coals are medium-hot (you can hold your hand 5 inches above the grill surface for about 3 seconds), place the chops on the grill and cook until they are well seared on both sides and done to your liking on the interior, 4 to 5 minutes per side for rare. (If there are flare-ups, move the offending chop briefly to the part of the grill with no coals.) To check for doneness, nick, peek, and cheat: Make a ¼-inch cut in the thickest part of the meat; it should be slightly less done than you like it. When they are done, remove the chops from the grill, cover them loosely with foil, and allow them to rest for 5 minutes.

4. Serve the chops accompanied by the relish.

See Grilled Peppered Lamb
Loin Chops (page 280) for
details on loin chops. Here
we are using double chops,
which means they are even
more expensive, but they
do make a very impressive
presentation.

Top loin chops, which do
not have the tenderloin
portion, are a fine substitute here, but be sure to
get double-thick versions.
If you can't get them, then
use the standard thickness
and follow the directions
on page 278 for cooking
them. Shoulder chops and
leg chops are also good,
but they should be cooked
over a hot rather than
medium-hot fire, for a
minute or so less per side.

Grilled Double-Thick Lamb Loin Chops with Roasted Peppers and Onions and Creamy Braised Garlic-Parmesan Vinaigrette

SERVES 4

Double-thick loin chops are about the most luxurious chop you can find. Super-tender and with a delicate but pronounced lamb flavor, they are a real delicacy. They are also huge by lamb chop standards, so this is a "sear and move" situation, in which we brown the chops over a hot fire, then move them to a cooler fire to finish cooking.

To save time, you can braise the garlic several days ahead of time, squeeze the garlic meat out of the cloves, put it in a bowl, cover it with a film of olive oil, and keep it in the refrigerator.

Serve these with Quick-Sautéed Broccoli Rabe with Garlic and Oil (page 430) and either risotto or a side dish of pasta.

FOR THE VINAIGRETTE

1 head garlic

3 tablespoons olive oil

1 tablespoon grainy mustard

2 tablespoons freshly grated Parmesan cheese

3 tablespoons fresh lemon juice (about 1 lemon)

2 tablespoons red wine vinegar

1/2 cup extra virgin olive oil

Kosher salt and freshly cracked black pepper to taste

Eight 8-ounce double lamb loin chops, at least 2 inches thick

Kosher salt and freshly cracked black pepper to taste

2 red or yellow bell peppers, cored, seeded, and halved

2 medium red onions, peeled and cut into 1/2-inch-thick slices

3 tablespoons olive oil

1/4 cup roughly chopped pitted black olives

1/4 cup roughly chopped fresh oregano

1. To make the vinaigrette, first braise the garlic: Preheat the oven to 400°F. Slice off the top 1/4 inch of the unpeeled head of garlic and place the garlic in the center of a foot-long sheet of foil. Pour the 3 tablespoons oil over the bulb, wrap it up tightly, and roast until the individual garlic cloves are soft to the touch, about 1 hour.

2. Remove the garlic from the oven and, as soon as it's cool enough to handle, break the individual cloves from the head and squeeze the meat out of each one into a small bowl. Add the mustard and cheese and mix well. In a separate bowl, combine the lemon juice and vinegar and add the extra virgin olive oil in a steady stream, whisking steadily. Add the garlic mixture, whisk together well, and season with salt and pepper. Cover and set aside.

3. Build a two-level fire in your grill, putting about three quarters of the coals on one side and about one quarter on the other side.

4. Sprinkle the chops generously with salt and pepper. When the fire has died down and the coals are hot on the side with more coals (you can hold your hand 5 inches above the grill surface for 1 to 2 seconds), place the chops on the grill and sear well, about 6 minutes per side. Move to the cooler side of the grill and cook, turning once, for 4 to 6 minutes more for rare. To check for doneness, nick, peek, and cheat: Make a ¼-inch cut in the thickest part of the meat; it should be slightly less done than you like it. When the chops are done to your liking, remove them from the grill, cover them loosely with foil, and let them rest for 5 minutes.

5. While the lamb is searing, coat the peppers and onions with the olive oil, being careful not to separate the onion slices into rings. (If it makes it easier, stick a toothpick or small wooden skewer horizontally through each slice to keep the rings together.) When you move the lamb to the cooler side of the grill, lay the peppers and onions on the grill right beside them and cook, turning once, until tender and nicely browned, 4 to 6 minutes.

6. In a medium bowl, separate the onions into rings. Thinly slice the peppers and add to the onions, along with the olives and oregano. Toss with about ¼ cup of the vinaigrette.

7. Serve the roasted vegetables with the chops, passing the remaining dressing on the side.

Here we are calling for
chops from the rib area of
the lamb, the lamb equivalent of the Delmonico
steak. Since these chops
are relatively thin, we are
using double-thick ones
here, each containing two
rib bones. Although not as
expensive as loin chops,
they are still going to set
you back a bit, but they are
really excellent little chops.
A slightly less costly
approach is to buy whole
racks and cut them into
2-bone chops.

If you don't mind the
expense, double loin chops
are an excellent substitute
in this recipe.

Broiled Double-Thick Lamb Rib Chops with Slicked-Up Store-bought Mint Jelly Sauce

SERVES 4

Lamb and mint are a very traditional English combination. But the straight mint jelly that is often served with lamb is a little too sweet for our taste. Add some fresh lemon juice for tartness, a bit of cardamom for a touch of exotic aromaticity, and some butter to smooth the whole thing out, and you've got the makings of a great but very quick and simple pan sauce.

This recipe is also great on the grill. But since a hot fire, which is what you should use, is a bit hotter than the broiler even set on high, cook the chops for about 1 minute less per side.

Serve these chops with Persian Rice (page 418) and a salad of tomatoes, scallions, black olives, and cilantro, tossed with a lemon vinaigrette.

FOR THE SAUCE

One 8-ounce jar mint jelly

¼ cup fresh lemon juice (about 1 lemon)

Seeds from 4 cardamom pods (or ¼ teaspoon ground cardamom)

2 tablespoons cold unsalted butter, cut into pieces

¼ cup fresh mint leaves, cut into very thin strips

8-ounce double lamb rib chops, 1½ inches thick

3 large cloves garlic, peeled and halved lengthwise

2 tablespoons olive oil

Kosher salt and freshly cracked black pepper to taste

1. Preheat the broiler, set on high if you have a choice.

2. Make the sauce: In a medium sauté pan, warm the jelly over low heat until it liquefies. Stir in the lemon juice and cardamom, then raise the heat, bring to a simmer, and simmer until the sauce is reduced by half, about 10 minutes. Remove from the heat and add the cold butter a little at a time, swirling the pan to blend it into the sauce. Stir in the mint leaves and set aside.

3. As soon as the sauce is done, cook the chops: Dry the chops with paper towels, rub them with the cut sides of the garlic cloves, brush with olive oil, and season with salt and pepper. Place them on the rack of the broiler pan about 3 inches from the heat source and cook until well seared on the outside and done to your liking on the inside, 5 to 6 minutes per side for medium-rare. To check for doneness, nick, peek, and cheat: Make a ¼-inch cut in the thickest part of the meat; it should be slightly less done than you like it. Remove the chops from the broiler and allow to rest for 5 minutes.

4. Serve the chops accompanied by the sauce.

Grilled Lamb Tenderloins on Greek Salad with Grilled Pita

SERVES 4 TO 6

Lamb and the other flavors of Greek cooking are pretty much inseparable. Here we rub a batch of lamb tenderloins with a straightforward but very flavorful and aromatic spice rub, grill them, then slice them and serve them on a classic Greek-style salad along with some simple grilled pita. You won't find a better simple lamb dish than this.

Serve this with some Hash Browns (page 412) for a light summer meal.

FOR THE SPICE RUB

3 tablespoons cumin seeds (or 1½ tablespoons ground cumin)

3 tablespoons coriander seeds (or 1½ tablespoons ground coriander)

2 tablespoons black peppercorns (or 1 tablespoon freshly cracked black pepper)

3 tablespoons kosher salt

8 lamb tenderloins, about 6 ounces each, trimmed

FOR THE GRILLED PITA

6 fresh pita breads, cut into eighths

3 tablespoons extra virgin olive oil

3 tablespoons kosher salt

FOR THE SALAD

1½ large cucumbers, peeled, seeded, and sliced ¼ inch thick

2 tomatoes, cored and diced large

1 small red onion, peeled and sliced paper-thin

½ cup feta cheese broken into small cubes

3 tablespoons fresh lemon juice (about 1 lemon)

¼ cup extra virgin olive oil

2 tablespoons roughly chopped fresh oregano

Kosher salt and freshly cracked black pepper to taste

THE CUT

A lamb tenderloin is a small piece of meat, only about 6 ounces, almost like a big fat pencil. It can be hard to get hold of, since most butchers cut the loin into loin chops rather than boning out the tenderloin separately. But, like tenderloin of pork or beef, it is super-tender and great on the grill, so it is worth asking the butcher for, even though you will probably have to give him a little lead time.

OTHER CUTS YOU CAN USE

You can easily substitute rib or loin lamb chops in this recipe. Simply grill them for about 2 minutes more per side than the tenderloin, then slice the meat up and put the slices on the salad.

1. Light a fire in your grill.

2. If using whole spices, combine the cumin, coriander, and peppercorns in a small heavy sauté pan and toast over medium heat, shaking the pan frequently to prevent scorching, until the spices become fragrant and darken, 2 to 3 minutes. Cool and grind in a spice grinder, coffee grinder, or mortar and pestle along with the salt. If using preground spices, combine them and the salt in a small bowl and mix well.

3. Dry the lamb with paper towels and rub it all over with the spice mixture, pressing gently to be sure it adheres. When the fire has died down and the coals are hot (you can hold your hand 5 inches above the grill surface for 1 to 2 seconds), place the lamb on the grill and cook until well seared on the outside and done to your liking on the inside, about 3 minutes per side for medium-rare. To check for doneness, nick, peek, and cheat: Cut into the meat and check to see if the center is slightly less done than you like it. When the tenderloins are done to your liking, remove them from the grill, cover them loosely with foil, and let them rest for about 5 minutes.

4. While the lamb is grilling, brush the pita triangles with the olive oil, sprinkle with the salt, and place around the edges of the fire, where the heat is lower. Grill on both sides until the edges darken and curl slightly, 2 to 3 minutes per side.

5. While the grilled lamb is resting, make the salad: In a medium bowl, combine the cucumbers, tomatoes, onion, and feta. In a small bowl, combine the lemon juice, olive oil, oregano, and salt and pepper and whisk well to combine. Pour the dressing over the cucumber mixture, toss gently, and spread on a large serving platter.

6. Slice the lamb into thick slices on the bias, arrange the slices on top of the salad, and serve with the pitas.

Grilled Lamb Shoulder Chops Greek-Style

SERVES 4

Shoulder chops are actually our favorite type of lamb chop. They aren't the most tender, and they certainly have a little gnarl and fat in them, but they have truly great lamb flavor, and we like all the little pieces of different muscles in them. Plus, they are far less expensive than other types of lamb chops and, after all, they are right next to the first rib chop. They are usually rather thin, so make sure you have a hot fire so they get some good sear on the outside before they have a chance to overcook on the inside.

Lamb and grilling are a classic combination in Greek cookery. So we like to grill up some shoulder lamb chops over a hot fire, then serve them very simply with that quintessential Greek flavoring combination of fresh oregano, fresh lemon juice, really good olive oil, and just a touch of garlic.

Serve these chops with grilled pita bread, tabbouleh, or Parsleyed New Potatoes (page 412), and some hard-cooked eggs.

Four 10- to 12-ounce lamb shoulder blade chops, ½ inch to ¼ inch thick
Kosher salt and freshly cracked black pepper to taste
¼ cup extra virgin olive oil
2 tablespoons roughly chopped fresh oregano
1 teaspoon minced garlic
½ lemon

1. Build a fire in your grill.

2. Dry the chops with paper towels and sprinkle them generously with salt and pepper. When the fire has died down and the coals are hot (you can hold your hand 5 inches above the grill surface for 1 to 2 seconds), place the chops on the grill and cook until well seared, 3 to 4 minutes per side. To check for doneness, nick, peek, and cheat: Make a ¼-inch cut in the thickest part of the meat; it should be slightly less done than you like it. When the chops are done, remove them from the grill, cover them loosely with foil, and let them rest for 5 minutes.

3. Meanwhile, in a small bowl, combine the olive oil, oregano, and garlic and mix well.

4. Spoon the garlic mixture over the lamb chops, squeeze the lemon on top of them, and serve hot.

THE CUT

The lamb shoulder blade chop comes from the top of the lamb shoulder, near the neck. It is roughly rectangular in shape and typically has lines of fat running through it. It also has pieces of two bones, the chine bone (backbone) and the blade bone. Like other cuts from the shoulder, it has a deep, rich lamb flavor. It is best suited for either braising, which makes it very tender, or high-heat grilling, which melts the interior fat and crisps up the fat on the edges of the chop. While it can certainly be chewy, it is not tough when cooked by these methods.

OTHER CUTS YOU CAN USE

The shoulder arm chop, also known as the round bone chop, is an excellent substitute in this recipe. It comes from the bottom of the lamb shoulder, near the leg, contains a round cross-section of the arm bone, and has slightly less fat than the shoulder blade chop. You can also use lamb loin or rib chops in this recipe.

BUTCHERSPEAK

If you buy shoulder chops in the supermarket, they are most likely going to be blade chops. If you go to a butcher, ask him for the arm chops, which are a bit less fatty but just as flavorful.

COOK ONCE, EAT TWICE

Leftover lamb from these chops makes a fantastic addition to a cold orzo salad.

Just as with other animals, the loin is a very tender part of the lamb. It is usually cut into loin chops, but if you talk nice to your butcher, he will bone out the loin and make the cut we are calling for here, a boneless whole loin of lamb. It is going to be very expensive, but you aren't going to find a cut of meat that is much more elegant, tender, and delicately flavored than this one.

OTHER CUTS YOU CAN USE

Lamb loin or rib chops are fine substitutes in this recipe. See pages 282 and 284 for general cooking times for these chops.

Parsley-Coated Grilled Lamb Loin with Smoky Eggplant Planks and Tomato-Fig Hobo Pack

SERVES 4

The loin is the primo, pure expression of lamb meat—no bone, virtually no connective tissue or fat, just lamb. You see it quite often in restaurants, but almost never in a supermarket. It is even rare in butcher shops, but if you make a point of calling in advance, you can get it. It is nice to serve at home because it's unusual, it's very easy to cook, and its tenderness is quite amazing.

As cooks all over the Middle East can attest, eggplant is great with lamb. Here we cut it lengthwise into planks, an approach that lets you grill it without any further preparation and also creates nice platforms for serving the lamb. The hobo pack of tomatoes and figs creates its own juice, which flows down over the lamb and eggplant when you serve it and gives the whole dish a nice rich flavor.

Serve this with your favorite rice dish—risotto, Simple Rice Pilaf (page 417) or Persian Rice (page 418), even Coconut Rice (page 418) and a mixed green salad.

FOR THE HOBO PACK

4 plum tomatoes, cored and halved

6 ripe figs, quartered

¼ cup extra virgin olive oil

Kosher salt and freshly cracked black pepper to taste

¼ cup roughly chopped fresh mint

3 tablespoons olive oil

¼ cup roughly chopped fresh parsley

2 tablespoons minced garlic

Kosher salt and freshly cracked black pepper to taste

1 whole boneless loin of lamb, about 2 pounds

FOR THE EGGPLANT

1 large eggplant, cut lengthwise into four 1-inch-thick slices

3 tablespoons olive oil

Kosher salt and freshly cracked black pepper to taste

1. Light a fire in your grill.

2. Make the hobo pack: Tear off four sheets of heavy-duty foil, each about 2 feet long, and stack them one on top of the other. Arrange the tomatoes and figs in the center of the top sheet, drizzle with the olive oil, and season with salt and pepper. Fold up the sheets of foil around the figs and tomatoes, one after another, turning the package a quarter turn between each sheet and making sure that each sheet is well sealed.

3. When the fire has died down and the coals are medium hot (you can hold your hand 5 inches above the grill surface for 3 to 4 seconds), place the hobo pack on the outside periphery of the coals, where the fire is less intense. Pile the coals up around it and cook for about 20 minutes, while you grill the lamb and eggplant.

4. In a small bowl, combine the olive oil, parsley, garlic, and salt and pepper and mix well. Dry the tenderloins with paper towels and slather them generously with the garlic mixture, then place them on the grill and cook until they are well seared on the outside and done to your liking on the inside, 4 to 5 minutes per side for medium-rare. To check for doneness, nick, peek, and cheat: Cut into the meat and check to see if the center is slightly less done than you like it. When the chops are cooked to your liking, remove them from the grill, cover them loosely with foil, and let them rest while you cook the eggplant.

5. Brush the eggplant planks with the olive oil and season with salt and pepper. Place on the grill and cook until golden brown on one side, 4 to 5 minutes. Flip them and grill on the other side the same way.

6. Arrange the grilled planks on a serving platter, slice the lamb on the bias, and arrange over the eggplant. Remove the tomatoes and figs from the foil and toss with the mint. Spoon the tomatoes and figs over the lamb and serve.

COOK ONCE, SERVE TWICE

In the unlikely event that you have any lamb left over, slice it paper-thin and serve it as a carpaccio-style appetizer, drizzled with good extra virgin olive oil and sprinkled with capers. Now, that's luxury.

Basically what you need here is several pieces cut from the loin of the lamb. The best approach is simply to ask your butcher to cut these 3- to 4-ounce pieces for you. You can also ask him to pound them to a ½-inch thickness while he's at it, but that's very easy (and kind of fun) to do at home.

OTHER CUTS YOU CAN USE

Boneless lamb leg is a good substitute in this recipe.

Sautéed Lamb Medallions with Red Wine–Pomegranate Sauce and Minted Vegetables

SERVES 4

This is really a veal treatment applied to lamb, which is pretty cool. What you do is take slices of the fine-grained lamb loin and pound them relatively thin, then quickly sauté them just long enough to give them a nice sear and cook them to medium-rare. It is a quick and simple approach, which features the pure flavor of the lamb. The subtle treatment of the vegetables matches the rather delicate taste of the lamb loin, and the red wine–pomegranate pan sauce adds depth and richness to the dish.

By the way, pomegranate molasses is one of those ingredients, like chipotle peppers, that is really worth searching out. It has a complex, tart-sweet flavor that can't really be duplicated, and there's no quicker way to add a touch of the exotic to all kinds of dishes than with a little of this dark red syrup. You can find it in any Middle Eastern grocery or mail-order it on the Net.

We would serve this with Rice Pilaf with Almonds and Currants (page 417).

> 10 pearl onions, peeled
> 1 cup baby carrots
> 1 cup fresh peas (or substitute thawed frozen peas)
> 3 tablespoons olive oil
> Eight 3- to 4-ounce pieces lamb loin, pounded to a ½-inch thickness
> Kosher salt and freshly cracked black pepper to taste
> 1 red onion, peeled and diced small
> 1 cup mellow red wine, such as merlot or zinfandel
> ¼ cup balsamic vinegar
> 2 tablespoons pomegranate molasses (or substitute 1 tablespoon regular molasses mixed with 1 tablespoon fresh lemon juice)
> 3 tablespoons unsalted butter
> ⅓ cup roughly chopped fresh mint

1. Blanch the vegetables: Fill a large pot or your sink with ice water. Bring a large pot of salted water to a boil over high heat. When the water is boiling, add the pearl onions and blanch for 2 minutes. Add the baby carrots and blanch for another 3 minutes. Add the peas and blanch for 30 seconds. Drain and immediately plunge the vegetables into the ice water to stop the cooking process, then drain again and set aside.

2. In a large sauté pan, heat the oil over medium-high heat until very hot but not smoking. Sprinkle the lamb medallions generously with salt and pepper. Add to the pan in a single layer, in batches if necessary to avoid crowding, and sear well, 2 to 3 minutes per side. To check for doneness nick, peek, and cheat: Make a ¼-inch cut into the thickest part of a medallion; it should be slightly less done than you like it. Transfer the lamb medallions to a platter as they are done and cover with foil to keep warm.

3. When all the meat is browned, pour off all but 2 tablespoons of the fat from the pan and return it to medium-high heat. Add the red onion and sauté, stirring occasionally, for about 1 minute. Add the wine and vinegar and bring to a boil, stirring to scrape up the browned bits on the bottom of the pan. Continue to boil until the liquid is reduced by about two thirds. Stir in the molasses, remove from the heat, and season with salt and pepper.

4. Meanwhile, in a medium sauté pan, melt the butter over medium-high heat. Add the onions, carrots, and peas and sauté for 2 to 3 minutes, until the vegetables are warmed through. Add the mint and season with salt and pepper. Serve the vegetables with the lamb medallions.

Indobob: Spice-Rubbed Grilled Lamb Skewers with Peanut-Herb Power Pack

SERVES 4

The name of this dish comes from an English-speaking Malay cook who served us a version of it at a street stall in Penang, Malaysia. It seems that Westerners had repeatedly asked him for shish kebabs, and since this was an Indonesian version of the Middle East classic, he called it an Indobob.

This recipe is actually pretty typical of the way that lamb is used in the Far East. Because it has such a demonstratively strong flavor, this meat matches up with other strong flavors and a wide palate of spices.

Serve this with white or brown rice, a watercress salad with lime vinaigrette, and Carrot-Ginger Hobo Pack (page 442).

THE CUT

As with stew meat, you are going to get better-quality lamb for skewers if you buy a larger cut and cut it into cubes yourself. In this particular instance, we are going to go with two different options for the cut. Most people will use leg, which is the classic choice for this type of preparation. But shoulder, while a little chewier, is also a bit more flavorful, so we like that just a bit better. Shoulder arm chops, shoulder blade chops, and shoulder roast are good choices.

⅓ cup chopped peanuts

3 tablespoons roughly chopped fresh mint

3 tablespoons roughly chopped fresh cilantro

3 tablespoons roughly chopped fresh basil

2 tablespoons minced fresh ginger

3 tablespoons sesame oil

2 tablespoons olive oil

⅓ cup curry powder

3 tablespoons kosher salt

2 tablespoons freshly cracked white pepper (or substitute black pepper)

2 pounds boneless lamb leg or shoulder, cut into ½-inch cubes

1. Light a fire in your grill.

2. Make the power pack: In a small bowl, combine all the ingredients and mix well; set aside.

3. In a large shallow bowl, combine the olive oil, curry powder, salt, and white pepper and mix well. Dry the lamb cubes with paper towels, add them to the bowl, and toss well to coat thoroughly. Thread the lamb onto skewers.

4. When the fire has died down and the coals are hot (you can hold your hand 5 inches above the grill surface for 1 to 2 seconds), place the kebabs on the grill and cook until well seared on the outside and done to your likeness on the inside, 2 to 3 minutes per side for rare. To check for doneness, nick, peek, and cheat: Cut into one of the cubes of meat; it should be slightly less done than you like it. When the meat is done, remove the skewers from the grill, cover loosely with foil, and let them rest for 5 minutes before serving.

5. Serve the lamb, passing the power pack for each person to add to taste.

Grilled Lamb and Peach Skewers with Cumin-Raisin Vinaigrette

THE CUT
See Indobob (page 291) for information on lamb meat for skewers.

SERVES 4

You might think that combining peaches and lamb in this way is a novel or even original idea. But, in fact, some version of this dish—peaches and lamb grilled together—has probably been served literally millions of times in the Middle East, where lamb and fruit are a classic combination and grilling is an everyday event. So if you have never tried this culinary pairing, you owe it to yourself to make this dish.

Serve with Simple Rice Pilaf (page 417), thick slices of grilled bread, and a salad of cucumbers, raisins, and walnuts with a yogurt dressing.

3 tablespoons kosher salt

3 tablespoons freshly cracked black pepper

3 tablespoons cracked coriander seeds (or 1½ tablespoons ground coriander)

¼ cup roughly chopped fresh mint

2 tablespoons minced garlic

¼ cup olive oil

2 pounds boneless lamb leg or shoulder, cut into 1-inch cubes

2 red bell peppers, cored, seeded, and cut into eighths

2 red onions, peeled and cut into eighths

2 peaches, pitted and cut into eighths

FOR THE VINAIGRETTE

¼ cup golden raisins

½ cup extra virgin olive oil

¼ cup fresh lime juice (about 2 limes)

3 tablespoons cumin seeds

Kosher salt and freshly cracked black pepper to taste

1. Light a fire in your grill.

2. In a medium bowl, combine the salt, pepper, coriander, mint, garlic, and olive oil. Dry the lamb cubes with paper towels, add to the bowl, and toss well to coat thoroughly. Thread the meat cubes onto four long skewers, alternating them with the peppers, onions, and peaches.

3. In a small bowl, combine the vinaigrette ingredients and whisk together well.

4. When the fire has died down and the coals are hot (you can hold your hand 5 inches above the grill surface for 1 to 2 seconds), place the skewers on the grill and cook until the vegetables are tender and the lamb is done to your liking, 3 to 4 minutes per side for rare. To check for doneness, nick, peek, and cheat: Cut into one of the cubes of meat; it should be slightly less done than you like it. Remove the skewers from the grill and allow to rest for 5 minutes.

5. You have two serving options: You can slide the ingredients off the skewers into a large bowl, add the vinaigrette, toss well, and serve. Or you can simply serve each person his or her own skewer, drizzled generously with the vinaigrette.

THE CUT

See Indobob (page 291) for information on lamb to use for skewers.

Broiled Sherried Lamb Skewers with Dried Apricots and Green Olive Dressing

SERVES 4

One of the hallmarks of North African cooking is the use of green olives as a flavoring. We particularly like the combination of green olives and apricots, another popular ingredient in the cooking of this region. The loamy, acidic bite of the olives and the mellow sweetness of the apricots set each other off perfectly. To provide another level of flavor, we add sherry, which has a pretty aggressive, musky undertone of its own. The result is a kind of new twist on the classic shish kebab.

Lamb leg is a fine choice for the meat cubes here, but we slightly prefer the shoulder. It does take a bit more time to cut shoulder meat into cubes because of the fat and connective tissue, but those same factors also give it a little more flavor—and make it cheaper.

We like to serve these by making a big batch of couscous or white rice, putting it on a platter, sliding everything off the skewers, and putting the platter in the middle of the table for guests to help themselves. It has a certain Berber air to it that makes it more fun to eat. Serve it with a salad of Romaine lettuce, oranges, and red onions along with lavash, pita bread, or any other flatbread you can find.

2 tablespoons minced garlic

1 to 3 teaspoons hot pepper flakes

3 tablespoons olive oil

1/2 cup dry sherry

3 tablespoons cracked coriander seeds

Kosher salt and freshly cracked black pepper to taste

2 pounds boneless lamb leg or shoulder, cut into 1-inch cubes

2 red bell peppers, cored, seeded, and cut into 1-inch squares

1 large red onion, peeled and cut into 1-inch chunks

12 dried apricots

FOR THE DRESSING

1/2 cup roughly chopped pitted green olives

1/4 cup extra virgin olive oil

1 teaspoon minced garlic

1/4 cup roughly chopped fresh parsley

2 tablespoons fresh lemon juice (about 1/2 lemon)

2 tablespoons finely chopped orange zest (orange part only) (optional)

Kosher salt and freshly cracked black pepper to taste

1. Preheat the broiler, set on high if you have a choice

2. In a medium bowl, combine the garlic, hot pepper flakes, olive oil, sherry, coriander, and salt and pepper and mix well. Dry the lamb with paper towels, then add it to the bowl, along with the peppers, onion, and apricots and toss gently until everything is well coated. Thread the meat onto four long skewers, alternating it with the peppers, onions, and apricots.

3. In a small bowl, combine the dressing ingredients and whisk to mix well. Set aside.

4. Place the skewers on the broiler pan and broil about 3 inches from the heat source until well seared on the outside and done to your likeness on the inside, about 5 minutes per side for rare. To check for doneness, nick, peek, and cheat: Make a 1/4-inch cut in the thickest part of the meat; it should be slightly less done than you like it. Remove the skewers from the heat, cover loosely with foil, and allow to rest for 5 minutes.

5. Drizzle the skewers generously with the green olive dressing and serve.

Technically called the lamb leg center slice, this is really a steak cut from the thick center section of the leg. You sometimes see this in supermarkets these days, but more than likely you will have to go to a butcher, buy a leg, and get him to cut some of these steaks for you. But that's no problem, because there are plenty of uses for the rest of the leg. For more information on this approach, see Getting a Leg Up (page 257). Do make sure, though, that the butcher cuts your steaks at least ¾ inch thick.

Lamb sirloin chops, which come from the upper section of the leg, are an excellent substitute here. You can also substitute shoulder chops or rib chops.

Grilled Lamb Leg Steaks on Eggplant Planks with Mint-Yogurt Sauce and Cucumber–Red Onion Relish

SERVES 4

Although it is sometimes called a leg chop, the cut of meat we're using here is really a big ol' lamb steak. The terminology comes from the days before electric band saws. In those times, a "chop" was any piece of meat that was separated from the carcass with a cleaver. Only relatively small cuts of meat could be produced this way. The larger cuts that had to be cut with a saw, including those from the center of the leg, were called steaks.

But as far as we're concerned, you can call this cut whatever you like, as long as you give it a try. It's worth going to a butcher for, because it is an exceptional piece of meat. It has more flavor than chops from the loin, less fat and connective tissue than chops from the shoulder, and it works well with all kinds of flavor footprints. Here we put the steaks in a Middle Eastern suit, serving them grilled on top of grilled eggplant planks with a straightforward minty yogurt sauce and a very simple relish. We think the whole combination works really well.

Serve this with couscous, Lima Beans with Bacon and Thyme (page 431), and a spinach salad with pomegranate seeds.

FOR THE SAUCE

1 cup plain yogurt

2 tablespoons honey

¼ cup roughly chopped fresh mint

FOR THE RELISH

1 red onion, peeled, halved, and thinly sliced

1 cucumber, peeled, seeded, and diced small

3 tablespoons extra virgin olive oil

3 tablespoons fresh lemon juice (about 1 lemon)

Kosher salt and freshly cracked black pepper to taste

3 tablespoons cracked coriander seeds

1 tablespoon kosher salt

1 tablespoon freshly cracked black pepper

Four 8- to 10-ounce lamb leg chops, ¾ to 1 inch thick (or substitute center-cut lamb leg steaks), trimmed of external fat

FOR THE EGGPLANT

1 small eggplant, cut lengthwise into 4 slices about ¾ inch thick

3 tablespoons olive oil

2 tablespoons minced garlic

Kosher salt and freshly cracked black pepper to taste

1. Light a fire in your grill.

2. Make the sauce: In a small bowl, combine the yogurt, honey, and mint and mix well. Cover and refrigerate until serving time.

3. Make the relish: In a small bowl, combine all the relish ingredients and mix well; set aside.

4. In a small bowl, combine the coriander, salt, and pepper and mix well. Rub the chops all over with this mixture, pressing lightly to be sure it adheres. When the fire has died down and the coals are hot (you can hold your hand 5 inches above the grill surface for 1 to 2 seconds), place the chops on the grill and cook until well seared and done to your likeness, 4 to 5 minutes per side for medium-rare. To check for doneness, nick, peek, and cheat: Make a ¼-inch cut in the thickest part of the meat; it should be slightly less done than you like it. Remove the chops from the heat, cover with foil, and allow to rest while you grill the eggplant.

5. Brush the eggplant slices with olive oil and sprinkle with the garlic and salt and pepper. Place them on the grill and cook until well browned, very soft, and moist all the way through, about 4 minutes per side.

6. Place an eggplant plank on each plate, top with a lamb chop, spoon a couple of tablespoons of sauce over the top, and serve, accompanied by the relish.

COOK ONCE, EAT TWICE

Chop any leftover lamb and eggplant into cubes, combine with any leftover relish, drizzle with any leftover sauce, and you'll be enjoying a great lamb salad.

Technically called lamb breast spareribs, these ribs are popularly known as Denver-style ribs or Denver rack. They have a good amount of gnarl and fat on them, but, like other such cuts, they respond very well to long, slow cooking over the indirect heat of a smoky fire, a situation in which the fat helps keep them moist. You are unlikely to find these in a supermarket, but most butchers will have them, and will be happy to sell them to you quite cheaply.

Denver Lamb Ribs Adobo with Fresh Pineapple-Chipotle Glaze

SERVES 4

Denver ribs are the lamb equivalent of pork spareribs. Like their pork counterparts, they are excellent for a barbecue-style slow-roast approach. Here we coat the ribs with a Latin-inspired spice rub, then put them off to the side of the grill and let them cook for a long time over low, indirect heat.

Again, don't be afraid to use big flavors with lamb, because the meat has the character to stand up to them. In this recipe, for example, we use hot and smoky chipotles, earthy cumin, tangy citrus, sweet molasses, and musky pineapple, and when you taste the dish, you'll see that all these flavors in no way overpower the meat.

Serve these with warm tortillas, some straight-up tomato salsa, and Spicy Latin Black Beans (page 423) or Spanish Rice (page 419).

FOR THE GLAZE

2 cups pineapple juice

1 cup red wine vinegar

3 tablespoons molasses

1 to 2 tablespoons minced canned chipotle peppers in adobo, or more to taste

2 tablespoons freshly cracked black pepper

2 tablespoons minced garlic

2 tablespoons cumin seeds (or 1 tablespoon ground cumin)

3 tablespoons paprika

2 tablespoons kosher salt

3 tablespoons freshly cracked black pepper

1 tablespoon dark brown sugar

¼ cup roughly chopped fresh cilantro

¼ cup fresh lime juice (about 2 limes)

Four 12- to 14-ounce racks of Denver lamb ribs

1. In a medium saucepan, combine all the glaze ingredients. Bring just to a boil over high heat, reduce the heat to medium-high, and simmer until the mixture is reduced to about 1 cup, about 30 minutes. Remove from the heat and set aside.

2. Start a fire well over to one side of a large kettle grill, using about enough coals to fill half of a large shoe box.

3. In a small bowl, combine the garlic, cumin, paprika, salt, pepper, sugar, cilantro, and lime juice and mix well. Rub the racks all over with this spice mixture, pressing lightly to be sure it adheres.

4. When the flames have died down and the coals are covered with white ash, place the racks on the grill on the side away from the coals, being careful that none of the ribs are directly over the coals. Put the lid on the grill with the vents open one quarter of the way. Cook for 1½ to 2 hours, adding a handful of fresh charcoal about every 30 minutes, until the meat is so tender it pulls very easily away from the bone. During the last 30 seconds of cooking, brush the racks with the glaze. Serve 1 rack to each person, passing the remaining glaze separately.

Stir-fried Lamb with Green Beans, Eggplant, and Peppers in Hoisin-Ginger Sauce

SERVES 4

Lamb is popular in China, so here we make a classic Chinese-style stir-fry dish with lamb, several vegetables that are widely used in Asian cooking, and a flavorful dressing featuring our favorite Chinese sauce, hoisin.

The key to stir-frying is to have all the ingredients cut up and the sauces ready before you begin, because once you start, you can't stop until the dish is ready to eat. So the best approach is to prepare all the ingredients and then line them up in little dishes next to the stove in the order that they will be added to the pan. This is what French cooks call *mise en place* and the Boy Scouts call being prepared. Either way, it's crucial for successful stir-frying.

To make the lamb easier to cut into thin slices, stick it in the freezer for about 20 minutes before you slice it.

Serve this over bowls of brown or white rice, and you've got a quick and easy meal going.

THE CUT

You can use cuts from either the leg or the shoulder for stir-frying, but we prefer leg because the shoulder has more fat and connective tissue. If you use the shoulder, though, do try to remove most or all of the fat when you cut it into strips, since the quick cooking of the stir-fry method doesn't allow a lot of time for the fat to render.

1 tablespoon Asian chili paste (or substitute 1 teaspoon each minced garlic, minced fresh chile pepper, and catsup)

¼ cup soy sauce

¼ cup rice wine vinegar

¼ cup hoisin sauce

2 tablespoons peanut oil

1 pound boneless lamb leg, partially frozen and cut into thin strips

Kosher salt and freshly cracked white pepper (or substitute black) to taste

¼ cup peanut oil

1 pound green beans, trimmed

1 cup eggplant diced small (about ½ small eggplant)

1 large red bell pepper, cored, seeded, and cut into very thin strips

1 red onion, peeled and diced small

2 tablespoons sesame oil

2 tablespoons minced fresh ginger

1 tablespoon minced garlic

4 scallions (white and green parts), very thinly sliced on the bias

1. In a small bowl, combine the dressing ingredients and whisk together well; set aside.

2. Sprinkle the lamb generously with salt and white pepper. Heat an extra-large heavy sauté pan over high heat for 1 minute. Add 2 tablespoons of the peanut oil and when it is smoking hot, add the lamb, in batches if necessary to avoid crowding, and cook, stirring constantly and vigorously, until the meat is just browned, about 1 minute. Transfer the lamb to a bowl and cover to keep warm.

3. Add the remaining 2 tablespoons oil to the hot skillet, add the green beans, and stir-fry over high heat, stirring constantly, for 2 minutes. Add the eggplant cubes and cook, stirring, for 2 minutes. Add the red pepper strips and onion and cook, stirring, for 2 minutes more. Make a well in the center of the pan, pushing the vegetables to the sides. Drizzle the sesame oil into the center of the pan, add the ginger and garlic, and cook, stirring, for 1 minute, stirring in the vegetables at the end.

4. Return the lamb to the pan and season with salt and white pepper. Pour the dressing over the top, add the scallions, and toss to combine. Serve at once, over bowls of hot steamed rice.

RECIPES FOR
SMALL TOUGH CUTS OF LAMB

Persian-Style Lamb and Eggplant Stew with Tomatoes, Raisins, and Saffron

Irish Lamb Stew, Straight Up

Lamb, Leek, and White Bean Stew with Oregano, Walnuts, and Hard Cheese

Aromatic Lamb Stew with Peaches and Fresh Mint

Curried Lamb Stew with Okra and Tomatoes

Layered Lamb, Onion, and Potato Casserole with Red Wine

New School Shepherd's Pie with Sweet Potato Crust

Spicy Lamb-and-Rice-Stuffed Squash with Dates, Mint, and Pine Nuts

10 STEPS TO GREAT LAMB STEWS

1. Dry the meat cubes.

2. Season the meat cubes generously.

3. Brown the meat cubes well, in batches if necessary.

4. Remove the meat from the pot, adjust the amount of fat in the pot, and sauté the aromatics and vegetables.

5. Deglaze the pot with some of the liquid.

6. Return the meat to the pot along with enough liquid to cover.

7. Bring to a simmer and skim off any film, then reduce the heat to low and simmer gently.

8. Check for doneness early and often.

9. Skim the film and fat from the liquid.

10. Add any final seasonings, season to taste with salt and pepper again, and serve.

Persian-Style Lamb and Eggplant Stew with Tomatoes, Raisins, and Saffron

SERVES 5 TO 6

Even though this layered dish could be called a casserole, we call it a stew in honor of its inspiration, a Persian-style *khoresh*, or stew. Lamb and eggplant have long been staples in the Middle East, where saffron is also a favored seasoning and fruit is frequently paired with meat. So here we have a little Persian, or Iranian, action going on.

As always with stews, an important key to achieving great flavor is to be sure to brown the meat well at the very beginning. Also, although you may think that you have more eggplant than you need here, persevere; it cooks down beautifully and creates a nice, rich, thick liquid for the stew.

Serve this with a Romaine salad with feta cheese, Persian Rice (page 418), and maybe some apricot chutney alongside.

2 pounds boneless lamb shoulder, cut into 1-inch cubes

Kosher salt and freshly cracked black pepper to taste

3 tablespoons olive oil, or more if needed

2 large eggplants, peeled and sliced into 1-inch rounds

2 onions, peeled and diced small

2 tablespoons minced garlic

5 plum tomatoes, cored and diced small

¾ cup dark raisins

1 teaspoon ground allspice

1 tablespoon ground coriander

1 teaspoon saffron threads, dissolved in ½ cup hot water

About 2 cups lamb or chicken stock (or see Stock Options, page 32)

¼ cup roughly chopped fresh mint

1. Preheat the oven to 300°F.

2. Dry the lamb with paper towels and sprinkle it generously with salt and pepper. In a large sauté pan, heat 2 tablespoons of the oil over medium-high heat until very hot but not smoking. Add the lamb to the pan in a single layer, in batches if necessary to avoid crowding, and brown well on all sides, about 15 minutes total; as the lamb is browned, transfer it to a bowl.

3. When all the lamb has been browned, add the remaining 1 tablespoon of oil to the pan, then add the eggplant slices in a single layer, in batches if necessary to avoid crowding, and brown well on both sides, about 5 minutes per side. As the eggplant is browned, transfer it to another bowl.

4. Pour off the fat or add oil to the pan as needed so you have a total of about 2 tablespoons in the pan. Add the onions and cook, stirring occasionally, until translucent, 7 to 9 minutes. Add the garlic and cook, stirring, for 1 minute more. Remove from the heat.

5. In a 5-inch-deep Dutch oven or other large ovenproof pot with a lid, layer the eggplant, lamb, and onions, starting and ending with the eggplant. Add the tomatoes, raisins, spices, salt and pepper to taste, and enough stock to just cover everything. (If you need more liquid, add some beer or more stock, but don't overdo it, as the tomatoes will give off liquid as they cook.) Bring to a simmer and skim any film from the surface of the liquid.

6. Cover the pot, place in the oven, and cook until the lamb is tender, 1½ to 2 hours. Serve hot, in bowls, sprinkling each portion with a bit of mint.

Irish Lamb Stew, Straight Up

SERVES 6 TO 8

Our usual approach to stews is to brown the meat and sauté the aromatics, then put everything in the pot together with the liquid and cook it until it's done. In the case of this Irish-style lamb and beer stew, though, we decided to roast the vegetables separately, then add them to the meat and liquid at the end. This approach results in vegetables with firmer texture and slightly more distinct flavors. We also used larger cubes of lamb than usual, so you get a more definitive meat presence. Together, these adjustments make the stew seem more substantial and just a bit more uptown than other versions of this very familiar dish.

Serve this with a plate of different kinds of pickles to add a little flavor jolt, Potatoes Macaire (page 414), and some Irish soda bread for sopping up the stewing liquid.

OTHER CUTS YOU CAN USE

Cuts from the lamb leg are also fine for stew meat. While they are more expensive and have a bit more of a tendency to dry out, they do have the advantage of having less fat and connective tissue, so they are easier to cut into cubes. Look for lamb leg sirloin chops or buy the shank portion of the whole leg. If you can't find a good shoulder or leg cut of lamb, you can always just pick up a package of "lamb stew meat" and check to see there's nothing too horrible in there.

THE CUT

See Persian-Style Lamb and Eggplant Stew (page 302) for details on lamb meat for stew.

3 pounds boneless lamb shoulder, cut into 2-inch cubes

Kosher salt and freshly cracked black pepper to taste

3 tablespoons vegetable oil

2 tablespoons unsalted butter

2 large onions, peeled and diced small

3 tablespoons minced garlic

About 3 cups dark beer, such as Guinness

3 tablespoons olive oil

2 pounds red or white waxy potatoes, washed and quartered lengthwise

1/2 pound carrots (about 5 carrots), peeled and cut into 1-inch rounds

1/2 pound parsnips (about 6 parsnips), peeled and cut into 1-inch rounds

1. Preheat the oven to 425°F.

2. Dry the lamb with paper towels and sprinkle it generously with salt and pepper. In a 5-inch-deep Dutch oven or other large ovenproof pot with a lid, heat the vegetable oil over medium-high heat until very hot but not smoking. Add the lamb in a single layer, in batches if necessary to avoid crowding, and brown well on all sides, about 15 minutes total; as the pieces are nicely browned, transfer them to a bowl.

3. Add the butter to the pot and melt over medium-high heat. Add the onions and cook, stirring occasionally, until translucent, 7 to 9 minutes. Add the garlic and cook, stirring, for 1 minute more.

4. Return the meat to the pot and add the beer. (The liquid should cover the other ingredients; if it does not, add more beer.) Bring to a simmer, stirring to dissolve any brown crusty stuff in the bottom of the pan. Skim any film from the surface of the liquid, then cover, reduce the heat to low, and simmer gently until the lamb is tender, 1½ to 2 hours.

5. While the stew is cooking, roast the vegetables: In a medium bowl, toss 1 tablespoon of the olive oil with the potatoes and salt and pepper to taste. Spread the potatoes on a baking sheet and roast, stirring frequently, until golden brown and tender, about 25 minutes. Do the same with the carrots and parsnips, tossing them with the remaining 2 tablespoons oil, spreading on one baking sheet, and roasting for about 17 minutes. Check for doneness by tasting the vegetables; they should be slightly underdone. Remove from the oven.

6. When the meat is tender, add the vegetables to the stew and simmer together for about 10 minutes more. Season with salt and pepper and serve.

Lamb, Leek, and White Bean Stew with Oregano, Walnuts, and Hard Cheese

SERVES 6 TO 8

THE CUT

See Persian-Style Lamb and Eggplant Stew (page 302) for details on lamb meat for stew.

Somewhat similar to the French country classic cassoulet, this hearty stew gets an extra flavor dynamic from the aged cheese and toasted walnuts sprinkled on the top after it is finished cooking. We like to serve the stew on top of big slabs of toasted country bread.

When you buy leeks, look for ones with a relatively high proportion of usable white and light green versus the dark green, which is too tough for cooking. That dark green portion is very good in stocks, though, so you might want to throw it in the freezer. Speaking of stock, we know that few people are likely to have lamb stock sitting around, so this might be a good opportunity to make some enriched chicken stock as described on page 32. Of course, you can also go the route of substituting beer or a mixture of red wine and water for the stock. And, by the way, if you are in a hurry or forget to soak the beans overnight, you can shortcut the process by using a good variety of canned beans; in that case, add them about 15 minutes before the stew is done.

Serve this with a simple arugula salad and Roasted Beets (page 435).

2 pounds boneless lamb shoulder, cut into 2-inch cubes

Kosher salt and freshly cracked black pepper

3 tablespoons olive oil

4 tablespoons (½ stick) unsalted butter

10 small or 5 large leeks (white and light green parts), well washed and halved lengthwise, then cut crosswise into ½-inch pieces

3 tablespoons minced garlic

4 plum tomatoes, cored and diced small

1 pound dried cannellini or Great Northern white beans, picked over, rinsed, soaked overnight, and drained (or substitute two 16-ounce cans beans, drained and rinsed)

3 bay leaves

About 4 cups lamb or chicken stock (or see Stock Options, page 32)

2 teaspoons finely chopped fresh oregano

6 to 8 large slices country bread (1 per serving), toasted

1 cup walnut halves, toasted in a dry sauté pan, shaken frequently, until fragrant, 4 to 5 minutes

8 ounces Parmesan, Asiago, or other hard aged cheese, very thinly sliced or coarsely grated

1. Dry the meat with paper towels and sprinkle it generously with salt and pepper. In a 5-inch-deep Dutch oven or other large heavy pot with a lid, heat the oil over medium-high heat until very hot but not smoking. Add the lamb in a single layer, in batches if necessary to avoid crowding, and brown well on all sides, about 12 minutes total; as the pieces get nicely browned, transfer them to a bowl.

2. Add the butter to the pot and melt over low heat. Add the leeks, cover, and cook until they are very soft but not browned, about 15 minutes. Uncover the pot, add the garlic, raise the heat to medium-high, and cook, stirring, for 2 minutes. Add the tomatoes and sauté, stirring, 5 minutes more.

3. Return the meat to the pot along with the beans, bay leaves, stock, and 1 tablespoon salt. (The liquid should cover all the ingredients; if it does not, add more stock or some beer.) Bring to a simmer, stirring to incorporate any brown crusty stuff in the bottom of the pot. Skim any film from the surface of the liquid, then cover, reduce the heat to low, and cook, skimming the film from the surface periodically, until the meat is very tender and the beans are cooked, 1½ to 2 hours. (If it seems as though the stew is getting too thick, add a little water.)

4. Remove the stew from the heat, stir in the oregano, and season with salt and pepper. Place the toasted bread in the bottom of soup bowls, ladle the stew over the top, sprinkle with the walnuts and cheese, and serve hot.

THE CUT

See Persian-Style Lamb and Eggplant Stew (page 302) for details on lamb meat for stew.

Aromatic Lamb Stew with Peaches and Fresh Mint

SERVES 6

We are big fans of the lamb stews of the Middle East. They are highly aromatic and often have an enticing sweetness that comes from cooking fruit along with the meat. To enhance that dynamic here, we sauté the peaches for a few minutes to caramelize them just a bit before adding them to the stew partway through the cooking process. That gives them a more complex, slightly sweeter flavor. Then for a little burst of fresh flavor, we add some lime juice and toss in some fresh mint about 20 minutes before the end. Although there are relatively few ingredients in this dish, it achieves a very nice layered flavor.

Serve this with Israeli couscous or Rice Pilaf with Almonds and Currants (page 478) and tabbouleh.

> 2 pounds boneless lamb shoulder, cut into 1-inch cubes
>
> Kosher salt and freshly cracked black pepper to taste
>
> 3 tablespoons olive oil, or more if needed
>
> 3 medium onions, peeled and diced small
>
> 2 tablespoons tomato puree
>
> About 3 cups lamb or chicken stock (or see Stock Options, page 32)
>
> 2 tablespoons vegetable oil
>
> 4 ripe peaches, pitted and quartered
>
> 1/3 cup fresh lime juice (2 to 3 limes)
>
> 1/3 cup roughly chopped fresh mint

1. Dry the lamb with paper towels and sprinkle it generously with salt and pepper. In a 5-inch-deep Dutch oven or other large heavy pot with a lid, heat the olive oil over medium-high heat until very hot but not smoking. Add the meat to the pot in a single layer, in batches if necessary to avoid crowding, and cook until well browned on all sides, about 15 minutes total; transfer the pieces to a platter as they are done.

2. Pour off the fat or add oil to the pot as needed so you have a total of about 2 tablespoons in the pot. Add the onions and sauté, stirring occasionally, until golden brown, 11 to 13 minutes. Add the tomato puree and cook, stirring, for 2 more minutes.

3. Return the meat to the pot and add the stock. (If there is not enough liquid to cover all the ingredients, add additional stock or red wine or beer.) Bring to a simmer, stirring to dissolve any brown crusty stuff in the bottom of the pot. Skim any film from the surface of the liquid, then cover, reduce the heat to medium-low so the stew is kept just at a low simmer, and cook for 1½ to 2 hours, skimming the film occasionally as it rises to the surface.

4. When the stew has cooked for about 1½ hours, heat the vegetable oil in a medium sauté pan over medium-high heat until hot but not smoking. Add the peach quarters and cook, stirring, until golden brown on both cut sides, about 5 minutes.

5. Add the sautéed peaches to the stew, along with the lime juice and salt and pepper to taste. Continue to cook until the meat is very tender, 20 minutes to 1 hour more.

6. Remove the stew from the heat, stir in the mint, season with salt and pepper if necessary, and serve hot.

THE CUT

See Persian-Style Lamb and Eggplant Stew (page 302) for details on lamb meat for stew.

Curried Lamb Stew with Okra and Tomatoes

SERVES 6

In India, where beef is forbidden to Hindus and pork to Muslims, goat and lamb are the meats of choice for nonvegetarians. According to Julie Sahni and other experts, many a fine Indian dish has been spoiled by a mistranslation—from English to English. It seems that Indians call goat meat "mutton." American and English cooks, seeing that term in recipes, have used the old tough lamb that we know as mutton with decidedly poor results. For this rather light stew, we'll stick to lamb.

Okra, a highly popular vegetable in India, goes into the pot shortly before the stew is finished cooking so that it stays relatively crisp. But if you like the rather slimy texture of long-cooked okra, which also helps thicken the stew, you can add it earlier, after about half an hour of cooking.

Serve this with basmati rice or plain long-grain rice and a carrot salad or a salad of cucumbers and tomato.

> 2 pounds boneless lamb shoulder, cut into 1-inch cubes
>
> Kosher salt and freshly cracked black pepper to taste
>
> 3 tablespoons olive oil, or more if needed
>
> 1 medium onion, peeled and thinly sliced
>
> 6 cloves garlic, peeled and thinly sliced
>
> 3 tablespoons minced fresh ginger
>
> 2 tablespoons curry powder
>
> 1 teaspoon cayenne pepper, or to taste
>
> 5 plum tomatoes, cored, peeled, and diced medium
>
> About 3 cups lamb or chicken stock (or see Stock Options, page 32)
>
> 1 pound small okra pods, stems trimmed and cut into rounds about ½ inch thick
>
> ¼ cup roughly chopped fresh cilantro
>
> ¼ cup fresh lime juice (about 2 limes)
>
> 1 cup sour cream

1. Dry the meat with paper towels and sprinkle it generously with salt and pepper. In a 5-inch-deep Dutch oven or other large heavy pot with a lid, heat the oil over medium-high heat until very hot but not smoking. Add the lamb in a single layer, in batches if necessary to avoid crowding, and brown well on all sides, about 15 minutes total; as the pieces are nicely browned, transfer them to a platter.

2. Pour off the fat or add oil to the pot as needed so you have a total of about 2 tablespoons in the pot. Add the onion and sauté, stirring occasionally, until golden brown, 11 to 13 minutes. Add the garlic, ginger, curry, and cayenne pepper and cook, stirring, for 1 minute.

3. Return the lamb to the pot, along with the tomatoes and stock. (The liquid should just cover the other ingredients; if it does not, add more stock, or beer.) Bring to a simmer and skim any scum off the top of the liquid, then cover the pot, reduce the heat to medium-low so the stew is kept just at a simmer, and cook, skimming the foam from the surface periodically, until the meat is tender, 1½ to 2 hours.

4. Add the okra and cook, stirring once or twice, for about 10 minutes more, until it is tender. Remove from the heat, stir in the cilantro and lime juice, and serve, garnishing each portion with a couple of tablespoons of sour cream.

Layered Lamb, Onion, and Potato Casserole with Red Wine

SERVES 6 TO 8

Here's one for all you fans of French country cooking. This is a pretty straight-forward French-style dish in which we first cook the lamb on top of the stove with red wine and the traditional French trio of aromatic vegetables, then layer it with potatoes and onions and bake the whole affair. Our friend Kay Rentschler, who helped out with a lot of the work of putting this book together, said that this dish reminds her of the type of peasant-style French dish that people would bring down to the village baker to bake in his oven on laundry day. Of course, one easy shortcut is to simply make a stew by adding the onions, potatoes, garlic, and thyme along with the lamb (Step 4 below). That still makes for an excellent dish; it's just a little less dense and more liquid than the casserole version.

Serve this with a green salad and a side of Roasted Winter Squash (page 435).

THE CUT
See Persian-Style Lamb and Eggplant Stew (page 302) for details on lamb meat for stew.

8 slices bacon, diced small

2 onions, peeled and diced small

1 carrot, peeled and diced small

1 stalk celery, diced small

1 head garlic, separated into cloves, peeled, and crushed

Olive oil as needed

2 pounds boneless lamb shoulder, cut into 1-inch cubes

Kosher salt and freshly cracked black pepper to taste

2 cups dry red wine

About 2 cups lamb or chicken stock (or see Stock Options, page 32)

FOR THE POTATOES AND ONIONS

3 pounds new or Red Bliss potatoes, thinly sliced

2 tablespoons minced garlic

¼ cup roughly chopped fresh thyme

2 tablespoons kosher salt

1 tablespoon freshly cracked black pepper

2 large onions, peeled, halved, and thinly sliced

1. In a 5-inch-deep Dutch oven or other large heavy ovenproof pot with a lid, cook the bacon over medium-high heat until it has rendered its fat but is slightly undercooked, about 5 minutes. Transfer to paper towels or a brown paper bag to drain.

2. Drain all but about 3 tablespoons of fat out of the pot, add the onions, carrot, and celery, and cook, stirring occasionally, until the onions are golden brown, 11 to 13 minutes. Add the garlic and cook, stirring, for 1 minute more. Using a slotted spoon, transfer the vegetables to a bowl, leaving as much fat in the pot as possible.

3. Pour off the fat or add oil to the pot as needed so you have a total of about 2 tablespoons in the pot. Dry the lamb with paper towels and sprinkle it generously with salt and pepper. Add the lamb to the pot in a single layer, in batches if necessary to avoid crowding, and brown on all sides, about 15 minutes total; transfer the pieces to the bowl with the vegetables as they are done.

4. When all the lamb has been browned, add the wine to the pot and bring to a simmer, stirring to incorporate any crusty brown bits stuck to the bottom of the pot. Return the bacon, vegetables, and lamb to the pot, and add the stock. (If all the ingredients are not covered by the liquid, add additional stock, or dark beer.) Bring to a simmer and skim any film from the surface of the liquid, then cover, reduce the heat to low, and simmer until the lamb is fork-tender, 1½ to 2 hours. When the lamb is done, remove the meat from the pot, then strain and reserve the cooking liquid. (*Note:* If you have decided for the stew option shortcut, adding the potatoes, onions, and thyme along with the lamb, don't bother—you're ready to eat.)

5. Preheat the oven to 325°F. Lightly oil a 3-quart casserole dish.

6. Place the potato slices in a large bowl. Add the garlic, thyme, salt, and pepper and mix well. Layer the lamb, onions, and potato mixture in the casserole: Start with half the lamb, then add half the onions, and half the potatoes, and repeat, so you end up with six layers, with potatoes on top. Pour the reserved cooking liquid over the top, cover the dish tightly with foil, place in the oven, and cook for 1 hour.

7. Remove the foil and continue cooking until the potatoes are very tender, about 30 minutes more. Serve hot.

New School Shepherd's Pie with Sweet Potato Crust

SERVES 6 TO 8

Shepherd's pie was originally created as a way to use the leftovers from a roast, and you can certainly substitute leftover roast lamb for the ground lamb called for in this version. But this dish is so delicious that you shouldn't wait until you have leftovers; ground lamb works just fine. You can also use the more traditional white potatoes instead of sweet potatoes, but we think our approach gives the dish a deeper, more interesting flavor.

This is one of the favorite staff dinners at the East Coast Grill and, like many other ground meat dishes, it's also very popular with kids.

Serve this with a big salad, and you're all set.

THE CUT

The story with ground lamb is approximately the same as with ground beef: For the best, buy a whole piece of meat and ask your butcher to grind it for you. Any cut from the shoulder or leg of the lamb will have about the right mixture of fat and meat; we slightly prefer the shoulder, because it has a little more flavor. If you buy prepackaged ground lamb in the supermarket, on the other hand, chances are good that it will be from the fattier parts of the lamb, like the breast or belly. But if that is the only option, go ahead and buy it rather than deciding not to make this or other ground lamb dishes. Just drain off any excess fat after sautéing the lamb and you'll be fine.

4 large sweet potatoes, peeled and cut into ½-inch cubes

1 cup half-and-half, warmed

Kosher salt and freshly cracked black pepper to taste

3 tablespoons olive oil

3 pounds ground lamb

3 tablespoons minced garlic

¼ cup roughly chopped fresh herbs: any one or a combination of thyme, parsley, and/or basil

2 red onions, peeled and diced small

2 carrots, peeled and diced small

1 cup fresh or thawed frozen peas

3 tablespoons catsup

3 tablespoons A-1 sauce

1 tablespoon unsalted butter

1. Bring a large pot of salted water to a boil. Add the sweet potatoes and cook until they are easily pierced with a fork but still offer some resistance, about 15 minutes. Drain the potatoes, place them in a large bowl, add the half-and-half and salt and pepper, and mash until the potatoes are smooth. The mixture should be fairly loose.

2. Preheat the oven to 400°F.

3. In a large sauté pan, heat 1 tablespoon of the oil over medium-high heat until hot but not smoking. Add the lamb and cook, stirring occasionally, until well browned, 8 to 10 minutes. (If using prepackaged ground lamb, you may need to drain off excess fat at this point.) Add the garlic and cook, stirring frequently, for 2 minutes more. Add the herbs and stir to mix well, then transfer the lamb to a bowl and set aside.

4. Wipe out the sauté pan, return it to medium-high heat, and heat the remaining 2 tablespoons oil until hot but not smoking. Add the onions and carrots and cook, stirring occasionally, until the onions are golden brown, 11 to 13 minutes. Add the peas, catsup, and A-1 sauce and cook, stirring frequently, for 4 minutes. Add the lamb mixture, stir to combine, and season with salt and pepper.

5. Spread the lamb mixture in a 3-quart casserole dish. Cover the top completely with the sweet potatoes, swirling the potatoes with the back of a spoon to add some surface texture. Dot with the butter, place in the oven, and bake until the lamb mixture bubbles and the potatoes are golden brown on top, about 40 minutes. Serve hot.

Spicy Lamb-and-Rice-Stuffed Squash with Dates, Mint, and Pine Nuts

THE CUT

See New School Shepherd's Pie (page 311) for information on ground lamb.

SERVES 4

Stuffed vegetables are a long and honorable tradition in Middle Eastern cuisines. Since lamb is the meat of choice there, it is very often used in the stuffing mixtures. Not coincidentally, it's ideal for this purpose, because its distinctive flavor does not get lost in the stuffing.

Although zucchini and eggplant are the most common stuffed vegetables, here we use acorn squash. We like it because it has a richer, deeper flavor than squashes that mature earlier in the season, like zucchini and summer squash.

Serve this with grilled pita bread and a salad of watercress, cucumbers, tomatoes, and feta cheese—or some purslane if you can get hold of it.

2 medium acorn squash

2 tablespoons vegetable oil

1 pound ground lamb

Kosher salt and freshly cracked black pepper to taste

2 tablespoons unsalted butter

1 medium onion, peeled and diced small

3 cloves garlic, peeled and minced

2 ripe tomatoes, cored and roughly chopped

$1/2$ teaspoon ground cinnamon

2 tablespoons cracked coriander seeds (or 1 tablespoon ground coriander)

$1\frac{1}{2}$ cups plain yogurt, mixed with 1 cup water until smooth

$1/2$ cup pitted dates, chopped small

$1/2$ cup pine nuts, toasted in a 350°F oven until lightly browned, about 10 minutes

1 cup cooked brown or white rice

$1/4$ cup finely chopped fresh mint

3 tablespoons finely chopped fresh parsley

1. Preheat the oven to 350°F.

2. Prebake the squash: Cut the squash lengthwise in half and scoop out the seeds. Rub the cut sides of both squash with the oil, then place cut side down in a baking dish and cook until quite tender, about 45 minutes. Let cool slightly.

3. As soon as the squash is cool enough to handle, scoop out the pulp into a bowl, leaving a ½-inch layer of pulp inside the shells. Place the shells right side up in the baking dish and set both pulp and shells aside.

4. Heat a large heavy sauté pan over high heat until very hot. Sprinkle the lamb generously with salt and pepper, then add tablespoon-sized chunks of the lamb to the pan (you will not need to add any oil), in batches so that the individual chunks are not touching. Let the lamb chunks brown undisturbed on one side, then turn and brown on the other side, about 2 minutes per side. Transfer to a paper towel–lined plate.

5. Pour off the fat from the pan, turn the heat down to medium, and add the butter. As soon as it is melted, add the onion and cook slowly, stirring occasionally, until very soft and golden, about 12 minutes. Add the garlic, tomatoes, cinnamon, and coriander and cook, stirring occasionally, for 5 minutes.

6. Return the browned lamb to the pan, along with the diluted yogurt, and stir to combine. Turn the heat down to very low and simmer for 10 minutes, stirring every few minutes. Uncover the pan and stir in the reserved squash pulp, along with the dates, pine nuts, rice, mint, and parsley. Season with salt and pepper.

7. Sprinkle the insides of the squash shells with salt and pepper, then spoon the filling into the cavities, creating a high rounded crown. Cover the baking dish loosely with aluminum foil and bake until the squash is heated through, about 20 minutes. Remove the foil and continue to bake until the top of the filling has browned slightly, about 10 minutes. Serve hot.

RECIPES FOR
ODD CUTS OF LAMB: OFFAL ET AL.

**Broiled Lamb Kidneys with Grainy Mustard Sauce and
Watercress and Tomato Salad**

Lamb Tongues on Toast with Bacon and Tomatoes

Unlike the more familiar veal kidneys, which consist of a number of pieces of meat gathered around a center of fat, lamb kidneys look like giant kidney beans. (Hence the name of the beans.) These kidneys are easy to trim—it involves scooping out the little center core of fat—but you might as well ask the butcher to do it for you.

Broiled Lamb Kidneys with Grainy Mustard Sauce and Watercress and Tomato Salad

SERVES 4

Less is more when cooking lamb kidneys, which are extremely delicate. Their most prized characteristic is their tenderness, which is maintained by under- rather than overcooking them. Here we broil them quickly, then make a simple mustard-butter-wine sauce with the pan drippings. Served with a simple watercress and tomato salad, this is a kind of elegant and unusual dish to serve to your more adventurous culinary pals.

8 lamb kidneys (about 1½ pounds total), split and trimmed of center fat

FOR THE SAUCE
8 tablespoons (1 stick) unsalted butter, at room temperature
¼ cup grainy mustard
3 tablespoons minced shallots
1 tablespoon roughly chopped fresh parsley
Kosher salt and freshly cracked black pepper to taste
1 cup dry red wine

FOR THE SALAD
2 bunches watercress, tough stems removed, washed, and dried
2 beefsteak tomatoes (about the size of a baseball), cored and quartered
¼ cup extra virgin olive oil
2 tablespoons fresh lemon juice (about ½ lemon)
Kosher salt and freshly cracked black pepper to taste

4 tablespoons (½ stick) unsalted butter, melted
Kosher salt and freshly cracked black pepper to taste

1. In a large pot of boiling salted water, parboil the kidneys for 1 minute. Drain, dry well, and set aside.

2. Preheat the broiler to high if you have a choice.

3. In a small bowl, combine the softened butter with the mustard, shallots, and parsley and mix well. Season with a little salt and pepper, cover, and set aside. (This butter can be made ahead and refrigerated. Bring to room temperature before using.)

4. In a large bowl, combine the watercress, tomatoes, olive oil, and lemon juice. Toss the salad gently, season with salt and pepper, and divide among four plates.

5. Dip the kidneys in the melted butter, season with salt and pepper, and place in a medium roasting pan. Broil 3 inches from the heat source until just nicely seared on one side, 3 to 4 minutes. Turn and continue cooking to the desired doneness, 3 to 4 minutes more for rare. To check for doneness, make a ¼-inch cut in one of the kidneys; it should be pink inside, but not raw looking. Transfer to a warm plate and cover to keep warm while you make the sauce.

6. Place the roasting pan on the stove over medium-high heat and add the wine. Bring to a simmer, stirring to dissolve the browned bits in the bottom of the pan. Cook until the wine is reduced by about half, 10 to 15 minutes. Stir in the reserved butter mixture, a little at a time, until all the butter is incorporated; the sauce should be thick enough to coat the back of a spoon. Season with salt and pepper.

7. Add the warm kidneys and any accumulated juices to the sauce and heat for 1 minute, then transfer to the plates with the salads and serve right away.

Lamb Tongues on Toast with Bacon and Tomatoes

SERVES 4

Okay, so now we're getting out there on the culinary fringe. But in many Arab countries, where "meat" means "lamb," every part of the animal is used, and the tongues are quite a delicacy. Italian cooks also like them. They have a very soft, almost silky texture and a more delicate flavor than any other part of the lamb. The down side to lamb tongue is that, like many organ meats, it requires quite a bit of advance preparation. Once that is done, though, you have some very unusual and tasty meat. Here we serve it on toast with a rich, smooth sauce of bacon, tomatoes, and sherry.

    4 lamb tongues
    1 tablespoon kosher salt
    1 large onion, peeled and thinly sliced

THE CUT

There is no mystery about this cut—it's the tongue of the lamb. It is often sold pickled, though, so locating fresh ones can be difficult. If there is a halal, or Orthodox Islamic, butcher in your town, that's a good place to try. Tongue also freezes very well, so if all you find is frozen ones, that's no problem.

This dish is actually very good made with beef or veal liver as well. Simply sauté the liver, then jump into the recipe at Step 3.

2 carrots, peeled and thinly sliced

2 stalks celery, diced small

¼ cup fresh lemon juice (about 1 lemon)

1 small bunch parsley, leaves roughly chopped and stems reserved

4 teaspoons fresh thyme leaves (or 2 teaspoons dried thyme)

2 whole cloves

FOR THE SAUCE

½ pound slab bacon, diced large

¼ cup minced shallots

4 plum tomatoes, cored and diced medium

2 tablespoons sherry

2 tablespoons cold unsalted butter, cut up

Kosher salt and freshly cracked black pepper to taste

4 large slices country bread, toasted and lightly buttered

1. Scrub the tongues with a vegetable brush under cold running water. Let them soak in cold water for 2 hours, then place them in a Dutch oven and add the salt and cold water to cover. Bring the water to a simmer, skimming the foam that rises to the surface. Add the onion, carrots, celery, lemon juice, parsley stems, thyme, and cloves and simmer, partially covered, until the tongues are tender, about 2 hours.

2. Drain the tongues and place them in a bowl of cold water to cool. As soon as they are cool enough to handle, peel them: Cut a slit down the back of each tongue from the base to the tip with a small paring knife. Run your fingers under the skin and separate it from the meat. Slice the meat crosswise into medallions, or lengthwise in half. Place on a platter, cover with foil, and place in the oven set on the lowest setting to keep warm while you make the sauce.

3. In a large sauté pan, cook the bacon over medium-low heat until crisp. Using a slotted spoon, transfer the bacon to the platter of tongue, leaving 3 tablespoons of the rendered fat in the sauté pan, and return the platter to the oven. Add the shallots to the pan and cook over low heat, stirring occasionally, until softened, 2 to 3 minutes. Raise the heat to medium-high, add the tomatoes, and cook, stirring occasionally, for 3 minutes more. Pour in the sherry and bring just to a simmer, then stir in the butter, a little at a time, until all of it is incorporated.

4. Add the tongue and bacon to the sauce and turn a few times to coat well. Season with salt and pepper, sprinkle with the chopped parsley, and serve on the buttered toast.

PORK: SWINE *of the* TIMES

If we were exiled to the proverbial desert island and had to choose only one kind of meat to eat for the rest of our lives, pork would have to get the nod. Not only does it have a wonderful, rich, distinctive taste, it is also the most versatile of meats.

Of course, it also helps that we were born, respectively, in Virginia and Iowa, two of the top rivals for pork epicenter of the United States.

As a kid, one of my (Chris's) absolute favorite moments was when the guys would show up at my parents' house on the beach to cook a whole pig. I knew that after they had dug the pit, laid the fire, and spent the night sitting around in lawn chairs drinking beers, telling outrageous stories, and every so often feeding the smoldering fire with hickory logs, we would be rewarded in the morning with outstanding pork barbecue. Crisp and crunchy on the outside, buttery soft and moist on the inside, with its rich, smoky flavor, it's one of my favorite childhood memories.

And, of course, there were those pork spareribs. After spending hours cooking slow and low, just out of reach of the flames from a hardwood fire, they'd be so tender that just a little tug would pull them right off the bone, the chewy interior meat rich as bacon on the tongue, the exterior sticky-sweet from caramelization.

Even that was just the beginning. A smoky, salty country ham from nearby Smith-field, where the pigs ate a diet of peanuts, was a fixture of my family's holiday table, and to this day, bacon and sausage are among my favorite foods.

Growing up in central Iowa, I (Doc) was raised on stories of how my grandfather would always wait until after the first freeze to butcher the pigs on the family farm. My mother and grandmother would then make sausages, put the hams in big boxes of salt to cure, brine a few other large cuts, and stash the rest in the cold house to stay frozen through the winter months. In celebration of the event, there would always be a fresh pork loin roast for dinner that Sunday.

That was a tradition that my grandmother continued long after Grandpa was dead and she had moved into town from the farm. When she took her pork loin roast out of the oven on a Sunday afternoon, its outer layer of crispy fat dark brown and glistening, it was a moment of glory. And when she cut it into thick slices and served it up with her braised red cabbage, the juicy pork had a rich, lingering, mellow taste that could not be matched by any other meat.

But the fact that we are both partial to pork does not exactly single us out among diners of the world. Pork is the most widely eaten of all red meats, and while lamb may have been the first animal to be domesticated, it is the pig that has been the best friend to humankind.

Pigs are remarkably easy to raise, demanding nothing more than table scraps, a bit of garbage, or the freedom to forage for their own food in fields or forests. Every single last part of the pig can be eaten, either as a dish in itself or as a flavoring for other dishes. With two litters a year, pigs are also rapid reproducers. Equally important, at least to the vast majority of humans who lived in the eras before mechanical refrigeration, pork is the easiest of all meats to preserve. Because of its low moisture content, it takes particularly well to salting and brining, and it can also readily be smoked or preserved in its own fat, in the manner of French confit.

Pigs were not native to America, but because they were ideal shipboard animals (if provisions ran low, they could be butchered and their meat preserved in salt brine for the rest of the voyage), they came here with the first European explorers. Put ashore, they thrived in the new country and spread out across its vast expanses along with the new settlers. Whenever an East Coast family set out for the new lands to the west, there were always a few pigs trotting alongside the wagons, finding their own food as they went.

When they were first brought here, pigs were raised much as they had been in the Old World, feeding on table scraps, garbage, and what they could forage from surrounding fields and forests. Back then, this was no great hardship, since the woods were filled with acorns, hazelnuts, and beechnuts. Even so, the pigs of that day were relatively lean and scrawny.

But shortly after the Native Americans had introduced the European settlers to corn, the colonists decided to try feeding it to their pigs for the last couple of months before slaughter. As it turned out, this not only increased the pigs' fat content, but also gave their meat a firmer texture and a richer flavor. In one of those serendipities that occur every once in a while in nature, pigs also proved to be amazingly efficient at converting corn to meat. It takes about five times as much corn to produce a pound of beef, for example, as it does a pound of pork.

When settlers began to fan out across the Midwest, this alliance of meat and grain really came into its own. The great Central Plains were ideal for raising corn, and farmers could afford to feed their pigs almost exclusively on it. Soon they had developed a new style of pig, far fatter than its ancestors. Meat from this porker came to dominate the American diet; in fact, our forefathers ate more pork than any other single foodstuff except wheat.

Most of the pork being eaten in America at that time was not fresh, but salted or cured. In those days, many homes had a barrel in the basement or root cellar where cuts of pork were kept submerged in a heavily salted brine throughout the year, to be pulled out and used as needed. This constant source of meat was the origin of the phrase "pork barrel," to denote expensive projects designed by politicians to reward supporters and curry favor with voters.

With the invention of the refrigerated railroad car in 1870, though, fresh pork began to be more common. The pigs that were being slaughtered and shipped across the country at that point were even fatter than their predecessors. Since they no longer had to be able to walk long distances to market, they could be bred for a higher proportion of lard to meat. This was very desirable, because in those days, lard was truly an all-purpose product. Not only was it the primary fat used in cooking and baking, it was also employed as fuel for lamps, as a lubricant, and even in munitions. As a result, a "good hog" was one that was almost 50 percent fat by weight, with a solid three-inch layer of fat along its back.

Not surprisingly, hogs bred and fed to produce a three-inch fat layer also produced meat heavily marbled with the artery-clogging substance. Even after lard began to be supplanted by vegetable-based oils and other products, Americans continued to favor very fatty pork for a time. But in the early 1960s, newly health-conscious diners began trying to reduce the amount of saturated fat in their diets, and pork began to drop from favor.

Seeing their market share dwindle, hog producers began a campaign to produce a leaner, more marketable product. By modifying feeding programs and crossing American "lard type" pigs with the leaner, longer-bodied "bacon type" pigs that breeders in Europe had been perfecting, they succeeded: Today's pork has, on average, about 50 percent less fat than it did in the early 1960s. Cuts from the loin have seen an almost 70 percent fat reduction during that period.

Of course this is good news for our health. It's not such great news, however, for our taste buds. Since fat is a carrier of flavor—a leaner pig is a less flavorful pig. But there are several ways to deal with this. To begin with, the new leaner version of pork should in general not be cooked as long as its predecessor. Fortunately, the near-total elimination of trichinosis means that it's possible to reduce cooking times without threatening your health. Choosing some of the more underused but tasty cuts of pork, cooking bone-in cuts, and searing them hard at the beginning of the cooking process are also good ways to increase the flavor potential of the new pork.

Finally, it is easy to boost the flavor quotient of today's pork by combining it with a whole range of other flavorful ingredients. Pork's relatively mild but still distinctive flavor is a perfect foil for everything from chile peppers and the bright, intense flavors of tropical foods to the more subtle palette of Mediterranean cuisines.

ABOUT CUTS OF PORK

Pork may no longer be America's #1 meat, but it is still a central part of our everyday diet. That means that you can buy a wide variety of good-quality cuts at any neighborhood supermarket, and the options for all kinds of cooking methods are many and exciting.

Unlike the steer, the calf, and the lamb, which we break down into four primary sections, we are going to break the pig into only three such sections. That's because in the pig, the loin and the rib are treated as one section rather than two.

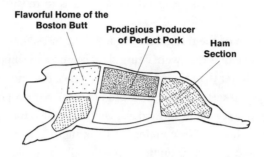

Starting from the front, we have the shoulder, which we like to call the Flavorful Home of the Boston Butt, perhaps the most versatile cut of meat of all. You can roast it, you can steak it, you can braise it, you can cut it into chunks and use it in stews. What the option play is to college football, the Boston Butt is to pork—many things can occur when you have a pork butt in the refrigerator. The Picnic Shoulder is another, slightly gnarlier cut from the front of the hog that is good for braising. The shoulder region also gives us the blade steak and the flavorful ham hock, often used to add flavor to a large pot of beans or greens.

Everything from the shoulder back to the start of the leg is included in the loin. Any way you slice it, this is the Prodigious Producer of Perfect Pork Section. The loin itself is a roast, known as the rack of pork, which can also be divided into several separate roasts including the blade loin roast, sirloin loin roast, center rib roast, and center loin roast. The pork tenderloin also comes from the loin, as do the many variations on pork chops: rib chops, loin chops, sirloin chops, and center-cut chops. From the belly, which we are including in the loin, come bacon and pork spareribs, and what more can we say about those fatty delights?

Finally we come to the leg, which is not called the round. If it were in lamb it would be leg of lamb, if it were in beef or veal it would be the steamship round. But in the pig it is ham.

Now let's look at cuts of pork from the point of view of how you cook them.

When it comes to roasts, you have what is perhaps the single most versatile and adaptable of all cuts of red meat, the center cut pork loin. It provides tender, fine-grained roasts both bone-in and boneless. The rib roast, also known as the rack of pork, is the equivalent of a beef prime rib, and you know how good that is. Perhaps the most neglected cut for roasting is the fresh ham, which is the uncured hind leg of the pig; it makes a magnificent roast whether cooked in the oven or in a covered grill.

The tenderloin, which is not only the most tender cut of pork but also the leanest, is another of our favorites for roasting. It is widely available these days, it's totally simple to cook, doesn't take long, and adapts to all sorts of flavor treatments. Because it's so small, it can also be grilled.

And speaking of cuts that are in a border zone and can be prepared using more than one type of cooking method, let's look at the Boston butt. This cut, which falls right on the dividing line between tough and tender large cuts of pork, may be the single most under-rated cut of red meat. It is just tender enough to roast, but also responds well to braising, and it has a tremendous amount of pork flavor. If that's not enough to send you in its direction, it's also inexpensive, and when you put it over the indirect heat of a smoky fire for 12 to 14 hours, it becomes the incomparable shredded pork barbecue.

And while we're on the subject of long, slow cooking, let's not neglect spareribs. Any of you who grew up in the South or the Midwest know the virtues of these slightly gnarly, ultra-flavorful beauties. They come from the part of the pig that is right underneath the bacon, and they have all the rich flavor that suggests, combined with the pleasure of eating meat on the bone. For those occasions when you want ribs in a hurry, baby backs are a good choice.

In addition to the Boston butt, other cuts from the shoulder area, such as the shoulder blade roast and the picnic shoulder, are not only fantastic for braising but they are also the best single source for cubes of pork to use in stews. We particularly enjoy pork stews because this is the way that cooks in the hot-weather world most often use pork. That makes pork stews the ideal vehicles for a wild variety of flavor combinations.

In the small tender department, where you'll find those cuts of pork that are cooked with dry heat, you've got to start with one of the most favored cuts of all, the chop. There are five varieties of chops cut from the loin of the pig. While each has its distinct character, they are all tender, flavorful, and easy to cook. Thick or thin, stuffed or spice-rubbed, grilled or sautéed or broiled, these are among the most versatile and tasty cuts of meat we know. Pork cutlets, fillet, and scalloppini, which are basically variations on the theme of chops without bones, provide yet other ways to enjoy this part of the pig.

Finally, to represent the cuts of pork that follow an earlier American tradition and are used primarily as flavorings, we have included recipes for ham hocks, both fresh and cured.

As we pointed out, it's generally not a good idea to cook pork as long or as hard as our grandparents did. Because of trichinosis, which was widespread in the days when hogs were fed largely on raw table scraps and other garbage, it used to be essential to cook all pork well-done. But since trichinosis is all but nonexistent in today's animals, pork does not need to be cooked any longer than other red meats.

Of course, if you prefer to continue to cook your pork to well-done, that's certainly your prerogative. As we've said elsewhere, we're not about to tell you how you should like your meat. You bought it, and you're entitled to cook it until it's as done as you like.

Our preference, though, is to cook tender cuts of pork to medium. That means leaving a bit of pink in the middle and removing roasts from the oven when the thermometer reads 147°F or so. Assuming you let the meat rest after you remove it from the heat, this actually gives you the best of both worlds. The internal temperature will continue to rise as the meat reposes and should reach almost 155°F in 10 to 15 minutes. This will result in meat that is free of harmful bacteria, but still blushingly pink, tender, and succulent.

As with other types of meat, we also prefer really thick versions of tender cuts of pork. In this case, that mainly applies to chops, and it's relatively easy to find chops that are 1½ to 2 inches thick in the supermarket. For some reason, they have caught on with the public while thicker cuts of other types of meat have not. But if you can't get hold of a thick chop, go ahead and buy the thinner version. You simply need to shorten the cooking time in the recipe and start checking for doneness particularly early to make sure you don't cook it more than you were intending to.

OUR TOP 5 FAVORITE CUTS OF PORK

1. **Boston butt**

2. **Spareribs**

3. **Tenderloin**

4. **Double-thick rib chop**

5. **Fresh ham**

BUYING PORK

It's easy to find good-quality pork in this country. Pigs are slaughtered young, so tenderness is not really an issue. Grading is another non-issue. Pork may be graded, but it has completely different rating categories than other meats, ranging from USDA 1 at the top to USDA 4 at the bottom. The grades have to do with the amount of lean versus fat on the pig, with the highest grade going to the highest proportion of lean to fat. However, since most markets sell only Grade 1 pork at this point, there's no reason to be concerned with it.

When buying pork, you should look for meat that is light to dark pink, rather than gray or red. Also be sure that the meat looks moist rather than dry, and that the external fat is smooth, creamy, and white. The meat should be fine-textured, with little or no fat streaked through the muscle itself, and, above all, it should be firm rather than mushy to the touch. Since there is a wide variety in the skill with which pork is butchered, you also want to look for cuts that look neatly severed, with no ragged edges.

Fresh pork will keep in the refrigerator, tightly wrapped, for three or four days. Because of its low water content, pork does not freeze quite as well as beef or lamb. It will keep in the freezer, again tightly wrapped (see page 27), for up to six months, but it is really best to use it after a month or six weeks.

Unlike lamb, pork is not generally imported; unlike beef, it is not yet sold under brand names. So buying it is a pleasure. It's pretty simple, it's pretty inexpensive, and it's wholly delicious.

RECIPES FOR
LARGE TENDER CUTS OF PORK

Maple-Glazed Fresh Ham with Hard Cider–Raisin Sauce

Grill-Roasted Rum-Brined Fresh Ham with Mango Salsa and Grilled Pineapples and Bananas

Cumin-Crusted Grilled Boneless Pork Loin with Grilled Avocados and Apple-Chipotle Salsa

Roast Pork Loin with Spicy Hoisin Sauce, "Peking Duck–Style"

Roast Pork Loin with Apricot-Sausage Stuffing and Rosemary-Garlic Jus

Ginger-Rubbed Rack of Pork with Chile-Lychee Sambal

Roast Sage-Garlic Pork Butt with Roasted Pineapple and Onions and Sweet Mustard Sauce

---

10 STEPS TO GREAT ROASTED PORK

1. Preheat the oven.

2. Dry the meat.

3. Season the meat well.

4. Put the roast on a rack in a roasting pan, set on the middle shelf of the preheated oven, and sear.

5. Turn down the oven temperature.

6. Add the vegetables, if any.

7. Check for doneness early and often.

8. Transfer the meat to a platter, cover loosely with foil, and allow to rest for 10 to 20 minutes, depending on size.

9. Pour off the excess fat from the pan, add stock, deglaze, and simmer to reduce the liquid.

10. Carve and serve, passing the jus separately.

What we are calling for here is basically an uncured bone-in half pork leg. You can get either the rump or shank section of the leg, each of which has its advantages. (Sometimes you will see a center-cut roast from the leg, but it is usually smaller than the roast we are looking for here.) The rump half, which is rounded, has a higher proportion of meat to bone, but we slightly prefer the shank half, which is tapered, because it is easier to carve and a bit less fatty. Although fresh hams are beginning to show up more often in supermarkets, you are likely to need to make a trip to the butcher shop to get this cut at this point. As usual with cuts of this size, it pays to call several days ahead to make sure you can get it.

OTHER CUTS YOU CAN USE

You can adapt this recipe to a cured ham if you like. (We suggest that you get a bone-in ham, since they tend to have more flavor.) Cured hams don't really need to be cooked, just warmed up. So instead of browning at 500°F and then roasting for a long time at 300°F, simply rub the flavoring paste on the ham, put it in a 300°F oven, and cook until it is heated all the way through, about 1½ hours.

Maple-Glazed Fresh Ham with Hard Cider–Raisin Sauce

SERVES 10 TO 12

There is a common misconception that *ham* refers only to the hind leg of a hog that has been cured and/or smoked. Well, that is a ham all right. On the other hand, so is that same hind leg if it is uncured and unsmoked. To distinguish it from the cured version, it has come to be called a "fresh ham," and it is a wonderful piece of meat. Sweet, tender, juicy, and full of pork flavor, it is also much cheaper than the more traditional loin roast, which makes it ideal for big, celebratory dinners. Make sure the ham you buy is bone-in and skin-on; the bone adds lots of flavor, and the crispy skin is our favorite part of the meal.

In this version, we rub the ham with a sweet and earthy spice paste, then finish up with a simple pan sauce with raisins and some reduced hard cider. We made this autumnal dish for Thanksgiving dinner last year, and it took the assembled crowd by storm.

Serve this with Au Gratin or Roesti Potatoes (page 410), Green Beans with Mushrooms and Almonds (page 429), and corn bread.

1½ cups dark raisins

½ cup dark rum

FOR THE SPICE PASTE

1 cup packed dark brown sugar

⅔ cup fresh sage leaves

4 teaspoons dry mustard

4 teaspoons finely grated lemon zest (yellow part only) (about 2 lemons)

8 cloves garlic, peeled

4 teaspoons kosher salt

4 teaspoons black peppercorns

One 8- to 10-pound bone-in fresh ham (half a leg), skin on

1 cup maple syrup

One 1-liter bottle hard apple cider (or substitute regular apple cider)

Kosher salt and freshly cracked black pepper to taste

1. Preheat the oven to 500°F.

2. In a small bowl, combine the raisins and rum. Set aside to soak while the ham cooks, at least 2 hours.

3. Make the spice paste: Place all the ingredients in a food processor fitted with a steel blade or in a blender and process until smooth.

4. Using a sharp knife, score the entire surface of the ham in a crosshatch pattern, cutting down just through the skin to the flesh underneath. (If you are cutting to the right depth, the skin will spread apart a bit as you cut.) Rub the ham all over with the spice paste, pressing it gently into the crosshatch cuts.

5. Put the roast on a rack in a roasting pan and roast for 20 minutes. Reduce the heat to 300°F. After 40 minutes more, begin painting the ham every 15 minutes or so with the maple syrup. Continue roasting until the ham is done the way you like it, 2 to 2½ hours total cooking time for medium to medium-well. To check for doneness, insert a meat thermometer into the dead center of the roast and let it sit for 5 seconds, then read the temperature: 126°F is medium-rare, 134°F is medium, 150°F is medium-well, and 160°F is well-done; we like to pull it at 147°F.

6. While the ham is cooking, put the cider in a medium saucepan and bring to a boil over high heat. Reduce the heat to medium-high and simmer vigorously until reduced by about half, about 20 minutes.

7. When the ham is done, remove it from the roasting pan, cover it loosely with foil, and allow it to rest for at least 20 minutes and up to 1 hour.

8. Tip the roasting pan so you can spoon off all the fat from the pan juices, then place the pan on the stove over two burners set at medium-high heat. Add the reduced apple cider and bring to a simmer, scraping the bottom of the pan to get up the browned bits. Skim any film off the surface and season the liquid as needed with salt and pepper. Add the rum-soaked raisins and stir to combine, then pour into a gravy boat.

9. Slice the ham into thick slices, drizzle with the cider-raisin sauce, and serve, passing any remaining sauce separately.

COOK ONCE, EAT TWICE

You are likely to have some leftovers from this big piece of meat, which is great, because it makes incredible sandwiches. The possibilities are legion. Layer it on rye bread with Swiss cheese, mustard, and roasted red peppers, for example, or put thick slices between pieces of whole wheat bread with some mango salsa.

THE CUT

See Maple-Gazed Fresh
Ham (page 326) for details
on fresh ham.

OTHER CUTS YOU CAN USE

You can substitute any
large pork roast from the
leg or shoulder here.
Boston butt is a good
option, for example.

Grill-Roasted Rum-Brined Fresh Ham with Mango Salsa and Grilled Pineapples and Bananas

SERVES 10 TO 12

Here's one for you outdoor cooking fanatics. We know you all say, "Oh, I've done chickens, I've done turkeys, I've done legs of lamb, I've done beef brisket." But have you ever done a fresh ham on the grill? We don't think so. So right now, we challenge you to give it a try.

What we are doing here is grill-roasting, not barbecuing, which means that we're cooking over a charcoal fire that's around 350°F, rather than the 220°F or so that is used for barbecuing. To help keep the meat moist during the rigors of grill-roasting, we first let it soak for at least 24 hours in a brine spiced with rum, nutmeg, and cloves. (This means, of course, that you have to get started at least a day ahead when you want to make this recipe. But if you should forget, you can skip the brine without harming the recipe. By no means fail to make this dish just because you don't have the time or inclination to brine.)

After brining the ham, we coat it with a West Indies–style rub that will give it a nice dark crust as it cooks. Then we serve it with mango salsa and some grilled bananas and pineapples, which are emblematic of the pork/fruit connection. Long before other meats were combined with fruits, pork was routinely served this way. So here we just add some smokiness to the concept.

All in all, this is an outstanding dish. Serve it to your fellow outdoor cooking nuts, and you're definitely going to be top dog in the backyard cooking sweepstakes.

For your big West Indian feast, serve this with Spicy Latin Black Beans (page 423) and a salad of tomatoes, hearts of palm, avocados, and red onions.

FOR THE BRINE (OPTIONAL)

3 quarts water

1 cup sugar

1 cup kosher salt

3 cups dark rum

25 whole cloves

2 teaspoons ground nutmeg

One 8- to 10-pound bone-in fresh ham (half a leg) with skin

4 ripe mangoes, peeled, pitted, and diced medium

2 small red onions, peeled and diced small

1 to 3 tablespoons minced jalapeño or other fresh chile peppers of your choice

½ cup fresh lime juice (about 4 limes)

½ cup pineapple juice

½ cup roughly chopped fresh cilantro

Kosher salt and freshly cracked black pepper to taste

FOR THE SPICE RUB

½ cup of your favorite hot sauce

2 tablespoons minced garlic

1½ tablespoons cumin seeds (or 1 tablespoon ground cumin)

1½ tablespoons coriander seeds (or 1 tablespoon ground coriander)

1½ tablespoons kosher salt

1½ tablespoons freshly cracked black pepper

1½ tablespoons dark brown sugar

FOR THE GRILLED PINEAPPLE AND BANANAS

8 tablespoons (1 stick) unsalted butter

½ cup packed dark brown sugar

5 bananas, unpeeled, halved lengthwise

1 pineapple, unpeeled, halved lengthwise and cut crosswise into half moons about ½ inch thick

¼ cup vegetable oil

1. In a bowl, pot, or clean bucket large enough to hold the ham, stir together the water, sugar, and salt until the sugar and salt completely dissolve. Add the rum, cloves, and nutmeg and mix well. Add the ham, making sure that it is completely submerged in the liquid; add additional water if necessary to cover. Allow the ham to brine in the refrigerator for 1 to 3 days, stirring the brine and turning the ham over each day.

2. Make the salsa: In a medium bowl, combine the mangoes, onions, jalapeños, lime juice, pineapple juice, cilantro, and salt and pepper and mix well. Set aside. (This can be made 2 to 3 days ahead of time, covered, and refrigerated.)

3. In another medium bowl, combine the ingredients for the spice rub and mix well. Remove the ham from the brine and pat dry. Rub it all over with the spice rub, pressing gently to be sure it adheres.

4. Start a fire well over to one side of a large kettle grill, using about enough coals to fill a shoe box. When the fire dies down and the coals are well lit, place the ham on the side away from the coals, being careful that

COOK ONCE, EAT TWICE

Cut any leftover pork into thick ham steaks and fry them up for breakfast, with some sautéed apples and buttered bread.

none of the meat is directly over the coals. Put the lid on the grill with the vents one quarter of the way open and cook, adding a handful of fresh charcoal about every 30 minutes, until the ham is done the way you like it. Start checking for doneness after about 2 hours, but expect that it may take up to 3 hours for a medium to medium-well piece of meat this large. To check for doneness, insert a meat thermometer into the center of the roast and let it sit for 5 seconds, then read the temperature: 126°F is medium-rare, 134°F is medium, 150°F is medium-well, and 160°F is well-done; we like to pull it at 147°F. When the ham is done, remove it from the grill, cover it loosely with foil, and allow it to rest for 20 to 30 minutes before carving.

5. Meanwhile, melt the butter in a small saucepan over medium heat. Add the brown sugar, stirring to dissolve, then remove from the heat. Rub the banana halves and pineapple slices lightly with the oil. Place the fruit cut side down on the grill over a medium fire for 2 to 3 minutes, or until the bananas are just golden and the pineapple slices have light grill marks. Flip the fruit over, brush on some of the brown sugar glaze, and grill for 1 minute more. Remove from the grill and drizzle with any leftover glaze.

6. Cut the ham into thick slices and serve, accompanied by the grilled fruit and mango salsa.

A BRINE IN ITS TIME

Brining pork is a good idea. We haven't included brines in most of the recipes here because we don't want to imply that is an essential step in cooking pork. But if you have the time, then we do encourage you to give any large cut of pork a soak. Contrary to popular opinion, bringing is not really about imparting a lot of new flavors; if you include spices and other flavoring in a brining solution, those flavors will work their way into the meat somewhat, but that's not really the point. The significant action that goes on during brining is the penetration of salt and, to a somewhat lesser extent, sugar into the meat as it soaks. When this happens, it causes the proteins in the meat to unwind a bit. As they do so, they interlock with each other and form a matrix that traps moisture inside the meat. As a result, the meat is juicer and more tender when it is cooked. The salt and sugar also enhance the inherent flavors of the pork, just as they would if you sprinkled them on the surface. But with brining, they penetrate much further into the meat, deepening on its flavor throughout. With today's lean pork, that's a very good thing. So if you've got the time and the space in your refrigerator, go ahead and brine those pork roasts. As a basic brine, we recommend a ratio of 2 quarts water to 1 cup kosher salt and ¾ cup sugar. An overnight brine is great, but even 4 to 6 hours works. Just be sure that when you do brine, you dry the outside of the pork well before you begin searing it.

Cumin-Crusted Grilled Boneless Pork Loin with Grilled Avocados and Apple-Chipotle Salsa

SERVES 4 TO 6

Of all the cuts of all the types of red meat, the center-cut pork loin may be the most versatile. Relatively lean, with a tender, fine-grained texture and some good pork flavor, this is the epitome of the new pork that breeders have worked so hard to produce over the past twenty years or so, and it makes one magnificent roast.

Here we take advantage of this cut's versatile nature to give it a Latin American treatment. Apples and pork are a classic, and we think that tart green apples and smoky chipotle chiles are another great pairing, so we decided to put the three together. As for the grilled avocados, the idea might make you blanch, as it did us the first time we heard of it, but they are actually fantastic. The smokiness imparted by the grilling fire matches perfectly with the mellow, buttery muskiness of the avocado.

FOR THE SALSA

2 Granny Smith apples, cored and diced medium

½ red onion, peeled and diced medium

1 to 3 tablespoons minced canned chipotle peppers in adobo, depending on your taste for heat

¼ cup fresh lime juice (about 2 limes)

¼ cup roughly chopped fresh cilantro

Kosher salt and freshly cracked black pepper to taste

⅓ cup kosher salt

⅓ cup freshly cracked black pepper

½ cup cumin seeds (or ¼ cup ground cumin)

2 tablespoons brown sugar

One 3-pound boneless center-cut pork top loin roast, external fat trimmed to ¼ inch

FOR THE AVOCADOS

4 avocados, halved and pitted

3 tablespoons olive oil

Kosher salt and freshly cracked black pepper to taste

THE CUT

This is basically the back of the pig from the shoulder to the leg. Since the muscles in this area don't do much work, this is a supremely tender cut. At the hip (sirloin) and shoulder (blade) end it has a little bit of sinew and connective tissue that make those sections very flavorful, but in the middle it is pure, tender boneless pork. If you wonder why the pork people came up with the advertising slogan, "The Other White Meat ..." this cut will give you the answer.

OTHER CUTS YOU CAN USE

The bone-in loin blade roast (from the portion of the loin nearest the shoulder) and bone-in loin sirloin roast (the portion of the loin nearest the hip) would also be very good here.

1. Light a two-level fire in your grill, using about enough charcoal to fill two shoe boxes and tapering the depth of the charcoal in the grill so that two thirds of the coals are on one side and one third on the other.

2. Make the salsa: In a medium bowl, combine all the ingredients. Mix well and set aside.

3. In a small bowl, combine the salt, pepper, cumin, and brown sugar and mix well. Dry the pork loin with paper towels and rub it all over with this mixture, pressing gently to be sure it adheres.

4. When the fire has died down and the coals in the hotter part are medium-hot (you can hold your hand 5 inches above the grill surface for 2 to 3 seconds), place the meat over the hottest part of the fire and cook until well seared, 8 to 10 minutes on each side. Move the pork to the cooler part of the grill, cover it with a disposable aluminum foil roasting pan, and cook until the pork is done the way you like it. To check for doneness, insert a meat thermometer into the dead center of the roast and let it sit for 5 seconds, then read the temperature: 126°F is medium-rare, 134°F is medium, 150°F is medium-well, and 160°F is well-done; we like to pull it at 147°F. When the meat is done, remove it from the grill, cover it loosely with foil, and let it rest for 10 to 20 minutes.

5. While the pork is resting, grill the avocados: Rub the cut side of the avocado halves with the oil and sprinkle generously with salt and pepper. Place the halves on the hotter side of the grill, cut side down, and cook for 3 to 5 minutes, or until you see grill marks. Remove from the grill and fill the centers of the avocados with the salsa.

6. Cut the pork loin into slices about 1 inch thick and serve, accompanied by the stuffed avocados.

Roast Pork Loin with Spicy Hoisin Sauce, "Peking Duck–Style"

SERVES 6 TO 8

This is your basic Asian-marinated pork, which we call "Peking Duck–Style" because the presentation—coating the meat with jazzed-up hoisin sauce and wrapping it up in pancakes—is fashioned after that famously elaborate Chinese dish. We like it because it is one of those situations where you pass around the various ingredients and let each person assemble his or her own dinner.

This dish requires some advance planning, since it involves marinating the pork overnight. If you forget to do this, though, don't despair; you can just make the marinade, reduce it on the stove, and baste the pork with it as it cooks and right after it comes out of the oven. You'll lose a little depth of flavor, but the dish will still be wonderful. (You can also serve this without the pancakes if you want; just cut the roast into slices about ½ inch thick and serve with the hoisin sauce on the side. Believe us, the pork still tastes great.)

We might serve this with a dish of egg noodles sprinkled with toasted sesame seeds and minced scallions and ginger.

FOR THE MARINADE

3 tablespoons peanut oil

⅓ cup roughly chopped fresh ginger

2 tablespoons minced garlic

1 tablespoon five-spice powder

½ cup honey

½ cup soy sauce

½ cup dry sherry

½ cup rice wine vinegar (or substitute white wine vinegar)

1 cup orange juice

3 tablespoons crushed Szechwan peppercorns (or substitute freshly cracked white pepper)

2 tablespoons sesame oil

One 4-pound boneless pork loin roast, external fat trimmed to ¼ inch

½ cup hoisin sauce

2 tablespoons Asian chile paste (or substitute 1 tablespoon each minced fresh chile peppers and minced garlic)

Mandarin pancakes or flour tortillas

FOR THE GARNISHES (AS YOU LIKE)

Thinly sliced scallions

Pickled ginger

Cilantro leaves

Very thinly sliced jalapeño peppers

1. Make the marinade: In a medium saucepan, heat the oil over medium-high heat until hot but not smoking. Add the ginger, garlic, and five-spice powder and cook, stirring, for 1 minute. Add the remaining marinade ingredients and bring to a simmer, then turn the heat to low and simmer gently for 15 minutes. Remove from the heat and allow to cool almost to room temperature. (If you're in a hurry, throw in a couple of ice cubes to speed the cooling.)

THE CUT

In recipes such as this one, you can use any one of several roasts from the loin, which is basically the upper back of the pig. The most deluxe option is the boneless top loin roast, which is the whole loin (see Cumin-Crusted Grilled Boneless Pork Loin, page 331, for more details). But often you will find large enough roasts cut from one of three sections of the loin. For the most tender meat with the best texture, choose a center-cut pork loin roast. For a bit more flavor but a little rougher texture, choose a boneless pork loin blade roast, which is the part of the loin nearest the shoulder, or a boneless pork loin sirloin roast, which comes from the loin nearest the leg. Any one of them will be excellent.

OTHER CUTS YOU CAN USE

You can substitute a boneless pork butt, a shoulder roast, or a fresh ham in this recipe.

COOK ONCE, EAT TWICE

Leftover pork from this dish makes excellent pork fried rice, and if you have any of the garnishes left over, you can toss them in there too.

2. Place the pork loin in a deep glass dish. Pour the cooled marinade over, cover it, and refrigerate it overnight, or for up to 3 days, turning several times.

3. Preheat the oven to 500°F.

4. Remove the pork from the marinade and set aside. In a medium saucepan, bring the marinade to a boil over medium heat, then reduce the heat and simmer the marinade vigorously until it is thick and syrupy, 30 to 40 minutes. Strain into a bowl and set aside.

5. Place the pork roast on a rack in a medium roasting pan and roast until well browned, about 20 minutes. Reduce the oven temperature to 300°F and continue to roast, brushing the pork with the reduced marinade every 15 minutes or so, until the meat is done the way you like it, about 50 minutes to 1 hour more for medium to medium-well. To check for doneness, insert a meat thermometer into the dead center of the roast and let it sit for 5 seconds, then read the temperature: 126°F is medium-rare, 134°F is medium, 150°F is medium-well, and 160°F is well-done; we like to pull it at 147°F. When the pork is done, remove it from the oven, cover it loosely with foil, and let it rest for 10 to 20 minutes.

6. While the pork is resting, combine the hoisin sauce and chile paste in a small bowl and mix well.

7. Thinly slice the pork and pass it on a platter along with the spicy hoisin sauce and mandarin pancakes or flour tortillas so guests can roll up their own, Peking duck–style. Pass any or all of the garnishes for people to include.

THE CUT

See Cumin-Crusted Grilled Boneless Pork Loin (page 331) for details on the boneless center-cut pork top loin.

Roast Pork Loin with Apricot-Sausage Stuffing and Rosemary-Garlic Jus

SERVES 6

This dish is great in the fall. It has a lot of rich, deep flavors that for some reason seem autumnal to us, and it is exactly the kind of thing you want on the table when you sense winter just over the horizon. It's also pretty elegant.

It takes a bit of time to make this recipe, but you don't have to do anything very complicated. Basically, you take a boneless center-cut pork loin, cut a large pocket in it, and fill it with a flavorful stuffing that includes sausage, so that it stays moist during roasting. Then, when the roast is done, you make a simple pan sauce from the drippings, expanding and deepening the flavors with rosemary, apricot preserves, and a whole head of roasted garlic. (Don't forget, by the way, to put the garlic in the oven with the roast when you reduce the temperature after the initial browning.)

If you want, you can make the whole process easier by simply skipping the brining step. Brining does give the pork a somewhat fuller flavor and a moister texture, so it's worth doing if you have the time, but the recipe also works great without it.

Serve this with roasted apples and Candied Sweet Potatoes (page 436) or Roasted Winter Squash (page 435).

FOR THE BRINE (OPTIONAL)

2½ quarts water

2 cups packed dark brown sugar

1 cup kosher salt

5 large sprigs fresh rosemary

10 garlic cloves, peeled and crushed

3 bay leaves, crumbled

One 3- to 4-pound boneless center-cut pork top loin roast, external fat trimmed to ¼ inch

FOR THE STUFFING

2 tablespoons olive oil

1 red onion, peeled and minced

½ pound Italian pork sausage, casings removed and well crumbled

1 tablespoon minced garlic

1½ cups minced dried apricots

1 large egg, lightly beaten

½ cup fresh bread crumbs

Kosher salt and freshly cracked black pepper to taste

1 head garlic, top ¼ inch sliced off

2 tablespoons olive oil

1½ cups chicken stock (or see Stock Options, page 32)

½ cup dry white wine

¼ cup apricot preserves

¼ cup fresh rosemary needles

Kosher salt and freshly cracked black pepper to taste

1. In a large bowl, roasting pan, or bucket large enough to hold the roast, combine the water, brown sugar, and salt and stir until the sugar and salt are completely dissolved. Add the remaining brine ingredients and mix well. Add the pork loin, making sure that it is completely submerged in the liquid (if it is not, add more water). Let the roast brine in the refrigerator for 24 hours, stirring the brine and turning the meat occasionally.

2. Make the stuffing: In a large sauté pan, heat the oil over medium-high heat until hot but not smoking. Add the onion and cook, stirring occasionally, until translucent, 7 to 9 minutes. Add the sausage and garlic and continue to cook, stirring occasionally, until the sausage is cooked through, 10 to 12 minutes. Remove from the heat and allow the mixture to cool almost to room temperature, then add the apricots, egg, bread crumbs, and salt and pepper, mixing well to combine. Cover and refrigerate the stuffing until you are ready to cook the pork.

3. Preheat the oven to 500°F.

4. Remove the pork from the brine and dry it well with paper towels. (Discard the brine.) To cut a pocket for the stuffing, make a lengthwise cut halfway through the thickness of the meat. Holding the knife inside the cut, turn the knife parallel to the cutting board and make horizontal cuts to the left and right of the original cut. Fill this cavity with the stuffing and close the meat up around it. Tie the roast with twine in several places so it will hold its shape, and sprinkle it generously with salt and pepper.

5. Place the roast on a rack in a roasting pan and roast for 20 minutes to brown the outside. Reduce the oven temperature to 300°F and continue roasting until the meat is done the way you like it, 40 to 60 minutes more for medium to medium-well. To check for doneness, insert a meat thermometer into the dead center of the roast and let it sit for 5 seconds, then read the temperature: 126°F is medium-rare, 134°F is medium, 150°F is medium-well, and 160°F is well-done; we like to pull it at 147°F.

6. Meanwhile, prepare the garlic: Place the whole unpeeled head of garlic in the center of a foot-long sheet of aluminum foil. Pour the olive oil over it, then wrap it up very tightly. When you reduce the oven temperature to 300°F, place the garlic in the oven and cook until the individual garlic cloves are soft to the touch, about 1 hour. Allow to cool to room temperature, then squeeze the pulp from the cloves into a bowl. Mash with a wooden spoon until very smooth and set aside.

7. When the pork is done, transfer it to a platter and cover it loosely with foil to keep warm while you make the sauce.

8. Discard any fat in the roasting pan and place the pan on the stove over two burners at medium-high heat. Add the stock and wine, stirring to dissolve the brown crusty stuff in the bottom of the pan, and simmer, stirring occasionally, until the liquid is reduced by half, about 5 minutes. Skim any scum from the top, then stir in the preserves, the garlic puree, and the rosemary and season with salt and pepper.

9. Slice the pork into ½-inch slices, drizzle with the sauce, and serve, passing the remaining sauce on the side.

COOK ONCE, EAT TWICE

If you have leftovers, try treating this like a Thanksgiving situation—make a sandwich with the meat and the stuffing.

Ginger-Rubbed Rack of Pork with Chile-Lychee Sambal

SERVES 8

Although cooks in Southeast Asia would be much more likely to cut their pork up for a stir-fry than to make a roast like this, the flavors of that part of the world are fantastic with pork. Here we coat a deluxe center rib roast with a pretty straight-up ginger-spice rub, roast it, and serve it with a sambal featuring that familiar tropical combination of hot and sweet. We urge you to make the effort to find lychees. These small fruits, native to Southeast Asia, have a hard red shell and a single seed. Their flesh has a smooth, almost slippery texture and a juicy sweetness that works really well in the sambal.

Serve this with Basic Fried Rice (page 420) and some green beans or broccoli seasoned with soy sauce.

- ⅓ cup minced fresh ginger
- ⅓ cup minced garlic
- ½ cup roughly chopped fresh cilantro
- ½ cup roughly chopped fresh mint
- 2 tablespoons kosher salt
- 2 tablespoons freshly cracked white pepper (or substitute black pepper)
- One 5- to 6-pound bone-in pork loin center rib roast

FOR THE SAMBAL

- One 12-ounce can lychees, diced small, with ½ cup of their juice
- ¼ cup fresh lime juice (about 2 limes)
- ¼ cup Vietnamese chile-garlic paste
- 5 scallions (white and green parts), thinly sliced
- Kosher salt and freshly cracked black pepper to taste

THE CUT

We are calling here for a bone-in center rib roast, which is a very nice cut of meat indeed. If this were beef, it would be a prime rib; if it were lamb, it would be rack of lamb. Tender and full of flavor, it is one of our favorite cuts. This roast can be cut with anywhere from 5 to 8 ribs, but to serve this many people, the 8-rib rack is what you'll need.

OTHER CUTS YOU CAN USE

Any of the bone-in loin roasts, including the loin blade roast (from the portion of the loin nearest the shoulder) and the loin sirloin roast (the portion of the loin nearest the hip), would also be good here. Be aware, though, that a bone-in blade roast is going to be pretty difficult to carve, since it has both the blade bone and the rib bones in it.

1. Preheat the oven to 500°F.

2. In a small bowl, combine the ginger, garlic, cilantro, mint, salt, and pepper and mix well. Dry the pork with paper towels and rub it all over with the spice mixture, pressing gently to be sure it adheres.

3. Place the pork on a rack in a roasting pan and roast for 20 minutes to brown. Reduce the oven temperature to 300°F and continue to cook until the pork is done to your liking, 1 hour to 1 hour and 10 minutes more for medium to medium-well. To check for doneness, insert a meat thermometer into the dead center of the roast and let it sit for 5 seconds, then read the temperature: 126°F is medium-rare, 134°F is medium, 150°F is medium-well, and 160°F is well-done; we like to pull it at 147°F. Remove from the oven, cover loosely with foil, and allow to rest for 20 minutes before carving into individual chops.

4. Meanwhile, make the sambal: In a small bowl, combine the lychees and the reserved juice, the lime juice, chile paste, and scallions and mix well. Season with salt and pepper.

5. Serve the pork chops with the sambal.

Roast Sage-Garlic Pork Butt with Roasted Pineapple and Onions and Sweet Mustard Sauce

SERVES 6 TO 8

Pork butt is one of those cuts of meat that to our mind has not received its proper due. It is inexpensive and easy to cook, and it has great flavor, but many people regard it as somehow a low-class piece of meat. No doubt this is because it contains a lot of sinews and intramuscular fat, but if you cook it properly, it is quite tender, and the fat helps keep it from drying out even if you have guests who insist that their pork be overcooked. The butt is very often braised, which is a fine treatment, but it is also just tender enough to be roasted, as we do here.

In this treatment, we rub the pork butt with garlic and fresh sage and pair it with the pineapple that always seemed to accompany pork not only in Polynesian restaurants but also on our family's dinner tables. Instead of just cubing the fruit and sticking it on top of the finished roast, though, we add it to the roasting pan with some red onions after the meat has browned so their flavors can mingle during the long low-heat roasting. Then, to add some flavor and character to the simple pan sauce, we stir in some grainy mustard, another classic pork match-up, at the end.

By the way, if you can't find a good pineapple in the market, you can substitute three good-sized mangoes or six or seven peaches. In either of those cases, use orange juice in place of the pineapple juice.

You might serve this with Roasted Winter Squash (page 435) or Roasted Carrots (page 435), dinner rolls, and classic stewed greens.

3 tablespoons minced garlic

3 tablespoons roughly chopped fresh sage

3 tablespoons kosher salt

3 tablespoons freshly cracked black pepper

One 5- to 6-pound boneless pork butt roast

1 small pineapple, peeled, cored, and cut into 2-inch chunks

3 red onions, peeled and quartered

FOR THE SAUCE

2 cups pineapple juice

¼ cup red wine vinegar

½ cup grainy mustard

Kosher salt and freshly cracked black pepper to taste

THE CUT

We are calling for a boneless pork butt roast here. This is one of the great misnomers of all time: The pork butt is not from the butt of the animal at all, but from the shoulder. (It got its name because in colonial times this type of pork cut was packed into barrels called "butts" for shipping or storage.) Basically, this is to pork what the chuck is to beef. Just like beef chuck, it has a lot of connective tissue, fat, and sinew, all of which make it quite tough, but also give it wonderful flavor. This is a supermarket cut, and it is some very cost-effective good eating. If you are making dinner for a smaller group, you can often find half butts, which weigh 3 to 4 pounds.

OTHER NAMES

Because this method of cutting the shoulder originated in colonial times in Boston, this cut has lots of city-specific nicknames, including Boston butt roast, boneless Boston shoulder, and boneless shoulder blade Boston roast.

Any boneless roast from the pork shoulder will work just fine here. Avoid shoulder cuts with the word "picnic" in them for this treatment, though. They are actually from the arm and foreleg of the pig rather than the shoulder, and are too tough for roasting. Another good substitute is a half fresh ham, from the hind leg of the pig.

1. Preheat the oven to 500°F.

2. In a small bowl, combine the garlic, sage, salt, and pepper and mix well. Dry the pork butt with paper towels. With the tip of a sharp knife, make 10 to 12 small cuts, about ½ inch long and ½ inch deep, evenly spaced over the surface of the pork and push some of the spice rub into each slit. (If you have any left over, rub it over the surface of the pork.)

3. Place the pork on a rack in a roasting pan and roast for 20 minutes to brown it. Reduce the oven temperature to 300°F, add the pineapple and onions to the roasting pan, and continue to cook until the pork is done to your liking, 1 hour to 1 hour and 10 minutes more for medium-well. To check for doneness, insert a meat thermometer into the dead center of the roast and let it sit for 5 seconds, then read the temperature: 126°F is medium-rare, 134°F is medium, 150° is medium-well, and 160°F is well-done; we like to pull it at 147°F. When the roast is done, remove it from the pan, along with the pineapple and onions, loosely cover with foil, and allow the meat to rest for about 20 minutes while you make the sauce.

4. Pour off the fat from the roasting pan and place the pan on the stove over two burners at medium-high heat. Add the pineapple juice and vinegar and bring to a simmer, stirring to dissolve the brown crusty stuff in the bottom of the pan. Continue to simmer until the liquid is reduced by half, about 5 to 7 minutes. Stir in the mustard, season with salt and pepper, and pour into a sauce boat.

5. Slice the pork roast and serve with the pineapple and onions, passing the sauce separately.

RECIPES FOR
LARGE TOUGH CUTS OF PORK

Soy-Braised, Hoisin-Glazed Pork Shoulder with Sesame-Ginger Dipping Sauce

Red Wine–Braised Pork Steaks with Peaches, Cinnamon, and Couscous

Traditional Dry-Rubbed St. Louis–Style Pork Spareribs

EZ–Style Adobo Pork Ribs with Molasses-Chile Barbecue Sauce

Authentic Eastern North Carolina Barbecued Pork Butt on Buns with Tidewater Slaw

Cheater-Style Indoor Barbecued Pork

---

10 STEPS TO GREAT BRAISED PORK

1. Dry the meat.

2. Season the meat well.

3. Sear the meat hard.

4. Remove the meat from the pot, adjust the amount of fat in the pot, and sauté the aromatics and vegetables.

5. Deglaze the pot with some of the liquid.

6. Return the meat to the pot along with enough liquid to cover it about halfway.

7. Bring to a simmer, skim the film, cover the pot, and place in a 300°F oven.

8. Check for doneness early and often: Look for "fork-tender."

9. Skim the fat and any film from the liquid and, if you want, remove the meat and reduce the liquid; season to taste.

10. Carve the meat and serve with the braising liquid on the side.

See Roast Sage-Garlic Pork Butt (page 339) for details about pork shoulder roast, also known as pork butt roast.

Any boneless pork shoulder roast will work just fine here. Since we are braising, you can use not only the Boston butt-style or shoulder blade roasts, but also the tougher cuts from the picnic shoulder, which are actually from the arm and foreleg. Cuts like fresh picnic shoulder or pork shoulder arm roast are incredibly cheap and can be very tasty when cooked this way. You could also substitute a half fresh ham from the hind leg of the pig.

Soy-Braised, Hoisin-Glazed Pork Shoulder Roast with Sesame-Ginger Dipping Sauce

SERVES 6

Pork is the meat of choice in China, and in fact throughout most of non-Muslim Asia. And while many American cooks tend to think of braising as a French, or at least European, cooking technique, it is very popular in Asia as well. Because pork shoulder is ideal for braising, this cut is a favorite in that part of the world. The rich, somewhat fatty meat is a perfect match for strong Asian flavors such as hoisin and soy sauce, both of which are central ingredients in this dish.

Be sure that you brown the meat well here, since that will add a wonderful, slightly caramelized flavor to the final roast.

Serve this with plenty of rice and some quick-sautéed eggplant or some mild mustard greens prepared in the manner of quick-sautéed Broccoli Rabe with Garlic and Oil (page 430).

3 tablespoons olive oil, or more if needed

One 4-pound boneless Boston butt or picnic shoulder

3 tablespoons freshly cracked white pepper (or substitute black), or more to taste

Kosher salt to taste

2 large red onions, peeled and thinly sliced

¼ cup minced garlic

¼ cup minced fresh ginger

1 tablespoon minced fresh chile peppers of your choice

½ cup soy sauce

½ cup rice wine vinegar or white vinegar

1 cup white wine

FOR THE DIPPING SAUCE

¼ cup sesame oil

3 tablespoons minced fresh ginger

3 tablespoons fresh lemon juice

1 teaspoon honey (or substitute sugar)

6 dashes Tabasco sauce

½ cup hoisin sauce

1 bunch scallions (white and green parts), thinly sliced

1. Preheat the oven to 300°F.

2. In a 5-inch-deep Dutch oven or other large ovenproof pot with a lid, heat the oil over medium-high heat until very hot but not smoking. Dry the meat with paper towels, rub it all over with the white pepper, sprinkle it generously with salt, and brown well on all sides, 8 to 10 minutes per side. Remove the meat from the pot and set aside.

3. Pour off the fat or add oil to the pot as needed so you have a total of about 2 tablespoons in the pot. Add the onions and cook, stirring occasionally, until translucent, 7 to 9 minutes. Add the garlic, ginger, and chiles and cook, stirring, for 1 minute. Add the soy sauce, vinegar, and wine and bring to a simmer, stirring to scrape up any browned bits in the bottom of the pot.

4. Return the pork to the pot. (The liquid should come about halfway up the sides of the pork; if it does not, add some water.) Bring the liquid to a simmer and skim any film from the top, then cover, place in the oven, and cook until the meat is tender, 2 to 2½ hours. To check for doneness, plunge a fork straight down into the meat and try to pull the fork out. If the fork slides out easily, the meat is done; if the meat hangs on to the fork, give it more time. When the meat is done, remove it from the liquid, cover it loosely with foil, and set it aside.

5. Taste the braising liquid, and if it needs more flavor, place the pot on the stove over medium-high heat and simmer to reduce the liquid. For a thicker sauce, reduce it until it coats the back of a spoon. Adjust the seasoning as needed.

6. Meanwhile, make the dipping sauce: Combine the sesame oil, ginger, lemon juice, honey, and Tabasco in a small bowl and mix well.

7. Cut the pork into thick slices, brush them generously with the hoisin sauce, sprinkle with the scallions, and serve, passing the dipping sauce and braising liquid on the side.

COOK ONCE, EAT TWICE

Shred any leftover pork, removing as much fat as possible in the process, heat it up with a bit of the braising liquid, and make some awesome Chinese-style shredded pork sandwiches.

Red Wine–Braised Pork Steaks with Peaches, Cinnamon, and Couscous

SERVES 4

North African flavors predominate in this dish, which is rather simple to make but delivers complex layers of taste. We particularly like the peaches, which give the braising liquid a nice sweetness. Although the addition of butter to the braising liquid at the very end creates a pleasant texture, it is by no means essential. Feel free to leave it out if you wish.

Since this dish already has its own starch in the form of flavored couscous, all it needs to make a terrific meal is grilled pita bread and a salad of Romaine lettuce, tomato, red onion, and feta cheese.

2 tablespoons olive oil, or more if needed

Four 10- to 12-ounce bone-in pork shoulder blade steaks, about 1 inch thick

Kosher salt and freshly cracked black pepper to taste

1 red onion, peeled and diced small

4 ripe peaches, peeled, pitted, and sliced into eighths

About 1 cup chicken stock (or see Stock Options, page 32)

1 cup dry red wine

1/2 teaspoon ground cinnamon

1 bay leaf

Pinch of dried thyme

FOR THE COUSCOUS

4 tablespoons (1/2 stick) unsalted butter

1 large onion, peeled and diced small

1 teaspoon minced garlic

1 3/4 cups instant couscous (about 1 box)

2 1/4 cups boiling water

2 teaspoons kosher salt

1 teaspoon red pepper flakes, or less to taste

2 tablespoons fresh thyme leaves (or 1 tablespoon dried thyme)

2 tablespoons grainy mustard

2 tablespoons unsalted butter, cut into 8 pieces

1. In a very large sauté pan, heat the oil over medium-high heat until very hot but not smoking. Dry the steaks with paper towels and sprinkle them generously with salt and pepper. Add them to the pan in a single layer, in batches if necessary to avoid crowding, and cook until well browned on both sides, 8 to 10 minutes; remove the steaks to a platter as they are done.

2. Pour off the fat or add oil to the pan as needed so you have a total of about 2 tablespoons in the pan. Add the onion and sauté, stirring occasionally, until translucent, 7 to 9 minutes. Add the peaches and sauté, stirring frequently, until they start to brown, about 5 minutes more. Add the chicken stock and wine and bring to a simmer, stirring to dissolve the brown crusty stuff in the bottom of the pan.

3. Return the steaks to the pan and add the cinnamon, bay leaf, and thyme. (The liquid should come halfway up the sides of the meat; if it does not, add more stock or water.) Skim any scum from the liquid, then reduce the heat to low and simmer, partially covered, until the steaks are tender, about 1 hour. To check for doneness, plunge a fork straight down into the meat and try to pull the fork out. If the fork slides out easily, the meat is done; if the meat hangs on to the fork, give it more time.

4. While the steaks are braising, make the couscous: In a medium saucepan, melt the butter over medium heat. Add the onion and cook, stirring occasionally, until translucent, 7 to 9 minutes. Add the garlic and cook, stirring, for 1 minute. Add the couscous and stir until it is well coated with butter, about 1 minute more. Add the boiling water and salt, remove the pan from the heat, cover, and let the couscous stand until all the liquid is absorbed, about 15 minutes.

5. When the steaks are tender, transfer them to a serving platter and cover them loosely with foil to keep warm. Skim the film from the cooking liquid and taste it. If it needs more flavor, place the pan over medium-high heat and simmer to reduce the liquid. When the liquid is slightly less thick than you want it, stir in the mustard, then swirl in the butter, a little at a time, until the sauce is shiny and thick. Remove from the heat and season with salt and pepper.

6. Transfer the couscous to a large serving bowl and add the red pepper flakes and thyme, fluffing with a fork to break up any lumps.

7. Top the steaks with sauce and serve, passing the couscous and any remaining sauce on the side.

BUTCHERSPEAK

This is a bit of an unusual cut nowadays, since this section of the hog is most often left intact as a Boston butt. But any good butcher should know what you are talking about if you ask for the cut by its formal name, the shoulder blade steak. If you just ask for a blade steak, he might confuse it with the blade chop from the loin, which is a similar cut but works better when cooked by dry heat methods.

Spareribs are long narrow pieces of meat and bone that come from the lower part of the hog's ribs and breastbone. "St. Louis–style" refers to a slab of ribs that has had the breastbone removed, which makes more uniform and more maneuverable on the grill.

Pork spareribs, breastbone off.

You can substitute the smaller pork back ribs (which come from the loin of the hog), but if you do, you'll want to cut the cooking time roughly in half.

Traditional Dry-Rubbed
St. Louis–Style Pork Spareribs

SERVES 8

Many people, when they grill ribs, use baby back ribs. But to me (Chris), those are not really ribs. Real ribs, also known as spareribs, come from the belly of the animal, right underneath the bacon. These ribs are not really all that tender, so they need some time on the grill, but when they come off, they have an amazing flavor.

The key is that you are cooking with indirect heat, so it's important to make sure that no part of the meat is directly over the coals. If it is, the fat dripping down off the ribs will cause the kind of fire you don't want. We're calling for four 2-pound racks of ribs here, so you need a big grill to keep the ribs away from the flames. Or you can, of course, cut the racks in half and cook a series of smaller racks.

Rather than slather the ribs with a tomato-based sauce, here we serve them "dry," accompanied by a vinegar-based sauce for drizzling on or dipping into. That gives the spice rub, which becomes a beautiful dark brown during cooking, a chance to shine.

This is your classic barbecue preparation, so serve the ribs with any or all of the following: coleslaw, baked beans, corn bread, watermelon, sweet potato salad, and sweet iced tea.

FOR THE RUB

¼ cup kosher salt

¼ cup freshly cracked black pepper

¼ cup chile powder

¼ cup ground cumin

½ cup sugar

½ cup paprika

Four 2-pound racks St. Louis–style pork spareribs

FOR THE SAUCE

½ cup white vinegar

2 tablespoons Tabasco sauce

2 tablespoons sugar

1 tablespoon kosher salt

1 tablespoon freshly cracked black pepper

1. Start a fire well over to one side using about enough charcoal to fill half a shoe box in a large kettle grill.

2. In a medium bowl, combine the rub ingredients and mix well. Dry the ribs with paper towels, then rub them thoroughly on all sides with this mixture, pressing gently to be sure it adheres.

3. In a small bowl, combine the sauce ingredients and mix well. Set aside.

4. When the coals are well lit, place the meat on the side away from the coals, being careful that none of it is directly over the coals. Put the lid on the grill with the vents open one quarter of the way. Cook for 3 to 4 hours, adding a handful of fresh charcoal about every 30 minutes, until the juice runs clear when you poke the meat with a fork and the meat is tender and pulls easily from the bone.

5. Remove the ribs from the grill and cut them apart between the bones. Serve the ribs "dry," with the sauce on the side.

COOK ONCE, EAT TWICE

When you reheat leftover ribs, it is important that you bring them back the same way they were cooked—slow and low. So reheat these babies in a 225°F oven, and they will be almost as delicious as when they first came off the grill.

In the trade, these are called "3 and down" pork spareribs. The "3 and down" means that each rack weighs 3 pounds or less, and the "spareribs" means that they come from the belly of the hog, right below the bacon. If you can get them, these are my #1 choice for ribs.

OTHER CUTS YOU CAN USE

You can definitely use St. Louis–style spareribs here, and, in a pinch, you could cut your cooking times in half and go with the pork loin back ribs, even though they're really a different animal.

EZ–Style Adobo Pork Ribs with Molasses-Chile Barbecue Sauce

SERVES 5

The "3 and down" spareribs used in this recipe are my (Chris's) absolute favorite type of ribs. These beauties are small enough to be manageable, but they have plenty of fat and incredible pork flavor. It just doesn't get any better than this in the rib department.

Here I'm taking a kind of nontraditional approach to these ribs. First I coat them with my dry adaptation of the Latin American adobo sauce, flavored with cumin, chili, oregano, and sour orange. Next I go the "cheater's route," putting the ribs in a low oven for 3 hours to cook them through, then laying them on the grill over a very low charcoal fire to give them a nice crust and some good smoke flavor. To finish it all off, there's a sweet-sour-hot barbecue sauce for drizzling or dunking.

These hyper-flavorful ribs go great with Latin-Style Black Beans and Rice (page 422) and a Costa Rican–style salad of cabbage, avocados, red bell peppers, and pineapple.

FOR THE FLAVORING PASTE

2 tablespoons minced garlic

2 tablespoons ground cumin

2 tablespoons chile powder

2 tablespoons dark brown sugar

3 tablespoons kosher salt

3 tablespoons freshly cracked black pepper

¼ cup roughly chopped fresh oregano

¼ cup roughly chopped fresh cilantro

6 tablespoons orange juice

2 tablespoons fresh lime juice (about 1 lime)

4 dashes Tabasco sauce

2 tablespoons olive oil

Two 3-pound racks pork spareribs

FOR THE SAUCE

⅓ cup molasses

½ cup catsup

¼ cup fresh lime juice (about 2 limes)

2 tablespoons ground cumin

½ cup roughly chopped fresh cilantro

1 to 3 tablespoons minced fresh chile peppers of your choice

1. Preheat the oven to 200°F.

2. In a food processor or blender, combine the paste ingredients and blend until smooth. Dry the ribs with paper towels, then rub them thoroughly with the paste. Place the ribs on two baking sheets and slow-roast for 3 hours, or until red juice comes out when you poke the meat with a fork and the meat is tender and pulls easily from the bone. Remove the ribs from the oven. They can go right onto the grill, stand out for a while, or be refrigerated, covered, for 2 days.

3. While the ribs are roasting, combine the sauce ingredients in a small bowl and mix well; set aside.

4. Light a fire in your grill. You want a very low charcoal fire with the rack set as high as possible.

5. Put the ribs on the grill and let them stay there as long as your patience allows. A light crust on the outside is the goal, and, depending on your fire, it can be achieved in 5 minutes per side or take up to 30 minutes per side, if you're into prolonging your guests' agony. Of course, the longer the ribs cook, the better. Brush them with the sauce during the last minute on the grill.

6. Cut the ribs apart between the bones and serve with the remaining barbecue sauce on the side.

COOK ONCE, EAT TWICE

If you are fortunate enough to have any of these ribs left over, reheat them in a low (250°F) oven and eat them with coleslaw. Or you can even just eat them room temp—we certainly have.

THE CUT

See Roast Sage-Garlic Pork Butt (page 339) for details about pork butt, also known as pork shoulder roast or Boston butt.

OTHER CUTS YOU CAN USE

Any of the roasts from the pork shoulder are fine here, although those with the word "picnic" in their name may be a little tough.

Authentic Eastern North Carolina Barbecued Pork Butt on Buns with Tidewater Slaw

MAKES ABOUT 15 SANDWICHES

This is the classic, the original item, real honest-to-goodness pulled pork barbecue. You've got to have your patience working in order to make this dish, with plenty of beer on hand and plenty of trash talk to make the long hours around the smoky fire pass more pleasantly.

For you short-cutters out there, another way to do this is to cook the pork butt for 4 to 8 hours in your covered grill with heavy smoke. (This is a place where the wood chips you see in all those grilling catalogues might actually come in handy.) Then you can take the meat out of the grill and put it in a 200°F oven to cook until it is tender. It will take almost as long, but you won't have to stand around and feed the fire the whole time—and while we think that's the whole point of the enterprise, we do understand that there are others who actually have more pressing things to do with their time.

These days, you see lots of recipes for this dish that tell you to cook the pork to a particular temperature, but that doesn't make sense to us. What you really want to do here is cook the meat *past* the point of mere doneness to the point of tenderness. That can only be determined by checking the texture, not the temperature.

Serve this with some other barbecue classics: watermelon, corn on the cob, potato salad, and banana cream pie.

FOR THE RUB

¼ cup kosher salt

¼ cup freshly cracked black pepper

¼ cup paprika

2 tablespoons granulated sugar

2 tablespoons brown sugar

2 tablespoons ground cumin

2 tablespoons chile powder

1 tablespoon cayenne pepper

Two 4- to 5-pound boneless pork butts

FOR THE SAUCE

1 cup white vinegar

1 cup cider vinegar

1 tablespoon sugar

1 tablespoon red pepper flakes

1 tablespoon Tabasco sauce

Kosher salt and freshly cracked black pepper to taste

FOR THE SLAW

1½ cups mayonnaise

½ cup white vinegar

⅓ cup sugar

1 tablespoon celery seeds

Kosher salt and freshly cracked black pepper to taste

1 head green cabbage, cored and finely shredded

2 carrots, peeled and grated

Cheap fluffy white buns

Hot sauce for garnish

1. Light a fire well over to one side of a large kettle grill, using about enough charcoal to fill half of a shoe box.

2. In a small bowl, combine the rub ingredients and mix well. Dry the pork butts with paper towels, then rub them on all sides with the rub, pressing gently to be sure it adheres.

3. In another small bowl, combine the sauce ingredients and mix well. Set aside.

4. When the fire has died down and the coals are covered with ash, place the meat on the side away from the coals, being careful that none of the meat is directly over the coals. Put the lid on the grill with the vents open one quarter of the way. Cook for 12 to 14 hours, adding a handful of fresh charcoal about every 30 minutes, until the meat is super-tender.

5. While the pork is on the grill, make the coleslaw: In a small bowl, combine the mayonnaise, vinegar, sugar, celery seeds, and salt and pepper, and mix well. In a large bowl, combine the cabbage and carrots. Pour the dressing over the mixture and blend well. Cover and refrigerate until serving time.

6. Remove the pork butts from the grill and chop or shred them, whichever you prefer. Mix the pork with the sauce to taste, and pile it onto the buns, top with the slaw, and garnish with hot sauce.

COOK ONCE, EAT TWICE

Pulled pork barbecue is among the most durable dishes out there. You can reheat it over and over, or you can freeze it and thaw it, and it will still taste great. It's the ideal thing to have in your freezer in case folks unexpectedly decide to come for the weekend and you want to feed them some real down-home food. Just make sure you have plenty of sauce on hand too.

See Roast Sage-Garlic
Pork Butt (page 339) for
details about pork butt,
also known as pork shoul-
der roast or Boston butt.

OTHER CUTS YOU CAN USE

Any of the roasts from the
pork shoulder would work
well here, although those
with the word "picnic" in
their name may be a little
tough.

Cheater-Style Indoor Barbecued Pork

SERVES 8 HUNGRY PEOPLE

One of the primary disadvantages of living in a cold climate is that it's hard to barbecue when snow is piled high on the ground. So we have worked very hard to come up with a solution for all of our climate-impaired barbecue brethren, and this is it.

While it is rank heresy to even suggest this among true aficionados, it is possible to approximate the taste of real barbecue in the oven. Notice that we said *approximate,* because of course you can't duplicate the exact flavor of meat that has spent 10 or 12 hours sitting over the smoky heat of a smoldering hickory fire. But you can produce a very reasonable, mighty tasty facsimile.

There is, of course, a trick to it. While the oven can hold a steady, even heat for as long as you want it to, it cannot provide the dominant flavor of smoke that is an essential part of barbecue. To mimic that, you have to add a nontraditional step to the barbecuing process, a precooking dunk in brine flavored with liquid smoke. Because this requires some setup and some soaking time, it is not really *quick* barbecue, but it is easy barbecue that can be done at any time of year.

Some cooks may balk at using liquid smoke, suspecting that, like many potions designed to mimic flavors, it is a witches' brew of chemicals and additives. Not so. In fact, it is made simply by burning hickory wood, condensing the resulting smoke, and filtering it to remove impurities. So you can use it without fear for your health, even though it may cause you to fear for your barbecue credentials.

Since the amount of brine required depends on the size and shape of the container being used for the brining process, it may not always be necessary to make the full amount of brine called for below. As with most unfamiliar dishes, you will have to go by trial and error the first time, but after that, you will know what you need before you begin.

FOR THE BRINE

1 gallon water

½ cup liquid smoke

1½ cups kosher salt

¾ cup dark brown sugar

One 5-pound boneless pork butt roast

¼ cup granulated sugar

¼ cup paprika

2 tablespoons ground cumin

1 tablespoon kosher salt

2 tablespoons freshly cracked black pepper

2 tablespoons chile powder

¾ cup white vinegar

3 to 4 tablespoons Texas Pete, Tabasco, or other hot sauce

1 tablespoon granulated sugar

Kosher salt and freshly cracked black pepper to taste

1. In a large bucket or other container that the pork butt will easily fit into, combine the water, liquid smoke, salt, and brown sugar and stir to dissolve the salt and sugar. Place the pork butt in the container, making sure there is enough brine so the butt is completely covered. Refrigerate for 24 to 48 hours, turning every 12 hours or so.

2. Make the spice rub: In a small bowl, combine the granulated sugar, paprika, cumin, salt, pepper, and chile powder and mix well.

3. Preheat the oven to 210°F.

4. Remove the pork from the brine, dry it well, and rub it all over with the spice mixture, pressing gently to be sure it adheres. Put the pork butt in a roasting pan, place in the oven, and cook for 10 to 12 hours, or until the pork is so tender that it will not grip a fork when you try to lift it.

5. Just before the pork is done, combine the vinegar, hot sauce, granulated sugar, and salt and pepper in a small bowl and mix well.

6. Remove the pork from the oven and, as soon as it is cool enough to handle, drain off the fat, then chop or shred the pork into bite-sized pieces. Add the vinegar mixture, mix well, and serve.

RECIPES FOR
SMALL TENDER CUTS OF PORK

10 STEPS TO GREAT GRILLED PORK

1. Build a two-level fire using hardwood charcoal.

2. Wait for the flames to die down and the coals to be covered with gray ash.

3. Check the temperature of the fire.

4. Dry the meat well.

5. Season the meat well.

6. Sear the meat hard over a hot fire.

7. Move the meat to the cooler part of the fire if it needs to cook more slowly (don't use the cover).

8. Flip the meat only once during cooking.

9. Check for doneness early and often (nick, peek, and cheat).

10. Remove the meat from the heat, cover with foil and allow to rest for 10 minutes, then serve it up.

Grilled Coriander-Crusted, Pickled Corn–Stuffed Double-Thick Pork Chops with Peach Chutney

Panfried Brined Loin Chops Stuffed with Walnuts and Stilton Cheese, with Spiced Apples

Macadamia Nut–Crusted Pork Chops with Pineapple-Ginger Catsup

White Pepper–Crusted Pork Loin Chops with Peanut-Ginger Power Pack

Sautéed Pork Cutlets with Cashew Slaw and Chile Flavor Booster

Grilled Pork Loin Fillets on Latin-Style Salad with Sour Orange–Oregano Dressing

Sautéed Pork Scallopini over Scallion Lo Mein with Soy-Braised Bok Choy

Grilled Boneless Pork Loin Chops with Green Olive–Red Onion Relish and Nectarine Chutney

Hoisin-Glazed Grilled Pork Blade Chops with Spicy Korean Vegetables

Grilled Thin Pork Chops with Avocado-Corn Salsa

Molasses-Glazed Pork Tenderloin with Seared Sweet-and-Sour Red Onions and Sage-Date Power Pack

Grilled Pork Tenderloin on a Salad of Grilled Potatoes and Red Onions

Grilled Baby Back Ribs, Buffalo-Style

Grilled Pork, Bacon, and Mango Skewers with
Guava-Chile Glaze

Grilled Pork and Fig Skewers with Sun-Dried
Tomato–Basil Relish

BBQ-Rubbed Grilled Fresh Ham Center Slice with
Watermelon-Pineapple Salad

10 STEPS TO GREAT SAUTÉED PORK

1. Use a big heavy sauté pan.

2. Dry the meat well.

3. Season the meat well.

4. Use only a small amount of oil.

5. Get the pan and the oil hot.

6. Don't overcrowd the meat in the pan.

7. Sear the meat hard.

8. Flip the meat only once while cooking.

9. Check for doneness early and often (nick, peek, and cheat).

10. Remove the meat from the heat, cover with foil, and allow to rest, then serve.

10 STEPS TO GREAT BROILED PORK

Check out sautéing: The steps are the same except you use a broiler pan instead of a sauté pan; preheat the broiler instead of getting the oil hot and skip the searing step.

Here we are calling for a double-thick version of our favorite pork chop, the loin rib chop. This chop is cut from the rib section of the loin, which is toward the shoulder. Because of this, it has a somewhat higher fat content than a true center-cut chop, which makes it both more flavorsome and less likely to dry out during cooking. Rib chops can be distinguished by the section of rib bone that runs along one side.

OTHER NAMES

Pocket pork chop.

OTHER CUTS YOU CAN USE

Any very thick chop from the loin, including the top loin chop and loin chop, will work just fine here.

BUTCHERSPEAK

To get chops this thick, you are probably going to have to go to a butcher. As long as you're there, you might want to ask the butcher to cut the pockets in the chops so you don't have to.

Grilled Coriander-Crusted, Pickled Corn–Stuffed Double-Thick Pork Chops with Peach Chutney

SERVES 4

We're talking corn, we're talking pickles, we're talking chutney—could there be any doubt that this recipe is right out of the South?

Pork and corn are an old standby combination to which we're adding coriander, one of our favorite spices. We definitely recommend that you buy whole coriander seeds and grind them up yourself, since the flavor is much clearer and stronger. It's easy to do this if you just buy an extra electric coffee grinder or a large pepper mill and keep it for spices rather than coffee or pepper.

For this recipe, you need some giant chops, thick enough to stuff. That means that we'll be using the "move and cover" method of grilling to avoid burning the outside of the meat before the inside is cooked through. Build a two-level fire, brown the chops well on both sides over the hotter part, move them to the cooler part, and cover them with a tin or disposable aluminum pie pan to cook through. (They can also be finished in a 350°F oven if for some reason you would rather do that.)

Serve this with Hominy with Cheddar, Chiles, and Sour Cream (page 438) or simple steamed green beans and a big green salad with blue cheese dressing. That's some good eating right there.

FOR THE CHUTNEY

2 tablespoons olive oil

1 large onion, peeled, halved, and thinly sliced

5 ripe but firm peaches, pitted and roughly chopped

1/4 cup packed dark brown sugar

2 tablespoons granulated sugar

2 teaspoons kosher salt

1 teaspoon freshly cracked black pepper

1/4 teaspoon ground allspice

3 tablespoons molasses

1/2 cup white vinegar

2 tablespoons fresh lemon juice (about 1/2 lemon)

Four 12- to 16-ounce pork loin rib chops, 2 to 2 1/2 inches thick

Kosher salt and freshly cracked black pepper to taste

⅓ cup cracked coriander seeds (or 3 tablespoons ground coriander)

2 ears corn, husked, blanched in boiling salted water for 2 minutes, drained, and kernels cut off the cob (about 1 cup kernels)

3 tablespoons finely chopped sweet pickles or pickle relish

2 tablespoons balsamic vinegar

1 teaspoon dark brown sugar

1 teaspoon celery seeds

1. Make the chutney: In a medium saucepan, heat the oil over medium-high heat until hot but not smoking. Add the onion and cook, stirring occasionally, until translucent, 7 to 9 minutes. Add the peaches and cook, stirring frequently, for 4 minutes. Add both sugars, the salt, pepper, allspice, molasses, and vinegar and bring to a simmer, then turn the heat down to low and simmer for 30 minutes, stirring occasionally. If necessary, add a small amount of water to prevent the mixture from burning. Remove the chutney from the heat, stir in the lemon juice, and set aside.

2. Build a two-level fire in your grill, using about enough charcoal to fill a large shoe box and tapering the depth of the charcoal in the grill so that two thirds of the coals are on one side and one third on the other.

3. Dry the pork chops with paper towels, sprinkle them generously with salt and pepper, and rub them with the coriander. In a medium bowl, combine the corn, pickles, vinegar, brown sugar, celery seeds, and salt and pepper to taste and mix well. Cut a pocket in the side of each pork chop: Insert a sharp thin-bladed knife, such as a boning knife, into the center of the side of the chop and, holding the knife in place, sweep the blade back and forth in a slight sawing motion to create a pocket without enlarging the opening. Pull the knife out, reinsert it in the same opening with the blade facing in the opposite direction, and repeat the sawing motion. Put one quarter of the corn mixture into the pocket in each chop.

4. When the fire has died down and the coals are medium-hot (you can hold your hand 5 inches above the grill surface for 3 to 4 seconds), place the chops over the hottest part of the fire and cook until well seared on both sides, about 8 minutes per side. Move the chops to the cooler part of the grill, cover with a metal pie pan or disposable aluminium pie plate, and continue to cook until the pork is done to your liking, 10 to 12 more minutes for medium to medium-well. To check for doneness, nick, peek, and cheat: Make a ¼-inch cut in the thickest part of the meat and take a peek; it should be slightly less done than you like it. When the meat is done to your liking, remove it from the heat, cover it loosely with foil, and let it rest for 10 minutes.

5. Serve each chop with a generous spoonful of the peach chutney.

COOK ONCE, EAT TWICE

Leftovers from this dish can be made into a really nice bread salad. Put the pork and the relish in a big bowl with some cubes of stale bread, thin out the peach chutney with some balsamic vinegar and olive oil, add it to the bowl, give it a toss, and you've got an exceptional lunch.

The top loin chop is to pork what New York strip or sirloin strip is to beef. It comes pretty much from the center portion of the loin, and it is a very tender chop that also has a good pork flavor. (See The Chop Shop, page 362, for more details on types of pork chops.)

OTHER CUTS YOU CAN USE

Rib loin chops, boneless or bone-in, are also great in this recipe. Basically, whatever center-cut chops from the loin your butcher has in this thickness will be fine.

Panfried Brined Loin Chops Stuffed with Walnuts and Stilton Cheese, with Spiced Apples

SERVES 4

We love blue cheese and meat together. We figure sometimes it's best to just be direct, so in this recipe we stuff a really good blue cheese right inside some extra-thick pork chops, adding some walnuts for crunch and richness. We then finish them with balsamic apples cooked in the pork juices. We'll wager you will end up using the apples with other pork dishes too. It's a nice way to dress up quickly sautéed thin pork chops, for example, when you don't have time to cook thick ones.

In this recipe, we brine the thick pork chops for 6 to 8 hours before cooking them. We like this technique because the treatment not only makes today's lean chops slightly more flavorful, but also helps keep them moist during high-heat cooking. But, as always, if you don't have the time or the inclination, you can skip the brining and still have a great dish. In that case, though, you might do better to use rib loin chops rather than the top loin chops we call for here.

Our friend Michael Otten, who faithfully tested dozens of recipes in this book just for the fun of it, came up with the method used here for making a large pocket in the double-thick chops with only a small opening in the exterior. Once you get the stuffing into the chop, it's unlikely to come out while the chops are cooking.

Serve this with Green Beans with Mushrooms and Almonds (page 429) or Braised Leeks (page 430), roasted sweet potatoes, and a simple green salad.

FOR THE BRINE (OPTIONAL)

5 cups water

½ cup kosher salt

¾ cup packed dark brown sugar

1 cup apple cider

2 bay leaves, crushed

6 cardamom pods, crushed

3 allspice berries, crushed

2 tablespoons freshly cracked black pepper

6 ounces Stilton or other blue cheese of your choice

3 ounces walnuts, toasted in a dry skillet over medium heat, shaking frequently, until fragrant, 3 to 5 minutes, and chopped

1 teaspoon freshly cracked black pepper

Four 10-ounce boneless pork top loin chops, about 1½ inches thick

Kosher salt and freshly cracked black pepper to taste

2 tablespoons vegetable oil

FOR THE SAUCE

2 large tart apples, cored and cut in eighths

¼ cup balsamic vinegar

¼ cup water

Generous pinch of ground allspice

Generous pinch of ground cardamom

Generous pinch of ground cinnamon

Kosher salt and freshly cracked black pepper to taste

1½ tablespoons cold unsalted butter, cut into small pieces

1. Make the optional brine: In a bowl large enough to hold the chops, stir together the water, salt, and sugar until the salt completely dissolves. Add the remaining brine ingredients and mix well, then add the chops, making sure that they are completely submerged in the liquid. Refrigerate for 6 to 8 hours.

2. Make the stuffing: Crumble the cheese into a small bowl, add the walnuts and pepper, and toss lightly to combine. (Cover and refrigerate if you are not planning to stuff the chops right away.)

3. Remove the chops from the brine and pat them dry with paper towels. Cut a pocket in the side of each pork chop: Insert a sharp thin-bladed knife, such as a boning knife, into the center of the side of the chop and, holding the knife in place, sweep the blade back and forth in a slight sawing motion to create a pocket without enlarging the opening. Pull the knife out, reinsert it in the same opening with the blade facing in the opposite direction, and repeat the sawing motion. Stuff each chop with one quarter of the blue cheese mixture. Fasten the slits closed with toothpicks and sprinkle the chops generously with salt and pepper.

4. In a large sauté pan, heat the oil over medium-high heat until very hot but not smoking. Add the chops and sear well, about 5 minutes per side. Reduce the heat to medium, cover the pan, and cook until done to your liking, about 10 minutes more for medium-well. To check for doneness, nick, peek, and cheat: Make a ¼-inch cut in the thickest part of a chop and take a peek; it should be slightly less done than you like it. When the chops are done, transfer them to a platter and cover them loosely with foil to keep warm.

5. Turn the heat back to medium-high. If the pan is dry, add another tablespoon of oil. Add the apples to the pan and sauté, turning occasionally, until browned on both sides, about 5 to 8 minutes. Add the vinegar and water and bring to a simmer, stirring to dissolve the brown crusty stuff in the bottom of the pan. Add the allspice, cardamom, cinnamon, and salt and pepper and simmer until the liquid is reduced by half, 5 minutes. Swirl in the butter, a little at a time, until the sauce is shiny and thick. Remove from the heat.

6. Remove the toothpicks from the chops, arrange some of the apples and sauce over each chop, and serve.

Macadamia Nut–Crusted Pork Chops with Pineapple-Ginger Catsup

SERVES 6

There's a Hawaiian kind of thing going on in this recipe, with the macadamia nut crust on the chops and the flavorful Pineapple-Ginger Catsup alongside. And, by the way, if you find it odd that we call a pineapple concoction a "catsup," this is actually nothing new. In the old days, a catsup was simply a vinegar-based sauce used to preserve all kinds of fruits and vegetables, from mushrooms to mangoes to (that's right) pineapples. It is only in the relatively recent past that this term has come to be reserved for the tomato-based condiment we know so well. If you don't feel like making the catsup, though, just sauté the pork chops with their rich macadamia crust and serve them with your favorite salsa.

Although we call for two sauté pans here, if you have a really giant, restaurant-sized pan that will comfortably hold all six chops in a single layer, go for it. The idea is just that the chops should not be too crowded, or they won't brown right.

You might serve this with plain rice or a grain salad and maybe even Simple Lentils (page 425).

FOR THE CATSUP

¼ cup olive oil

1 red onion, peeled, halved, and thinly sliced

1 red bell pepper, cored, seeded, and roughly chopped

1 green bell pepper, cored, seeded, and roughly chopped

¼ cup minced fresh ginger

1 tablespoon minced garlic

1 tablespoon minced fresh chile peppers of your choice

3 tablespoons curry powder

1 large pineapple, peeled, cored, and cut into ½-inch chunks (about 4 cups)

½ cup dark raisins

1¼ cups white vinegar

½ cup orange or pineapple juice

1 cup packed dark brown sugar

Kosher salt and freshly cracked black pepper to taste

Six 10- to 12-ounce bone-in pork loin chops, 1 to 1½ inches thick

Kosher salt and freshly cracked black pepper to taste

½ cup macadamia nuts or peanuts, toasted in a dry skillet over medium heat, shaken frequently, until fragrant, 3 to 5 minutes, and crushed

2 tablespoons unsalted butter

2 tablespoons vegetable oil

COOK ONCE, EAT TWICE

The catsup recipe here makes considerably more than you will use with these chops. That's a good thing, though, because it will keep, covered and refrigerated, for several weeks. That way, you're ready to instantly add a ton of flavor to a quick sautéed pork chop or even a nice grilled steak any time you want.

1. Make the catsup: In a large saucepan, heat the oil over medium-high heat until hot but not smoking. Add the onion and bell peppers and sauté, stirring occasionally, until the onion becomes translucent, 7 to 9 minutes. Add the ginger, garlic, chile peppers, and curry powder and sauté, stirring, for 1 minute. Add the pineapple, raisins, vinegar, juice, and brown sugar and bring to a boil. Reduce the heat to low and simmer, stirring occasionally, until the liquid has thickened slightly, 10 to 15 minutes. Season with salt and pepper, remove from the heat, and allow to cool slightly. Puree briefly in a blender, leaving the catsup slightly chunky; cover and set aside.

2. Dry the pork chops with paper towels and sprinkle generously with salt and pepper. Rub them all over with the crushed macadamias, pressing gently to be sure they adhere. Divide the butter and oil equally between two sauté pans and heat over medium heat until the butter has melted. Add 3 chops to each sauté pan and cook until done to your liking, 5 to 7 minutes per side for medium-well. To check for doneness, nick, peek, and cheat: Make a ¼-inch cut in the thickest part of one of the chops; it should be slightly less done than you like it. Remove the chops from the pans, cover with foil, and let them rest for about 5 minutes.

3. Serve the chops, passing the catsup on the side.

THE CHOP SHOP

All pork chops come from the loin of the hog. This is basically the upper back from the shoulder to the leg, the most tender part of the animal. As a result, all pork chops are quite tender. But there are differences between chops cut from various parts of the loin, which is, after all, quite a large part of the hog. These differences are significant enough to make it worth knowing which is which. Basically there are five types of chops. The problem is that they are not always properly labeled, so you don't always know exactly what you are getting. But there are some visual clues that can help.

Chops taken from the two extreme ends of the loin are relatively rare in supermarkets. The blade chop, also called the pork chop end cut, comes from the section of the loin right next to the shoulder. The sirloin chop, sometimes called the pork sirloin steak, is taken from the end of the loin right next to the hip. Both of these have more connective tissue, more fat, and a higher ratio of bone to meat than chops from the center section of the loin.

Much more common are the three types of chops that can be labeled "center cut"–the rib chop, loin chop, and top loin chop. While these chops shade into one another as you move along the loin, there are definitely distinctions. The rib chop comes from the part of the loin nearer the shoulder, which means it has a little bit more fat than the other center-cut chops. It can be distinguished by the small curved section of rib bone that runs along one side. The loin chop, which is most often simply labeled "center cut," comes from the center and rear center sections of the loin. It contains portions of the top loin muscle and the tenderloin muscle, divided from each other by a bone that is the distinguishing mark of this type of chop. The top loin chop is essentially a loin chop without the tenderloin section. Because pork tenderloin is such a popular piece of meat, this is the way most center-cut chops are butchered these days.

For many people, a helpful way of keeping these three straight is to think of them in terms of what they would be if they came from a cow. So here it is: a rib chop is like a rib-eye steak; a top loin chop is like a top loin steak, also known as a New York strip or sirloin strip; and a loin chop is like a T-bone or porterhouse.

Our particular favorite is the rib chop. Now that pork is so lean, the little extra fat on this chop is a definite advantage. It not only gives the meat more flavor, but also makes it less likely to dry out during cooking.

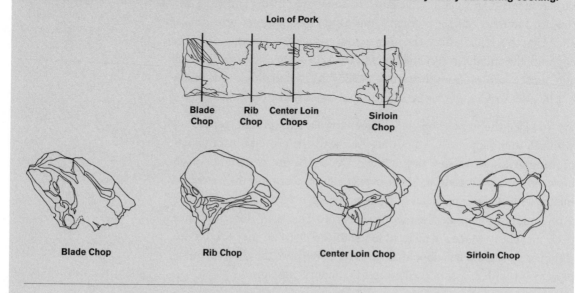

Loin of Pork

Blade Chop — Rib Chop — Center Loin Chops — Sirloin Chop

Blade Chop   Rib Chop   Center Loin Chop   Sirloin Chop

White Pepper–Crusted Pork Loin Chops with Peanut-Ginger Power Pack

SERVES 4

THE CUT

See Macadamia Nut–Crusted Pork Chops (page 360) for details on the pork loin chop and other cuts that can be substituted for it. As usual, when you're looking for chops this thick, it's a good idea to call the butcher and make sure he has some on hand.

Pepper-crusting meat is a technique I (Chris) really like. Like a spice rub, a coating of pepper gives the meat a super-flavorful crust and creates a real contrast in flavor and texture between the inside and the outside. For an Asian take, I use white pepper here. This is a very straightforward dish with plenty of flavor that you can make when you come home and want a quick dinner that's not boring. If you make the power pack ahead of time (it will keep, covered and refrigerated, for 3 to 4 days), you can have this on the table in about 20 minutes.

Serve this with brown rice and maybe some Roasted Asparagus (page 427).

FOR THE POWER PACK

¼ cup finely chopped roasted unsalted peanuts

2 tablespoons minced fresh ginger

1 jalapeño or other small chile pepper, minced

4 scallions, (white and light green parts), very thinly sliced

2 tablespoons finely chopped fresh mint

2 tablespoons sesame oil

1 teaspoon sugar

Four 10-ounce pork loin chops, about 1½ inches thick

Kosher salt to taste

2 tablespoons freshly ground white pepper (or substitute black pepper)

1 tablespoon vegetable oil

1. In a small bowl, combine all the power pack ingredients and mix well; set aside.

2. Sprinkle the chops generously with salt and rub all over with the white pepper, pressing gently to be sure it adheres.

3. In a large sauté pan, heat the vegetable oil over medium-high heat until hot but not smoking. Add the chops and brown well on both sides, 5 to 7 minutes per side. Turn down the heat to medium-low and continue to cook until the chops are just lightly pink in the center, 3 to 4 minutes. To check for doneness, nick, peek, and cheat: Make a ¼-inch cut in one of the chops at the thickest point; it should be slightly less done than you want it to be. Remove the chops from the heat, cover loosely with foil, and let them rest for 5 minutes.

4. Stir the peanut-ginger mixture, spoon a portion over each chop, and serve.

Sautéed Pork Cutlets with Cashew Slaw and Chile Flavor Booster

SERVES 4

Asian flavors predominate in this dish, in which thin pork cutlets are sautéed quickly, then placed on top of a spicy cabbage slaw with lots of crunchy cashews in it, and finally topped with an intense flavor booster at the last minute. The result is a lot of flavor and interesting textures for not that much work.

As for the cut of meat, some of you might be wondering why the same piece of pork is sometimes called a chop, sometimes a cutlet, and sometimes a fillet. To be honest, it's a combination of logic and caprice. Technically speaking, a chop is a relatively small piece of meat taken from the rib section of an animal and usually including part of the rib bone. So when this piece of meat has a bone, it's definitely a chop. In the old days, a chop *without* a bone was called a fillet, which is defined as a boneless piece of meat (or fish). But nowadays we also call it, more simply, a boneless chop. As for the cutlet, that is a very thin, tender piece of meat usually taken from the rib or leg of an animal. So a chop that is pounded thin can become a cutlet. And there you have it: same piece of meat, three names.

Whatever you call it, the pork here is thin and tender, so we cook it at high heat to get it nicely browned on the outside before it overcooks on the inside. To accomplish that, make sure that your oil is hot before you put the cutlets in the pan.

Serve this with brown or white rice and some Braised Fennel (page 438).

FOR THE FLAVOR BOOSTER
2 to 3 jalapeños, thinly sliced
¼ cup fish sauce (or substitute 2 tablespoons sesame oil)
2 tablespoons soy sauce
Pinch of sugar

These cutlets are made from boneless pork top loin chops that have been pounded to a thickness of about ½ inch. The fine-grained texture of these chops makes them ideal for this purpose.

OTHER CUTS YOU CAN USE
Any center-cut pork loin chop is great here, and the sirloin cutlet and loin blade chop will also work fine. (See The Chop Shop, page 362, for more information about various types of pork chops.)

FOR THE SLAW

2 cups shredded green cabbage

1 cup peeled and shredded carrots (about 1 large or 2 small carrots)

½ cup bean sprouts of your choice (optional)

½ cup cashews, toasted in a 350°F oven for 5 to 7 minutes

2 tablespoons minced fresh ginger

1 tablespoon minced fresh chile peppers of your choice, or to taste

1 teaspoon minced garlic

2 tablespoons cracked coriander seeds (or 1 tablespoon ground coriander)

¼ cup sugar

¼ cup fresh lime juice (about 2 limes)

¼ cup soy sauce

¼ cup molasses

½ cup peanut oil

Kosher salt and freshly cracked black pepper to taste

Four 8-ounce boneless pork top loin chops

Kosher salt and freshly cracked black pepper to taste

2 tablespoons olive oil

COOK ONCE, EAT TWICE

You can use any leftover pork in a quick stir-fry with garlic, carrots, bell peppers, and onions, serving any leftover slaw on the side. If you have any booster left, put that in the stir-fry too. In fact, you might want to make a double or triple batch of the flavor booster while you're at it, since it keeps well if covered and refrigerated, and it adds a ton of flavor to any dish in just seconds.

1. Make the chile booster: In a small bowl, combine all the ingredients and mix well to dissolve the sugar; set aside.

2. Make the cashew slaw: In a very large bowl, combine the cabbage, carrots, bean sprouts, if using, and cashews and mix well. In a food processor or blender, combine the ginger, chiles, garlic, coriander, sugar, lime juice, soy sauce, molasses, peanut oil, and salt and pepper and process until well blended. Pour this dressing over the vegetables, toss to coat thoroughly, and set aside.

3. Dry the chops with paper towels, place them between two sheets of plastic wrap, and, using a meat mallet or other blunt instrument, such as the bottom of a sauté pan, pound them to a thickness of about ½ inch. Now they are cutlets. Sprinkle them generously with salt and pepper.

4. In a large sauté pan, heat the oil over medium-high heat until hot but not smoking. Add the cutlets, in batches if necessary to avoid crowding, and cook until well browned and done to your liking, 3 to 4 minutes per side for medium-well. To check for doneness, nick, peek, and cheat: Make a ¼-inch cut in the thickest part of the meat; it should be slightly less done than you like it. Remove the cutlets from the pan, cover them loosely with foil, and let them rest for 5 minutes before serving.

5. To serve, place some of the cashew slaw on each plate, top with a pork cutlet, and top the pork with a spoonful of the flavor booster.

Pork loin fillets, which we call for in this recipe, are basically boneless top loin chops. You should be able to find these in most supermarkets, because the ones we are using here are less than an inch thick. But you still want to have *some* thickness on these chops, so avoid the very thin versions.

OTHER CUTS YOU CAN USE

Boneless rib chops are excellent in this recipe. You can also substitute fillets cut from the super-tender and readily available pork tenderloin. Farther down the tenderness scale, boneless sirloin chops or blade chops are also OK.

Grilled Pork Loin Fillets on Latin-Style Salad with Sour Orange–Oregano Dressing

SERVES 4

Sometimes people tell us that they think meat is too heavy to eat when it's really hot outside. But that doesn't make sense to us, since people in the tropics eat meat, particularly pork. So it stands to reason that there are many ways to combine meat with other ingredients in dishes that are perfect for summer meals. This is one of them.

In this dish, fillets sliced from the tender and relatively lean pork loin are grilled quickly with a little cumin and then served on top of a super-fresh salad with an array of Latin American flavors going on. This salad is actually a good illustration of the fact that greens, while important to any salad, don't have to be the primary ingredient.

Serve this with Latin-Style Black Beans and Rice (page 422), fried plantains or yucca, and some watermelon and you've got a great meal.

FOR THE DRESSING

¼ cup fresh orange juice (about ½ orange)

¼ cup fresh lime juice (about 2 limes)

⅓ cup olive oil

¼ cup red wine vinegar

1 teaspoon minced garlic

2 teaspoons sugar

⅓ cup roughly chopped fresh oregano

Kosher salt and freshly cracked black pepper to taste

FOR THE SALAD

2 ears corn, husked

2 avocados, peeled, pitted, and diced large

2 tomatoes (about the size of a baseball), cored and diced large

1 red onion, peeled and diced small

1 cup cooked (or drained canned) black beans

1 bunch arugula, trimmed, washed, and dried

Kosher salt and freshly ground black pepper to taste

Four 6-ounce boneless pork loin fillets, about ¾ inch thick

Kosher salt and freshly cracked black pepper to taste

2 tablespoons ground cumin

1. Light a fire in your grill.

2. In a medium bowl, combine all the dressing ingredients and whisk together well; set aside.

3. Make the salad: Blanch the corn in boiling salted water for 2 minutes, drain, and cool under cold running water. Slice the kernels off the ears. (You should have about 1 cup of kernels.) Place the kernels in a large bowl, add all the remaining salad ingredients, and set aside.

4. Dry the pork fillets with paper towels, sprinkle them generously with salt and pepper, and rub them all over with the cumin, pressing gently to be sure it adheres.

5. When the fire has died down and the coals are medium-hot (you can hold your hand 5 inches above the grill surface for 3 to 4 seconds), place the fillets on the grill and cook until well seared on one side, about 5 minutes. Turn and continue cooking to the desired doneness, about 5 minutes total cooking time for medium-well. To check for doneness, nick, peek, and cheat: Make a ¼-inch cut in the thickest part of the meat and take a peek; it should be slightly less done than you like it. When the meat is done to your liking, remove it from the grill, cover it loosely with foil, and let it rest for 5 minutes.

6. Pour enough of the dressing over the salad to moisten the ingredients and toss well. Place a portion of the salad on each plate and top with a fillet.

These scallopini are basically boneless pork top loin chops pounded to a ¼-inch thickness. As with cutlets, the smooth, fine-grained texture of the pork loin makes it ideal for this treatment.

OTHER CUTS YOU CAN USE
Any boneless pork loin chop will work fine here. (See The Chop Shop, page 362, for more information about particular types of pork chops.) You could even use a fresh ham steak from the leg of the hog, although it might not have as fine a grain and therefore not be quite as easy to pound.

Sautéed Pork Scallopini over Scallion Lo Mein with Soy-Braised Bok Choy

SERVES 4

Because pork combines so well with Asian flavors such as soy and ginger, it's ideal for Asian-style noodle dishes, which we like a lot. Here we cook some lo mein–style noodles, braise some bok choy in a flavorful soy-ginger sauce, and then quickly cook some pieces of thin pork loin to lay over the top, all of which makes for a nice combination of textures as well as flavors.

Although we are not ordinarily big fans of baby vegetables, bok choy is an exception. Since the miniature versions of these Asian cabbages are very tender, you can just cut them into quarters and cook them; that way, you get both leaves and stems in the same serving. Plus they look neat on the plate, sort of like an Asian version of baby artichokes.

Some of you might also notice that we're adding yet another term to the trio of *chop, cutlet,* and *fillet,* which all apply to what is basically the same cut of pork loin. To put it simply, *scallopine* is the Italian term for a cutlet pounded quite thin, usually breaded. (We figure the more terms you know for any piece of meat, the more fun it is.)

It's important here that you pound the pork down to no more than ¼ inch thick so it will cook quickly and evenly. Besides, if the pork is thicker than that, it somehow seems too clunky for the rest of the dish.

1 pound flat noodles, such as linguine, fettuccine, or lo mein

5 tablespoons sesame oil

Eight 4-ounce boneless pork top loin chops (or four 8-ounce chops, sliced horizontally in half)

3 tablespoons peanut oil

1 pound baby bok choy, trimmed and quartered

2 tablespoons minced fresh ginger

1 tablespoon minced garlic

¼ cup soy sauce

¼ cup water

¼ cup rice wine vinegar

1 teaspoon dark brown sugar

½ to 1 teaspoon red pepper flakes

Kosher salt and freshly cracked black pepper to taste

¼ cup toasted sesame seeds

½ cup chopped scallions (green and white parts)

1. Bring a large pot of salted water to a boil over high heat. Add the noodles and cook until just barely tender, 3 to 5 minutes. Drain, refresh under cold water, and drain again.

2. Place the noodles in a large bowl, add 2 tablespoons of the sesame oil, and toss to coat. Cover and refrigerate until ready to use. (You can do this several hours ahead if you want.)

3. Dry the chops with paper towels, place them between two sheets of plastic wrap, and, using a meat mallet or other blunt instrument, such as the bottom of a sauté pan, pound them to a thickness of about ¼ inch. Now they are scallopini. Set them aside.

4. In a large sauté pan, heat 1 tablespoon each of the sesame and peanut oil over medium-high heat until hot but not smoking. Add the bok choy and cook, stirring occasionally, until golden brown, about 3 minutes. Add the ginger and garlic and cook, stirring, for 2 minutes. Add the soy sauce, water, vinegar, brown sugar, and red pepper flakes and bring to a simmer. Lower the heat to medium, partially cover the pan, and simmer, turning occasionally, until the bok choy is very tender, about 15 minutes.

5. While the bok choy is braising, put another large sauté pan over medium-high heat, add the remaining 2 tablespoons peanut oil, and heat until it is hot but not smoking. Sprinkle the scallopini generously with salt and pepper and add them to the pan in a single layer, in batches if necessary to avoid crowding, and cook until well browned on both sides and just cooked through, 3 to 4 minutes per side; remove them to a platter as they are done. When all the meat has been browned, cover the platter with foil and set aside.

6. Pour off and discard any peanut oil left in the pan. Return the pan to medium-high heat and add the remaining 2 tablespoons sesame oil. Add the noodles, sesame seeds, and scallions, tossing with tongs until the mixture is well combined. Transfer the noodles to a platter.

7. To serve, arrange the bok choy around the noodles, then cut the pork into slices about ½ inch wide and lay them on top of the noodles. Drizzle the bok choy braising liquid over the pork and serve.

Boneless top loin chops are the New York strip of pork chops. Taken from the top loin muscle of the loin, they are very tender and although they are mild, they do have good pork flavor. This is "the other white meat" in action. You don't need really thick chops here, but do try to get them around an inch thick or so; otherwise, overcooking them is hard to avoid.

Any "center cut" pork chop of the right thickness will be great in this recipe, as will loin rib chops or even loin sirloin cutlets.

Grilled Boneless Pork Loin Chops with Green Olive–Red Onion Relish and Nectarine Chutney

SERVES 4

We think the southern Mediterranean flavors of this relish—green olives, red onions, a bit of garlic, and some red pepper flakes—complement pork really well. As an added advantage, this is one place that you can use pimiento-stuffed olives to great effect.

To balance the olive relish, we have the sweet-sour aspect of the nectarine chutney, with its strong undercurrent of coriander. Of course, you can leave the chutney out if you want and still have an excellent dish. But this recipe makes quite a lot of chutney and it keeps well, covered and refrigerated, so you might want to go ahead and make it—then you'll have a super-tasty condiment in reserve for another dinner.

Serve this with Simple Rice Pilaf (page 417) and a Tomato Hobo Pack (page 443).

FOR THE CHUTNEY

2 tablespoons olive oil

2 onions, peeled and diced small

8 ripe nectarines, peeled, pitted, and cut into sixths

1 medium red bell pepper, cored, seeded, and diced small

6 tablespoons dark brown sugar

$\frac{1}{4}$ cup granulated sugar

1 tablespoon molasses

$\frac{1}{4}$ cup dark raisins

$\frac{1}{2}$ cup fresh orange juice (about 1 orange), or more if needed

$\frac{1}{2}$ cup white vinegar

2 teaspoons kosher salt

1 tablespoon freshly cracked black pepper

1 tablespoon cracked coriander seeds (or $1\frac{1}{2}$ teaspoons ground coriander)

2 tablespoons fresh lemon juice (about $\frac{1}{2}$ lemon)

1 teaspoon roughly chopped fresh mint

FOR THE RELISH

$\frac{1}{2}$ cup roughly chopped pitted green olives (with pimientos is OK)

$\frac{1}{2}$ small red onion, peeled and thinly sliced

2 tablespoons balsamic vinegar

¼ cup extra virgin olive oil

1 teaspoon red pepper flakes

1 teaspoon minced garlic

Kosher salt and freshly cracked black pepper to taste

Four 8-ounce boneless pork top loin chops, about 1 inch thick

Kosher salt and freshly cracked black pepper to taste

COOK ONCE, EAT TWICE

If you have any chops left over, cut them into small chunks, mix them with any leftover relish, and serve the combination over white rice, with the chutney on the side.

1. Make the chutney: In a large sauté pan, heat the oil over medium-high heat until hot but not smoking. Add the onions and cook, stirring occasionally, until translucent, 9 to 11 minutes. Add the nectarines and bell pepper and cook for 3 to 4 minutes, stirring occasionally. Add both sugars, the molasses, raisins, orange juice, vinegar, salt, pepper, and coriander and bring to a simmer, then reduce the heat to low and cook, stirring occasionally, until thickened, 30 to 45 minutes. Add a small amount of water or orange juice if the chutney begins to stick to the bottom of the pan. Remove from the heat and allow the chutney to cool for 10 minutes, then stir in the lemon juice and mint and set aside.

2. Light a fire in your grill.

3. While the fire is heating up, make the relish: In a medium bowl, combine all the ingredients and mix well; set aside.

4. Dry the chops with paper towels and sprinkle them generously with salt and pepper. When the fire has died down and the coals are medium-hot (you can hold your hand 5 inches above the grill surface for 3 to 4 seconds), place the chops on the grill and cook until well seared on one side, 5 to 7 minutes. Turn and continue cooking to the desired doneness, 5 to 7 minutes more for medium-well. To check for doneness, nick, peek, and cheat: Make a ¼-inch cut in the thickest part of the meat and take a peek; it should be slightly less done than you like it. When the meat is done, remove it from the grill, cover it loosely with foil, and let it rest for 5 minutes.

5. Top each chop with a tablespoon or two of the relish and serve, passing the chutney separately.

The blade chop comes from the section of the loin right next to the shoulder. This means that it has more connective tissue and a little more fat than cuts from the center of the loin, but it also has more flavor. We like it for that reason, and also because we don't mind a little gnarliness in our chops.

OTHER NAMES

Pork chop end cut, pork blade steak.

OTHER CUTS YOU CAN USE

Any center-cut pork loin chop (rib, loin, or top loin chop) would be a good substitute here. You can also use shoulder blade chops, although that is getting a bit far into the tough area for grilling.

Hoisin-Glazed Grilled Pork Blade Chops with Spicy Korean Vegetables

SERVES 4

We really like the pairing of hoisin sauce and pork. In fact, we really like hoisin sauce in general. One of the most popular sauces of Chinese cooking, it is a thick, sweetish, dark red mixture made from soybeans, garlic, vinegar, sugar, chile peppers, and various spices. Think of it as the Chinese version of catsup, but with stronger flavors.

To go along with the hoisin-brushed chops, we take a page from the Korean *kimchee* book and make what amounts to quick pickled vegetables. Letting them sit in salt for a couple of hours draws some moisture out of the vegetables, which makes them kind of tender-crisp and also intensifies their flavors a bit. Just be sure you rinse them really well before adding the other ingredients.

Serve this with brown rice and you're all set for a slightly exotic, light summer meal.

FOR THE VEGETABLES

3 cucumbers, unpeeled, cut lengthwise into thirds, seeded, and cut into finger-sized pieces

1 carrot, peeled and cut into finger-sized pieces

1 red bell pepper, cored, seeded, and cut into thin strips

1/2 cup kosher salt

1 bunch watercress, tough stems trimmed, washed, and dried

1 tablespoon minced garlic

1 tablespoon minced fresh ginger

1 tablespoon minced fresh chile peppers of your choice, or less to taste

2 tablespoons sugar

1/4 cup white vinegar

1 tablespoon paprika

2 teaspoons freshly cracked white pepper (or substitute black pepper)

1/4 cup sesame seeds, toasted in a 350°F oven for 5 minutes

Four 10- to 12-ounce pork blade chops, about 1 inch thick

Kosher salt and freshly cracked black pepper to taste

1/2 cup hoisin sauce

1. Make the vegetables: Rub the cucumbers, carrot, and bell pepper all over with the salt, put in a bowl, cover, and refrigerate for 2 hours. Rinse very well and drain.

2. In a large bowl, combine the vegetables with the watercress, garlic, ginger, chiles, sugar, vinegar, paprika, and pepper and mix well. Sprinkle with the toasted sesame seeds and set aside.

3. Light a fire in your grill.

4. Dry the pork chops and sprinkle them generously with salt and pepper. When the fire has died down and the coals are medium-hot (you can hold your hand 5 inches above the grill surface for 3 to 4 seconds), place the chops on the grill and cook until well seared on one side, 5 to 7 minutes. Turn and continue cooking to the desired doneness, 5 to 7 minutes more for medium-well. During the last 30 seconds of cooking, brush the chops liberally with the hoisin sauce. To check for doneness, nick, peek, and cheat: Make a ¼-inch cut in the thickest part of the meat and take a peek; it should be slightly less done than you like it. When the chops are done to your liking, remove them from the grill, cover them loosely with foil, and let them rest for about 5 minutes.

5. Serve the chops accompanied by the Korean vegetables.

COOK ONCE, EAT TWICE
Leftover pork from this dish is another excellent candidate for pork fried rice, and you can serve the leftover spicy vegetables on the side.

For this particular treatment, we like chops with a little bit more fat on them. (The hot fire makes it crispy and, to us, it makes the chops taste kind of like bacon.) First choice is a pork loin blade chop, which comes from the part of the loin closest to the shoulder. The sirloin chop, from the opposite end of the loin near the hip, is also good.

Any thin-cut pork chop will work fine in this recipe.

Grilled Thin Pork Chops with Avocado-Corn Salsa

SERVES 4

We have been saying over and over again, "Thick, thick, thick is the way to go with meat." So why, you may ask, are we suddenly going thin? Well, it's because sometimes, with certain cuts and the right type of heat, thin is good.

I (Chris) was in Guadalajara, Mexico, a few years ago, walking down the street, and I stopped at one of those open-air restaurants where they were cooking thin pork chops over a really hot fire. They got them on the fire and off again so quickly that instead of overcooking, they just got beautifully seared, and with the fat and the smokiness, they tasted like bacon. Some time later, I was stuck in a supermarket situation and super-thin pork chops were all I could get, so I decided to cook them that way and ended up really loving them.

The key here is to have a super-hot fire, then take the pork chops with their flavorful marinade and get them on and off in a hurry. Six minutes is about the total cooking time here.

That means this is a great dish to make when you have a lot of people coming over. You can make the salsa the day before, then cook up the pork chops in a hurry. (If you don't get the salsa made, you can always pinch-hit by accompanying the chops with some chunked avocadoes dressed with a simple lime vinaigrette.)

Serve this with a tomato salad, Latin-Style Black Beans and Rice (page 422), and a Sweet Potato–Raisin Hobo Pack (page 441).

1 tablespoon minced garlic

2 tablespoons cumin seeds (or 1 tablespoon ground cumin)

1 tablespoon red pepper flakes, or to taste

1/2 cup fresh lime juice (about 4 limes)

Kosher salt and freshly cracked black pepper to taste

Eight 6-ounce pork loin blade or pork sirloin chops, about 1/2 inch thick

FOR THE SALSA

3 ears corn, husked

3 ripe but firm avocados, peeled, pitted, and diced large

1 red onion, peeled and diced small

1 red bell pepper, cored, seeded, and diced small

1/3 cup olive oil

1/4 cup red wine vinegar

1 tablespoon minced garlic

4 to 8 dashes Tabasco sauce

1 tablespoon ground cumin

1 teaspoon chile powder

¼ cup roughly chopped fresh oregano

½ cup lime juice (about 4 limes)

Kosher salt and freshly cracked black pepper to taste

COOK ONCE, EAT TWICE

If you have any chops left over, the meat is fantastic mixed into rice and beans.

1. In a large bowl, combine the garlic, cumin, red pepper flakes, lime juice, and salt and pepper and mix well. Add the pork chops, cover, and refrigerate, turning the chops over once, for about 30 minutes. (If you didn't think ahead, you can dunk them for as little as 5 minutes.)

2. Light a fire in your grill.

3. Meanwhile, make the salsa: Blanch the corn in boiling salted water for 2 minutes, drain, and cool under cold running water. Cut the kernels off the cobs and place them in a medium bowl. Add all the remaining salsa ingredients, mix well, and set aside.

4. Remove the chops from the lime juice mixture. When the fire has died down and the coals are very hot (you can hold your hand 5 inches above the grill surface for only 1 second), place the chops on the grill and sear well on one side, about 3 minutes. Turn and continue cooking to the desired doneness, about 3 minutes longer for medium-well. To check for doneness, nick, peek, and cheat: Make a ¼-inch cut in the thickest part of one of the chops and peek inside; it should be slightly less done than you like it. Remove the chops from the grill, cover loosely with foil, and let them rest for 5 minutes.

5. Serve the chops accompanied by the salsa.

Just as with beef, the tenderloin is the most tender cut of pork. It is also very low in fat—about the same per serving as a boneless, skinless chicken breast. Since it is relatively small, it is sold whole—in fact, these days you often see two of these mini-roasts sold together in a Cryovac package. The tenderloin has a little less pork flavor than other fattier cuts, but it is convenient and readily available and tasty and easy to cook. We like it a lot.

Molasses-Glazed Pork Tenderloin with Seared Sweet-and-Sour Red Onions and Sage-Date Power Pack

SERVES 4 TO 5

If you have not cooked with pork tenderloin, we very strongly encourage you do to so. Tenderloins are easy to find in any market, and they are sort of mini-roasts, which is cool. They weigh anywhere from 12 to 16 ounces, and they are not only quick and easy to cook, they are also incredibly tender.

This recipe takes a pretty straightforward approach to the tenderloin, in which we sear it stovetop and then finish cooking it in a high-heat oven. This is a technique that you see very often in professional kitchens. The key is to make sure you get it really nice and brown when you sear it. During the last few minutes of cooking, we put a simple molasses glaze on the pork (don't put it on earlier, or it will burn), then serve it on some sweet-sour onions and top it with a power pack of unctuously sweet dates moderated with earthy sage.

This seems like a fall dish to us, so we would serve it with German-Style Braised Red Cabbage (page 434) and some applesauce or (even better) peach sauce.

3 tablespoons olive oil

2 red onions, peeled and thinly sliced

⅓ cup molasses

¼ cup dry red wine

Three 12- to 14-ounce pork tenderloins, trimmed of external fat

Kosher salt and freshly cracked black pepper to taste

3 tablespoons balsamic vinegar

FOR THE POWER PACK

⅓ cup chopped pitted dates

¼ cup roughly chopped fresh sage

1 teaspoon minced garlic

2 tablespoons extra virgin olive oil

1. Preheat the oven to 450°F.

2. In a large ovenproof sauté pan, heat 2 tablespoons of the oil over medium-high heat until hot but not smoking. Add the onions and cook, stirring occasionally, until they are golden brown, 11 to 13 minutes. Remove the onions to a bowl.

3. Combine the molasses and wine in a small bowl; set aside.

4. Dry the tenderloins with paper towels and sprinkle them generously with salt and pepper. Add the remaining 1 tablespoon oil to the pan, return to medium-high heat, and heat until the oil is hot but not smoking. (*Note:* If your pan is not large enough to comfortably hold the 3 tenderloins, use two smaller pans.) Add the tenderloins and sear well on all sides, about 12 minutes total.

5. When the tenderloins are well browned, place the pan in the oven and roast, brushing the tenderloins generously with the molasses mixture after about 8 minutes, until they are done to your liking, 10 to 14 minutes for medium-well. To check for doneness, insert a thermometer into the dead center of the meat and wait for 5 seconds, then check the temperature: It should be 150°F. Or you can nick, peek, and cheat: Make a ¼-inch cut in the thickest part of the meat and take a peek; it should be slightly less done than you like it. When the pork is done, remove it from the oven, brush once more with the molasses mixture, cover loosely with foil, and let rest for 10 minutes.

6. Meanwhile, add the balsamic vinegar to the onions and toss to combine thoroughly. In a small bowl, combine the dates, sage, garlic, and olive oil and mix well.

7. Slice the pork into slices about 1 inch thick. Place the onions on individual serving plates or a platter, top with the sliced pork, and sprinkle with the date mixture.

THE CUT

See Molasses-Glazed Pork Tenderloin (page 376) for details about pork tenderloin.

Grilled Pork Tenderloin on a Salad of Grilled Potatoes and Red Onions

SERVES 4 TO 5

Pork tenderloins are superb on the grill. As is fitting with this very adaptable cut, the approach is simple. You just put them over the hot part of your two-level fire and sear them well, rolling them around every once in a while to be sure they get evenly brown. Then you move them to the cooler part of the fire to let them finish cooking.

In this recipe, we grill some onions and potatoes on the hotter part of the fire after the tenderloin moves over to the cooler part, then toss them with lettuce and a spicy dressing to make a salad base for the tenderloin. It's pretty easy, and it all comes together well.

Serve this with corn on the cob and a Mushroom and Kale Hobo Pack (page 443). For dessert, try some grilled peaches with honey and cinnamon.

FOR THE DRESSING

¾ cup olive oil

¼ cup balsamic vinegar

1 tablespoon celery seeds

1 tablespoon cracked coriander seeds (or 1½ teaspoons ground coriander)

1 teaspoon minced garlic

1 tablespoon sugar

2 tablespoons grainy mustard

1 teaspoon red pepper flakes, or to taste

Kosher salt and freshly cracked black pepper to taste

Three 10- to 12-ounce pork tenderloins, trimmed of external fat

Kosher salt and freshly cracked black pepper to taste

2 medium red onions, peeled and cut into ½-inch-thick rounds

10 small new potatoes (about the size of a golf ball), cooked in boiling salted water until easily pierced with a fork, about 15 minutes, and drained

2 tablespoons olive oil

1 head lettuce of your choice, washed, dried, and torn into bite-sized pieces

1. Using enough charcoal to fill a large shoe box, light a two-level fire in your grill, putting about three quarters of the coals on one side and about one quarter on the other side.

2. In a small bowl, whisk all the dressing ingredients together well, then set aside.

3. Dry the tenderloins with paper towels and sprinkle them generously with salt and pepper. When the fire has died down and the coals are hot on one side (you can hold your hand 5 inches above the grill surface for 1 to 2 seconds) and medium-hot on the other (you can hold your hand 5 inches above the grill surface for 3 to 4 seconds), place the tenderloins on the hot part of the grill and cook, turning once or twice, for 12 to 15 minutes, long enough to develop a brown crusty sear on the outside. Move the tenderloins to the cooler side of the grill and cook, turning occasionally, for 10 to 12 minutes longer. To check for doneness, nick, peek, and cheat: Make a ¼-inch cut in the thickest part of the tenderloin and peek inside; it should be slightly less done than you like it. When the tenderloins are done to your liking, remove them from the grill, cover them loosely with foil, and let them rest for 10 minutes before slicing.

4. Meanwhile, after you move the tenderloins over to the cooler side of the grill, brush the onions and potatoes with the olive oil, sprinkle them with salt and pepper, and place them on the hotter part of the grill. Cook until golden brown, 2 to 3 minutes per side for the potatoes and 5 to 7 minutes per side for the onions. Transfer the vegetables to a large bowl.

5. Add the lettuce to the potatoes and onions. Whisk the dressing well and add it to the bowl, using just enough to moisten the ingredients, then toss gently.

6. Place a portion of salad on each plate. Cut the tenderloin into slices about 1 inch thick, lay several on top of each salad, and serve.

Pork loin back ribs are
known as "baby backs" for
a reason: They are much
smaller than true spareribs.
These ribs come from the
blade and center sections
of the loin and are more
tender, if less flavorful, than
spareribs.

Grilled Baby Back Ribs, Buffalo-Style

SERVES 6 AS AN APPETIZER

We've done this before and we'll do it again, because we really like it: grilling something and then cutting it up and tossing it in a Buffalo wings mixture. The combination of the spicy mix and the smoke flavor really works well; in this case, it makes for an appetizer that people are wild about. You have to use the baby back ribs here, because they are tender enough to grill in a relatively short time. Just be sure that you don't have the ribs directly over the fire while they're cooking.

As long as you've got the fire going, you might want to stick a couple of New Potato Hobo Packs (page 442) in the coals to serve alongside the ribs.

2 slabs baby back ribs (20 bones), about 3 pounds total

1/3 cup extra virgin olive oil

15 dashes Tabasco sauce, or more to taste

1 tablespoon minced garlic

1/3 cup roughly chopped fresh herbs: any one or a combination of sage, oregano, thyme, basil, and/or parsley

Kosher salt and freshly cracked black pepper to taste

Your favorite blue cheese dressing (optional)

Celery sticks (optional)

1. Start a fire well over to one side of a large kettle grill, using about enough coals to fill a large shoe box.

2. When the coals are well lit and covered with gray ash, place the meat on the side of the grill away from the coals, being careful that none of the meat is directly over the coals. Put the lid on the grill with the vents open one quarter of the way and cook for 20 minutes. Flip the ribs and cook them for an additional 20 minutes.

3. Meanwhile, in a large bowl, combine the olive oil, Tabasco, garlic, herbs, and salt and pepper to taste and mix well.

4. When the ribs are done, remove them from the fire and cut them apart. Toss them with the sauce mixture to coat thoroughly, then serve with blue cheese dressing and celery sticks if you want.

Grilled Pork, Bacon, and Mango Skewers with Guava-Chile Glaze

SERVES 4

Although it may sound a bit weird at first, grilled mango is really fantastic. Here we combine it with guava, which is a typical flavor pairing in parts of Polynesia, where pork is also the meat of choice. To celebrate that, these skewers have a double dose of pork, with bacon strips as well as cubes of loin.

Try to get slab bacon if you can. Because the bacon won't cook all the way through on the skewers, we first partially cook it on the stove, then cut it into pieces for skewering. Once the skewers are on the fire, be careful that the bacon doesn't burn; we are using a slightly cooler fire than usual to help with this potential problem, but you may need to move the skewers off to the side once or twice during cooking.

To keep the Polynesian theme going, serve this with macadamia nuts, rice pilaf, and roasted true yams, which are a large, starchy tuber.

FOR THE GLAZE

4 ounces guava jelly

2 tablespoons fresh lime juice (about 1 lime)

1 to 2 tablespoons minced fresh chile peppers of your choice

1 tablespoon minced fresh ginger

¼ cup roughly chopped fresh cilantro

Kosher salt and freshly cracked black pepper to taste

4 slices thick-cut slab bacon

2 pounds boneless pork loin, cut into 1-inch cubes

Kosher salt and freshly cracked black pepper to taste

Twelve 1-inch cubes fresh mango (2 mangoes)

2 red bell peppers, cored, seeded, and cut into 1-inch pieces

1. Light a fire in your grill.

2. Make the glaze: In a small saucepan, dissolve the guava jelly over medium heat. When it has turned to liquid, add the lime juice, chiles, and ginger and stir to combine. Remove from the heat, stir in the cilantro, season to taste with salt and pepper, and set aside.

3. In a large sauté pan, cook the bacon over medium heat for 4 to 5 minutes (you don't want to cook it completely), then drain on paper towels or a brown paper bag and cut into pieces about 1 inch long.

THE CUT
Although we usually call for cubes of pork shoulder meat as the #1 choice for skewers, here we use the leaner and slightly more tender loin, since the bacon provides plenty of fat and flavor. The easiest thing to do is just buy some boneless pork loin chops about an inch thick and cut them into cubes.

OTHER CUTS YOU CAN USE
Cubes of any pork shoulder meat will also work very well here. In fact, you can cut up just about any type of pork, including the tenderloin, and use it on these skewers. If you ever see tenderloin tips in the supermarket, grab them and make this dish with them.

Chop up any leftovers from this dish into a kind of chunky hash and serve it on top of rice and beans.

4. Dry the pork cubes with paper towels and sprinkle them generously with salt and pepper. Thread the meat onto skewers, alternating it with the mango, bacon, and red peppers.

5. When the fire has died down and the coals are medium-hot (you can hold your hand 5 inches above the grill surface for 3 to 4 seconds), place the kebabs on the grill and cook for 5 to 8 minutes per side for medium. During the last 30 seconds or so of cooking, brush the kebabs with the glaze. To check for doneness, nick, peek, and cheat: Make a ¼-inch cut in the thickest part of the meat and take a peek; it should be slightly less done than you like it. When the meat is done to your liking, remove the kebabs from the grill, cover them loosely with foil, and allow them to rest for about 5 minutes.

6. Drizzle the skewers with the remaining glaze and serve.

THE CUT

The relative tenderness of pork makes the exact cut you use for skewers less crucial than with beef. Our first choice, though, is boneless pork shoulder, since it has enough fat to stay moist over the grilling fire.

OTHER CUTS YOU CAN USE

Tenderloin tips run a close second for this recipe—they are extremely tender and relatively inexpensive, if you can find them. You can also use cubed boneless rib chops, although there you're starting to stray into more expense than it might be worth.

Grilled Pork and Fig Skewers with Sun-Dried Tomato–Basil Relish

SERVES 4

If you're looking for a quick and simple recipe with lots of flavor, ideal for a casual weekend cookout, this is an A-#1 candidate. Figs, which go great with pork in any fashion, are truly wonderful on the grill. Our friend Mike Otten liked the Italian-inspired relish so much that he made an extra batch to eat as a spread on toasted bread. You might want to try that too. It will keep for several days, covered and refrigerated.

Serve this with a Mediterranean White Bean Salad (page 424) and maybe a side of pasta with pine nuts and broccoli rabe.

FOR THE RELISH

½ cup thinly sliced sun-dried tomatoes

1 teaspoon minced garlic

½ cup fresh basil leaves, cut into long thin slices

¼ cup extra virgin olive oil

¼ cup pine nuts, toasted in a 350°F oven for 5 minutes (shake the pan frequently)

2 tablespoons balsamic vinegar

Kosher salt and freshly cracked black pepper to taste

2 pounds boneless pork butt or other pork shoulder cut, cut into 1-inch cubes

Kosher salt and freshly cracked black pepper to taste

8 fresh figs

1 red onion, peeled and cut into 1-inch chunks

3 tablespoons olive oil

1. Light a fire in your grill.

2. In a small bowl, combine all the relish ingredients and mix well; set aside.

3. Dry the pork cubes with paper towels and sprinkle them generously with salt and pepper. Thread onto skewers, alternating the pork with the figs and onion cubes. Brush the kebabs lightly with the olive oil.

4. When the fire has died down and the coals are medium-hot (you can hold your hand 5 inches above the grill surface for 3 to 4 seconds), cook the skewers for 3 to 4 minutes per side (a total of 12 to 16 minutes) for medium. To check for doneness, nick, peek, and cheat: Make a ¼-inch cut in the thickest part of the meat and take a peek; it should be slightly less done than you like it. When the meat is done to your liking, remove the skewers from the grill, cover loosely with foil, and let the meat rest for 5 minutes.

5. Leave the kebabs assembled or slide the ingredients off onto a platter, and serve with the relish.

A pork leg (fresh ham) center slice is basically a cross-section of the hind leg of the hog, the part that is usually smoked or cured to become a ham. To get a piece this thick, you're definitely going to have to call your butcher. But it's worth it, because this is a neat cut of meat. Like the whole fresh ham, it is tender and very sweet and juicy. (If you can't get this cut, though, go ahead and make the recipe using any of the substitutes suggested here.)

Country-style ribs are a great substitute here, since they belong to that relatively exclusive category of cuts that respond well both to slow moist cooking and to quick high-heat cooking on the grill. Loin blade chops and loin sirloin chops also work well here, and relatively thin center-cut loin chops would also be fine. If you use any of these substitutes, you'll need 8 ribs or chops, each weighing about 6 ounces and about ¾ inch thick.

BBQ-Rubbed Grilled Fresh Ham Center Slice with Watermelon-Pineapple Salad

SERVES 4 TO 6

This is a pretty straight-up barbecue-style approach that we apply to a non-traditional cut. What we're using is a thick slice from the part of the hog that is usually made into ham. My (Doc's) grandmother occasionally used to make a very thin version of this cut that she called ham steak and served with pan gravy, a dish that is still on the menu in family-style restaurants throughout the Midwest. But here we're using a much thicker piece of pork. After rubbing the meat with a standard barbecue spice rub, we sear it really well over a hot fire, then finish it up over a cooler fire. It tastes great, has excellent texture, and is fun to serve, because few people use this cut of meat, so they're usually surprised by it. If you have a favorite BBQ sauce, go ahead and brush it on the pork when it comes off the grill if you like.

We both had grandfathers who liked to eat watermelon with salt and pepper on it, so savory watermelon salads are favorites of ours. This one, with the sweet pineapple and the tartness of fresh lime juice and red wine vinegar, is a particularly refreshing version and goes great with the grill-barbecued pork.

Serve this with thick slices of grilled bread and Creamed Corn (page 433).

FOR THE BBQ RUB

¼ cup paprika

2 tablespoons sugar

2 tablespoons ground cumin

2 tablespoons freshly cracked black pepper

2 tablespoons kosher salt

2 tablespoons chile powder

One 2-pound pork leg (fresh ham) center slice, about 1 inch thick

FOR THE SALAD

1½ cups seeded large watermelon chunks

1½ cups large pineapple chunks

1 red onion, peeled, halved, and thinly sliced

2 tablespoons roughly chopped fresh oregano (or substitute fresh parsley)

1¼ cup fresh lime juice (about 2 limes)

2 tablespoons red wine vinegar

Kosher salt and freshly ground black pepper to taste

COOK ONCE, EAT TWICE
Slice up any leftover pork, put it between two slices of bread, slather on a little barbecue sauce, and that's one great sandwich right there. Or you can just brown the meat in a frying pan and eat it with eggs for a hearty breakfast.

1. Using about enough coals to fill a large shoe box, light a two-level fire in your grill, putting about three quarters of the coals on one side and one quarter on the other side.

2. Make the rub: Combine all the ingredients in a small bowl and mix well.

3. Dry the pork with paper towels and rub it generously with the barbecue rub. When the fire has died down and the coals in the hotter part of the grill are medium-hot (you can hold your hand 5 inches above the grill surface for 3 to 4 seconds), place the pork over the hot part of the fire. Cook until it is well seared on both sides, 4 to 5 minutes per side. Move the meat to the cooler side of the grill, cover it with a metal pie pan or disposable aluminum pie pan, and cook until tender, about 5 minutes per side. To check for doneness, nick, peek, and cheat: Make a ¼-inch cut in the thickest part of the meat and take a peek; it should be slightly less done than you like it. When the meat is done, remove it from the heat, cover it loosely with foil, and let it rest for 5 minutes before serving.

4. Meanwhile, make the salad: In a large bowl, combine all the ingredients and toss gently.

5. Cut the ham slice into thick wedges and serve accompanied by the salad.

RECIPES FOR SMALL TOUGH CUTS OF PORK

10 STEPS TO GREAT PORK STEWS

1. Dry the meat cubes.

2. Season the meat cubes generously.

3. Brown the meat cubes well, in batches if necessary.

4. Remove the meat from the pot, adjust the amount of fat in the pot, and sauté the aromatics and vegetables.

5. Deglaze the pot with some of the liquid.

6. Return the meat to the pot along with enough liquid to cover.

7. Bring to a simmer and skim off any film, then reduce the heat to low and simmer gently.

8. Check for doneness early and often.

9. Skim the film and fat from the liquid.

10. Add any final seasonings, season to taste with salt and pepper again, and serve.

Orange-Stewed Country-Style Pork Ribs with Sweet-and-Sour Red Cabbage Slaw

West Indies–Style Pork Stew with Plantains, Lime, and Chiles

Spicy Pork Stew with Tomatoes and Okra over Jalapeño-Cheddar Grits

Mango-Stewed Pork with Fried Sweet Potatoes

Fragrant Winter Pork Stew with Fennel, Pears, and Sauerkraut

Malaysian-Inspired Pork Stew with Coconut Milk and Aromatic Garnishes

Spicy Stewed Pork with Eggplant, Chiles, and Sesame Spinach

Gingered Pork Curry with Seven Garnishes

Orange-Stewed Country-Style Pork Ribs with Sweet-and-Sour Red Cabbage Slaw

SERVES 4

Despite their name, country-style ribs are actually a form of chop. Because they have a good deal of fat as well as a piece of bone, they are great for long, slow cooking methods like stewing. As an added advantage, they are quite cheap.

We really like Latin flavors with pork, and this dish has plenty of them, with the sour orange, chipotles, and cumin flavoring the stewed liquid. Chipotles, which are dried, smoked jalapeños, are worth seeking out. We like the canned version in adobo sauce, which is a vinegary liquid that keeps the peppers moist.

We would serve this with Latin-Style Black Beans and Rice (page 422) and Fried Plantains (page 56) or corn on the cob.

3 tablespoons olive oil, or more if needed

8 country-style pork ribs, about 6 ounces each

Kosher salt and freshly cracked black pepper to taste

3 tablespoons ground cumin

2 large red onions, peeled and thinly sliced

2 tablespoons minced garlic

1 to 3 tablespoons minced canned chipotle peppers in adobo, according to your taste for heat

1 cup orange juice

½ cup red wine vinegar

One 12-ounce bottle beer, or more as needed

FOR THE SLAW

½ cup fresh lime juice (about 4 limes)

1 tablespoon dark brown sugar

1 tablespoon ground coriander

½ head red cabbage, finely shredded

1 cup fresh diced pineapple

Kosher salt and freshly cracked black pepper to taste

½ cup roughly chopped fresh cilantro

1. In a large sauté pan, heat the oil over medium-high heat until very hot but not smoking. Dry the ribs with paper towels, sprinkle them generously with salt and pepper, and rub them all over with the cumin. Add them to the pan in a single layer, in batches if necessary to avoid crowding, and cook until well browned, 4 to 5 minutes per side; transfer the ribs to a platter as they are done.

2. Pour off the fat or add oil to the pan as needed so you have a total of about 2 tablespoons in the pan. Add the onions and cook, stirring occasionally, until golden brown, 11 to 13 minutes. Add the garlic and chiles and cook, stirring, for 1 minute more.

3. Return the ribs to the pan and add the orange juice, vinegar, and beer. (The liquid should cover the ribs; if it does not, add beer to cover.) Bring to a simmer and skim any film from the top of the liquid, then reduce the heat to low, cover, and cook until the ribs are very tender, 50 minutes to 1½ hours.

4. While the ribs are cooking, make the slaw: Combine the lime juice, brown sugar, and coriander in a small bowl. In a large bowl, combine the cabbage and diced pineapple. Pour the dressing over the cabbage mixture and mix well. Season with salt and pepper, then cover and refrigerate until serving time.

5. When the ribs are done, remove them from the pan, cover them loosely with foil, and set them aside. Skim the fat from the stewing liquid. Taste the liquid, and if it needs more flavor, continue to simmer to reduce. For a thicker sauce, reduce it until it coats the back of a spoon. Stir in the cilantro and season with salt and pepper.

6. Serve the ribs topped with some of the sauce, passing the slaw on the side.

THE CUT

See Spicy Pork Stew with Tomatoes and Okra (page 390) for details on pork stew meat and other cuts you can use in this recipe.

West Indies–Style Pork Stew with Plantains, Lime, and Chiles

SERVES 6

Full of vibrant Caribbean flavors, this stew is another demonstration of the primacy of pork in cuisines throughout much of the hot-weather world. If you don't have access to plantains, you can substitute sweet potatoes in this recipe, but before you do so, be sure to check out any Latin markets in your area. They are certain to have not only plantains but also a number of interesting root vegetables that you may not be familiar with but that bear investigation.

Serve this with Latin-Style Black Beans and Rice (page 422) or Spicy Latin Black Beans (page 423), maybe fried yucca, and a side of ripe mangoes with lime juice.

¼ cup olive oil, or more if needed

2 pounds boneless pork shoulder, cut into 2-inch cubes

Kosher salt and freshly cracked black pepper to taste

2 medium onions, peeled and diced small

1 tablespoon minced garlic

2 tablespoons cumin seeds (or 1 tablespoon ground cumin)

1 to 3 tablespoons minced fresh chile peppers of your choice, depending on your taste for heat

6 plum tomatoes, roughly chopped

About 1½ cups chicken stock (or see Stock Options, page 32)

1 cup orange juice

½ cup red wine vinegar

¼ cup dark rum

2 tablespoons dark brown sugar

2 slightly ripe plantains, peeled and cut into chunks

¼ cup roughly chopped fresh oregano

2 limes, cut into 6 wedges each

1. In a 5-inch-deep Dutch oven or other large heavy pot with a lid, heat the oil over medium-high heat until very hot but not smoking. Dry the pork with paper towels and sprinkle it generously with salt and pepper. Add it to the pot in a single layer, in batches if necessary to avoid crowding, and cook until well browned on all sides, about 15 minutes total; transfer the pieces to a platter as they are done.

2. Pour off the fat or add oil to the pot as needed so you have a total of about 2 tablespoons left in the pot. Add the onions and cook, stirring occasionally, until golden brown, 11 to 13 minutes. Add the garlic, cumin, and chiles and cook, stirring, for 1 minute. Add the tomatoes and cook, stirring, for 1 minute more.

3. Return the pork to the pot and add the stock, orange juice, vinegar, rum, brown sugar, and salt and pepper to taste. (If there is not enough liquid to completely cover the ingredients, add more stock.) Bring to a simmer, cover, and cook for 30 minutes. Add the plantains and continue cooking, stirring occasionally, until the sauce thickens and the pork is tender, about 1½ hours more. When the pork is fork-tender, stir in the oregano and season with salt and pepper.

4. Serve the stew over plain white rice, with the lime wedges for squeezing.

While you sometimes find cubed "pork for stew" in supermarkets, it is not as common as veal or beef stew meat. This is actually somewhat of an advantage, because it forces you to buy a cut of meat and cube it up yourself. This in turn means you will be getting the cut that is best for stewing, rather than cubes from an assortment of cuts, what you are most likely to get when you buy precut stew meat.

As with beef, we prefer pork from the shoulder area for stewing. Because this section of the animal gets a lot of exercise, it has a good deal of connective tissue, which translates to flavor during long, slow cooking. It also has enough fat to stay moist over the course of the cooking. So any of the shoulder cuts—most of which will have the word "Boston" in the name—are fine: pork butt, Boston butt, boneless Boston shoulder, boneless shoulder blade, or just Boston butt. Cuts with the word "picnic" in the name, such as picnic shoulder, which come from farther down the leg, are tougher but also fine for stew meat.

Spicy Pork Stew with Tomatoes and Okra over Jalapeño-Cheddar Grits

SERVES 6

With its pork, okra, and tomatoes and its flavorings of garlic, paprika, and cayenne (plus filé gumbo if you can find it), this dish has strong Creole-style roots. So it has plenty of flavors going on, and to add to the mix, we serve it over that old Southern favorite, grits, with Cheddar cheese and jalapeños.

Now, we know that some of you out there will be tempted to avoid this recipe because you don't like okra. Don't. You can leave it out and still have a great dish, or you can go ahead and add the okra and you'll probably find that it tastes a lot better than you thought. The key is to buy small pods, no longer than two inches, which are both tender and tasty.

All you need to make this a meal is a green salad and maybe some corn bread.

3 tablespoons olive oil, or more if needed

2 pounds boneless pork shoulder, cut into 2-inch cubes

Kosher salt and freshly cracked black pepper to taste

2 onions, peeled and diced small

3 tablespoons minced garlic

1 tablespoon paprika

1 tablespoon cayenne pepper

2 tablespoons gumbo filé powder (optional)

6 plum tomatoes, peeled, cored, and diced medium

3 cups chicken stock (or see Stock Options, page 32)

1 pound small okra (the pods no larger than 2 inches long), cut into 1-inch pieces (or substitute frozen okra)

2 tablespoons roughly chopped fresh thyme (or 1 teaspoon dried thyme)

2 tablespoons roughly chopped fresh oregano (or 1 teaspoon dried oregano)

FOR THE GRITS

4 tablespoons (½ stick) unsalted butter

1 small onion, peeled and diced small

1 to 3 minced jalapeño chiles, depending on your taste for heat

1½ cups fresh corn (from 3 ears)

4 cups water

½ teaspoon kosher salt, plus more to taste

1 cup quick-cooking grits

½ cup grated sharp Cheddar cheese

Freshly cracked black pepper to taste

1. In a 5-inch deep Dutch oven or other large heavy pot, heat the oil over medium-high heat until very hot but not smoking. Dry the pork well with paper towels and sprinkle it generously with salt and pepper. Add it to the pot in a single layer, in batches if necessary to avoid crowding, and brown well on all sides, 12 to 15 minutes in all; transfer the pieces to a platter as they are done.

2. Pour off the fat or add oil to the pot as needed so you have about 2 tablespoons in the pot. Add the onions and cook, stirring occasionally, until golden brown, 11 to 13 minutes. Add the garlic, paprika, cayenne, and filé powder, if using, and cook, stirring, for 1 minute more.

3. Return the pork to the pot and add the tomatoes and chicken stock. Bring to a simmer and cook, uncovered, stirring from time to time, until the sauce thickens and the pork is tender, about 1½ hours. Add the okra and simmer for 20 minutes more. Stir in the herbs and season with salt and pepper.

4. Meanwhile, after you add the okra to the stew, start making the grits: In a medium sauté pan over medium heat, melt 2 tablespoons of butter. Add the onion and sauté, stirring occasionally, until translucent, 7 to 9 minutes. Add the chiles and corn and cook, stirring, for 1 minute more. Remove from the heat and set aside.

5. Bring the water to a boil in a medium saucepan over high heat. Add the salt and, stirring constantly, sprinkle the grits into the water. Reduce the heat to low, cover, and cook for about 5 minutes, stirring once. Remove the pan from the heat and stir in the sautéed onion and corn mixture, the cheese, and the remaining 2 tablespoons butter. Season with salt and pepper.

6. Serve the grits in individual bowls, topped with the pork stew.

Mango-Stewed Pork with Fried Sweet Potatoes

SERVES 6

We really like the combination of mango, pork, and coriander; it's a trio in which each ingredient seems to set off the other, bringing out real depths of flavor. Since this recipe takes its inspiration from the French-speaking islands of the Caribbean, where curry is popular, we also add a little curry powder to the mix.

Don't forget that when the stew has been cooking for a while, you need to put the sweet potatoes in the oven so they can cook at the same time. These potatoes are simple to make and really taste great—we're pretty sure that once you've made them, you'll be serving them with plenty of other dishes too.

We don't like to say that a dish "demands" or "cries out for" something, because food can't talk. But if we did, we would say that this dish "demands" to be served with Latin-Style Black Beans and Rice (page 422), because they are perfect together.

2 tablespoons minced garlic

1 tablespoon red pepper flakes, or to taste

3 tablespoons cracked coriander seeds

2 pounds boneless pork shoulder, cut into 1-inch cubes

Kosher salt and freshly cracked black pepper to taste

5 tablespoons olive oil

2 large red onions, peeled and thinly sliced

2 red bell peppers, cored, seeded, and thinly sliced

3 tablespoons minced fresh ginger

2 small mangoes, peeled and diced large (2 cups)

1 cup mango juice (or substitute orange juice)

About 1 cup dry white wine

¼ cup red wine vinegar

2 tablespoons curry powder

1 tablespoon dark brown sugar

FOR THE SWEET POTATOES

2 large sweet potatoes

¼ cup vegetable oil

Kosher salt and freshly cracked black pepper to taste

1. In a small bowl, combine the garlic, red pepper flakes, and coriander and mix well. Dry the pork with paper towels, sprinkle it generously with salt and pepper, and toss with the spice mixture.

2. In a 5-inch-deep Dutch oven or other large heavy pot with a lid, heat 3 tablespoons of the oil over medium-high heat until very hot but not smoking. Add the pork in a single layer, in batches if necessary to avoid crowding, and cook until it is well browned on all sides, about 15 minutes in all; as the meat is browned, transfer it to a platter.

3. Discard the oil in the pot. Add the remaining 2 tablespoons oil to the pot and heat over medium-high heat until hot but not smoking. Add the onions and peppers and sauté, stirring occasionally, until the onions are golden brown, 11 to 13 minutes. Add the ginger and mangoes and sauté, stirring, for 3 minutes more.

4. Return the meat to the pot and add the mango juice, wine, vinegar, curry powder, and sugar. (If the liquid does not completely cover the ingredients, add enough wine so that it does.) Bring to a simmer and skim any film off the top of the liquid, then cover, reduce the heat to low, and cook gently until the meat is tender, about 1½ to 2 hours.

5. When the pork has been cooking for about 1 hour, preheat the oven to 350°F. Place the sweet potatoes on a small baking sheet and bake until they can be easily pierced with a fork or skewer but still offer some resistance, 30 to 45 minutes. Remove the potatoes from the oven and allow them to cool slightly. As soon as they are cool enough to handle, cut them lengthwise into quarters; set aside.

6. When the stew is almost done, heat the vegetable oil in a large sauté pan over medium-high heat until it is very hot but not smoking. Add the sweet potatoes and fry until they are brown and crisp, 5 to 8 minutes. Season generously with salt and pepper.

7. Serve the pork covered with the sauce, accompanied by the sweet potatoes.

See Spicy Pork Stew with
Tomatoes and Okra (page
390) for details on pork
stew meat and other cuts
you can use in this recipe.

Fragrant Winter Pork Stew with Fennel, Pears, and Sauerkraut

SERVES 6 TO 8

With caraway seeds, allspice berries, sauerkraut, and pears, this dish is full of Eastern European flavors. We think of it as a variation on goulash, that classic Hungarian stew more frequently made with beef. As with other pork stews, you can buy a piece of boneless pork shoulder and cube it up yourself, which is the best option, or you can simply buy packaged pork stew meat, which will also work fine.

Unlike other stews, this one is actually best served the day it is made, because the fennel and pears soften overnight. Serve this with a hot German potato salad, Baked Stuffed Potatoes (page 415), or a wedge of iceberg lettuce topped with Thousand Island dressing.

6 ounces slab bacon, rind removed and diced small (or substitute 6 to 8 slices regular bacon)

2 pounds pork shoulder, trimmed of fat and cut into 2-inch cubes

Kosher salt and freshly cracked black pepper to taste

2 large onions, peeled and diced small

2 large fennel bulbs, fronds removed, cored, and thinly sliced

2 cups dry white wine

1 pound sauerkraut, rinsed and drained

2 tablespoons caraway seeds

6 allspice berries (or 1 teaspoon ground allspice)

3 bay leaves

About 2 cups chicken stock (or see Stock Options, page 32)

3 pears, peeled, cored, diced large, and tossed with juice of $\frac{1}{2}$ lemon to prevent browning

$\frac{1}{2}$ cup sour cream

$\frac{1}{2}$ cup grainy mustard

1. In a 5-inch-deep Dutch oven or other large heavy pot with a lid, cook the bacon slowly over medium heat until it is crisp and golden brown, 6 to 8 minutes. Transfer the cooked bacon to a large bowl, leaving the fat in the pot.

2. Dry the pork well with paper towels and sprinkle it generously with salt and pepper. Raise the heat to medium-high and add the pork to the pot in a single layer, in batches if necessary to avoid crowding, and cook until well browned on all sides, about 15 minutes; transfer the pieces to the bowl with the bacon as they are done.

3. When all the pork has been browned, pour off all but 2 tablespoons of fat from the pot, add the onions and fennel, and cook, stirring occasionally, until the onions are translucent, 9 to 11 minutes. Add the wine and bring to a simmer, stirring to dissolve the brown crusty stuff in the bottom of the pot.

4. Return the pork and bacon to the pot and add the sauerkraut, caraway seeds, allspice, bay leaves, and stock. (If the liquid does not cover all the other ingredients, add enough stock to cover.) Bring to a simmer, skim any film off the surface, then cover, reduce the heat to low, and simmer gently for 1 hour. Add the pears, then continue to cook until the meat is fork-tender, 30 minutes to 1 hour more.

5. Meanwhile, in a small bowl, combine the sour cream and mustard and mix well.

6. Serve the stew in shallow bowls, garnishing each with a dollop of the mustard cream.

THE CUT

See Spicy Pork Stew with Tomatoes and Okra (page 390) for details on pork stew meat and other cuts you can use in this recipe.

Malaysian-Inspired Pork Stew with Coconut Milk and Aromatic Garnishes

SERVES 6

In Southeast Asia, soups and stews are a big part of any cook's repertoire. This particular version is inspired by the flavors of Malaysia, where over the centuries cooks of Malay, Indian, and Chinese backgrounds have created a unique cuisine. With lots of garlic, a bit of curry powder, coconut milk, and the Southeast Asian herb trio of basil, mint, and cilantro, it hits a lot of taste buds with every bite.

Make sure that you use unsweetened coconut milk, which is made by steeping fresh coconut meat in hot water and then straining it, rather than the sweetened product used in tropical drinks. Cans of the unsweetened version are available in most Asian groceries and many supermarkets—or you can make your own. To do so, place equal quantities of coconut meat and boiling water in a food processor or blender, puree, strain the resulting mixture through cheesecloth, and discard the solids—and you've got your coconut milk.

This stew is great with white rice and a salad that includes one or more of the bitter Asian greens like tatsoi, mizuna, or baby mustard greens. If you can't get any of those greens, try using some arugula or dandelion greens in the salad along with regular lettuce.

3 tablespoons finely minced garlic

2 tablespoons curry powder

2 tablespoons ground cumin

1 tablespoon paprika

1 tablespoon cayenne pepper, or less to taste

2 pounds boneless pork shoulder, cut into 1-inch cubes

Kosher salt and freshly cracked black pepper to taste

5 tablespoons olive oil

2 large red onions, peeled, halved, and thinly sliced

3 tablespoons minced fresh ginger

3 plum tomatoes, cored and diced small

¼ cup soy sauce

1¼ cups unsweetened coconut milk

1 cup dry white wine

¼ cup roughly chopped fresh basil

¼ cup roughly chopped fresh mint

¼ cup roughly chopped fresh cilantro

½ cup roughly chopped roasted unsalted peanuts

3 tablespoons fresh lime juice (about 1½ limes)

5 dashes Tabasco sauce, or to taste

1 teaspoon brown sugar

1. In a large bowl, combine the garlic, curry powder, cumin, paprika, and cayenne pepper and mix well. Dry the pork cubes with paper towels, sprinkle them generously with salt and pepper, add to the bowl with the spice mixture, and toss to coat well.

2. In a 5-inch-deep Dutch oven or other large heavy pot with a lid, heat 3 tablespoons of the oil over medium-high heat until very hot but not smoking. Add the pork in a single layer, in batches if necessary to avoid crowding, and cook until it is well browned on all sides, about 10 minutes; transfer the meat to a platter as it is done.

3. Discard the oil in the pot, add the remaining 2 tablespoons olive oil, and heat over medium-high heat until hot but not smoking. Add the onions and sauté, stirring occasionally, until golden brown, 11 to 13 minutes. Add the ginger and tomatoes and cook, stirring, for 2 minutes more.

4. Return the meat to the pot and add the soy sauce, coconut milk, and wine. (The liquid should just cover the dry ingredients; if it does not, add a bit more wine—but don't overdo it, because the tomatoes will add liquid as they cook.) Bring to a simmer and skim any film off the surface, then cover, reduce the heat to low, and cook gently until the meat is very tender, 1½ to 2 hours.

5. In a small bowl, combine the garnish ingredients and mix well.

6. Place a generous helping of the stew in each bowl, top with a couple of tablespoons of the garnish, and serve hot.

THE CUT

See Spicy Pork Stew with Tomatoes and Okra (page 390) for details on pork stew meat and other cuts you can use in this recipe.

Spicy Stewed Pork with Eggplant, Chiles, and Sesame Spinach

SERVES 4

To us, pork seems like the most versatile of the red meats. It matches up very well with flavor footprints from around the world, particularly from Asia. Here we take advantage of that by stewing pork cubes in a mixture of soy sauce, vinegar, and white wine that we flavor with garlic, ginger, and red pepper flakes, with some cilantro added at the end for freshness and some peanuts for crunch. Eggplant not only adds its own flavor, but helps to thicken the stew as well. When you look at the eggplant before cooking it, you may think you have too much, but don't worry—it will cook down just right.

You can skip the sesame spinach if you like, but we really like the contrasting freshness it provides to the long-cooked stew—and it doesn't take much time to prepare.

Serve this over white rice.

3 tablespoons olive oil, or more if needed

1 pound pork shoulder, cut into 1-inch cubes

Kosher salt and freshly cracked white pepper to taste (or substitute black pepper)

2 tablespoons minced garlic

3 tablespoons minced fresh ginger

1 tablespoon red pepper flakes

1 red onion, peeled and diced small

1 red bell pepper, cored, seeded, and diced small

1 large eggplant, peeled and diced small

1 tablespoon sugar

¼ cup white vinegar

¼ cup soy sauce

About ½ cup dry white wine

FOR THE SPINACH

2 tablespoons sesame oil

1 tablespoon minced garlic

1 tablespoon minced fresh ginger

1½ pounds spinach, trimmed, well washed, and dried

2 tablespoons white or rice wine vinegar

Kosher salt and freshly cracked white pepper to taste (or substitute black pepper)

¼ cup roughly chopped fresh cilantro

¼ cup roughly chopped roasted unsalted peanuts

1. In your largest sauté pan, heat the olive oil over medium-high heat until very hot but not smoking. Dry the pork well with paper towels and sprinkle it generously with salt and white pepper, then add to the pan and cook, stirring occasionally, until browned on all sides, about 12 to 15 minutes. Add the garlic, ginger, and red pepper flakes and continue to cook, stirring, for 1 minute more. Transfer the pork to a platter.

2. Add oil or pour off the fat from the pan so you have about 2 tablespoons in the pan. Return the pan to medium-high heat, add the onion, bell pepper, and eggplant, and cook, stirring occasionally, until the onion is golden, 11 to 13 minutes.

3. Return the pork to the pan and add the sugar, vinegar, soy sauce, and white wine. (The liquid should cover all of the ingredients; if it does not, add more wine or water.) Bring to a simmer, skim any film from the surface, then reduce the heat, cover, and cook until the pork is fork-tender, about 1½ hours. Season with salt and pepper.

4. Meanwhile, when the stew is almost done, make the spinach: In a large sauté pan, heat the sesame oil over medium-high heat until hot but not smoking. Add the garlic and ginger and stir once, then add the spinach and sear it for about 1 minute, stirring constantly. Add the vinegar and toss two or three times, then remove the pan from the heat and season the spinach with salt and white pepper.

5. Serve the stew in bowls, sprinkling each bowl with cilantro and chopped peanuts, and either serve the spinach separately or lay a generous helping of spinach on top of each bowl of the stew, over to one side.

THE CUT

See Spicy Pork Stew with Tomatoes and Okra (page 390) for details on pork stew meat and other cuts you can use in this recipe.

Gingered Pork Curry with Seven Garnishes

SERVES 6

One of the cool things about ordering curries in Indian restaurants when we were younger was that sometimes you got lots of little bowls of garnishes—peanuts, currants, coconut, bottled Major Grey's chutney, and so on—to add as you liked. When we got older and started doing some traveling in Asia, we found this to be a very common approach in that part of the world. In much of Southeast Asia, for example, platters of whole herb leaves and freshly sliced vegetables are routinely set out for adding to soups and stews.

Here we take that approach in a dish that we have chosen to call a "curry" because it contains many of the spices typically present in dishes known by that name in the West. The dish also includes fish sauce, a fermented fish product that is an important part of the flavor footprint of Southeast Asia. Don't be put off by the smell of uncooked fish sauce. It mellows as it cooks, and it actually works much like salt, deepening the flavor of the dish without having a distinct taste presence of its own. Of course, you can leave it out if you want; in that case, substitute soy sauce in the jalapeño garnish.

3 tablespoons olive oil, or more if needed

2 pounds boneless pork shoulder, cut into 1-inch cubes

Kosher salt and freshly cracked black pepper

2 small red onions, peeled and diced small

1 to 3 tablespoons minced red chile peppers of your choice

1 red bell pepper, cored, seeded, and diced small

1 green bell pepper, cored, seeded, and diced small

3 tablespoons minced garlic

3 tablespoons minced fresh ginger

3 plum tomatoes, cored and diced small

1 tablespoon ground cumin

1/2 teaspoon turmeric

1 tablespoon paprika

2 tablespoons ground coriander

2 tablespoons freshly cracked white pepper (or substitute black pepper)

2 stalks lemongrass, chopped into several large pieces (so you can remove them after cooking)

3 tablespoons Thai fish sauce (*nam pla*)

About 1 cup chicken stock (or see Stock Options, page 32)

½ cup dry white wine

½ cup pineapple juice

FOR THE GARNISHES

5 jalapeño peppers, cut into very thin rounds

¼ cup Thai fish sauce (*nam pla*)

½ cup roughly chopped roasted unsalted peanuts

½ cup grated unsweetened coconut, toasted in a small sauté pan, shaking
frequently, until aromatic, 3 to 4 minutes

½ cup fresh cilantro leaves

½ cup fresh mint leaves

½ cup thinly sliced scallions (white and green parts)

3 limes, quartered

COOK ONCE, EAT TWICE

While stews are excellent "make-ahead-and-reheat" dishes, the wild array of flavors in this one make it particularly well suited to that approach. Prepare a new batch of the varied garnishes just before you serve the stew, and they will add a layer of fresh flavors.

1. In a 5-inch-deep Dutch oven or other large heavy pot with a lid, heat the oil over medium-high heat until hot but not smoking. Dry the pork and sprinkle it generously with salt and pepper. Add it to the pot in a single layer, in batches if necessary to avoid crowding and cook until well browned on all sides, about 15 minutes total; transfer the pieces to a platter as they are done.

2. Pour off the fat or add oil to the pot as needed so you have a total of about 2 tablespoons in the pot. Add the onions, chiles, and bell peppers to the pot and cook, stirring occasionally, until the onions are translucent, 7 to 9 minutes. Add the garlic, ginger, and tomatoes and cook, stirring, for 2 minutes. Add the cumin, turmeric, paprika, coriander, 2 tablespoons salt, the white pepper, and lemongrass and cook, stirring constantly, for 3 minutes longer.

3. Return the pork to the pot and add the fish sauce, chicken stock, wine, and pineapple juice. (If there is not enough liquid to completely cover the ingredients, add more stock.) Bring to a simmer, skim any film from the surface, then reduce the heat to low and simmer gently until the pork is fork-tender, 1 to 1½ hours. When the meat is done, remove and discard the lemongrass.

4. Prepare the garnishes: In a small bowl, combine the jalapeños with the fish sauce and stir to mix well. Place each of the remaining garnishes in a small bowl.

5. Serve the curry over bowls of steaming white rice, and let your guests help themselves to the garnishes.

RECIPES FOR
ODD CUTS OF PORK: OFFAL ET AL.

**Pot Likker–Braised Fresh Ham Hocks with Collard Greens
and Potatoes**

**Smoked Ham Hocks with Indian-Spiced Green
Split Peas**

Pot Likker–Braised Fresh Ham Hocks with Collard Greens and Potatoes

SERVES 8

This dish is worth making for the pot likker alone. That's the name given to the liquid that collard greens have been cooked in, and it has always been one of my (Chris's) favorite things. In fact, I've long been a big fan of greens, but recently my appreciation for their proven track record with regards to both health and flavor has taken a quantum leap. Make this dish in the middle of the winter with some corn bread to sop up the leftover pot likker, and you will have a hearty, delicious, down-home treat.

FOR THE GREENS

2 pounds collard greens, stemmed and well washed (or substitute turnip greens or kale)

6 slices bacon

1 large onion, peeled and diced large

½ cup cider vinegar

2 tablespoons kosher salt

2 tablespoons freshly cracked black pepper

½ teaspoon red pepper flakes

2 fresh ham hocks, about 1 pound each, trimmed of most external fat

2 tablespoons vegetable oil

Kosher salt and freshly cracked black pepper to taste

2 pounds new potatoes, washed and halved

1. In a large stockpot, bring 1 gallon of water to a boil. Add the collards, bacon, and onion and stir several times, then reduce the heat to low and add the vinegar, salt, pepper, and pepper flakes. Cover and simmer for 2 hours. Remove the greens with tongs, drain them, and set them aside. Skim the fat from the liquid (the "pot likker") and leave it in the stockpot over very low heat.

2. Preheat the oven to 500°F.

3. In a deep roasting pan, toss the ham hocks with the oil, then sprinkle generously with salt and pepper. Roast for 20 minutes to brown, then reduce the oven temperature to 300°F. Remove the hocks from the pan and skim off the fat that has accumulated in the pan, leaving the meat

THE CUT

What you want to use here is a fresh hock from the front leg of the hog. This is the same part of the animal as the shank of the veal, and it is actually sometimes called a pork shank. It is a tough piece of meat, with a lot of connective tissue and a fair amount of internal fat, but, like other cuts of this nature, it has a tremendous amount of flavor. While it is very often smoked, you can find it fresh in many butcher shops, and to us, the fresh version has a little nicer flavor. It is very rich and, when cooked by slow moist heat, ends up with a cool silky texture. Be sure you trim away as much of the external fat as possible, though, or the dish will be too fatty.

OTHER NAMES

Pork shank, shoulder hock.

OTHER CUTS YOU CAN USE

You can substitute smoked pork hocks, which are easier to find, for the fresh hocks called for here. Or, if you're a bold cook, try using smoked pig's feet, also known as trotters.

juices behind. Put the hocks back in the pan and add enough pot likker to cover them about halfway. Cover the pan tightly with foil and braise in the oven for 1½ hours.

4. Add the greens and potatoes to the pan, cover again, and cook until the hocks and potatoes are tender, another 30 minutes to 1 hour. To check for doneness, stick a fork straight down into the meat and try to pull the fork out. If the fork slides out easily, the meat is done; if the meat hangs on to the fork, give it more time.

5. To serve, spoon the greens onto a serving platter and moisten them slightly with pot likker. Pull the meat from the hocks, set it on top of the greens, and surround with the potatoes.

THE CUT

Ham hocks are the lower portion of the leg of the pig, usually cut into pieces 2 to 3 inches long. Hocks are full of fat, gristle, and connective tissue, along with some very flavorful meat, and are typically smoked or cured, or both.

Smoked Ham Hocks with Indian-Spiced Green Split Peas

SERVES 4

In years past, many poor families raised a pig or two in their backyard. When that pig was butchered, not a single part of it was allowed to go to waste. The feet and ears got pickled (taken together, they were known as "souse"), all the little trimmings got ground up and made into sausage, even the meat from the head was transformed into head cheese. Hocks, which are basically the ankle of the pig, were traditionally smoked and then cooked up with a mess o' greens or used to add rich flavor to large pots of hearty soups like split pea.

Here we work a little change on that tradition by cooking the ham hocks separately, then serving them on top of a bowl of split peas flavored with Indian spices. The best approach is to take a forkful of meat from the hock, load up some of the peas on top, and eat it.

Like other cuts of meat that have plenty of fat and gristle, ham hocks require long cooking and taste even better if they are cooked a day ahead. This advance cooking also gives you a chance to skim off the top layer of fat that accumulates after the hocks (and the reserved cooking liquid we use here) cool down. However you choose to approach it, though, this is a great dish for a cold winter's day, particularly since it requires you to keep pots simmering on the stove for hours.

For an extra treat, top each ham hock with some Batter-Fried Onion Rings (page 437), or serve the onion rings alongside.

FOR THE HOCKS

4 large meaty smoked ham hocks

2 medium onions, peeled and quartered

2 carrots, peeled and diced large

2 stalks celery, diced large

1 tablespoon minced garlic

2 bay leaves

2 allspice berries (or substitute ¼ teaspoon ground allspice)

10 black peppercorns

Stems from 1 bunch parsley

Kosher salt and freshly cracked black pepper to taste

FOR THE PEAS

2 tablespoons olive oil

1 yellow onion, peeled and diced small

1 tablespoon minced fresh ginger

1 tablespoon minced garlic

½ teaspoon turmeric

½ teaspoon ground cumin

½ teaspoon ground coriander

1 teaspoon freshly cracked black pepper, plus more to taste

1 pound green split peas, picked through and washed

Kosher salt to taste

2 carrots, peeled and diced medium

1. In a large stockpot, combine all the ingredients for the hocks, cover with water, and bring to a simmer over high heat. Reduce the heat to medium-low and cook, uncovered, until the hocks are falling-off-the-bone tender, about 3 hours. To check for doneness, plunge a fork straight down into the meat and try to pull the fork out. If the fork slips right out, the meat is done; if the meat hangs on to the fork at all, give it more time.

2. When the hocks are done, let them cool in the cooking liquid, then transfer them to a saucepan, along with enough of the cooking liquid to cover (about 2 cups). Strain the remaining cooking liquid into a bowl and add enough water to make a total of 6 cups liquid. (Or refrigerate the hocks and liquid until you are ready to cook the peas.)

3. Make the peas: In a large sauté pan, heat the oil over medium-high heat until hot but not smoking. Add the onion and cook, stirring occasionally, until translucent, 7 to 9 minutes. Add the ginger, garlic, and spices and cook, stirring, for 1 minute more. Add the 6 cups reserved diluted cooking liquid and bring to a simmer, then add the split peas and salt. Simmer gently, uncovered, until the peas are just tender, about 30 minutes, adding more water if necessary. Add the diced carrots and continue cooking until the carrots are tender and the peas are falling apart, about 20 minutes more.

4. During the last 10 minutes of cooking time for the peas, remove the skins from the hocks, then reheat them in their cooking liquid over low heat.

5. To serve, divide the split peas among four soup bowls and top each with a ham hock. Ladle some of the cooking liquid over each one and serve.

FAVORITE CLASSIC *Side* DISHES

There are certain side dishes that over the years have proved their mettle as crowd-pleasing accompaniments to meat. To make the meal complete, we've assembled for you here the recipes for our Top 10 Classic Side Dishes in each of the following categories: Potatoes, Rice and Beans (On Their Own and Together), Green Vegetables, Non-Green Vegetables, and Hobo Packs. Tasty and trusty, each of them will serve you well.

TOP 10 SIMPLE CLASSIC POTATO DISHES

Potatoes Anna

Roesti Potatoes

Au Gratin Potatoes (Gratin Dauphinois)

French Fries

Hash Browns

Parsleyed New Potatoes

Mashed Potatoes

Potatoes Macaire

Roasted Potatoes

Baked Stuffed Potatoes

Potatoes Anna

SERVES 6

The trick here is to slice the potatoes very thin and very evenly. A mandoline or other slicing machine is a big help.

12 tablespoons (1½ sticks) unsalted butter, melted
6 large baking potatoes, peeled and very thinly sliced
Kosher salt and freshly cracked black pepper to taste

1. Preheat the oven to 425°F.

2. Put 6 tablespoons of the melted butter in a heavy medium sauté pan (preferably cast iron). Arrange a layer of potato slices, overlapping slightly, in concentric circles to cover the bottom of the pan. Top with a little more melted butter and season with salt and pepper. Continue layering the potatoes, butter, and seasonings in this fashion.

3. Lightly butter a lid that will fit snugly inside the pan, and place it directly on top of the potatoes. Place the pan on a baking sheet and bake for 20 minutes. Remove the lid and continue baking for 25 to 30 minutes more, until the potatoes are golden brown on the top and sides.

4. To serve, place a large serving plate over the potatoes and invert the potatoes onto the plate, then cut the potatoes into wedges.

Roesti Potatoes

SERVES 6

This recipe differs from Potatoes Anna (page 409) only in that the potatoes are shredded rather than very thinly sliced, which makes them less work and easier to cook.

8 tablespoons (1 stick) unsalted butter, melted
6 large baking potatoes, peeled and shredded
Kosher salt and freshly cracked black pepper to taste

1. Preheat the oven to 425°F.

2. In a heavy medium sauté pan (preferably cast iron), melt the butter over medium heat. Add the potatoes, tossing until they are well coated with the butter. Season with salt and pepper and gently press down on the potatoes with a spatula to form a large flat cake. Reduce the heat to low and cook until the potatoes are tender and golden brown on the bottom, 30 to 40 minutes.

3. Place a large plate over the potatoes and invert the potatoes onto the plate. Slide the potatoes, browned side up, back into the pan and continue cooking until the second side is well browned, 10 to 15 minutes more.

4. Place a serving plate over the potatoes and invert the pan again. Cut the potatoes into wedges and serve.

Au Gratin Potatoes (Gratin Dauphinois)

SERVES 6 TO 8

1 clove garlic, peeled and halved
1 tablespoon unsalted butter, at room temperature
6 large baking potatoes, peeled and thinly sliced
3 cups half-and-half or milk or a mix of the two
Pinch of freshly grated nutmeg (optional)
Kosher salt and freshly cracked black pepper to taste
1 cup grated Gruyère or other mild grating cheese

1. Preheat the oven to 350°F.

2. Rub the surface of a 2-quart baking dish with the garlic halves. Coat the dish with the butter and set it aside.

3. In a large saucepan, combine the potatoes, half-and-half, nutmeg, and salt and pepper and bring to a simmer over medium heat. Cook gently, stirring occasionally, until the liquid thickens slightly, about 5 minutes.

4. Transfer the potato mixture to the baking dish and sprinkle the grated cheese over the top. Bake until the cheese is melted and golden and the potatoes are tender when pierced with a fork, about 45 minutes. Serve the potatoes in the baking dish, hot from the oven.

French Fries

SERVES 6

These are the hands-down favorite of Chris's nephew Tommy, a seventeen-year-old vegetarian who knows a thing or two about French fries.

2 quarts vegetable oil

6 large baking potatoes, peeled, cut into 1/2-inch-thick strips, and soaked in cold water for 30 minutes

Kosher salt to taste

1. In a 5-inch-deep Dutch oven or other large heavy pot, heat the oil to 325°F. Meanwhile, drain the potatoes and dry very well with paper towels. When the oil comes up to temperature, carefully drop a handful of potato strips at a time into the oil and cook them for about 2 minutes. Transfer the potatoes to a paper towel–lined baking sheet to drain.

2. After all of the potatoes have been allowed to cool, heat the oil to 375°F. Fry the potatoes again, in small batches, until they are crisp and golden brown, 2 to 3 minutes. Drain again on paper towels, season to taste with salt, and serve immediately.

FOR STRAW POTATOES
Cut the potatoes into julienne strips less than 1/8 inch thick.

FOR POTATO CHIPS
Cut the potatoes into slices less than 1/8 inch thick.

FOR POTATOES O'BRIEN

Add ¼ cup each green and red bell peppers, diced small, before you add the potatoes to the sauté pan.

FOR HOME FRIES

After melting the butter, add 1 small onion, peeled and diced small, and sauté until translucent, about 7 minutes. Add an additional 2 tablespoons olive oil before you add the potatoes to the pan.

Hash Browns

SERVES 6

4 tablespoons (½ stick) unsalted butter, at room temperature

2 tablespoons olive oil

8 medium all-purpose potatoes, boiled, peeled, and diced small

Kosher salt and freshly cracked black pepper to taste

1 tablespoon unsalted butter, melted

1. In a heavy medium sauté pan, melt 2 tablespoons of the butter with 1 tablespoon of the olive oil over medium heat. Spread the potatoes in an even layer in the pan, pressing down on them slightly with a spatula. Season with salt and pepper and cook until the potatoes begin to brown on the bottom, 6 to 7 minutes, shaking the pan occasionally to prevent sticking. Pour the melted butter over the top of the potatoes.

2. Place a large plate over the pan and invert the potatoes onto the plate. Add the remaining 2 tablespoons butter and 1 tablespoon olive oil to the pan, slide the potatoes back in, and brown on the other side, about 5 minutes more. Season with salt and pepper and slide onto a platter. Serve immediately.

Parsleyed New Potatoes

SERVES 6

24 new potatoes, well washed

5 tablespoons unsalted butter

3 tablespoons finely chopped fresh parsley

Kosher salt and freshly cracked black pepper to taste

In a large saucepan, cover the potatoes with cold salted water. Bring to a boil, reduce the heat to low, and simmer until the potatoes are tender, 13 to 15 minutes. Drain the potatoes and return to the pan, along with the butter, parsley, and salt and pepper. Toss to combine well and serve immediately.

Mashed Potatoes

SERVES 6

6 large baking potatoes, peeled and quartered

6 tablespoons (¾ stick) unsalted butter, at room temperature, plus more for serving

¾ to 1 cup milk or cream, warmed

2 tablespoons sour cream, at room temperature

Kosher salt and freshly cracked black pepper to taste

1. In a large saucepan, just cover the potatoes with cold salted water. Cover the pan, bring to a boil, and boil until the potatoes are tender, about 20 minutes. Drain the potatoes and return to the hot pan. Place over medium heat briefly, shaking the pan, to dry the potatoes.

2. Remove the pan from the heat and add the butter, ¾ cup milk, and the sour cream. Season well with salt and pepper. Mash the potatoes until they are smooth, adding more milk if the potatoes seem dry. Give the potatoes a final, vigorous stir with a whisk to fluff them, and transfer to a serving bowl. Top with more butter and sprinkle with salt and pepper. Serve immediately.

FOR ROASTED-GARLIC MASHED POTATOES

Roast a head of garlic by slicing off the top, placing it on a length of aluminum foil, and drizzling it with olive oil. Close up the foil around the garlic and roast it in a preheated 400°F oven for 50 to 60 minutes. When the garlic is soft and golden brown, pop the cloves out of their skins. Add them to the potatoes before mashing.

FOR HORSERADISH MASHED POTATOES

Add ½ to ¾ cup freshly grated horseradish (depending on its strength and your taste) or 3 tablespoons prepared horseradish to the potatoes before mashing.

FOR BLUE CHEESE MASHED POTATOES

Add the full cup of milk or cream and omit the sour cream. Add ½ cup crumbled blue cheese before mashing.

Potatoes Macaire

SERVES 6

This is also a great way to use leftover mashed potatoes.

6 large baking potatoes, peeled and quartered

3 scallions (white and green parts), minced

6 tablespoons unsalted butter (¾ stick), at room temperature

½ cup milk or cream, warmed

Kosher salt and freshly cracked black pepper to taste

2 tablespoons vegetable oil

1. In a large saucepan, barely cover the potatoes with cold salted water. Bring to a boil and cook until the potatoes are tender, about 20 minutes. Drain the potatoes and return to the hot pan. Place over medium heat briefly, shaking the pan, to dry the potatoes.

2. Remove the pan from the heat, add the scallions, 4 tablespoons of the butter, the milk, and salt and pepper, and mash the potatoes until smooth. Form the potatoes into 6 cakes.

3. In a large sauté pan, melt the remaining 2 tablespoons of butter with the oil over medium heat. Add the potato cakes, in batches if necessary to avoid crowding, and fry until golden brown on both sides, 3 to 4 minutes per side. Serve immediately.

ROASTED POTATOES WITH BLACK OLIVES

Add ½ cup pitted and roughly chopped briny black olives to the potatoes before cooking.

Roasted Potatoes

SERVES 6

6 medium Red Bliss or baking potatoes, peeled and cut lengthwise into sixths

¼ cup olive oil

7 to 8 sprigs fresh thyme or rosemary

Kosher salt and freshly cracked black pepper to taste

1. Preheat the oven to 450°F.

2. In a large bowl, toss the potatoes with the olive oil, thyme sprigs, and salt and pepper. Place the potatoes on a baking sheet and roast, turning after about 20 minutes, until they are golden brown and tender, 30 to 40 minutes. Serve immediately.

Baked Stuffed Potatoes

SERVES 6

3 large baking potatoes

Vegetable oil

½ cup sour cream

½ cup milk, warmed

6 tablespoons minced fresh chives

4 tablespoons unsalted butter (½ stick), at room temperature

Kosher salt and freshly cracked black pepper to taste

1. Preheat the oven to 400°F.

2. Wash the potatoes and dry them well. Rub them with oil and bake until soft, about 1 hour. Let cool slightly. (Leave the oven on.)

3. As soon as the baked potatoes are cool enough to handle, cut them lengthwise in half and hollow them out, leaving no more than a ¼-inch thickness of potato in each shell. Place the potato innards in a medium bowl. Place the shells on a baking sheet, return to the oven, and bake until they are crisp, 10 to 15 minutes. Remove from the oven.

4. While the shells are baking, add the sour cream, milk, 4 tablespoons of the chives, 3 tablespoons of the butter, and salt and pepper to the potatoes and mash until smooth.

5. Turn the oven to broil. Fill the crisped shells with the potato mixture, dot with the remaining 1 tablespoon butter, and sprinkle with the remaining 2 tablespoons chives. Return the stuffed potatoes to the baking sheet and broil until the potatoes are piping hot and the tops are golden brown, 7 to 9 minutes. Serve at once.

FOR BACON-CHEESE STUFFED POTATOES

When you mix the potato innards with the sour cream and other ingredients, add 8 strips of bacon, cooked until crisp and broken into bits, and ¾ cup shredded Cheddar cheese. Sprinkle the finished potatoes with 2 tablespoons freshly grated Parmesan cheese.

TOP 10 SIMPLE CLASSIC RICE AND BEAN DISHES
(on their own and together)

Simple Rice Pilaf

Persian Rice

Coconut Rice

Spanish Rice

Basic Fried Rice

Hoppin' John

Latin-Style Black Beans and Rice

Spicy Latin Black Beans

Mediterranean White Bean Salad

Simple Lentils

Simple Rice Pilaf

SERVES 4

2 tablespoons unsalted butter

1 medium onion, peeled and diced large

1½ cups long-grain white rice

2½ cups chicken stock (or see Stock Options, page 32)

Kosher salt and freshly cracked black pepper to taste

¼ cup roughly chopped fresh parsley

1. In a medium saucepan, melt the butter over medium heat. Add the onion and cook, stirring occasionally, until translucent, 7 to 9 minutes. Add the rice and cook, stirring to coat completely with the butter, for 1 minute.

2. Add the stock and salt and pepper and bring to a simmer, then reduce the heat to low, cover, and cook gently until the rice is tender and the liquid is absorbed, checking for doneness after 15 minutes. Remove from the heat, remove the lid, and cover the pan with a towel. Cover the towel with the lid and allow to stand for 5 minutes.

3. Stir in the parsley and serve.

FOR RICE PILAF WITH ALMONDS AND CURRANTS

With the parsley, add ¼ cup almonds, toasted in a dry skillet over medium heat, shaking frequently, until fragrant, 3 to 5 minutes, and ¼ cup currants.

FOR RICE PILAF WITH LIME ZEST, PINE NUTS, AND AROMATIC SPICES

With the onion, add 2 tablespoons pine nuts. With the stock, add ½ teaspoon red pepper flakes, ½ teaspoon each ground cardamom and cinnamon, and 2 teaspoons finely minced lime zest (green part only). With the parsley, add ⅓ cup golden raisins.

Persian Rice

2 cups long-grain white rice

Kosher salt and freshly cracked black pepper to taste

10 tablespoons unsalted butter

1 small onion, peeled, halved, and thinly sliced

1. Bring a large pot (about 4 quarts) of salted water to a boil. Add the rice and cook, uncovered, for 10 minutes. Drain, season with salt and pepper, and set aside.

2. In a large nonstick skillet, melt 6 tablespoons of the butter over medium-high heat. Add the onion and cook, stirring frequently, until translucent, 7 to 9 minutes. Add the rice and press down on it with a spoon or spatula to form a smooth, even surface. Cover tightly, reduce the heat to low, and cook, undisturbed, for 50 minutes.

3. About 10 minutes before the rice is done, melt the remaining 4 tablespoons butter. Uncover the rice, drizzle the butter over it, cover, and cook for the remaining 10 minutes.

4. To serve, uncover the rice, place a large platter over the top of the skillet, and invert the rice onto it. The bottom layer of rice should be beautifully browned and crunchy.

Coconut Rice

SERVES 4

2 tablespoons vegetable oil

1 small onion, peeled and diced small

1 cup long-grain white rice

1 cup chicken stock (or see Stock Options, page 32) or water

1 cup unsweetened coconut milk

Kosher salt and freshly cracked black pepper to taste

1. In a large sauté pan, heat the oil over medium-high heat until hot but not smoking. Add the onion and cook, stirring frequently, until translucent, 7 to 9 minutes. Add the rice and continue to cook, stirring frequently, for 1 minute.

2. Add the chicken stock and coconut milk, bring to a simmer, and add the salt and pepper. Reduce the heat to low, cover, and cook gently until the rice is tender and the liquid is absorbed, 15 to 18 minutes. Remove from the heat, remove the lid, and cover the pan with a towel. Cover the towel with the lid and allow to stand for at least 5 minutes. Serve hot or at room temperature.

Spanish Rice

SERVES 4 TO 6

3 tablespoons olive oil

1 small onion, peeled and diced small

1 small green bell pepper, cored, seeded, and diced small

1 tablespoon minced garlic

1 cup long-grain white rice

1¾ cups chicken stock (or see Stock Options, page 32)

1 cup chopped drained canned tomatoes

1 tablespoon chile powder

Kosher salt and freshly cracked black pepper to taste

1. Preheat the oven to 350°F.

2. In a large ovenproof sauté pan, heat the oil over medium-high heat until hot but not smoking. Add the onion and green pepper and cook, stirring frequently, until the onion is translucent, 7 to 9 minutes. Add the garlic and cook, stirring, for 1 minute. Add the rice and stir to coat it thoroughly with the oil. Add the stock, tomatoes, chile powder, and salt and pepper and bring to a boil.

3. Stir the rice mixture once, cover, and transfer the pan to the oven. Cook until the rice is tender, about 25 minutes. Uncover the pan and allow the rice to stand for about 5 minutes, then fluff the rice with a fork and serve immediately.

Basic Fried Rice

¼ cup vegetable oil

2 tablespoons minced fresh ginger

1 tablespoon minced garlic

1 cup (uncooked) long-grain white rice

1¾ cups water

2 tablespoons sesame oil

½ red bell pepper, cored, seeded, and diced large

½ green bell pepper, cored, seeded, and diced large

1 bunch scallions (white and green parts), thinly sliced

3 tablespoons soy sauce

Kosher salt and freshly cracked black pepper to taste

1. In a medium saucepan, heat 2 tablespoons of the vegetable oil over medium heat until hot but not smoking. Add the ginger and garlic and cook, stirring occasionally, for 2 minutes. Add the rice and cook, stirring occasionally, for 2 more minutes. Add the water, cover, reduce the heat to low, and cook until the water is absorbed and the rice is tender, 15 to 18 minutes. Remove from the heat, remove the lid, and cover the pan with a towel. Cover with the lid and set aside for a few minutes.

2. In a large sauté pan, heat the sesame oil and the remaining 2 tablespoons vegetable oil over medium heat until hot but not smoking. Add the peppers and cook, stirring occasionally, for 2 minutes. Add the cooked rice and cook for a few minutes to heat through, stirring occasionally. Add the scallions and soy sauce and stir until the soy is thoroughly mixed in. Season with salt and pepper and serve.

Hoppin' John

1 cup dried black-eyed peas, picked through and rinsed

1 smoked ham hock, 8 to 12 ounces

1 large onion, peeled and diced small

1 teaspoon red pepper flakes

3 sprigs fresh thyme

2 bay leaves

1½ cups long-grain white rice

Kosher salt and freshly cracked black pepper to taste

1. In a 5-inch-deep Dutch oven or other large heavy pot with a lid, combine the peas, ham hock, onion, pepper flakes, thyme, and bay leaves over medium-high heat and add enough water to cover by 2 inches. Bring to a simmer, cover loosely, and cook until the peas are tender, 1 to 1½ hours.

2. Remove the ham hock from the pot and set aside. Bring the cooking liquid to a full boil and reduce to about 3 cups. Remove the thyme sprigs and bay leaves.

3. When the ham hock is cool enough to handle, remove the meat, cut it into small chunks, and return them to the pot. Add the rice, stirring well to combine, season with salt and pepper, cover, and simmer until the rice is tender and all the liquid is absorbed, 15 to 20 minutes. Allow to stand, covered, for 5 to 10 minutes, then serve hot.

Latin-Style Black Beans and Rice

SERVES 4

1 tablespoon olive oil

1 small yellow onion, peeled and diced small

1 tablespoon minced garlic

½ red bell pepper, cored, seeded, and cut into long thin strips

1 teaspoon ground cumin

1 cup long-grain white rice

1⅔ cups water or chicken stock (or see Stock Options, page 32)

1 teaspoon kosher salt, plus more to taste

2 cups cooked black beans or one 16-ounce can black beans

½ cup roughly chopped fresh cilantro

Freshly cracked black pepper to taste

1. In a medium saucepan, heat the oil over medium-high heat until hot but not smoking. Add the onion and cook, stirring occasionally, until translucent, 7 to 9 minutes. Add the garlic, bell pepper, and cumin and cook, stirring occasionally, for 2 minutes. Add the rice and cook, stirring, for 1 minute. Add the water and salt and bring just to a simmer, then reduce the heat to medium-low, cover, and cook until the water is absorbed and the rice is tender, about 15 minutes.

2. When the rice is cooked, add the beans, mix well, and cook for about 5 minutes, stirring occasionally, to heat the beans through. Add the cilantro, season with salt and pepper, and serve.

Spicy Latin Black Beans

1 pound dried black beans, picked through and rinsed

1 tablespoon minced canned chipotle peppers in adobo

1½ tablespoons cumin seeds

1 small yellow onion, peeled and diced small

1 tablespoon minced garlic

2 teaspoons kosher salt, plus more to taste

Freshly cracked black pepper to taste

1 cup roughly chopped fresh cilantro

3 tablespoons sliced scallions (white and green parts)

⅓ cup shredded Cheddar or Monterey Jack cheese (optional)

1. In a medium saucepan, combine the beans, chipotles, cumin, onion, and garlic over medium-high heat and add enough water to cover by 2 inches. Bring to a simmer, partly cover, and cook until the beans are tender, about 2 to 2½ hours, adding more water as necessary. After the beans have cooked for 30 minutes, add the salt.

2. When the beans are tender, season with salt and pepper, top with the cilantro, scallions, and cheese, if desired, and serve hot.

Mediterranean White Bean Salad

SERVES 6

1 pound dried cannellini, Great Northern, navy, or other white beans, picked through and rinsed

1 tablespoon kosher salt

FOR THE VINAIGRETTE

½ cup extra virgin olive oil

3 tablespoons red wine or sherry vinegar

1 tablespoon finely minced garlic

1½ tablespoons roughly chopped fresh thyme or oregano (or 2 teaspoons dried)

1 teaspoon Dijon mustard

Kosher salt and freshly cracked black pepper to taste

2 ripe tomatoes, cored and diced medium

2 scallions (white and green parts), thinly sliced

1. Put the beans in a 5-inch-deep Dutch oven or other large heavy pot with a lid and add water to cover by 2 inches. Place over medium-high heat and bring to a simmer, reduce the heat to low, partly cover, and cook the beans until tender, 1 to 1½ hours; add the salt after the beans have cooked for 30 minutes. When the beans are tender, drain, put into a large bowl, and set aside to cool slightly.

2. While the beans are cooking, make the vinaigrette: In a small bowl, whisk together the olive oil, vinegar, garlic, herbs, and mustard, season with salt and pepper, and set aside.

3. When the beans have cooled slightly, add the tomatoes and scallions to the bowl. Add the vinaigrette and toss well to combine. Check the seasoning and add more salt and pepper if necessary. Allow the salad to cool to room temperature before serving, or refrigerate until ready to serve.

Simple Lentils

SERVES 4

8 ounces (about 1 cup) green, brown, or du Puy lentils, picked through and rinsed

Kosher salt and freshly cracked black pepper to taste

1 small red onion, peeled and diced small

2 medium tomatoes, cored and diced small

1 small carrot, peeled and diced small

1 cup roughly chopped fresh parsley

1/3 cup olive oil

1/4 cup fresh lemon juice (about 1 lemon)

1/4 cup pine nuts, toasted in a 350°F oven until lightly browned, about 10 minutes (optional)

1. In a medium saucepan, combine the lentils, 3 cups water, and salt and pepper. Bring to a rapid boil over high heat, reduce the heat to medium, and simmer until the lentils are tender to the bite but not mushy, about 30 minutes. Drain and set aside to cool to room temperature.

2. Meanwhile, in a medium bowl, combine the onion, tomatoes, carrot, and parsley.

3. Add the cooled lentils to the vegetables and mix well.

4. In a small bowl, whisk together the oil and lemon juice. Add to the lentil mixture, toss well, and stir in the pine nuts, if using them. Serve warm, at room temperature, or chilled.

TOP 10 SIMPLE CLASSIC GREEN VEGETABLE DISHES

Roasted Asparagus

Quick-Sautéed Spinach with Garlic

Brussels Sprouts in Brown Butter

Minted Fresh Peas

Green Beans with Mushrooms and Almonds

Crispy Fried Okra

Braised Leeks

Sautéed Broccoli with Garlic and Oil

Creamed Spinach

Lima Beans with Bacon and Thyme

Roasted Asparagus

SERVES 4 TO 6

25 to 30 spears asparagus, bottom ¼ inch trimmed and washed

¼ cup olive oil

Kosher salt and freshly cracked black pepper to taste

1. Preheat the oven to 500°F.

2. Place the asparagus in a roasting pan just large enough to hold the spears in a single layer. Drizzle with the olive oil and toss to coat well, then season liberally with salt and pepper. Roast until the asparagus is just tender, 8 to 10 minutes. Serve warm or at room temperature.

Quick-Sautéed Spinach with Garlic

SERVES 4

¼ cup extra virgin olive oil

1¼ pounds spinach, trimmed, well washed, and dried

3 cloves garlic, peeled and very thinly sliced

1 lemon, halved

Generous pinch of red pepper flakes

Kosher salt and freshly cracked black pepper to taste

1. In your largest sauté pan, heat the oil over high heat until very hot, almost smoking. Add the spinach and cook, stirring furiously, for about 1 minute; the spinach should turn bright green and wilt slightly. Add the garlic and continue to cook, stirring rapidly, for 30 seconds.

2. Remove the spinach from the heat, squeeze the lemon over the top, and add the red pepper and salt and black pepper. Toss well and serve.

Brussels Sprouts in Brown Butter

SERVES 4

1 pound Brussels sprouts, well washed and stems trimmed

3 tablespoons unsalted butter

Kosher salt and freshly cracked black pepper to taste

1. Bring a large pot of salted water to the boil. Fill a large bowl with ice and water. Cook the sprouts in the boiling water until just tender, about 4 minutes. When the sprouts are done, drain and plunge them into the ice water; wait a few minutes, then drain them well and halve or quarter them.

2. In a large sauté pan, heat the butter over medium heat until foamy. Add the sprouts, season lightly with salt and pepper, and toss to coat them with the butter. Keep tossing until the butter begins to brown lightly and the sprouts are heated through. Serve immediately.

Minted Fresh Peas

SERVES 4

2 cups fresh peas

1 tablespoon unsalted butter

¼ cup roughly chopped fresh mint

Kosher salt and freshly cracked black pepper to taste

1. Bring a medium pot of salted water to the boil. Fill a large bowl with ice and water. Blanch the peas in the boiling water for 30 seconds, drain, plunge into the ice water to stop the cooking process, and drain again.

2. In a medium sauté pan, melt the butter over medium heat and add the peas. Sauté them for about 2 minutes, stirring occasionally, then stir in the mint, season with salt and pepper, and serve immediately.

Green Beans with Mushrooms and Almonds

SERVES 4

1 pound green beans, trimmed

2 tablespoons unsalted butter

2 tablespoons olive oil

⅔ cup thinly sliced white mushrooms

⅔ cup slivered blanched almonds, toasted in a sauté pan over medium heat, shaken frequently, until fragrant, 3 to 5 minutes

Kosher salt and freshly cracked black pepper to taste

1. In a large saucepan, bring 1 inch of salted water to a boil over medium-high heat. Add the beans, cover, and steam until just tender, about 10 minutes. Drain well, rinse with cold water to stop the cooking, and drain again.

2. While the beans are steaming, in a large sauté pan, melt the butter with the oil over medium-high heat. Add the mushrooms, toss to coat well, and cook, stirring occasionally, until tender and slightly browned, 5 to 7 minutes. Add the almonds and green beans to the pan, season with salt and pepper, toss well, and serve.

Crispy Fried Okra

SERVES 4

1 pound small okra pods (2 inches or less in length)

Vegetable oil for deep-frying

About ⅔ cup coarsely ground cornmeal

Kosher salt and freshly cracked black pepper to taste

1. Bring a medium pot of salted water to the boil. Fill a large bowl with ice and water. Blanch the okra in the boiling water for 2 minutes, drain, plunge into the ice water to stop the cooking process, and drain again.

2. In a large deep saucepan, heat 1 inch of oil until hot but not smoking. Dry the okra well on paper towels and dredge in the cornmeal, shaking off the excess. In batches, add only enough okra to the hot oil to form a single layer and cook until golden, about 3 minutes. Drain on paper towels, season generously with salt and pepper, and serve immediately.

Braised Leeks

SERVES 4 TO 6

These leeks can also be served chilled or at room temperature, tossed with a simple vinaigrette.

> 4 cups chicken stock (or see Stock Options, page 32)
>
> 6 medium leeks (white and tender green parts only root end trimmed but intact), halved lengthwise and thoroughly washed
>
> 3 tablespoons roughly chopped fresh herbs: any one or a combination of parsley, oregano, chervil, thyme, and/or chives
>
> Kosher salt and freshly cracked black pepper to taste

1. In a saucepan large enough to hold all the leeks in a single layer, bring the stock to a simmer over medium-high heat. Add the leeks, cover the pan, and simmer until the leeks are fork-tender, 15 to 20 minutes.

2. Transfer the leeks to a serving platter, sprinkle with the herbs and salt and pepper, and serve.

Sautéed Broccoli with Garlic and Oil

FOR BROCCOLI RABE WITH GARLIC AND OIL

Substitute 1 large bunch broccoli rabe, washed, trimmed, and cut into 1-inch pieces, for the broccoli.

SERVES 4

> 1 large bunch broccoli, washed, trimmed, and separated into florets
>
> 2 tablespoons olive oil
>
> 1 tablespoon minced garlic
>
> ¼ teaspoon red pepper flakes
>
> Kosher salt and freshly ground black pepper to taste

1. In a large pot of boiling, generously salted water, cook the broccoli until it is just tender, 2 to 3 minutes. Drain the broccoli, run under cold water to stop the cooking, and drain again.

2. In a medium sauté pan, heat the olive oil over medium-high heat until it is hot but not smoking. Add the garlic and red pepper flakes and cook, stirring, for about 15 seconds, until the garlic begins to color. Add the broccoli and sauté, tossing to coat with the oil, until it is heated through, about 1 minute. Season with salt and pepper and serve immediately.

Creamed Spinach

2 pounds spinach, trimmed and washed well

½ cup heavy cream

1 tablespoon unsalted butter

Pinch of grated nutmeg

Kosher salt and freshly cracked white pepper to taste

1. In a large sauté pan, toss the spinach over high heat until wilted (the water clinging to the leaves should be enough liquid to cook it in), 3 to 4 minutes.

2. Gently squeeze the spinach to remove the excess liquid, then roughly chop and return it to the pan. Add the cream, butter, nutmeg, and salt and white pepper and bring just to a boil. Reduce the heat and simmer until the cream has thickened, about 3 minutes. Adjust the seasonings and serve hot.

Lima Beans with Bacon and Thyme

SERVES 4 TO 6

3 slices thick-cut bacon, roughly chopped

1 small yellow onion, peeled and diced small

1 tablespoon minced garlic

1 pound lima beans, thawed if frozen

½ cup chicken stock (or see Stock Options, page 32)

Kosher salt and freshly cracked black pepper to taste

2 tablespoons roughly chopped fresh thyme

1. In a 5-inch-deep Dutch oven or other large heavy pot, cook the bacon over medium-low heat until it is brown and crisp, 8 to 10 minutes. Transfer the bacon to paper towels or a brown paper bag to drain.

2. Pour off all but about 2 tablespoons of fat from the pot and return it to medium-high heat. Add the onion and cook, stirring occasionally, until translucent, 7 to 9 minutes. Add the garlic and cook, stirring, for 1 minute more. Add the beans, stock, and salt and pepper and bring to a simmer, then reduce the heat to low and cook until the beans are just tender, about 10 minutes (5 minutes if you are using frozen beans).

3. Stir in the thyme and reserved bacon, then increase the heat to reduce any liquid left in the pot. Serve immediately.

TOP 10 SIMPLE CLASSIC (NON-GREEN) VEGETABLE DISHES

Creamed Corn

Grilled Corn on the Cob

German-Style Braised Red Cabbage

Mashed Turnips

Roasted Winter Squash

Roasted Carrots

Candied Sweet Potatoes

Batter-Fried Onion Rings

Braised Fennel

Hominy with Cheddar, Chiles, and Sour Cream

Creamed Corn

2 tablespoons unsalted butter

½ red onion, peeled and diced small

½ red bell pepper, cored, seeded, and diced small

4 ears corn, husked and kernels cut off the cob (or substitute 2½ cups thawed frozen corn)

⅔ cup heavy cream

Kosher salt and freshly cracked black pepper to taste

In a medium sauté pan, melt the butter over medium heat. Add the onion and bell pepper and cook, stirring frequently, until the onion is translucent, 7 to 9 minutes. Add the corn, cream, and salt and pepper and cook, stirring once, until slightly thickened, for 3 to 4 minutes. Serve immediately.

Grilled Corn on the Cob

SERVES 4 TO 6

12 ears corn, husked

Unsalted butter for serving

Kosher salt and freshly cracked black pepper to taste

4 limes, cut into wedges (optional)

1. Build a fire in your grill.

2. Fill your sink or a large pot with ice and water. In a large pot, bring 2 quarts of lightly salted water to a rolling boil over high heat. Add the corn and blanch for 1 minute. Drain and plunge into the ice-water bath to stop the cooking process; drain again.

3. When the fire has died down and the coals are medium-hot (you can hold your hand 5 inches above the grill surface for 3 to 4 seconds), put the corn on the grill and cook for 3 to 4 minutes, rolling often, until golden brown. Remove the corn from the grill, spread with butter, sprinkle liberally with salt and pepper, and drizzle each ear with a squeeze of lime, if desired. Serve immediately.

German-Style Braised Red Cabbage

SERVES 6

4 slices bacon, roughly chopped

½ teaspoon caraway seeds

1 small onion, peeled and diced small

1 medium head red cabbage, cored and shredded

2 apples, peeled, cored, and diced medium

2 tablespoons molasses

¼ cup red wine vinegar

¼ cup dry white wine

Kosher salt and freshly cracked black pepper to taste

1. In a 5-inch-deep Dutch oven or other heavy pot with a lid, cook the bacon over medium-low heat until the fat is rendered. Add the caraway seeds, increase the heat to medium, and cook, stirring, until the seeds are fragrant, about 2 minutes. Add the onion and cook, stirring frequently, until translucent, 7 to 9 minutes.

2. Add the cabbage, apples, molasses, vinegar, wine, and salt and pepper and stir to combine the ingredients well. Bring to a simmer, cover, and cook until the cabbage is very tender, about 1½ hours. Adjust the seasoning if necessary and serve immediately.

Mashed Turnips

SERVES 4 TO 6

1½ pounds Macumber or other turnips, peeled and cut into even-sized chunks about 1½ inches square

¼ cup plain yogurt

¼ cup fresh lemon juice (about 1 lemon)

1 tablespoon minced garlic

¼ cup chopped fresh parsley

Kosher salt and freshly cracked black pepper to taste

1. In a large pot of boiling salted water, cook the turnips just until easily pierced with a fork, 6 to 8 minutes; do not overcook. Drain well.

2. Place the turnips in a large bowl and add the remaining ingredients. Mash roughly with a potato masher, adjust the seasoning, and serve at once.

Roasted Winter Squash

SERVES 4

One 2- to 3-pound butternut or acorn squash, or 2 smaller squash, halved lengthwise and strings and seeds removed

Kosher salt and freshly cracked black pepper to taste

2 tablespoons unsalted butter, melted, plus extra if desired

2 tablespoons dark brown sugar

1. Preheat the oven to 400°F.

2. Place the squash halves cut side up on a baking sheet, sprinkle with salt and pepper, and brush with the melted butter. Crumble the brown sugar over the squash and bake until tender, about 1 hour, basting occasionally with more melted butter if desired. Serve hot.

Roasted Carrots

SERVES 4

2 pounds carrots, peeled and cut into 2-inch lengths (fatter pieces halved lengthwise)

1 medium red onion, peeled and cut into 1-inch wedges

2 tablespoons olive oil

2 tablespoons fresh rosemary needles

Kosher salt and freshly cracked black pepper to taste

1. Preheat the oven to 425°F.

2. In a roasting pan large enough to hold the vegetables comfortably, toss the carrots and onion with the oil, rosemary, and salt and pepper so that they are well coated. Spread them out evenly in the pan and roast, turning after about 20 minutes, until cooked through, about 50 minutes. Serve hot.

FOR ROASTED BEETS
Substitute beets for the carrots and thyme or oregano for the rosemary; trim and halve the beets before roasting.

Candied Sweet Potatoes

SERVES 4

3 pounds sweet potatoes (about 4 large), washed

3 tablespoons unsalted butter

Kosher salt and freshly cracked black pepper to taste

⅓ cup coarse-cut orange marmalade

3 tablespoons brown sugar

Pinch of ground cardamom

2 tablespoons rum (optional)

1. Preheat the oven to 350°F.

2. Place the sweet potatoes on a small baking sheet and bake until they are still firm but not hard in the center, about 45 minutes. Let cool slightly. (Leave the oven on.)

3. As soon as the sweet potatoes are cool enough to handle, peel them and cut them crosswise into quarters. Butter a casserole dish just large enough to hold the potatoes in a single layer, using 1 tablespoon of the butter. Arrange the potatoes in the dish and sprinkle with salt and pepper.

4. In a small saucepan, combine the marmalade, brown sugar, cardamom, rum, if using, and the remaining 2 tablespoons butter and cook over medium heat, stirring occasionally, until the mixture is melted and smooth. Pour over the sweet potatoes and bake until they are well glazed, about 20 minutes, basting occasionally with the liquid in the dish. If desired, baste again and broil for 20 to 30 seconds before serving.

The Cuts:

Beef

CHUCK

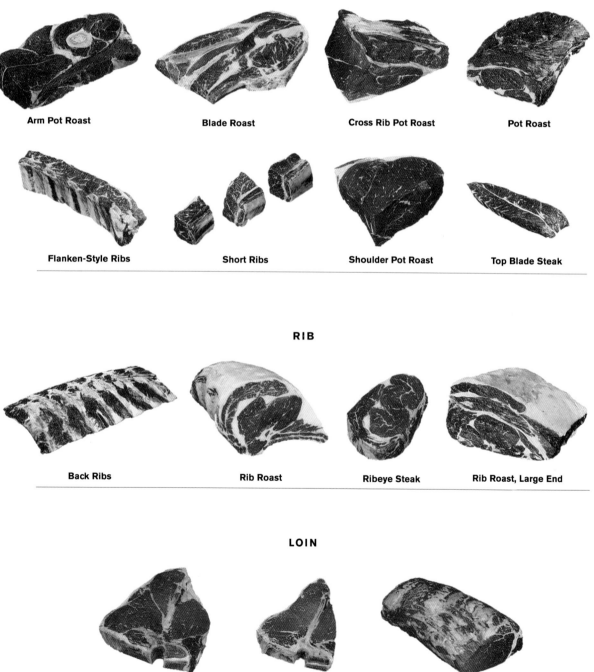

Arm Pot Roast

Blade Roast

Cross Rib Pot Roast

Pot Roast

Flanken-Style Ribs

Short Ribs

Shoulder Pot Roast

Top Blade Steak

RIB

Back Ribs

Rib Roast

Ribeye Steak

Rib Roast, Large End

LOIN

Porterhouse Steak

T-Bone Steak

Tenderloin Roast

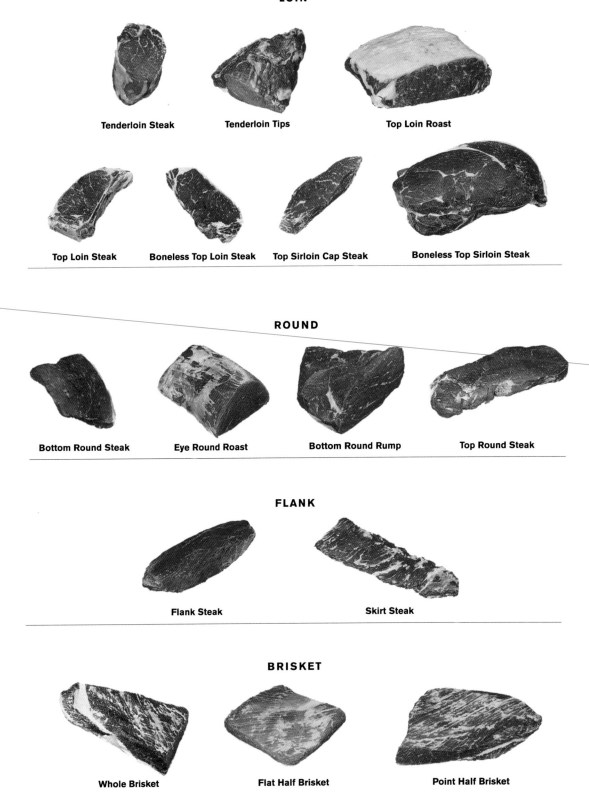

LOIN

Tenderloin Steak   **Tenderloin Tips**   **Top Loin Roast**

Top Loin Steak   **Boneless Top Loin Steak**   **Top Sirloin Cap Steak**   **Boneless Top Sirloin Steak**

ROUND

Bottom Round Steak   **Eye Round Roast**   **Bottom Round Rump**   **Top Round Steak**

FLANK

Flank Steak   **Skirt Steak**

BRISKET

Whole Brisket   **Flat Half Brisket**   **Point Half Brisket**

The Cuts:

Veal

SHOULDER

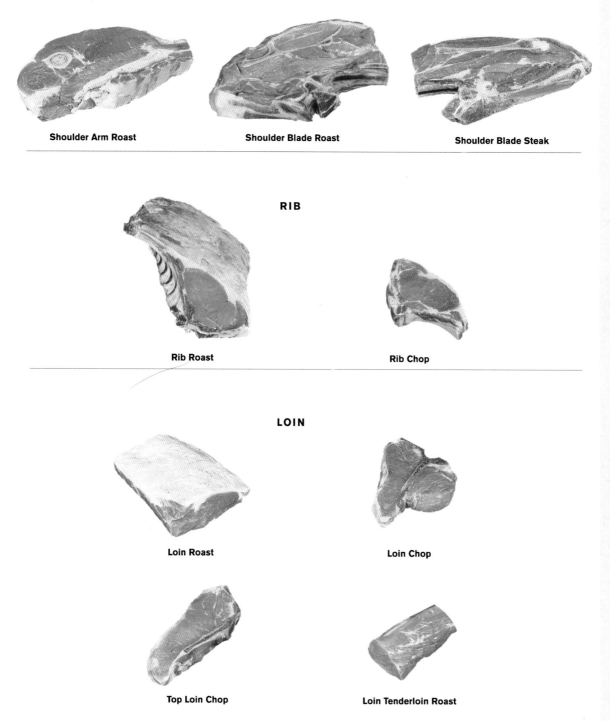

Shoulder Arm Roast

Shoulder Blade Roast

Shoulder Blade Steak

RIB

Rib Roast

Rib Chop

LOIN

Loin Roast

Loin Chop

Top Loin Chop

Loin Tenderloin Roast

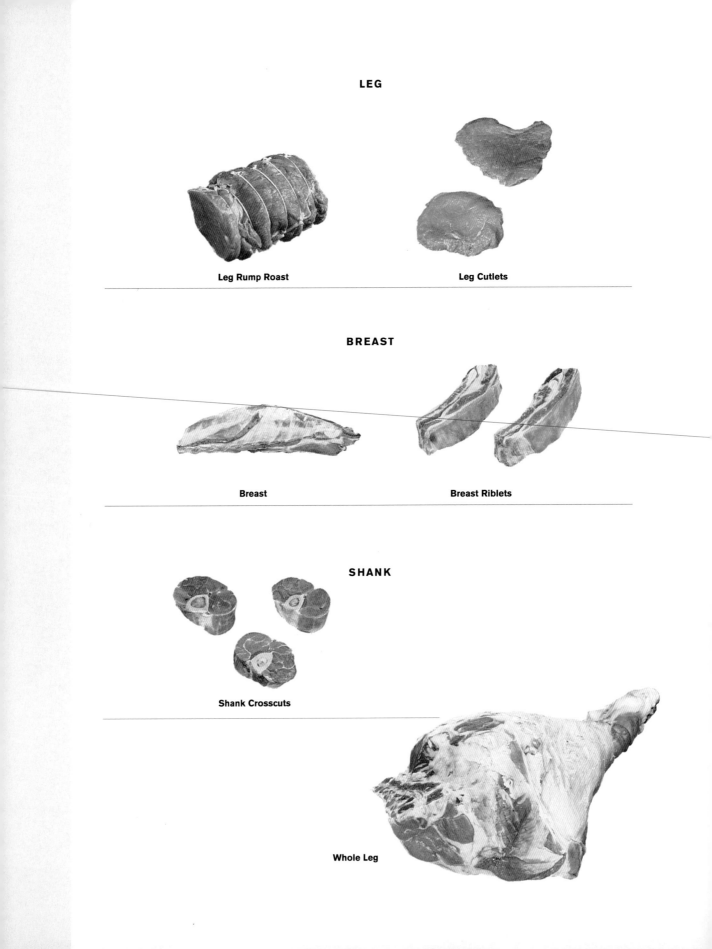

LEG

Leg Rump Roast

Leg Cutlets

BREAST

Breast

Breast Riblets

SHANK

Shank Crosscuts

Whole Leg

The Cuts:

Lamb

SHOULDER

Whole Square Cut

Arm Chop

Blade Chops

Boneless Roast

RIB

Rib Roast

Crown Roast

Rib Chop

Frenched Rib Chop

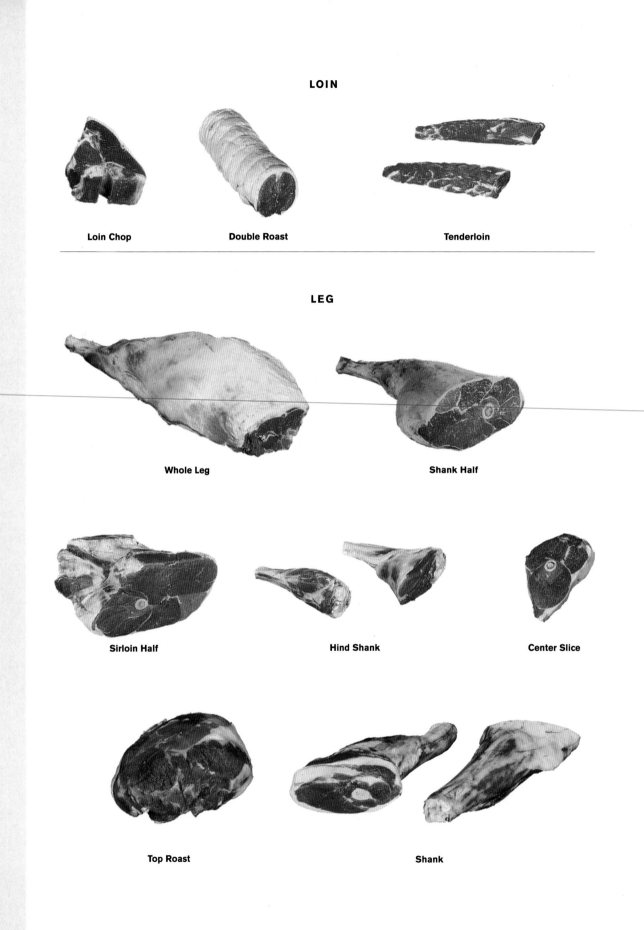

LOIN

Loin Chop   Double Roast   Tenderloin

LEG

Whole Leg   Shank Half

Sirloin Half   Hind Shank   Center Slice

Top Roast   Shank

The Cuts:

Pork

SHOULDER

Boston Blade Roast

Blade Steak

Hocks

LOIN

Back Ribs

Blade Roast

Blade Chop

Center Rib Roast

Country Style Ribs

Rib Chop

Rib Chop for Stuffing

Loin Chop

Sirloin Roast

Sirloin Chop

LOIN

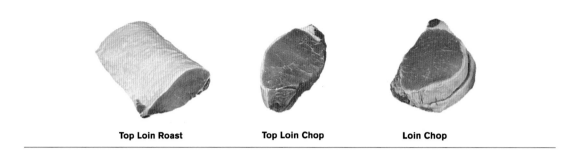

Top Loin Roast   **Top Loin Chop**   **Loin Chop**

LEG

Fresh Ham Rump Half   **Shank Half**   **Center Slice**

SIDE

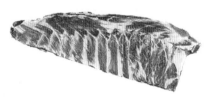 

Spareribs   **Spareribs**

Batter-Fried Onion Rings

SERVES 4

1 cup all-purpose flour
1½ teaspoons kosher salt
One 12-ounce bottle beer
10 dashes Tabasco sauce
2 yellow onions, peeled, sliced ¼ inch thick, and separated into rings
Vegetable oil

1. Preheat the oven to 225°F.

2. Make the beer batter: In a large bowl, combine the flour and salt. Add the beer all at once, along with the Tabasco, and mix well until the batter is combined and slightly frothy. Set the batter aside to rest for at least ½ hour, or up to 2 hours. Drop the onions into a bowl of ice water to soak while the batter is resting.

3. In a 5-inch-deep Dutch oven or other large, heavy pot, heat 2 inches of vegetable oil to 375°. Remove the onion slices from the ice water and dry them thoroughly with paper towels. Dip them in the batter a few at a time, drop gently into the oil, and fry until they are crisp and golden brown. As they are done, transfer to a paper towel–lined baking sheet, sprinkle with kosher salt, and put in the oven to keep warm while you finish frying the rest.

Braised Fennel

SERVES 4 TO 6

3 tablespoons unsalted butter

2 tablespoons olive oil

2 medium fennel bulbs, stalks trimmed, cored, and cut lengthwise into sixths

1 cup chicken stock (or see Stock Options, page 32)

3 tablespoons fresh lemon juice (about 1 lemon)

Kosher salt and freshly cracked black pepper to taste

1. In a large sauté pan, melt the butter with the olive oil over medium-high heat. Add the fennel and sauté until golden brown on all sides, 9 to 11 minutes.

2. Add the chicken stock, lemon juice, and salt and pepper, bring to a simmer, cover, and cook until the fennel is just tender, about 20 minutes. Uncover and allow the liquid in the pan to reduce and become syrupy, 3 to 5 minutes more. Serve immediately, with the pan juices poured over the top.

Hominy with Cheddar, Chiles, and Sour Cream

SERVES 4

Two 30-ounce cans hominy, drained and rinsed

⅔ cup sour cream

1 to 2 tablespoons minced fresh chile peppers of your choice, or less to taste

6 ounces Cheddar cheese, grated

Kosher salt and freshly cracked black pepper to taste

1. Preheat the oven to 350°F.

2. Spread one third of the hominy in the bottom of a small baking dish. Spread half the sour cream, half the chiles, and half the cheese on top. Season with salt and pepper. Repeat to form a second layer, and top with the remaining hominy. Bake uncovered until the top is golden, about 30 minutes. Serve hot.

HOBO **PACKS**

Hobo packs are basically a throwback to my (Chris's) Boy Scout days. The regulation version—which consists of carrots, onions, hamburger, and a lot of catsup all wrapped up in foil and stuck in the ashes to cook—was the first thing I ever cooked for my peers. It was a big success, so the memory of it has stuck with me over the years. As I have cooked for different audiences, I've expanded on and modified the technique, but the basics remain the same.

I'm fond of hobo packs for several reasons. First, the process is incredibly easy. Second, this is a very adaptable cooking method, equally suitable for the backyard grill, the fireplace in your living room, or a driftwood fire on the beach. And, third, it is a very exciting cooking method. Every time you set a hobo pack in the ashes, it's the beginning of a true culinary adventure. The possible incineration of dinner provides built-in drama, and the smoky, ash-seared flavor of the food that emerges from the foil is the payoff.

Hobo packs are particularly good accompaniments to grilled meats. Not only do they taste great, but, since you've got the fire lit anyway, it's very little extra work to wrap up some vegetables, stick them in the coals, and cook your side dish at the same time.

The two keys to an exceptional hobo pack are to wrap the food very well in the foil and to place the package in the coals in the cooler part of the fire, then pile the coals up around (but not on top of) it. For each of the hobo pack combinations here, follow the general directions below.

To Prepare: Combine all the ingredients in a large bowl and toss gently to combine. Tear off four sheets of heavy-duty foil, each about 2 feet long, and stack them one on top of the other. Arrange the combined ingredients in the center of the top sheet and season with salt and pepper. Fold up the sheets of foil around the vegetables, one after the other, turning the package one quarter turn between each sheet and making sure that each sheet is well sealed around the vegetables.

To Cook: Place the hobo packs in the coals around the periphery of the fire, where the heat is less intense. Pile the coals up around the packs and cook until the vegetables are tender, as indicated in the individual recipe. Remove from the coals, unroll the foil, and serve hot.

TOP TEN HOBO PACK SIDE DISHES

Potato and Eggplant Hobo Pack with Lemon

Spicy Yellow Squash Hobo Pack with Lime

Sweet Potato–Raisin Hobo Pack

New Potato Hobo Pack with Pearl Onions and Spinach

Butternut Squash Hobo Pack with Spinach and Apricots

Carrot-Ginger Hobo Pack with Scallions

Tomato Hobo Pack with Basil and Garlic

Mushroom and Kale Hobo Pack

Autumn Vegetable Hobo Pack

Ash-Roasted Garlic

POTATO AND EGGPLANT HOBO PACK WITH LEMON

COOKING TIME
35 to 40 minutes

SERVES 6

4 baking potatoes, washed and thickly sliced

2 lemons, very thinly sliced

10 cloves garlic, peeled and smashed

1 small eggplant, diced small

$1/2$ cup olive oil

Kosher salt and freshly cracked black pepper to taste

SPICY YELLOW SQUASH HOBO PACK WITH LIME

COOKING TIME
20 to 25 minutes

SERVES 6

4 small yellow squash, cut lengthwise into sixths

10 cloves garlic, peeled and smashed

2 tablespoons minced fresh chile peppers of your choice, or to taste

1 lime, very thinly sliced

$1/2$ cup roughly chopped fresh basil

$1/2$ cup roughly chopped fresh cilantro

2 tablespoons vegetable oil

2 tablespoons sesame oil

Kosher salt and freshly cracked black pepper to taste

SWEET POTATO–RAISIN HOBO PACK

COOKING TIME
25 to 30 minutes

SERVES 6

4 sweet potatoes, washed and quartered lengthwise

2 red onions, peeled and quartered

5 stalks celery, diced small

$1/2$ cup dark raisins

4 tablespoons ($1/2$ stick) unsalted butter, at room temperature, cut into small pieces

$1/4$ cup molasses

Kosher salt and freshly cracked black pepper to taste

NEW POTATO HOBO PACK WITH PEARL ONIONS AND SPINACH

SERVES 6

12 new potatoes (about the size of a golf ball), washed

24 pearl onions, unpeeled, root ends trimmed

½ pound spinach, trimmed, well washed, and dried

¼ cup roughly chopped fresh sage

⅓ cup olive oil

1 teaspoon red pepper flakes

Kosher salt and freshly cracked black pepper to taste

BUTTERNUT SQUASH HOBO PACK WITH SPINACH AND APRICOTS

SERVES 6

3 cups butternut squash diced large

½ pound spinach, trimmed, well washed, and dried

1 cup thinly sliced dried apricots

⅓ cup packed dark brown sugar

4 tablespoons (½ stick) unsalted butter, at room temperature, cut into small pieces

Kosher salt and freshly cracked black pepper to taste

CARROT-GINGER HOBO PACK WITH SCALLIONS

SERVES 6

6 large carrots, peeled and cut into 1-inch rounds

One 2-inch finger of fresh ginger, peeled and cut into matchsticks

6 scallions (white and green parts), thinly sliced

⅓ cup soy sauce

¼ cup olive oil

Kosher salt and freshly cracked black pepper to taste

TOMATO HOBO PACK WITH BASIL AND GARLIC

COOKING TIME
15 to 20 minutes

SERVES 6

4 tomatoes (about the size of a baseball), cored and quartered

2 red onions, peeled and quartered

15 cloves garlic, peeled and smashed

$\frac{1}{2}$ cup roughly chopped fresh basil

$\frac{1}{3}$ cup olive oil

Kosher salt and freshly cracked black pepper to taste

MUSHROOM AND KALE HOBO PACK

COOKING TIME
15 to 20 minutes

SERVES 4 TO 6

1 pound white mushrooms (or substitute the exotic mushrooms of your choice), trimmed

2 red onions, peeled and quartered

10 cloves garlic, peeled and smashed

$\frac{1}{4}$ cup chopped fresh herbs: any one or a combination of parsley, sage, rosemary, and/or thyme

$\frac{1}{3}$ cup olive oil

8 large leaves kale, washed and roughly chopped

Kosher salt and freshly cracked black pepper to taste

AUTUMN VEGETABLE HOBO PACK

COOKING TIME
35 to 40 minutes

SERVES 6

2 red onions, peeled and quartered

1 medium turnip, peeled and cut into bite-sized pieces

3 parsnips, peeled and cut into 1-inch rounds

2 medium beets, peeled and cut into bite-sized pieces

5 cloves garlic, peeled and smashed

$\frac{1}{4}$ cup roughly chopped fresh herbs: any one or a combination of fresh sage, thyme, and/or oregano

$\frac{1}{3}$ cup olive oil

Kosher salt and freshly cracked black pepper to taste

ASH-ROASTED GARLIC

This is not exactly a side dish, but roasted garlic has dozens of uses, and cooking it in the ashes gives it great flavor. It's particularly nice as a condiment with grilled steak or lamb chops or as an addition to mashed potatoes. Once the garlic is roasted, just wait until it is cool enough to handle and squeeze the flesh out of each clove.

4 large heads garlic, top quarter sliced off
¼ cup extra virgin olive oil
Kosher salt and freshly cracked black pepper to taste

INDEX

Acorn squash, *see* squash, acorn
adobo:
  Denver lamb ribs, with fresh
    pineapple-chipotle glaze,
    298–99
  pork ribs with molasses-chile
    barbecue sauce, EZ-style,
    348–49
African-style beef and tuber stew
  with toasted spices, 128–29
aged meat, 26–27
Agriculture Department, U.S.
  (USDA)
  cooking guidelines of, 28
  grading by, 9, 41, 44, 46, 324
  meat inspection and, 9
almonds:
  green beans with mushrooms
    and, 429
  rice pilaf with currants and,
    417
Alsatian-style orange-braised veal
  shoulder with sweet-and-
  sour braised cabbage and
  fennel slaw, 186–87
anchovies, spicy pan-seared veal
  loin medallions with green
  olives and, 205–6
A-1 (sauce):
  hollandaise, black pan-seared
    tournedos with asparagus,
    crab and, 91–92
  parsley butter, Texas-style
    ground beef casserole with
    sweet potato crust and,
    138–39

apple(s):
  -chipotle salsa, cumin-crusted
    grilled boneless pork loin
    with grilled avocados and,
    331–32
  green, lazy Sunday pot roast
    with caraway and, 69–70
  spiced, panfried brined loin
    chops stuffed with walnuts
    and Stilton cheese with,
    358–60
  Stilton-stuffed, simple veal
    rump roast with, 172–73
apricot(s):
  butternut squash hobo pack
    with spinach and, 442
  dried, broiled sherried lamb
    skewers with green olive
    dressing and, 294–95
  -lemon chutney, smooth,
    couscous-stuffed lamb loin
    with, 264–66
  -mint sauce, crown roast of
    lamb with saffron rice and,
    248–50
  -sausage stuffing, roast pork loin
    with rosemary-garlic jus and,
    334–37
artichoke hearts, sautéed
  medallions of veal with
  lemon, thyme and, 201–2
arugula:
  fennel, and oranges under
    grilled peppered lamb leg top
    with white bean-roasted red
    pepper relish, 260–61

a hot open-faced veal meat loaf
  sandwich with blue cheese-
  tomato relish and, 224–25
asparagus:
  black pan-seared tournedos
    with crab, A-1 hollandaise
    and, 91–92
  roasted, 427
au gratin potatoes (gratin
  Dauphinois), 410–11
autumn vegetable hobo pack, 443
avocado(s):
  -corn salsa, grilled thin pork
    chops with, 374–75
  grilled, cumin-crusted grilled
    boneless pork loin with
    apple-chipotle salsa and,
    331–32

Bacon:
  broiled veal loin chop with
    exotic mushrooms, sherry
    and, 194–95
  -cheese stuffed potatoes, 415
  grilled Polynesian-style
    tenderloin tip kebabs with
    pineapple, peppers and,
    104–5
  grill-roasted rib roast (prime
    rib) with potato-garlic hobo
    pack, sour cream, and bits of,
    44–45
  lamb tongues on toast with
    tomatoes and, 317–18
  lima beans with thyme and,
    431

ground meat:
    safety concerns with, 28
    see also beef, ground; lamb,
        ground; veal, ground
Gruyère, in au gratin potatoes
    (gratin Dauphinois),
    410–11
guava-chile glaze, grilled pork,
    bacon, and mango skewers
    with, 381–82

Ham, fresh, 322
    BBQ-rubbed grilled center-slice,
        with watermelon-pineapple
        salad, 384–85
    grill-roasted rum-brined, with
        mango salsa and grilled
        pineapples and bananas,
        328–30
    maple-glazed, with hard
        cider–raisin sauce, 326–27
ham, Smithfield, 319–20
    -raisin jus, honey-and-bourbon-
        glazed roasted loin of veal
        with crusty sweet potatoes
        and, 170–71
    veal birdies Tidewater-style,
        with backfin crab, lemon-
        caper sauce and, 208–9
ham hocks, 322, 323
    with collard greens and
        potatoes, pot likker-braised
        fresh, 403–4
    in Hoppin' John, 421
    smoked, with Indian-spiced
        green split peas, 404–6
hanger steak, 39, 116
hangover-style tripe stew, 151–52
hash:
    corned beef and sweet potato,
        with red wine-caramelized
        onions, 148–49
    a severe tongue hashing with
        turnips and Swiss chard,
        156–57
hash browns, 412
Hawaiian-style macadamia
    nut–crusted pork chops with
    pineapple-ginger catsup,
    360–61
hazelnut-crusted veal tenderloin
    with roasted grapes and port,
    192–93
head cheese Reuben, 158
heart (grilled beef), Peruvian-style
    you gotta have, 149–50
herb(s)(ed):
    aromatic, Southeast Asian-style
        veal cakes with two dipping
        sauces and, 222–23

-crusted grilled top round steak
    "London broil-style" with
    maître d'hôtel butter and
    smoky balsamic onions,
    106–7
-peanut power pack, spice-
    rubbed grilled lamb skewers
    with (Indobob), 291–92
potato dumplings and
    horseradish sauce, old-
    fashioned braised beef with,
    61–63
see also specific herbs
hobo packs, 439–44
    ash-roasted garlic, 444
    autumn vegetable, 443
    butternut squash, spinach, and
        apricots, 442
    carrot-ginger-scallions, 442
    of fig, prosciutto, and spinach,
        grilled veal T-bones with,
        200–201
    mushroom, pepper-crusted
        grilled strip loin steak with
        homemade steak sauce and,
        96–98
    mushroom and kale, 443
    new potato, pearl onions and
        spinach, 442
    potato, eggplant, and lemon,
        441
    potato-garlic, grill-roasted rib
        roast (prime rib) with sour
        cream, bacon bits and, 44–45
    spicy yellow squash and lime,
        441
    sweet potato-raisin, 441
    on toast, marrow, 153
    tomato, basil, and garlic, 443
    tomato-fig, parsley-coated
        grilled lamb loin with smoky
        eggplant planks and, 288–89
hoisin (sauce):
    aromatic ginger and beef broth
        with traditional Southeast
        Asian garnishes and, 136–37
    -ginger sauce, stir-fried lamb
        with green beans, eggplant,
        and peppers in, 299–300
    -glazed, soy-braised pork
        shoulder roast with sesame-
        ginger dipping sauce, 342–43
    -glazed grilled pork blade chops
        with spicy Korean vegetables,
        372–73
    spicy, "Peking duck–style" roast
        pork loin with, 332–34
hollandaise, A-1, black pan-seared
    tournedos with asparagus,
    crab and, 91–92

home fries, 412
hominy with Cheddar, chiles, and
    sour cream, 438
honey:
    -and-bourbon-glazed roasted
        loin of veal with crusty sweet
        potatoes and Smithfield ham-
        raisin jus, 170–71
    spicy mint, fennel-crusted flank
        steak with orange-black olive
        relish and, 114–15
hoppin' John, 421
horseradish:
    -grainy mustard sauce,
        barbecued whole beef brisket
        with pastrami-style rub and,
        70–72
    mashed potatoes, 413
    -mustard sauce, seared veal
        kidneys with roasted pears
        and, 239–40
    sauce, old-fashioned braised
        beef with herbed potato
        dumplings and, 61–63
hot, sweet, and sour bone sauce,
    Flintstones-style BBQ beef
    ribs with, 80–81

Indian:
    -spiced beef-stuffed red onions
        with fresh coconut-ginger
        chutney and simple yogurt
        sauce, 140–42
    -spiced green split peas with
        smoked ham hocks,
        404–6
Indobob: spice-rubbed grilled
    lamb skewers with peanut-
    herb power pack,
    291–92
Irish lamb stew, straight-up, 303–4

Jalapeño-Cheddar grits, spicy
    pork stew with tomatoes and
    okra over, 390–91
jam, yellow tomato-ginger, grill-
    roasted whole loin of beef
    with, 52–53
jus:
    light basil, rack of veal with
        chestnut stuffing, brandied
        oranges and, 166–68
    rosemary, garlic-studded,
        mustard-crusted roasted
        shoulder of lamb with cherry
        tomato-ginger confit and,
        266–67
    rosemary-garlic, roast pork loin
        with apricot-sausage stuffing
        and, 334–37

pork loin, 322
  cumin-crusted grilled boneless, with grilled avocados and apple-chipotle salsa, 331–32
  fillets, grilled, on Latin-style salad with sour orange–oregano dressing, 366–67
  roast, with apricot-sausage stuffing and rosemary-garlic jus, 334–37
  roast, with spicy hoisin sauce, "Peking duck–style," 332–34
pork (loin) chops, 324, 362
  cutlets, sautéed, with cashew slaw and chile flavor booster, 364–65
  grilled boneless, with green olive–red onion relish and nectarine chutney, 370–71
  grilled coriander-crusted, pickled corn-stuffed double-thick, with peach chutney, 356–57
  grilled thin, with avocado-corn salsa, 374–75
  macadamia nut-crusted, with pineapple-ginger catsup, 360–61
  panfried brined, stuffed with walnuts and Stilton cheese, with spiced apples, 358–60
  scallopini, sautéed, over scallion lo mein with soy-braised bok choy, 368–69
  white pepper–crusted, with peanut-ginger power pack, 363–64
pork picnic shoulder, 4, 322, 323
  in soy-braised, hoisin-glazed roast with sesame-ginger dipping sauce, 342–43
pork rib roast (rack of pork), 323
  ginger-rubbed, with chile-lychee sambal, 337–38
pork shoulder, 322
  blade roast, 323
  blade steaks, red wine-braised, with peaches, cinnamon, and couscous, 344–45
  in gingered curry with seven garnishes, 400–401
pork skewers:
  guava-chile glazed grilled bacon, mango and, 381–82
  sun-dried tomato-basil relish with grilled fig and, 382–83
pork spareribs, 319, 323
  EZ-style adobo, with molasses-chile barbecue sauce, 348–49

traditional dry-rubbed St. Louis–style, 346–47
pork stew (stewed pork), 323
  with coconut milk and aromatic garnishes, Malaysian-inspired, 396–97
  with eggplant, chiles and sesame spinach, spicy, 398–99
  with fennel, pears, and sauerkraut, fragrant winter, 394–95
  with mango and fried sweet potatoes, 392–93
  with plantains, lime, and chiles, West Indies–style, 388–89
  ribs, country-style orange, with sweet-and-sour red cabbage slaw, 387–88
  with tomatoes and okra, spicy, over jalapeño-Cheddar grits, 390–91
pork tenderloin, 322–23
  grilled, on a salad of grilled potatoes and red onions, 378–79
  molasses-glazed, with seared sweet-and-sour red onions and sage-date power pack, 376–77
  port, hazelnut-crusted veal tenderloin with roasted grapes and, 192–93
porterhouse steak, 5, 13, 38, 39, 40
  for two, Mr. Perfect, 89–90
potato(es):
  Anna, 409
  au gratin (gratin Dauphinois), 410–11
  bacon-cheese stuffed, 415
  baked stuffed, 415
  chips, 411
  dumplings, herbed, old-fashioned braised beef with horseradish sauce and, 61–63
  and eggplant hobo pack with lemon, 441
  French fries, 411
  -garlic hobo pack, sour cream, and bacon bits, grill-roasted rib roast (prime rib) with, 44–45
  grilled, and red onions salad, grilled pork tenderloin on a, 378–79
  hash browns, 412
  lamb, and onion casserole with red wine, layered, 309–11
  Macaire, 414
  mashed, 413
  O'Brien, 412

pot likker–braised fresh ham hocks with collard greens and, 403–4
  roasted, 414
  roasted, with black olives, 414
  roesti, 410
  straight-up roasted whole leg of lamb with lemon, garlic, and oregano over onions and, 252–53
  straw, 411
potato(es), new:
  hobo pack with pearl onions and spinach, 442
  parsleyed, 412
  rump roast on a bed of red onions, leeks and, 58–59
  pot likker–braised fresh ham hocks with collard greens and potatoes, 403–4
pot roast, 38
  balsamic-braised, with tomatoes, lemons, raisins, and black olive-pine nut relish, 66–68
  with caraway and green apples, lazy Sunday, 69–70
  old-school Yankee, with root vegetables and fresh tomato-fennel relish, 65–66
power packs:
  lemon-pistachio, tomato-braised veal shanks with pumpkin risotto and, 182–84
  peanut-ginger, white pepper-crusted pork loin chops with, 363–64
  peanut-herb, spice-rubbed grilled lamb skewers with (Indobob), 291–92
  sage-date, molasses-glazed pork tenderloin with seared sweet-and-sour red onions and, 376–77
Prime meat, 9, 41, 246
prime rib, *see* rib roast
prosciutto, grilled veal T-bones with a hobo pack of fig, spinach and, 200–201
Puerto Rican vinegar-braised flank steak with cabbage, corn and yucca salad, 77–79
pumpkin risotto, tomato-braised veal shanks with lemon-pistachio power pack and, 182–84

R aisin(s):
  balsamic, grilled veal flank steak on Texas toast with yellow tomato chutney and, 216–17

-blue cheese relish, a hot open-faced veal meat loaf sandwich with arugula and, 224–25

-braised veal shanks with pumpkin risotto and lemon-pistachio power pack, 182–84

-cucumber relish, mango-braised lamb shoulder with sweet toasted spices and, 275–77

curried lamb stew with okra and, 308–9

-fennel relish, fresh, old-school Yankee pot roast with root vegetables and, 65–66

-fig hobo pack, parsley-coated grilled lamb loin with smoky eggplant planks and, 288–89

hobo pack with basil and garlic, 443

jalapeño-Cheddar grits under spicy pork stew with okra and, 390–91

lamb tongues on toast with bacon and, 317–18

North African-style braised lamb shanks with lemons, green olives and, 269–70

old-school Southern-style beef stew with corn, bacon and, 130–31

onions, and peppers and crunchy parsley-bread crumb shake, old-style chunky beef and beer stew with, 122–23

Persian-style lamb and eggplant stew with raisins, saffron and, 302–3

sauce, spicy, basil-crusted meat loaf with brandy, walnuts and, 145–46

simply brown veal stew with peppers, capers and, 227–28

and watercress salad, broiled lamb kidneys with grainy mustard sauce and, 316–17

tomatoes, oven-dried, veal steamship round with green olives and, 174–76

tomatoes, roasted:

garlic-, very impressive roasted lamb saddle with peach-pomegranate sauce and, 262–64

-garlic relish, Chianti-and-balsamic-braised lamb shanks over creamy Parmesan polenta with, 270–72

tongue(s):

hashing with turnips and Swiss chard, a severe, 156–57

lamb, on toast with bacon and tomatoes, 317–18

tournedos, black pan-seared, with asparagus, crab, and A-1 hollandaise, 91–92

tripe stew, hangover-style, 151–52

truffle oil, scrambled eggs on toast with calf's brains and, 233–34

turnips:

black pepper-crusted wine-braised short ribs with garlic and, 74–75

Macumber, beer-braised veal breast with greens and, 180–81

mashed, 434

a severe tongue hashing with Swiss chard and, 156–57

Veal, 12, 159–240

cuts of, 5–8, 160–63

grades of, 9, 164

great, 10 steps to, 165, 177, 188, 189, 218

recipes for large tender cuts of, 165–76

recipes for large tough cuts of, 177–87

recipes for odd cuts of, 232–40

recipes for small tender cuts of, 188–217

recipes for small tough cuts of, 218–31

stock, 33

see also brains, calf's; calf's liver; *specific cuts*

veal, ground:

in Southeast Asian-style cakes with aromatic herbs and two dipping sauces, 222–23

see also veal meat loaf

veal, rack of, 161, 162

with chestnut stuffing, brandied oranges, and light basil jus, 166–68

rosemary-crusted roasted, with exotic mushrooms, white wine, and lemon, 168–69

veal birdies, 162

mango-stuffed, with cognac–green peppercorn sauce, 210–11

Tidewater-style, with Smithfield ham, backfin crab, and lemon-caper sauce, 208–9

veal breast, 162

barbecued Latin-Style with sour orange–chipotle barbecue sauce, 178–79

beer-braised, with Macumber turnips and greens, 180–81

veal chops, 162

veal flank steak, 162

grilled, on Texas toast with yellow tomato chutney and balsamic raisins, 216–17

seared, with roasted pears and horseradish-mustard sauce, 239–40

veal loin, 161, 162

honey-and-bourbon-glazed, with crusty sweet potatoes and Smithfield ham-raisin jus, 170–71

medallions, spicy pan-seared, with anchovies and green olives, 205–6

see also veal flank steak; veal T-bones; veal tenderloin(s)

veal loin chop(s), 162

broiled, with exotic mushrooms, bacon, and sherry, 194–95

grilled, with spicy green olive and sun-dried tomato relish, 196–97

veal meat loaf, 163

hot open-faced sandwich with arugula, blue cheese-tomato relish and, 224–25

veal rib chops, 161–62

simple, with smoky portobello relish, 197–98

see also veal, rack of

veal riblets (short ribs), 162

pepper-crusted, braised with red onions over mushroom risotto, 220–21

stewed with beer, bacon, and beans, 219–20

veal round (or leg), 161, 162

grilled, sweet potato, and red onion kebabs in the piccata style, 214–15

paillard with pancetta, white mushrooms, and Madeira, 203–4

panfried cutlets in the German style, 206–7

sautéed medallions, with artichoke hearts, lemon, and thyme, 201–2

see also veal birdies; veal rump roast; veal steamship round